THE PERFECT DISTANCE

TRAINING FOR LONG-COURSE TRIATHLON

TOM RODGERS

BOULDER, COLORADO

DEDICATION

To Tuula, who miraculously reappeared after twenty-five years and finally marched from the finish line on Ali'i drive in Kona into marriage with me.
From love comes the greatest endurance.

The Ultrafit Multisport Training Series
The Perfect Distance: Training for Long-Course Triathlon

1830 North 55th Street
Boulder, Colorado 80301-2700 USA
303/440-0601 · Fax 303/444-6788 · E-mail velopress@insideinc.com

Cover design and interior composition by Erin Johnson Design.
Cover photo by Timothy Carlson.
Interior photos by Tuula Rodgers.
Illustrations: page 142, Todd Telander; pages 182 and 184, Ed Jenne.
Tables 9.4 and 9.6 are taken with permission from *Going Long*, by Joe Friel and Gordon Byrn (VeloPress).

Distributed in the United States and Canada by Publishers Group West

Library of Congress Cataloging-in-Publication Data
Rodgers, Tom.
The perfect distance : training for long-course triathlon / Tom Rodgers.
— 1st ed.
p. cm.
ISBN-13: 978-1-931382-94-6 (pbk. : alk. paper)
ISBN-10: 1-931382-94-8
1. Triathlon—Training. I. Title.
GV1060.73.R63 2006
796.42'57—dc22

For information on purchasing VeloPress books, please call 800/234-8356 or visit www.velopress.com.

06 07 08 09 / 10 9 8 7 6 5 4 3 2 1

CONTENTS

FOREWORD

I have my own definition of triathlon—the evolution of synergistic motion. *The Perfect Distance* provides a success formula for maximizing this definition. Whether it is the proper equipment, nutrition, allied training (such as weight training), or the prevention or healing of possible sports injuries, Tom Rodgers covers it all in complete detail. Tom also incorporates the "availability" factor in the training time spent by his clients; since most of the triathletes come from the age group ranks of the sport and want a balanced life, there is a limit to how many hours a week they can train. Through the "availability" concept of training, the athlete can maximize their training by implementing the custom-designed program.

Endurance sports, and especially triathlon, have been an enormously positive influence on my life for the past 30 years. Tom has put together the complete guide to the half-Ironman. His approach to the preparation for racing this distance will provide athletes with a thorough plan to best maximize their physical and mental capabilities. While triathlon has seen a tremendous growth in the past 10 years in all distances, from sprint to full Ironman, the half-Ironman creates a special venue of opportunity for both seasoned veterans of the sport and novice athletes who want to increase their racing distance. This new book will certainly meet those needs. Rodgers exemplifies the theories that he coaches and teaches in his own outstanding performances at all distances, and especially the half-Ironman, Ironman, ultra-distance triathlons, and ultra-distance bicycle races.

Over the years of my involvement in the sport I have become very concerned with the high volume of training and racing done by some athletes. In some cases I feel that rather than reaping the benefits from a healthy lifestyle, athletes develop an unhealthy obsession. With the new popularity of the half-Ironman distance, the professional manner with which Tom has approached proper training may be a remedy for my concern. I do know that he has given every possible thought toward this goal of performance, balance, and injury-free participation. This book will provide timely insight to the half ironman distance, especially since the first-ever Ironman 70.3 World Championship was held in November 2006, another example of how this distance has moved to center stage in this great sport.

This book should not only be on all triathletes' shelves, but on their bedside table as well. While Tom has practiced what he preaches, he can also relay it to us mere mortals as we strive to maximize our efforts in endurance athletics. Tom has delivered an outstanding "how-to" book for our sport.

Mike Greer
Race Director, Buffalo Springs Lake Ironman 70.3 Triathlon
Former USA Triathlon Executive Director, currently serving on its Board of Directors

PREFACE

It was once said that training to go fast for a long time in three distinctive sports, the basis of long-course triathlon, was asking the impossible. But if you're reading this book, you think differently.

When folks started attempting longer distance triathlons, moving beyond the hour-long beach races in the California 1970s, some thought they were crazy. Relative to the social consensus of that time they probably were. Soon, however, triathletes found that not only could they race for extremely long periods, they could actually go *fast* in all three sports if they had the proper training and strategy.

Pioneers like Joe Friel and others who outlined periodization for multisport athletes did a magnificent job, and we all have benefited immensely. Yet there is still some progress to be made with the *design science* of training. We already have a plethora of plans, workouts, and methods available. Pick up a magazine for a few dollars, buy a book for a little more, or head to the internet and you will find a hundred training plans and thousands of workouts at the click of a mouse. All of these plans and workouts at your fingertips is not unlike the temptation of calorie-rich foods—it's easy to gorge yourself without getting the best nutrition.

It was not always so easy. In the early days of long-course triathlon, people did not yet know how to train properly for multisport events of four, five or even ten hours. Everything was experimental and one had to possess creative vision in order to devise any workable plan. And the sport's pioneers did just that, learning from their counterparts in the individual sports and weaving a unique fabric. No, they did not have all the scientific research that we now possess almost thirty years into the sport, but neither did they get lost in what Carl Jung termed the "mythology of facts"—reams of hard data without an underlying purpose.

This book is my attempt to integrate hard facts with an attitude of elegant design. With all the technical information available, one common problem is that triathletes want to apply those concepts right away and "drive them down the course." This is not unlike pedaling off on a new bike before taking the care to adjust the fit. We find a ready-made training plan and then go out and execute it without much thinking in between.

For beginners this is somewhat inevitable, but at some point you must develop a coherent vision of where you are going. Without vision, triathletes will become very tired (or quite bored) without getting very fit.

A training plan is a static form, a step-by-step procedure of finite elements meant to build fitness for a specific event. The process of formulating effective plans, executing them, and then reflecting upon the results is dynamic. A level higher still is vision, where we see the underlying purpose of the process. Most athletes need to spend more energy on the vision and process, and spend less time obsessing about the finite plan, which may or may not succeed. The mind leads and the body follows, and as we mature we learn to think more and act more thoughtfully.

I do not know of an athlete who can repeatedly execute the same plan in different situations successfully. In fact, the most successful athletes seem to be the ones who are willing to change their plan from year to year, or even week by week. There is nothing random or chaotic about this change—they seem to know exactly what they are doing despite a metamorphic plan. They have developed the necessary vision to see a little into the future, to sense when a plan will work for them and when it should be scrapped for something better.

This does not mean you should wake up every morning and change your training. Sometimes you indeed have to do the same thing over and over for countless weeks, months, or years until you get it right. But your *attitude* must never become crystallized or locked in time. Your mind must remain flexible, fluid, mercurial. (Remember that mercury is a fluidic metal which often changes form, that Mercury was the god of speed ... and speed is what racing is all about.)

In *The Perfect Distance,* I've taken some time to develop a design science of training (Chapters 1–3). Please be patient as I think you'll find the design process to be interesting reading, and if you can absorb this approach to creative, visionary thinking, you'll have a lot more success applying the more detailed information. Chapters 4 and 5 will get you into the planning.

That being said, I think you'll find as much technical information in this volume as you would expect in any other about triathlon. Chapters 6 through 8 cover the three sports, and Chapter 9 approaches all-important fourth event of nutrition from a physical and mental perspective. As with training, controlling what you eat is largely a problem of taming your mind and desires. Chapter 10 includes advanced concepts in the three sports and is geared toward the more experienced triathlete who wants to finish at or near the top of their division. Chapter 11 details practical racing strategies for beginners and experts alike, including a sample spreadsheet table of a veteran age-grouper's race plan. We include real-world examples of preparation taken from different skill levels in Chapter 12. Last, but not least, is the role of strength training and flexibility in endurance sports, with specific exercises in Chapter 13. And yes, we do include long lists of specific swim, bike, run, and combined workouts in the appendices.

Racing is all about *rush-rush-rush*—the competition will not wait for you. But training and building fitness requires patience and adherence to principles first, results second. Success *will* come, like a butterfly landing upon your shoulder, but you can't force it.

Tom Rodgers
Arlington, Texas

ACKNOWLEDGMENTS

I'd like to thank my wife, Tuula, who put up with the occasional irritations of a pressured writer, perhaps not so rarely. She contributed the fine photos in this book and is the best cheerleader an endurance athlete could ever want.

We all owe a debt to Joe Friel, who brought the theories of periodization to multisport training, and practically invented the triathlon coaching profession. On a personal level, Joe has also been an encouragement in my own writing. Other coaches that have inspired and educated me include Gordo Byrn, Ken Mierke, Richard Strauss, Dirk Friel, Phil Maffetone, and many others too numerous to mention. Top endurance athletes like fellow Texan Lance Armstrong, Mark Allen, Dave Scott, Scott Tinley, Paula Newby-Fraser, Natascha Badmann, and numerous others have been inspirational.

The fine editors and publishers at VeloPress have been encouraging and patient, as much of this book was written during some of the most stressful times of my life, times when the fatigue of ultradistance training and coaching sometimes weighed heavier than the love of writing.

All the athletes I've enjoying training with, racing with, and coaching have been my perpetual teachers, and this from all levels of the sport. One of these, Justin Daerr, who I was able to watch grow from a beginning teenage runner to triathlete to elite professional in only a few years, is proof positive dedication and adherence to fundamentals can take you anywhere you want to go in this sport. He also suggested the title for this book, *The Perfect Distance.*

Thanks to all the tireless half-Iron race directors, such as Mike Greer who created the Buffalo Springs Lake Ironman 70.3 and went on to become interim director of USA Triathlon, as well others at USAT and the World Triathlon Corporation who had the vision to grow the perfect distance of a 1.2-mile swim, 56-mile bike, and 13.1-mile run—much to the benefit to all who love to race it.

And I'd like to thank you, the long-course racers out there who never, ever, ever give up, keeping your bold spontaneity and love of the extreme. As the English poet Robert Browning said, "A man's reach should exceed his grasp—or what's a heaven for?"

CHAPTER 1

The Renaissance of the Half-Iron Distance

The reports of my death are greatly exaggerated.
—Mark Twain

When I decided to train for my first triathlon, I chose the Buffalo Springs Lake Half-Ironman® in Lubbock, Texas (now officially titled an Ironman 70.3 race). It was and is one of the toughest "halfs" in the world, very popular among my fellow Texans and the whole world. I knew little or nothing about triathlon beyond the "Julie Moss crawling in Kona" episode on ABC-TV. I had recently finished my first marathon run and was looking for something long and tough to challenge me further.

There was a great crop of guest speakers who also raced. In 1998 the legendary Scott Tinley stood before us, showing photos from his upcoming book and telling wonderful stories. I soaked up every word like a sponge.

He began, "Welcome to the great Buffalo Springs half-Ironman race, a dying breed in the world of triathlon." He lamented that Olympic- and sprint-distance racing was becoming dominant, eating up all the market and forcing the half-Iron races out of existence. At the time, this statement was an accurate assessment of triathlon: The big Ironman race in Hawaii, a few others in foreign countries, dwindling half-Iron races, and a movement toward shorter racing everywhere else.

Tinley would certainly agree that the prognosis for the long-course triathlon has happily reversed. He underestimated the fact that explosive growth in multisport racing would encompass all distances. In the last few years, the half-Iron distance race has returned with a preeminent constellation of races in the triathlon zodiac. There is now a national half-Iron distance championship series with twenty races. Not to be outdone, the brand-conscious folks at the World Triathlon Corporation (WTC) have created their 70.3 Ironman series with qualifying slots leading up to a world championship in the 1.2-mile swim, 56-mile bike, and 13.1-mile run triathlon. This book answers the rejoicing of pro and age-group athletes alike for the renaissance of this fun yet challenging discipline.

THE REALITY OF LONGER DISTANCES

Beginning and experienced endurance athletes know that longer distances involve a "reality check" for your goals and abilities. Unlike short-course racing, you cannot bluff or muscle your way through based on talent or with insufficient training. The longer distances require an organized training plan, some knowledge of physiology, and a realistic race strategy. Casual runners, cyclists, or swimmers can show up at a sprint triathlon without much preparation and usually finish standing up, having a good time, if not necessarily a fast time. If you try this approach in a marathon run or a half-Iron triathlon, you are probably in for a world of hurt, if indeed you finish standing up at all.

Reading this book and applying its tested principles should give you the ability to plan your training and enjoy the racing experience.

THE PERFECT DISTANCE

You might wonder why, with all the variety of triathlons out there ranging from 20 minutes to 30-plus hours, I call half-Iron racing "The Perfect Distance." The book title came from a triathlete I helped in Texas who went on to great things in the pro ranks. The phrase instantly struck a chord with me because the half-Iron distance:

- Stresses the fundamental principles of triathlon training common to all distances.
- Balances the "training triad" of endurance, force, and speed (see Chapter 2 on training fundamentals).
- Facilitates transition from the beginning to the intermediate level by progressing from sprint- and Olympic-distance experience.
- Provides the "Noble Middle Path" connecting the shorter and longer disciplines of triathlons.
- Significantly decreases the probability of overtraining or injury that often accompanies full Ironman or marathon running preparation.
- Saves time and money compared to longer races' entry fees, rapid registration fill-up, travel time and distance, and recovery, allowing the athlete more competitive possibilities per season—and often more fun as well.
- Requires only a moderate amount of weekly training hours, allowing busy professionals, spouses, parents, and students to get on with life in the "real world" outside of triathlon without undue stress or strain.
- Releases many of the same "joyous achievement" endorphins found when completing Ironman or marathon running races, but without as much bodily pain—more good vibes, less suffering.
- Gives athletes over 70 or those with severe physical challenges (such as wheelchair or amputee athletes) a much better chance of finishing within the time cutoffs. Such success might encourage them to attempt a previously unthinkable full Ironman race.
- Allows entry of athletes under 18 years of age. Many young athletes, despite suggestions to the contrary, wish to experience longer distances early in their careers.
- Provides veteran triathletes a sufficient challenge to measure long-range fitness and rehearse for longer efforts in a full Ironman. Half-Iron race completion is almost a "required exam" before attempting your first Ironman and can continue to serve as the perfect tune-up a few months before the longer race in future seasons.
- Allows expert age-group and pro triathletes to qualify for the Ironman world championships without the time-consuming recovery of a full Ironman qualifier.
- Opens a gateway for elite short-course athletes to cross over to longer distances without abandoning their specialized anaerobic training. They can pick up some extra prize money or sponsorship

exposure, or use the half-Iron race as a stepping-stone to elite Ironman racing. Several world and Olympic champions follow this path into their 30s, and some have excelled at both disciplines.

If all the above reasons are not enough, then just do it to have fun! I've had several treasured achievements in my racing career, but I don't think I've ever had any more fun than I did that first half-Ironman race at Buffalo Springs Lake.

WHAT YOU BRING TO THE TABLE

Because the half-Iron distance has diverse benefits, it brings a wide spectrum of talent and lifestyle to the starting line. Before going further, you should ask yourself where you fall in this large spectrum. We will state some broad categories with the understanding that it's impossible to label every individual. More than one of these may apply to you, but as a coach I've found that you will likely fall into one of these groups.

Endurance Athlete without Triathlon Experience

Although some may think it bold to attempt a half-Iron race as your first triathlon, coaches actually get a significant number of applicants wanting to compete in a full Ironman without prior experience. It's preferable to get some experience doing shorter races before attempting the half-Iron distance, but it's okay if you have already chosen a half-Iron race many months or a year in the future. You can plan for this as your important "A" race, and find one more "B" or "C" race of shorter distance to help you prepare. Many of my clients who are beginners have finished a half-Iron race within six to twelve months after entering the sport. I did it in three months at the age of 37 with only six months' prior running experience, and not very fast running at that.

It's not so important which endurance discipline you come from, but rather how long the racing distances are and your average weekly training hours. Someone who has successfully completed a marathon run with little or no walking, or someone who can ride a bike 100 miles, will adjust more quickly than someone who races 800 meters or has never been on a bike longer than one hour per day. Distance swimmers racing 400–1,500 meters or farther have developed more capacity for long-course racing than those who only sprint 50–100 meters.

If you have no experience in any of the three endurance phases of triathlon, that's okay. You can still do a half-Iron race, but you will have to be more patient and adjust your goals to be in line with your strengths and limiters. Most age-group triathletes start without a formal background in the three sports, and sometimes they go on to be perennial champions in their division. Triathlon's growth is such that many will choose it as their first-ever endurance sport.

The joy of finishing a long-course race is profound.

Just about everyone in this category should be training to finish the race, without much regard for exact time. Obviously, if you were a professional cyclist or swam in the Olympics, your splits are going to be different from someone still learning those disciplines. You will still need a balanced approach to the three phases of the event in order to finish strong.

The good news is you may never again progress as rapidly or have as much fun as you do in the first year of triathlon. Your times may improve for years, but the satisfaction for the newcomer is profound.

Beginning Triathlete Moving Up in Distance

This group is the fastest growing for half-Iron racing, perhaps the fastest growing in all the sport. These folks are the reason why race directors are opening up half-Iron races almost as quickly as those expensive coffee shops on every corner.

You may have been in the sport for six months or many years. You've done a few sprint- and perhaps Olympic-distance races, finished okay, and now want more. You've seen the television coverage and read the stories about full Ironman races, but you're not ready yet.

Since these athletes have a reasonably precise idea of their talents and abilities in the sport, it is easier to predict how they will perform in the longer challenge. Although they are exploring new territory in a race of five to seven hours, they can begin their training with a realistic goal of completion within a moderate time span.

Important questions include:

- How have you been handling your existing training plan, if any?
- How did you perform in prior races, including overall time, splits, and the "feel" of the race?
- Can you realistically increase your training hours to prepare for a race at least twice as long as previous efforts?

Fortunately, you do not have to train twice as many hours to race twice as far, or else marathon runners and Ironman specialists would burn out in their first year. For the half-Iron distance, moderate increases in training volume are not the most difficult adjustment.

Veteran Triathlete Moving Up in Distance

It's tough to draw a definite boundary that makes you a "veteran." Like beginners, we are all learning more about the sport every year, but it's safe to say that if you've been training regularly for over a year and have done a few races, you are no longer a beginner. Even without coaching or book-learning, you would have learned enough from the experience itself.

You have been thinking of doing a half-Iron race for some time and have already done some speculative planning. You are sure you want to do it, you know when and where you'd like to do it, but you need a more detailed road map to get you through the training and the race planning.

As with the beginning triathletes, you have experience in shorter races to draw upon and a good baseline of training information. Even if you did not keep a detailed log of training, heart rates, and so on, you remember the perceived exertion of shorter and longer efforts and the degree of intensity that you find comfortable—or not so comfortable.

You may have friends that have already done the half-Iron race, and they are a valuable source of information. But keep in mind that every athlete is unique, and even the same athlete is different from season to season. You have to take yourself as you are now and move on from there.

Veteran Triathlete with Long-Course Experience Seeking Improvement

When it comes to long-course racing, you can say, "Been there, done that, have the T-shirt." But if you're reading this book, you would like to do it faster next time—to go for that Personal Best or beat your local rival. Maybe you've excelled at short-course racing but never "hit the nail" when it comes to the longer stuff. Now is the time to examine your full potential, create a realistic plan for improvement, and race with both heart and mind.

Veteran Triathlete Training for Full Ironman

You may well have done a half-Iron race before, but now you've set your sights on the longer race, and you are using this event as a gauge of your long-range endurance and perhaps a dress rehearsal for the big event months later.

Note the time span, "months later": You want to give yourself plenty of time between a half-Iron tune-up race and a full Ironman A race. It's not that the half-Iron race takes a particularly long time to recover from, but rather that the critical weeks of high-volume Ironman training should not be broken up with the shorter, more intense half-Iron distances. You will read stories about top Ironman professional triathletes doing a famous half-Iron race a couple of weeks before racing in an Ironman, but they are usually in the early-season Base period. They may be doing incredibly high volumes and not tapering at all for this race, performing at what is for them merely a high aerobic intensity.

For the rest of us mortals, the half-Iron race should be placed at least five to six weeks or more before the upcoming Ironman. This choice is difficult for many age-group athletes who love their regional half-Iron race, but it falls too close to their farther-distance A race. If you've already chosen to race an Ironman, the rest of your season usually revolves around it.

The good news is that many half-Iron courses work as a scale model of a corresponding full Ironman course. A good example is Buffalo Springs Lake in Lubbock, Texas, which resembles the heat, wind, and hills of Kona. And the two races are four months apart, plenty of time in the same season. As the list of half-Iron races grows, it's easier to find one that meets your scheduling and course-simulation needs.

Expert Triathlete Seeking Age-Group Victory, Pro Podium, or Kona Slot

Welcome to the top of the pyramid. You've done plenty of half-Iron racing and probably some full Ironman races. Now you are going for all the marbles: Victory in your age group, an overall pro podium place, and along with it a Kona slot. There was a time when qualifying at a half-Ironman race was the primary method of getting to the Hawaii Ironman®. But with the proliferation of North American and overseas races, the large majority of the qualifying slots are reserved for those who finish a full Ironman race near the top of their age group. To qualify for Kona at a half-Ironman race, now termed a "70.3 Ironman," you must usually finish first or second in your age group or the pro division.

If you are racing at this high level, the half-Iron race becomes a more anaerobic experience. Not as anaerobic as Olympic style-racing, but still with a considerably higher heart rate than the Ironman. The training and race strategy are different for this type of athlete, since to win the race overall requires something around four hours, and even the masters division on a tough course may require 4:25 or faster.

But racing 20 percent faster does not mean training with 20 percent more intensity. The fundamentally aerobic nature of half-Iron training remains, with a little more anaerobic work in training and a lot more audacity on race day.

COACHING AND SELF-COACHING

Due to the prodigious efforts of pioneers like Joe Friel, Gale Bernhardt, and many others who founded the USA Triathlon coaching committee, there are good standards for coaches in this sport and training systems for coaches of various levels of experience and degrees of specialization. Along with the explosive growth of triathlon participants, there has been a parallel increase in the number of coaches.

But the most important discovery in triathlon—coaching, training, racing, and promotion—came from outside the sport. Maybe you guessed: It's the Internet. As with the rest of its effects, the Internet has been both a blessing and a curse when it comes to training, racing, and coaching. That old warning of "too much information" needs to be respected. For every good piece of triathlon training information and physiology, there are at least one or two more pieces of overgeneralization, dated theory, or downright falsehoods.

Looking for coaches has become seemingly easy. Just put in the word "triathlon training" in Google and you will get dozens of choices and also find a dozen or so coaches spending thousands of dollars to advertise their services every month in just this one search engine. If you look at endurance coaching as a kind of health care service, you can see that looking for quality has not become any easier, and can even be more difficult with so many choices.

You should take the same level of care in choosing a triathlon coach as you take when choosing where to buy pharmaceuticals or which medical doctor will examine you or perform surgery. In fact, when you consider the amount of time and money you will spend in this sport, especially at the longer distances—the risks you will take, the changes you will put your body through—you might find that triathlon choices are the most important health care decisions you will make in the coming years.

The person who tries to link all of this together into a useful process is your coach. He or she is an advocate who can advise you independently of all the race directors, nutritional vendors, bike manufacturers, electronic device inventors, magazine publishers, and other well-meaning (or perhaps selfishly motivated) entities who want to influence your path in multisport.

The most common question that always comes up with beginning athletes is, "What about my training plan? How can I get a training plan for my favorite race?" One of my colleagues humorously answered this question by saying, "You can get a training plan in a triathlon magazine for only $4.95." But he wasn't trying to be funny at all. Most of the Internet and print ads for coaches don't say much at all about the individual, but simply push the key words "training plans, training plans, training plans" over and over. When it comes to training and choosing a coach, many athletes cannot see the forest for the trees.

The most important thing in coaching is relationship: The personal, almost intimate relationship between coach and athlete, and the relationship between training, racing, and lifestyle. A precisely formulated training plan using all the latest and greatest in human physiology is not worth the paper it is printed on (or the telephone cable it is transmitted upon) without the quality of these relationships.

For some reason we expect great coaches when it comes to team sports like football, basketball, or soccer—the legend of the coach motivating the team's mind and heart to achieve great things. But since endurance sports are usually individual, we tend to view the coach as someone who just organizes the athlete's training plan. Can you name the coaches of any of the medal winners in the marathon run, 1,500m swim, or triathlon? But you can probably name several top coaches in team sports. Yet most triathlon champions have shown an intense loyalty to their coaches and have sometimes met with overtraining and failure when straying too far from their coach's methods.

Your endurance coach will become an important partner in your lifestyle as a serious athlete. Coaches are human beings with strengths and limiters just like their athletes. They have bills to pay, families to raise, and are usually very pressed for time—just like you are when you try to fit in all your training.

The dilemma is that coaches who really know what they are doing are always in demand and must show great discipline in limiting their clientele. Some people think you can scale coaching in a cookie-cutter fashion as with other products and services, but in fact it may be the least replicable type of service.

In the end you have to find someone you trust, and someone who has the ethical makeup and "heart" to truly care about your progress. No, this is not an easy thing to do. Just as most triathletes rarely buy the right bike frame when they begin, many do not find the right coach or outgrow a certain coach after they progress to a different level. An honest coach will notice when this is true and will recommend a better choice, just as a competent medical doctor would send you to a specialist or surgeon as required.

Most coaches have different price levels for different levels of attention. Like most things in life, you get what you pay for. Expecting total concentration and personal attention from a coach while only paying for his lowest level of service is like expecting first-class airline seating and service for the economy seat price.

Many top coaches only offer one high level of pricing nowadays. Yet many good, experienced coaches have openings and reasonably priced plans to meet your needs. As with other triathlon expenses, you need to choose a program based on your own financial resources. But if you have a choice between spending money on a resort hotel suite at the race or the fastest, coolest new race wheels, you would do better to spend that money first on a good coach.

In fact, for those new to the sport the cost of coaching might actually result in a net savings. I probably spent $10,000 in unnecessary expenses when I began in triathlon, whereas a top coach would have only cost me a third of that amount, and would have saved me at least $5,000. And, of course, I would have raced better and had more fun.

Committing to the Plan

Once you have chosen a coach, established clear communication, and devised a seasonal and weekly plan, you should stick to it. Second-guessing your coach in midstream is like second-guessing a surgeon or arguing with your lawyer during the trial proceedings. Yes, you should ask many questions and understand the purpose for all you do, but once that is achieved, you should follow the coach's methods faithfully.

Some athletes change the program but are a bit shy about talking about it. Weeks or months go by when the coach does not really know what the athlete is doing. Most coaches are flexible when it comes to lifestyle issues and modifying the plan based on family and work issues. That's usually not the problem. But when the athlete tries to tweak the intensity or volume without communication, the overall balance is disrupted, usually with bad results.

When in doubt, ask your coach. It's okay to disagree, and sometimes compromise is required on both sides. It's when my athletes stop calling me or stop e-mailing that I begin to worry. As the great athlete and coach Gordo Byrn says, "If I'm not talking to you, I'm not coaching you."

Sometimes my athletes start conversations with questions like, "Am I bothering you? Do you have time to talk about this?" Of course I do! Coaching is what I do for a living, and talking directly to my athletes is one of the most rewarding, joyful aspects of the job. Coaches are not the help desk at your phone company or bank. We actually enjoy helping you!

Responsibility is a two-way street. Your coach must take responsibility for the plan and methods used, and you should take responsibility for questioning and understanding the process, and then using it to the best of your ability.

Self-Coaching

Despite the wealth of information and motivation available from a personal coach, most of the readers of this book will be self-coaching. That's okay. I started reading triathlon books and coaching myself for a few years before hiring a personal coach.

I've been a self-taught learner most of my life. Even in a university education, I found myself mostly learning from books and individual problem-solving rather than from lectures or any one teacher. Certainly, training for sports like triathlon calls for a lot of solitude, and some triathlon champions train alone 90 percent of the time, especially for races where drafting is not allowed on the bike leg. So I have some sympathy for self-coached athletes.

I also believe the half-Iron distance discipline lends itself to self-coaching more than the longer full Ironman or even the specialized Olympic-style of draft-legal racing. Since it involves fundamental principles, moderate pacing, and moderate training volume, it's possible for an individual to judge intensity and manage a plan better than someone who is training twenty-five or more hours per week, or perhaps training at 90 percent of their maximum heart rate. I prepared for my first half-Ironman without any outside assistance beyond one book and some Internet articles, and a little folklore from other experienced triathletes.

If anything, self-coached athletes need to be even more organized than those with a coach who shares the planning load. Tools like heart rate monitors (HRMs), software training logs, online training systems (such as the TrainingPeaks.com system developed by Joe Friel) are essential for gauging your progress. I once described training without a heart rate monitor as trying to comb your hair or tie a necktie without a mirror. Yes, you can sometimes get away without one, but you'll look much better if you can see what you are doing. Since we are dealing with cardiorespiratory endurance sports, you need some reflection of your "aerobic image," and HRMs and related software help you do this. Later developments like power meters on the bike and GPS pacing on the run have also been very helpful to many athletes. These devices get easier to use every day, and you don't have to be a "techno geek" to learn how to use them. We are now into the second or third generation of training software—it's "speeding up" as quickly as the race times.

In order to succeed, you must have a plan: For the season, for the microcycles of your weekly training, and for the specific race distance. You must learn the basics of exercise physiology. And you need to learn when to take risks and push the envelope and when to rest and recover. This book will give you the tools to coach yourself and improve, and should you move on to personal coaching, you'll be much better equipped to communicate with your coach.

CHAPTER 2

Physiology and Psychology of Training

Despite all attempts to control the conditions of an experiment, the organism does what it damn well pleases.
—Harvard Law of Biology

One of the reasons I choose to call the half-Iron distance "perfect" is that it emphasizes the most fundamental aspects of training. Whereas Iron-distance training focuses mostly on endurance, and Olympic-distance or shorter races focus on speed, the half-Iron distance lies at the core of all triathlon. Almost all the great triathletes have at least attempted it and often excelled.

If you can learn to train and race effectively at the half-Iron distance, you are well on your way to excelling at *any* multisport event: Short, long, triathlon, or duathlon. You can maintain excellent fitness for any of these events year-round by spending 80–90 percent of your training time on fundamentals, which is the essence of half-Iron preparation.

THE LAW OF PERIODICITY AND THE PROCESS OF PERIODIZATION

The most important concept in training is the Law of Periodicity. This notion of rhythmic ebb and flow is fundamental to all of science, from the smallest subatomic particles to the largest cosmologies with distant galaxies at the edge of the "event horizon" of human knowledge. In the early twenty-first century, humans measure physical periods ranging from:

- **1/9,192,631,770th of a second**, the radiant transition time between the two hyperfine levels of the ground state of the cesium 133 atom. This measurement is so precise that astronomers must now add a "leap second" to the calendar every few decades.
- **11.2–20 billion years**, the recently estimated age of the universe. Despite the vastness of this number, cosmologists state that there is still two-thirds of this universe we are theoretically unable to see.

You can rest assured that we will be dealing with much simpler periods in this book, but it's good to keep in mind that this law is not new. It comes from the oldest human science, measuring the periodic movement of heavenly bodies.

In human physiology, we are dealing with periods of hours, days, weeks, or years. Athletes have always trained to some sort of regular periodic pattern, but until recently they had only a vague notion of how these patterns worked. The first observation started when we were running after or away from something. Fatigue set in and we had to slow down or stop. After a period of recovery, we felt better and could run again. The faster we ran, the more time we needed to recover before we could run fast once again. Since human migration and hunting required us to run, and we ate a naturally balanced diet with plenty of time to rest, hunters grew to be progressively faster runners. Nature ensured that humans were good endurance athletes without any conscious notion of "training." Though we lack the speed and strength of many animals, our ability to sustain a steady effort for hours, days, or weeks at a time is unparalleled in land mammals.

The Greek athlete Milo of Croton applied this notion of periodic growth to strength development around 542 B.C., carrying a calf every day until it grew into a bull. His periodic, progressive training must have worked since he went on to win five Olympic wrestling championships through age 40. Since he was said to be a follower of Pythagoras, the inventor of the periodic music scale and the triangular mathematical theorem, perhaps Milo possessed a clearer notion of scientific training than we might expect from an ancient athlete.

The fundamental equation of periodic training is simple to write, but very challenging to perform:

Training = Stress + Rest

The most important component of this equation is rest, but no one is going to get rich writing a triathlon book about rest. While those ancient hunters were chasing game or Milo was carrying that bull, they were not getting any faster or stronger. They were in fact breaking down tissue in their cardiovascular and muscular systems. It was only later during rest that any gains took place. After a certain period of rest and recovery, they noticed that the next time they ran or lifted they improved. Over a long period of time, this effect is tremendous, and the process is called *supercompensation,* where the body responds to stress by becoming more tolerant to the stressful activity, more efficient. Without rest there is no time to compensate and no training effect. A composer once said, "The music is the space between the notes," and indeed the training effect is caused by the space between workouts.

The body does not know or care about the type of stress. It reacts by burning fuel, secreting hormones, and breaking down tissues to respond to the crisis at hand. This stress causes discomfort and fatigue, and eventually we want to slow down and get some rest. Using our human brains, we can override these bodily messages and continue farther and farther into the valley of fatigue, and this was a useful tool if we were running from a lion or hurling a spear at dinner. The fight-or-flight mechanism is deeply ingrained and has much to do with why people start racing in the first place. In modern life, the mere *perception* of stress can affect the body as much as the primitive life-or-death conditioning.

The problem for athletes arises when we associate this mechanism with fear: Fear of losing, fear of not working hard enough, fear of not impressing our training partners, fear of looking too fat or too weak, fear of injury or accidental death, and so on. We all suffer from these fears, and they can be transformed into a very positive training force when brought under control. Control is another way of saying we "periodize" these stresses and emotions. There is a time to let go and rest, and rest more than we think. As Joe Friel said, "Train hard, rest harder."

MODERN TRAINING WITH PERIODIZATION

When we apply the Law of Periodicity to create a specific structure with cycles, attributes, and specific goals for each period, we call this process *periodization.* Note that the Law of Periodicity and the training equation are basic principles, but periodization is a creative process that applies these principles. Other athletes and coaches have applied the principles in different ways, so just because training has some variety and structure does *not* mean it uses the process of periodization.

In the second half of the twentieth century, we learned a lot more about the physiological processes that support training. Competition between superpowers in science and technology became evident in athletics just as it did with space travel. Struggling for international validation, the Soviet-bloc nations dedicated funding and technology to athletics as if it were a defense project, and indeed many of their athletes were ostensibly military officers. Their best doctors and scientists were assigned to individual athletes on a daily basis. Measurement of training, physiology, and resulting performance gains became a seven-days-a-week, 365-days-a-year proposition. They found that performance improved quickly when training followed a wave pattern of workouts. Before this development, most top athletes followed a mixed approach, where intensity was constant, and often quite high, throughout the year.

By the 1960s, a Romanian sports scientist, Tudor Bompa, refined this wave pattern with specific goals for various periods, thus becoming known as the "Father of Periodization." The results were displayed for the whole world to see in competition, but it was not until his publication of *Theory and Methodology of Training* that these techniques became widely known to Western athletes.

Central to the theory of periodization is the progression from general to specific training: As the training season evolves, workouts become more and more relevant to the specific sport and distance involved, while crosstraining in other disciplines declines. Related to specificity is the individuality of each athlete: Strengths and limiters determine the specific skills that require greater or lesser attention. Triathletes whose slowest event is the swim would spend more time on stroke drills early in the swim season and later focus more time on intervals related to their target distance. A cyclist who has trouble with climbing would lift weights early in the season but focus more on actual hill climbing as races approached.

As appealing as periodization may seem, it is not a standard that all top athletes follow. Some have done quite well with a mixture of workouts that do not follow periodization. Some age groupers think they are following periodization when in fact they are still using mixed training. Some are following periodized training plans, but they are so warped toward one end of the spectrum that they are of little use to the large majority of athletes.

Since this book focuses on half-Iron training and fundamentals, we will favor a classic model of periodization created with the flexibility of modern design methods. Not only does this model have the maximum chance of improving most athletes' performance, it is also the safest in terms of avoiding injury and overtraining. Reviewing the overall history of long-course racing, you'll find that elite athletes straying from the balanced approach may have had dramatic success for a year or two, but were forced back "down to earth" by injury or overtraining problems. They were unable to escape the Law of Periodicity, the inevitable ebb and flow of fitness. Despite attempting to delay the inevitable, they were forced to rest more and balance their lives whether they liked it or not.

NUTS AND BOLTS OF FITNESS

As with many structures in nature, fitness rests on a triangular foundation, a balancing of three types of energy: endurance, force, and speed (Figure 2.1).

These energies can complement one another or work in opposition. You can apply this triad to just about any sport from power lifting

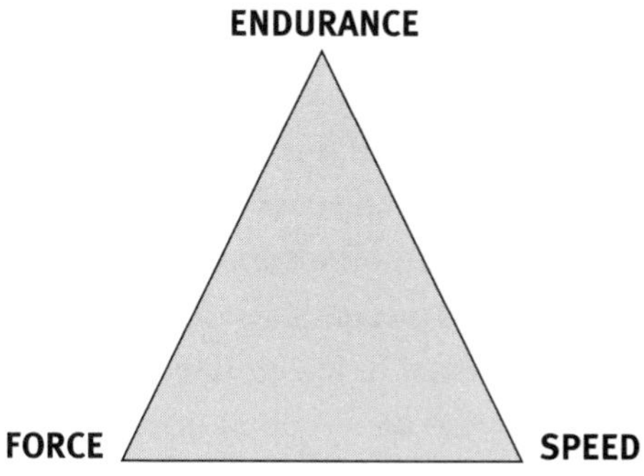

FIGURE 2.1
Training triad

to American football to Formula 1 auto racing, but it has special relevance to triathlon, where three different sports are performed over a range of intensities.

From a physiological perspective, anything over an 800m run is an aerobic endurance event, stressing fat burning and oxygen processing over sugar burning and anaerobic energy sources. In triathlon, where a one-hour race is still termed a "sprint," we really don't consider the emphasis on endurance until we get to the half-Iron distance. These are mere distinctions of the human mind since the body doesn't care what distance you plan to race. It simply moves and burns fuel in the most efficient way possible from moment to moment. Conceptual learning requires us to categorize into discrete chunks, but the biological reality is that all the processes work together, blending into one another.

Endurance

Endurance is the capacity to extend an activity over a long period of time with minimal fatigue. It involves an aerobic (oxygen-based) level of exertion, burning mostly fat and a little sugar. We place it at the top of the training triad for half-Iron preparation because this is the first popular triathlon distance where it is truly dominant. There are few if any athletes who could muscle their way through this event, or could exploit superior speed in one event to the exclusion of effective training for the other two. If you want to excel at this distance or finish standing up on your first try, you'd better have plenty of endurance. On the other hand, it does not require the extreme volume and time commitment that the full Iron distance requires. It is well within the endurance abilities of most amateur athletes.

Force

Force is the ability to accelerate mass, to overcome resistance. Although it is not the same as force applied by weight lifters or football linemen, strength *is* important to the long-course triathlete and to endurance athletes in general. Its most important application for triathletes is *muscular endurance* (Figure 2.2), a combination of strength and endurance. This attribute is demonstrated in longer time trials, open-water swims, climbing hills or fighting the wind, and in maintaining running form at the end of longer races.

Weight lifting can conjure muscular images made popular by Arnold Schwarzenegger or the bulk of an NFL linebacker. Coaches usually have

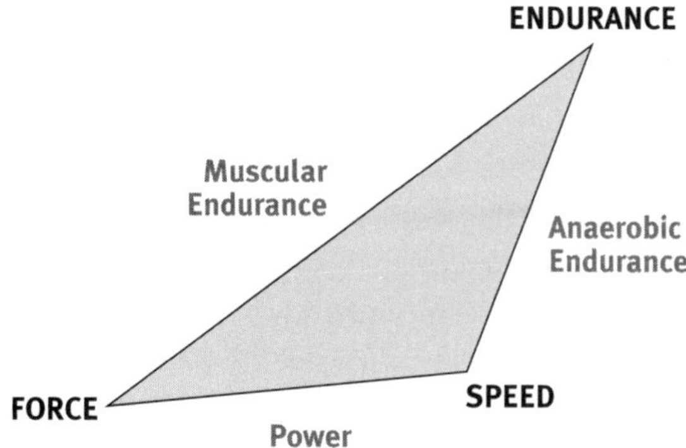

FIGURE 2.2

Sides of the training triad. Note the relative size and importance of the qualities.

to reprogram athletes to the endurance model of strength training, which emphasizes more repetitions with lower weight, a smaller and more specific group of exercises, and a parallel periodization that complements event-specific training. The good news is that it doesn't take many hours per week to develop this strength, just consistency. Athletes also build strength on the bike, in the water, and on the run by specific drills, which are as important as weight lifting. For triathletes, core strength in the abdominals, hips, and lower back are indeed more important than strength in the outer arms and legs.

Speed

Since the prize goes to the person with the highest average speed for the entire course, all triathletes need to work on this quality. But it means more than just training near race pace or going as fast as you can as often as possible. It means improving economy and the efficiency of motions that lead to faster racing speed. Developing speed requires performing drills and working on techniques at a relatively slow pace. Just as golfers have to slow down their swing to improve mechanics and therefore hit the ball farther in competition, endurance athletes have to deconstruct their swim stroke, pedal stroke, and running form in order to rebuild them into a more efficient "vehicle" for racing. Many athletes will achieve their aerobic potential after a few years of consistent training, but economy is something you work on your entire athletic career, a lifetime project. And more economical means safer and less prone to injury. Good form also minimizes the performance losses for the aging athlete.

The problem with economy drills is that they are not as glamorous or difficult as the anaerobic speed work of track intervals, hammerhead peloton rides, or swim sprints. They require slow, patient work more akin to golf or tennis. But research and our own experience shows economy is the most productive area in terms of increasing racing speed.

Competitive swimmers seem to do disproportionately well in long and short triathlons, considering the relatively brief contribution of the swim to the overall race time. The likely reason? They learn early to consistently perform stroke drills and work on technique (economy) in every practice session. When they move on to learn cycling and running, they have no problem extending regular technique drills and controlled intervals to these other sports. The rest of us need to learn similar discipline in working smarter, not just harder, in all three triathlon sports.

TRAINING FOR ENDURANCE

I propose endurance as the most important "angle" of the triathlon training triad, and even more so for the half-Iron distance. This kind of endurance involves mostly aerobic processing and burns primarily fat for fuel. But how much is truly aerobic? Any running event over 800 meters requires an aerobic effort. A one-hour race is about 85 percent carbohydrate burning. As for the half-Iron distance, fat burning is closer to 50 percent. But remember that carbohydrates are required to jump-start the fat-burning process, so really you could say 75 percent or more of a five-hour race requires aerobic fat burning.

Even though we've known these proportions for decades, many triathletes still think they need to train 30 percent of the time at anaerobic heart rates in order to race faster, dedicating up to a third of their training time for less than 10 percent of their racing energy. Imagine someone investing 30 percent of their money in a stock that provided less than 10 percent of their investment profits—they would quickly change stocks or fire their broker. Yet people will persistently emphasize anaerobic training for years and years without changing, indeed resisting advice to the contrary. Why is this so?

The reason is mostly cultural, especially for North American athletes. Endurance sports are not taught very well in our secondary schools, and if they are, as in the case of swimming, they emphasize shorter distances of 50–400 meters. The widely televised team sports emphasize short bursts of speed, and our university programs support mostly these sports. When we think of a runner, most Americans are much more likely to know who won the 100- or 200m dash in the Olympics than who won the marathon or the 10,000m running event. Yet for adult amateur athletes, endurance events are 90 percent of the competition. Adults are not lining up to qualify for the Boston 100-yard dash or the Hawaii quarter-mile run, yet our training psychology is still heavily influenced by sprinting events, including the related disciplines of weight lifting and stretching.

Combined with our work ethic is the neurological stimulation we receive from going all out. Anaerobic work can make us feel "high" in a similar way that children spin around and hyperventilate when playing. Even though it's risky and sometimes painful, we crave this intense stimulation in our normal training, not just in our racing where it belongs. We want to win the track interval against our running partners or pull away on the Saturday group ride, even though there are no awards.

This "need for speed" can't be entirely bad, or we would not be motivated to race in the first place. The trick is to know when to hold back and how to maintain a steady pace in long-term training the way you must maintain a steady pace in a long-course race, saving energy until the final parts of the race where it really matters. Just as actors or musicians save their most intense emotions for a real audience performance, triathletes must save their greatest intensity for real racing.

Once we establish that aerobic training should account for the lion's share of training time, certain questions arise:

1. What is aerobic training and how is it defined?
2. What exactly happens during anaerobic or non-oxygen-based training?
3. Are the two forms of energy mutually exclusive or do they work together?

Aerobic Training

Aerobic training involves the red or "slow-twitch" muscle fibers used during activities lasting five to fifteen minutes or longer. These muscle fibers convert fat to energy. Fatigue sets in when there is insufficient glucose to sustain the conversion of fat to energy. Aerobic training still requires some carbohydrates to sustain the fat-burning process. Examining the human body, we have about 90 minutes' worth of glycogen fuel (carbohydrates) stored in our muscles for training or racing. Anything beyond that requires mostly fat burning. How much fat do we have to spare? Even a very lean endurance athlete has more than 119 hours of fat to burn. This explains the ability of ultradistance athletes to run more than 100 miles or cycle more than 3,000 miles with only brief sleep breaks. They have become so efficient at fat burning that they have an almost endless fuel supply. For the rest of us mortals going shorter distances, we learn to conserve our glycogen stores for the end of the race when they can most improve our finishing time.

Anaerobic Training

Anaerobic training uses the white or "fast-twitch" muscle fibers used during activities of one to three minutes. These muscle fibers convert glucose directly to energy, a process called glycolysis. Whereas aerobic training requires at least a little sugar to keep it going, anaerobic training requires no fat to create short bursts of energy. There is a third energy system available, the creatine phosphate system, but this relates to even shorter bursts than glycolysis, only a few seconds, and therefore has little application to long-course training.

Combination of Aerobic and Anaerobic Systems

Neither aerobic nor anaerobic training are mutually exclusive, and in fact both processes are constantly going on in our bodies. Even while you read this page, the breakdown of carbohydrates is creating lactic acid in the muscles, a hallmark of anaerobic training. But at lower intensities and heart rates lactate is quickly removed from the bloodstream without discomfort. We call the point where lactate can no longer be removed as quickly as it's being created the *lactate threshold,* which some experts also call the *anaerobic threshold.*

Even if you understand acid-base chemistry, you might still ask, "What does this have to do with my actual training?" We can simplify the aerobic-anaerobic harmony by relating them more directly to their fuel sources, the energy burned by the muscles that actually propel us forward in a race:

- **Aerobic:** burning more fat and less sugar (glucose) for energy
- **Anaerobic:** burning more sugar (glucose) and less fat for energy

TABLE 2.1 RESPIRATORY QUOTIENT FOR AN ELITE TRIATHLETE

HEART RATE	RQ	PERCENT FAT	PERCENT SUGAR
127	.79	70	30
133	.80	67	33
135	.82	60	40
137	.83	56	44
141	.84	53	47
146*	.82	60	40
153	.85	50	50
153	.85	50	50
155	.87	42	58
164**	.87	42	58
169	.90	32	68

** near aerobic threshold (AeT)　** near lactate threshold (LT)*

Note: The repeated heart rate of 153 was the heart rate collected at two distinct times.

We can measure the glucose and fat the body is using at different training intensities. The respiratory quotient (RQ) is the amount of carbon dioxide exhaled divided by oxygen consumed. The lower the RQ, the more fat you are burning. A higher RQ means you are burning more sugar. An RQ of around 0.85 indicates a 50/50 split between fat and glucose burning (see Table 2.1 where two separate measurements recorded a heart rate of 153 despite passage of time and increase in perceived exertion—not so surprising for a very fit athlete).

Although it's unlikely that most readers will have their RQ tested in a lab, athletes should always keep the fat-sugar ratio in mind. Experienced long-course athletes like Mark Allen claim they can actually feel when the body is kicking over to more fat burning in long sessions. Certainly all of us can feel when we are well into the sugar-burning phase because we begin to suffer. The trick is to learn the fine line where you are nearing the top of the fat-burning intensity, to become more efficient there without going beyond it.

ESSENTIAL PHYSIOLOGY

Aerobic Threshold

We introduced a new term in Table 2.1, aerobic threshold (AeT). As with the anaerobic threshold, some writers will describe this differently, but we'll define it here as a point where fat burning clearly predominates and lactate accumulation is so low as to cause no discomfort, though longer efforts over two hours may cause muscular or joint soreness regardless of speed. For most long-course athletes, this value is around 20 heartbeats per minute below the lactate threshold. This intensity is the key to building endurance for long-course events and indeed should characterize the majority of training volume for triathletes.

The problem with recommending this intensity is that some think it means going slow, that it's a training method for lazy people. While it may mean a short-term reduction in average training speed, the goal is to actually maintain or increase speed at a very efficient heart rate, to go faster while still burning mostly fat. It may seem counterintuitive, but to race faster you have to become efficient at training slower, and this requires as much discipline as hammering hard workouts. After some months of disciplined aerobic threshold training, you'll find this heart rate challenging if maintained for a long period, and your speed will be faster while burning less glycogen. And when you need those extra bursts of intensity to climb hills, fight the wind, or pass another cyclist or runner, your heart rate will recover more rapidly to nominal levels.

Lactate Threshold

This concept is one of the most important, but perhaps one of the least understood in physiology. This confusion is caused more by semantics than by complicated blood chemistry. The muscles generate lactic acid when processing carbohydrate, including a positive hydrogen ion, and the resulting salt product is called lactate. This lactate is neutralized by the body and can be reused for energy. At some point, exertion increases to the point where the body can no longer keep up, and lactate begins to accumulate. The 50/50 point, where lactate production is equal to lactate removal, is called the lactate threshold (LT). This intensity is associated with a heart rate, which we call the lactate threshold heart rate. If you use a bike power meter, there is a corresponding wattage, and if you swim intervals in a consistent pool (with the same length, wave suppression, and water temperature), there is an associated pace.

Recent studies are eliminating the notion of lactic acid as the "bad guy" when it comes to muscle soreness, fatigue, or recovery delay. The villain is now thought to be the positive hydrogen ions created by burning carbohydrate. That doesn't mean you won't feel some discomfort when training or racing at your LT heart rate or when doing intervals at that intensity, but it can be attributed to other sources. Reduction in pain and soreness can result from improved mechanics (economy) and neurological learning as much or more than lactate tolerance.

We'll still do interval work and it will be challenging, but our goal will not be simply to tolerate lactic acid. The "no pain, no gain" training philosophy that has permeated team and endurance sports is thankfully fading away in the light of new science. Controlled, consistent intensity is the key to long-term improvement.

Strictly speaking, LT should mean the same thing as anaerobic threshold, but since many athletes focus on shorter endurance events like 10K running, criterium racing, or short time-trial cycling, the term anaerobic threshold has been used to refer to training intensities used to build anaerobic endurance. If you examine the heart rate of a good 10K runner or fast criterium cyclist, you'll find they can usually maintain a heart rate of five to fifteen beats per minute *over* their lactate threshold for the entire event. Even a good 40km time trialist (not in a triathlon) will maintain a heart rate considerably over their LT. If you read books by Joe Friel or other Ultrafit series authors, you'll see the term used correctly, but you may read other interpretations on the Internet or in other books. For this reason, we'll stick to the term lactate threshold.

Lactate Threshold Heart Rate (LTHR) is the maximum effective heart rate for training in long-course events, though you may occasionally exceed it in climbing hills or with other short-term stresses. The anaerobic endurance training used by champion road cyclists and 10–30km runners has little applicability to long-course triathlon. Fortunately, if you do your interval training at or below LT, you'll still be able to race a sprint triathlon, 10K running race, or a shorter bike race rather well, maybe even better than if you trained at higher heart rates. The fastest you'll need to go to race "the perfect distance" may indeed be "the perfect training" for many other endurance events.

Lactate threshold is relatively easy to test. Go out and ride a thirty-minute bike time trial, all-out, and you can estimate your bike LTHR very closely. There are similarly easy tests for the swim and the run. And if you want to be even more precise, there are field testing units that can measure the lactate levels with more precision, and these are within the price range of serious amateur athletes. The alternative methods such as VO_2max testing are more expensive, require equipment costing thousands of dollars, and are sometimes inconsistent when performed by different labs or even the same lab in a six-month period.

Once you've determined your LTHR, power, and/or swim pace, you can quickly determine the other training zones from a simple table lookup. Since your LTHR will change as fitness improves (or declines), you can regularly update these ranges with minimum hassle. Since you're already doing some training at LT for your race, you don't have to wear yourself out just testing performance. Save the "blissful suffering" for race day.

VO_2max (Maximum Volume of Oxygen Processing)

This value is commonly called aerobic capacity, but its maximal nature means it occurs at what most of us would find very anaerobic intensity. It is commonly measured during a graded exercise test where the athlete progressively increases intensity to exhaustion while being measured by a metabolic analyzer. The resulting value is milliliters (cubic centimeters) of oxygen per minute, per kilogram of body weight:

$$VO_2\text{max} = \frac{\text{Oxygen volume/time}}{\text{body mass}}$$

The upper part of this equation is mostly determined by genetics: heart rate and stroke volume, hemoglobin density, mitochondrial density, and muscle fiber composition. But it can be improved by training, and not just by maximal efforts. Aerobic threshold training can actually improve VO_2max, especially for the beginning to intermediate athlete—it just takes longer. But there comes a point when athletes will reach 99 percent of the maximum value of the upper numerator, and this may come rather early in the triathlete's career.

That leaves the lower part of the equation: body mass. This factor is the one most age-group athletes can definitely improve upon, and rapidly at that. If you simply lose five pounds before your next major race, your VO_2max immediately goes up. Very few age-group triathletes are too thin.

There are very few nutrients that can do much more than a balanced diet to improve performance. But there's plenty of stuff out there we should stop eating, or at least reduce our consumption of significantly.

Some athletes fear weight training because they think it will raise their body mass, thereby lowering their VO_2max and reducing speed. We want to avoid the kind of weight lifting that simply builds bulk muscle mass, but studies have shown that weight training can actually reduce overall weight and body fat percentage. The kind of strength training stressed in this book should not cause a weight increase unless you are truly underweight or strength-deficient.

VO_2max testing

As the cost of metabolic analyzers has come down, more athletes have access to VO_2max testing. This may be a mixed blessing for long-course athletes, since it can actually reduce confidence if the numbers don't pan out, and there are inevitable comparisons with famous athletes who possessed legendary aerobic capacity dating back to their teenage years. There are tables that suggest how fast, or how slow, we should be running based on our VO_2max. The other problem is that equipment may not be consistent from lab to lab, or even with the same tester from year to year. You may get just as useful a test result from your local coach as you would from a university sports medicine research center—or you may not.

If you do have the time and money to invest in VO_2max testing, it's probably better to wait until you have at least two years' experience in the sport. Unless your training is very inconsistent, your aerobic capacity may improve dramatically during this period. Once it begins to level off after extended training, the values are more valid. Stick with one lab and/or tester that you trust so that your baseline values will relate to future changes. You can also expect your values to decrease about 1 percent per year after age 40, though intelligent training can reduce this number.

And one more time: Don't compare your aerobic capacity to other famous athletes or even your local training partners or rivals. If the highest VO_2max won races, marathoner Frank Shorter would not have won Olympic gold and silver medals. Don't limit your own progress or goals because you think your VO_2max is too low to go any faster. One world-class Ironman claims to have never had his VO_2max tested because he did not want to hurt his confidence or have excuses for poor performance.

He focuses instead on things like lactate threshold power and economy, and indeed that should be the emphasis for all long-course triathletes.

ONE SPORT, THREE PHASES

Perhaps one of the most difficult things for the beginner to understand is that, as Paula Newby-Fraser says, "Triathlon is one event with three phases." When triathlon began over a quarter century ago, there were inevitable comparisons to the Olympic examples of biathlon, pentathlon, and decathlon, where talented athletes trained in varying disciplines and were awarded prizes based on their point totals in each individual event. And indeed these were great all-around athletes, though not quite world-class in any individual event. The idea of balanced training in different sports certainly applies to these Olympians as well as triathletes. But with the exception of biathlon, where shooting and skiing occur without a gap, the comparison breaks down. Not all the decathlon events are endurance sports, and there is a considerable recovery time between each event. If you have a bad day on the run, there is nothing that will prevent you from winning the discus and taking the lead. You can be weak in 30 percent of the decathlon events, yet still win the gold medal. Interestingly, you'll find more biathletes from the European military tradition placing high in long-course triathlons than you will Olympic decathletes or pentathletes.

Triathlon is unique in that each sport blends directly into the other, and each one affects the other dramatically in a race and consistently throughout the training season. To win the overall title at a modern long-course event, you had better be good in all three sports. Nowadays, winning even a masters age-group division precludes a one-sport weakness. Talented athletes from other sports have taken a crack at the Ironman® Hawaii, thinking perhaps their towering one-sport abilities would make it easier, and all have come away humbled by the experience, not just from the race itself, but from the difficulty of training.

Now that triathlon has reached a state of maturity, we can safely say it is unique and its own sport. It requires training discipline and organization like no other, notwithstanding some universal principles of physiology found in all endurance sports. If you want to win your age group or even finish your first half-Iron race in a respectable time, you must treat all three sports with respect and a balanced approach. This balance is difficult to learn. Since most of us have come from other endurance sports where we developed at least a modicum of skill, we tend to have a preference for one sport. You can't eliminate this preference entirely, but you can avoid an addiction to one sport or an aversion for another. There is a noble middle path between likes and dislikes, and triathlon racing rewards the athlete who can follow this path.

The good news is that this balanced approach can reduce the risk of injury, burnout, and overtraining found in singular endurance sports. And this blending brings great joy in mastery. It is said we now live in a multitasking culture, where different types of work are occurring simultaneously and not just in a linear progression. Triathlon is an athletic symbol of this cultural shift, hence its growing popularity.

STRENGTHS AND LIMITERS

Apply the concept of balance to the notion of strengths and limiters. When I first read Joe Friel's use of the phrase "strengths and limiters," it reminded me of the term "positives and deltas" we used at NASA in project management. The Greek character delta (Δ) denotes change in math and science, or the need for change in project management. The word choice avoids saying weak or negative. This positivity is good practice for athletes, since confidence is the most important advantage in racing. The mind is very amenable to suggestion, and even a hint of negativity can slow you down. The goal is to be realistic.

Some sports or skills can be called limiters because this term implies change. What was once a limiter can be turned into a strength, and a strength not maintained or ignored can quickly become limiting. Athletes coming from a one-sport specialty may find their talent actually lies in another sport, and success breeds love for that new sport, and still more delightful practice.

Even though most of us will admit that change is inevitable and that we have limiters, it's very difficult for adults to change their basic nature, hence difficult to convince triathletes to work on their limiters. It's a chicken-or-egg question about how the limiter developed in the first place: People don't like to do things they are not good at, and people are not good at things they don't practice. You have to walk that fine line between likes and dislikes. You can't outsource your swimming stroke technique or your end-of-race running form to a contractor—you have to do it yourself. Outside consulting may help you gain knowledge, but you must do the work, and starting is the hardest part.

Despite the ubiquity of personal computers, e-mail, and the Internet, most people have not learned to type very well. Using action-packed computer graphics and clicking with a mouse can be fun—typing drills are quite boring. But after six months of dedication to typing drills, you no longer need to think about typing on your computer; you can type twice as fast without additional effort, you make fewer mistakes, and in fact have more time to enjoy images, sounds, or video. Some aspects of triathlon will involve a rather boring phase of repetitive drills, where improvement builds slowly. But consistent application to drills can dramatically increase speed. And once you get into the habit, those little weekly gains become a reward in themselves.

Diagnosing your limiters is relatively easy. Working on them consistently is hard, not in the physiological sense but on a mental level. In Zen Buddhist monasteries, students are sometimes assigned to sit and stare at a large boulder or a brick wall for hours and hours. No other instruction or motivation is given: Just sit there and observe. After weeks or months of this, the student often becomes bored and anxious, and begins to question the purpose of it all. Some will just give up. Others will continue until a kind of acceptance sets in, a peaceful calm where their conscious mind can be turned off, and they access other energy or understanding.

As colorful and exciting as we try to make triathlon training, sometimes you need the patience to stare at a brick wall. Even though the brick wall doesn't change, rest assured that you will indeed change, and that your ability to focus and improve limiters will develop.

CHAPTER 3

Training Design

In God we trust—all others bring data.

—Plaque downstairs from Mission Control at NASA's Johnson Space Center in Houston, Texas

DESIGN SCIENCE

We have defined periodization as a methodical process for organizing training, applying certain laws of physiology. When designing a training plan, there are several possible methods:

- **Bottom-up Design:** This training design begins with minor details and works up toward a centralized, hierarchical structure. It moves from the specific to the general. Many athletes using mixed training employ this approach, and beginners are probably doing it by default. There may or may not be a link between lower-level workouts and the overall annual plan.
- **Top-down Design:** This approach assumes a set hierarchy moving from the general to the specific, and usually implies a centralized, top-level goal at the top of the pyramid (Figure 3.1). Begin with an annual training plan: insert races of relative importance (A, B, or C races), and call this the *macrocycle* of design. Then move down to individual two- to twelve-week blocks of training, usually termed

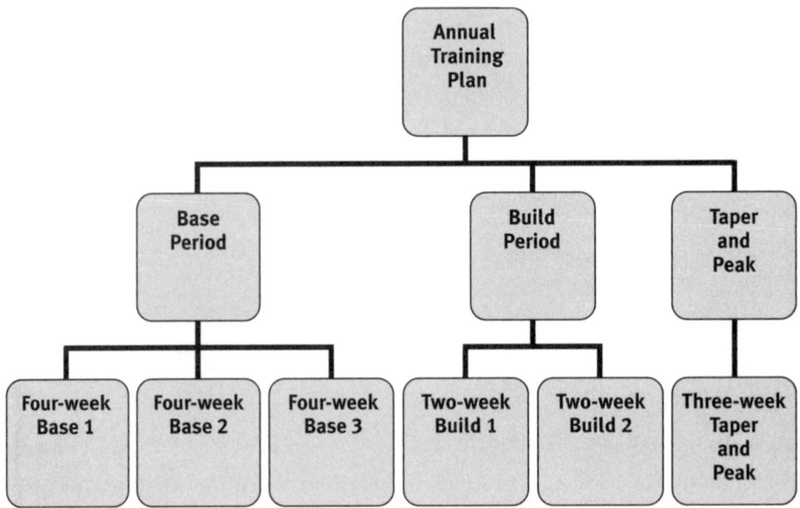

FIGURE 3.1
Typical top-down hierarchy for training design

Preparation, Base, Build, Peak, and Race periods, with a more restful Transition phase between these *mesocycles* of design. Then design individual training weeks (or longer multiday segments), *microcycles,* including a few breakthrough workouts with their various phases. This method is the one promoted by most coaches and publications for periodization design. Long-range planning and full knowledge of your schedule for six to twelve months is preferred. For some very serious athletes, it may include a five-year plan. There are advantages to this method for those who must commit to races a year in advance, a common requirement of most North American Ironman races. And it suits rare athletes who can plan their entire lifestyle around training and racing. Fortunately, this obsessive time management is *not* required for most half-Iron distance races, nor do the tapering and recovery periods take weeks or months to complete.

- **Inside-out Design:** In the mid-1980s, systems engineers found that the practical aspects of large-scale project management were limited by the bottom-up or top-down approaches. As smaller personal computers and distributed networks replaced large, centralized mainframes, and software development became more intuitive and less rigidly analytical, vertical hierarchies and plans were found to be too restrictive. The faster pace of change and unpredictability made

> them impractical. On the other hand, a consistent method of organization was still required, but with more flexibility, modularity, and better communication between levels of a plan. Pioneers like Grady Booch called this method *object-oriented* design, where blocks and their relationships in the grand scheme are designed from the inside out (Figure 3.2).

What does this mean for triathlon training? The traditional labels of macrocycle, mesocycle, and microcycle are still valid, and the various phases of Preparation, Base, Build, Peak, and Race are still used. All the periodic laws of physiology still hold. But we can be more flexible about how we move in and out of them and employ newer, more creative methods of organization. This flexible design trend has found new application in the biological sciences, from physiology to botany to

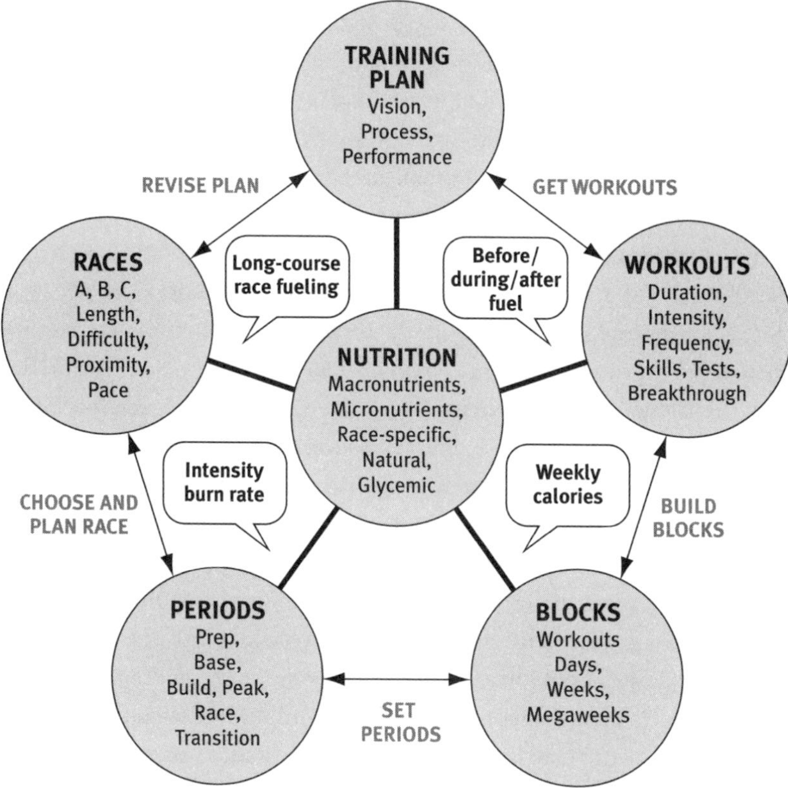

FIGURE 3.2
Object-oriented training design with flexible relationships

molecular genetics. Although the human mind may create vertical hierarchies, the human body responds organically to the real world. We should employ a design principle more in tune with nature's process.

In reality, coaches and top athletes are already doing this. The original notions of top-down design using periodization have been modified, tweaked, and transformed regularly due to new research and the intensity of competition. There has simply been a lag in design methods in an expert endurance community swamped with new discoveries. It's time to start using new terms to describe these new methods of training design.

With all the technology and information sources available to even the amateur athlete, the design of a long-course training plan can be as complex as the training of an astronaut for a long-term space mission. An elite triathlete may in fact be five years ahead of university studies or NASA research into extreme physiology. As with other paradigm shifts, this method should make our training design *simpler,* not more complex, than the older systems. We should be able to design and maintain our training plan with less time and minimize the workout time required to achieve a goal.

Athletes attempting the half-Iron distance have more flexibility in registering, training, and racing than those focused on full Iron-length racing. Many lack the extreme time commitment and forecast scheduling for a full Iron-distance race: more reasons to use a flexible, inside-out approach to training design.

All the objects in Figure 3.2 relate to one another. Only the basic connections are shown, and many others are possible. Although the Training Plan object appears on top, one could rotate the diagram or change the order of the individual elements. You can visualize the objects progressing in a clockwise cycle or backtrack to the previous object during the season. There is no requirement to follow a linear sequence in building the plan or in executing it. In fact, the order should evolve naturally as training progresses. This evolution can vary from athlete to athlete, from season to season, and perhaps even from race to race. In the real world, athletes are already doing this, or wish they could if only they were not constrained by the old linear-sequential model.

The objects complement one another. Planning is itself a part of training: It sharpens the mind and uses valuable workout time. Racing is itself a testing workout and affects future planning. And perhaps most important, nutrition has central and equal status to other aspects of training and racing. Most coaches stress the importance of nutrition, but it has usually been relegated to a sidebar position, a fourth discipline of triathlon, and athletes often consider it last in the design process. Our experience shows that it is the most important element for the large majority of endurance athletes. Even world champions with highly disciplined eating habits report that their worst race performances can be traced to lapses in hydration, nutrition, or both. Nutritional design affects every step of the process. One of the most common coaching questions is "What should I eat?" Most of the answer involves what you should *not* eat, and we'll explore that further in Chapter 9.

DESIGNING A WORKOUT

Athletes often come to coaches anxious to receive a long-range training plan, a complex schedule of workouts with an almost magical power to create fitness and promote speed. Many believe that that's all there is to coaching and intelligent race preparation: the detailed training plan. After some time under tutelage an athlete finally asks, "How should I be doing this particular workout?" And this is the most important question. If you were investing for your future, you might read the *Wall Street Journal* or surf the Internet for exclusive stock tips. Yet what really affects your retirement income is how much you're spending on that morning coffee-shop latte or that sports car monthly payment. Conserve money (or energy) on individual transactions (or workouts), and your wealth (or fitness) improves.

The critical workout attributes include intensity, duration, frequency, and volume.

Intensity

Intensity is the degree of exertion, which is measured by:

- **Perceived exertion:** how hard does it feel?
- **Heart rate:** the heart's reaction to stress in bodily systems
- **Power:** currently measured by watts generated on a bike
- **Speed:** useful in controlled environments like a pool or running track

Intensity is the most important attribute of a workout, for good or ill; unfortunately, most athletes believe that volume is more important, or at least they train that way.

Now is the time to bring up the subject of training zones. It took me two or three years of intensive study, plus multiple half-Iron, Iron-distance, and ultradistance races before I finally understood the zones as applied by coaches like Joe Friel. As with lactate threshold, the confusion comes more from terminology than reality. You'll see some systems, including those taught in USA Triathlon coaching classes, use only three zones: recovery, aerobic, and anaerobic. You also see terms like "tempo" referring sometimes to hard anaerobic pace, and sometimes to a more controlled high-aerobic or Zone 3 pace. We'll stick to the consistent numbering and terms used by Friel.

For today's endurance athletes, the most common way to delineate training zones is the heart rate monitor. There are many pros and cons about heart rate training, but it still serves as the most important tool for the long-course athlete in gauging effort in multiple sports. Even though power meters have revolutionized road cycling and time trialing for triathlons, and GPS or inertial running systems have benefited runners, the least expensive and most reliable tool for most situations is still the heart rate monitor.

Heart rate is even more important for the long-course athlete, since it is tied to the fuel burning rate. HRMs are more accurate tools around the aerobic threshold, which is where 80 percent or more of long-course training takes place, and they are still very useful in the high aerobic and subthreshold zones.

Let's correct a common fallacy about heart rate and heart rate training. Some may think that a heart rate monitor measures the stress and fatigue on the heart muscle, that higher rates mean the heart muscle is tired or overworked. A healthy heart has muscle fibers unlike any in the rest of the body. It can beat for three days at near maximum rates without failing. Barring disease, the heart can continue indefinitely. Heart rate reflects the overall fatigue in the respiratory and muscular systems, the processing of oxygen, fuel, and energy to produce motion. We know that we will burn all available glycogen and experience muscle failure long before the heart gives up, since near maximum efforts are rarely possible for over ten minutes. Think of the heart muscle itself as a kind of monitor on the stress level of the rest of the body, and your electronic HRM as just a screen display of information the heart is collecting on the various energy systems.

Although power meters have been around awhile on training bikes, we are only beginning to see them determine race pace on the bike. The lightest, most precise units are still expensive and rarely found on the racing bikes of age-group triathletes. We won't be throwing away our heart rate monitors anytime soon. I like to see triathletes learn to use the heart rate monitor first, mostly via intuitive observation, and many are already using it. Then we add power metering and other tools if available. For bike testing, the power meter is invaluable for gauging progress either indoors or outdoors.

TABLE 3.1 TRAINING ZONES IN RELATION TO WORKOUTS, RACES, AND RPE

ZONE	DESCRIPTION	EXAMPLES	RPE	EXERTION
1	Recovery	Easy 1-hour bike spin, slow, continuous swim, slow jog or walk, golf	6–8	Very, very light
2	Extensive Endurance	Long 3–5 hour bike, moderately paced stroke drill, long run	9–11	Light
3	Intensive Endurance	Early pace for half-Iron bike, half-Iron run, tempo intervals, beginner half-Iron run pace	12–14	Somewhat hard
4	Subthreshold	Ending race pace for half-Iron bike, half-Iron run	15	Hard
5a	Threshold	30-min bike time trial, 8×800m run intervals, Olympic-distance tri bike pace, 6×400m swim intervals, elite half-Iron run	16	Hard
5b	Anaerobic Endurance	Road cycling race, 10K run race, sprint triathlon, 12×100m swim intervals, 12×400m run intervals, climb 12–15% grade on bike	17–18	Very hard
5c	Power	All-out 100m dash, road cycling sprinter finish, track cycling sprint, 50m all-out swim sprint	19–20	Very, very hard

TABLE 3.2 CYCLING TRAINING ZONES IN RELATION TO HEART RATE

ZONE 1 Recovery	ZONE 2 Extensive Endurance	ZONE 3 Intensive Endurance	ZONE 4 Sub-Threshold	ZONE 5A Super-Threshold	ZONE 5B Anaerobic Endurance	ZONE 5C Power
90–108	109–122	123–128	129–136	**137**–140	141–145	146–150
91–109	110–123	124–129	130–137	**138**–141	142–146	147–151
91–109	110–124	125–130	131–138	**139**–142	143–147	148–152
92–110	111–125	126–130	131–139	**140**–143	144–147	148–153
92–111	112–125	126–131	132–140	**141**–144	145–148	149–154
93–112	113–126	127–132	133–141	**142**–145	146–149	150–155
94–112	113–127	128–133	134–142	**143**–145	146–150	151–156
94–113	114–128	129–134	135–143	**144**–147	148–151	152–157
95–114	115–129	130–135	136–144	**145**–148	149–152	153–158
95–115	116–130	131–136	137–145	**146**–149	150–154	155–159
97–116	117–131	132–137	138–146	**147**–150	151–155	156–161
97–117	118–132	133–138	139–147	**148**–151	152–156	157–162
98–118	119–133	134–139	140–148	**149**–152	153–157	158–163
98–119	120–134	135–140	141–149	**150**–153	154–158	159–164
99–120	121–134	135–141	142–150	**151**–154	155–159	160–165
100–121	122–135	136–142	143–151	**152**–155	156–160	161–166
100–122	123–136	137–142	143–152	**153**–156	157–161	162–167
101–123	124–137	138–143	144–153	**154**–157	158–162	163–168
101–124	125–138	139–144	145–154	**155**–158	159–163	164–164
102–125	126–138	139–145	146–155	**156**–159	160–164	165–170
103–126	127–140	141–146	147–156	**157**–160	161–165	166–171
104–127	128–141	142–147	148–157	**158**–161	162–167	168–173

Note: The lactate threshold heart rate is in bold in Zone 5A column.

CONTINUED

TABLE 3.2 CONTINUED

ZONE 1 Recovery	**ZONE 2** Extensive Endurance	**ZONE 3** Intensive Endurance	**ZONE 4** Sub-Threshold	**ZONE 5A** Super-Threshold	**ZONE 5B** Anaerobic Endurance	**ZONE 5C** Power
104–128	129–142	143–148	149–158	**159**–162	163–168	169–174
105–129	130–143	144–148	149–159	**160**–163	164–169	170–175
106–129	130–143	144–150	151–160	**161**–164	165–170	171–176
106–130	131–144	145–151	152–161	**162**–165	166–171	172–177
107–131	132–145	146–152	153–162	**163**–166	167–172	173–178
107–132	133–146	147–153	154–163	**164**–167	168–173	174–179
108–133	134–147	148–154	155–164	**165**–168	169–174	175–180
109–134	135–148	149–154	155–165	**166**–169	170–175	176–181
109–135	136–149	150–155	156–166	**167**–170	171–176	177–182
110–136	137–150	151–156	157–167	**168**–171	172–177	178–183
111–137	138–151	152–157	158–168	**169**–172	173–178	179–185
112–138	139–151	152–158	159–169	**170**–173	174–179	180–186
112–134	140–152	153–164	161–170	**171**–174	175–180	181–187
113–140	141–153	154–160	161–171	**172**–175	176–181	182–188
113–141	142–154	155–161	162–172	**173**–176	177–182	183–189
114–142	143–155	156–162	163–173	**174**–177	178–183	184–190
115–143	144–156	157–163	164–174	**175**–178	179–184	185–191
115–144	145–157	158–164	165–175	**176**–179	180–185	186–192
116–145	146–158	159–165	166–176	**177**–180	181–186	187–193
116–146	147–159	160–166	167–177	**178**–181	182–187	188–194
117–147	148–160	161–166	167–178	**179**–182	183–188	189–195
118–148	149–160	161–167	168–179	**180**–183	184–190	191–197

CONTINUED

TABLE 3.2 CONTINUED

ZONE 1 Recovery	ZONE 2 Extensive Endurance	ZONE 3 Intensive Endurance	ZONE 4 Sub-Threshold	ZONE 5A Super-Threshold	ZONE 5B Anaerobic Endurance	ZONE 5C Power
119–149	150–161	162–168	169–180	**181**–184	185–191	192–198
119–150	151–162	163–170	171–181	**182**–185	186–192	193–199
120–151	152–163	164–171	172–182	**183**–186	187–193	194–200
121–152	153–164	165–172	173–183	**184**–187	188–194	195–201
121–153	154–165	166–172	173–184	**185**–188	189–195	196–202
122–154	155–166	167–173	174–185	**186**–189	190–196	197–203
122–155	156–167	168–174	175–186	**187**–190	191–197	198–204
123–156	157–168	169–175	176–187	**188**–191	192–198	199–205
124–157	158–169	170–176	177–188	**189**–192	193–199	200–206
124–158	159–170	171–177	178–189	**190**–193	194–200	201–207
125–159	160–170	171–178	179–190	**191**–194	195–201	202–208
125–160	161–171	172–178	179–191	**192**–195	196–202	203–209
126–161	162–172	173–179	180–192	**193**–196	197–203	204–210
127–162	163–173	174–180	181–193	**194**–197	198–204	205–211
127–163	164–174	175–181	182–194	**195**–198	199–205	206–212

So for now we will consider the training zones from the intuitive Borg Rating of Perceived Exertion or RPE (Table 3.1) and from heart rate relative to lactate threshold (Tables 3.2 and 3.3). We will consider more advanced power-training methods in Chapter 7 on cycling.

Duration

Duration is the length of an individual workout. Athletes often measure workouts by how far they run, bike, or swim. Egos are boosted by claiming long 100-plus-mile bike rides or 20-plus-mile runs. But our experience shows duration measured in minutes or hours is a better tool for

TABLE 3.3 RUNNING TRAINING ZONES IN RELATION TO HEART RATE

ZONE 1 Recovery	ZONE 2 Extensive Endurance	ZONE 3 Intensive Endurance	ZONE 4 Sub-Threshold	ZONE 5A Super-Threshold	ZONE 5B Anaerobic Endurance	ZONE 5C Power
93–119	120–126	127–133	134–139	**140**–143	144–149	150–156
94–119	120–127	128–134	135–140	**141**–144	145–150	151–157
95–120	121–129	130–135	136–141	**142**–145	146–151	152–158
95–121	122–130	131–136	137–142	**143**–146	147–152	153–159
96–122	123–131	132–137	138–143	**144**–147	148–153	154–160
96–123	124–132	133–138	139–144	**145**–148	149–154	155–161
97–124	125–133	134–139	140–145	**146**–149	150–155	156–162
97–124	125–134	135–140	141–146	**147**–150	151–156	157–163
98–125	126–135	136–141	142–147	**148**–151	152–157	158–164
99–126	127–135	136–142	143–148	**149**–152	153–158	159–165
99–127	128–136	137–143	144–149	**150**–153	154–158	159–166
100–128	129–137	138–144	145–150	**151**–154	155–159	160–167
100–129	130–138	139–145	146–151	**152**–155	156–160	161–168
101–130	131–139	140–146	147–152	**153**–156	157–161	162–169
102–131	132–140	141–147	148–153	**154**–157	158–162	163–170
103–131	132–141	142–148	149–154	**155**–158	159–164	165–172
103–132	133–142	143–149	150–155	**156**–159	160–165	166–173
104–133	134–143	144–150	151–156	**157**–160	161–166	167–174
105–134	135–143	144–151	152–157	**158**–161	162–167	168–175
105–135	136–144	145–152	153–158	**159**–162	163–168	169–176
106–136	137–145	146–153	154–159	**160**–163	164–169	170–177
106–136	137–146	147–154	155–160	**161**–164	165–170	171–178

Note: The lactate threshold heart rate is in bold in Zone 5A column.

CONTINUED

TABLE **3.3** CONTINUED

ZONE 1 Recovery	ZONE 2 Extensive Endurance	ZONE 3 Intensive Endurance	ZONE 4 Sub-Threshold	ZONE 5A Super-Threshold	ZONE 5B Anaerobic Endurance	ZONE 5C Power
107–137	138–147	148–155	156–161	**162**–165	166–171	172–179
108–138	139–148	149–155	156–162	**163**–166	167–172	173–180
109–139	140–149	150–156	157–163	**164**–167	168–174	175–182
109–140	141–150	151–157	158–164	**165**–168	169–175	176–183
110–141	142–151	152–158	159–165	**166**–169	170–176	177–184
111–141	142–152	153–159	160–166	**167**–170	171–177	178–185
111–142	143–153	154–160	161–167	**168**–171	172–178	179–186
112–143	144–154	155–161	162–168	**169**–172	173–179	180–187
112–144	145–155	156–162	163–169	**170**–173	174–179	180–188
113–145	146–156	157–163	164–170	**171**–174	175–180	181–189
114–145	146–156	157–164	165–171	**172**–175	176–182	183–191
115–146	147–157	158–165	166–172	**173**–176	177–183	184–192
115–147	148–157	158–166	167–173	**174**–177	178–184	185–193
116–148	149–158	159–167	168–174	**175**–178	179–185	186–194
117–149	150–159	160–168	169–175	**176**–179	180–186	187–195
117–150	151–160	161–169	170–176	**177**–180	181–187	188–196
118–151	152–161	162–170	171–177	**178**–181	182–188	189–197
118–152	153–162	163–171	172–178	**179**–182	183–189	190–198
119–153	154–163	164–172	173–179	**180**–183	184–190	191–199
120–154	155–164	165–173	174–180	**181**–184	185–192	193–201
121–154	155–165	166–174	175–181	**182**–185	186–193	194–202
121–155	156–166	167–175	176–182	**183**–186	187–194	195–203
122–156	157–167	168–176	177–183	**184**–187	188–195	196–204

CONTINUED

TABLE 3.3 CONTINUED

ZONE 1 Recovery	**ZONE 2** Extensive Endurance	**ZONE 3** Intensive Endurance	**ZONE 4** Sub-Threshold	**ZONE 5A** Super-Threshold	**ZONE 5B** Anaerobic Endurance	**ZONE 5C** Power
123–157	158–168	169–177	178–184	**185**–188	189–196	197–205
123–158	159–169	170–178	179–185	**186**–189	190–197	198–206
124–159	160–170	171–179	180–186	**187**–190	191–198	199–207
124–159	160–170	171–179	180–187	**188**–191	192–199	200–208
125–160	161–171	172–180	181–188	**189**–192	193–200	201–209
126–161	162–172	173–181	182–189	**190**–193	194–201	202–210
126–162	163–173	174–182	183–190	**191**–194	195–201	202–211
127–163	164–174	175–183	184–191	**192**–195	196–202	203–212
127–164	165–175	176–184	185–192	**193**–196	197–203	204–213
128–165	166–176	177–185	186–193	**194**–197	198–204	205–214
129–165	166–177	178–186	187–194	**195**–198	199–205	206–215
129–166	167–178	179–187	188–195	**196**–199	200–206	207–216
130–167	168–178	179–188	189–196	**197**–198	199–207	208–217
130–168	169–179	180–189	190–197	**198**–201	202–208	209–218
131–169	170–180	181–190	191–198	**199**–202	203–209	210–219
132–170	171–181	182–191	192–199	**200**–203	204–210	211–220

consistently building fitness. It lessens the distance obsession, which can force athletes to train longer than they should. Since course conditions and athlete speed are highly variable, especially for cycling and longer runs, distance is not a consistent measurement of exertion. We convince our athletes to strive for "five-hour rides at or below aerobic threshold intensity" instead of pushing 100 miles or even farther in successive workouts. Some days 90 miles may seem quite hard, other days 103 miles might seem easy, or you might climb for 20 miles at only 10–15mph. Your body has no speedometer or GPS devices: The biochemical processes only understand time and intensity of reactions. The exception to this rule is swimming, where a lane-divided pool of regular length and temperature produces consistent times for a given workout. Even in the water, athletes are encouraged to work on quality rather than just pounding out more meters or yards in the workout.

Frequency

Frequency is the number of times a workout is performed, usually within the individual sport. Frequency is the rhythm or composition of individual workouts within the training symphony. In an individual workout, it can also refer to the number of intervals. Frequency is constrained by lifestyle outside of multisport: How many times can a workout be scheduled per week or period? Since workouts have a significant overhead of warm-up, cool-down, stretching, showering, transportation, and so on, frequency is largely dependent on free time. Repetition trains the nervous system in essential skills, which makes it a powerful factor in improving efficiency and speed. For fundamental long-course training, frequency is probably the least variable factor: Once you have established a workable pattern, it's best to keep to it. The body thrives on regularity.

Volume

Volume is the duration of individual workouts multiplied by their frequency. We list this factor last for a reason. It is overemphasized by many triathletes, who cling to the notion of very long workouts as essential to endurance fitness. They begin their weekly training plan design with a large volume goal. Yet studies and our own experience indicate that long-term increases in speed are promoted by doing the *least* amount of volume required for the race distance. There is an inevitable tendency to go farther and farther with each succeeding workout as fitness improves, but this approach works best only in the early season. Fortunately, the half-Iron distance does not require the volume of the full Iron distance or allied disciplines of ultrarunning or ultracycling. Speed and volume are like a seesaw, where increases in one cause a decrease in the other. For the half-Iron distance, we are seeking a balanced approach. Even when we consider the professional athlete with almost unlimited training hours for a full Iron-distance race, many report their personal best times by reducing volume by 10 percent or more. Athletes often ask, "How long should I train for this event?" And I answer, "How long do you have to train? How much training can your body and more importantly your lifestyle handle?" The total hours are usually less than expected.

Most athletes will quickly notice symptoms of overtraining caused by excessive intensity: soreness, injury, slow recovery time. But many will continue very high volume without noting symptoms for many months, staying at or below aerobic threshold. Either their speed will begin to decrease, or they will ease into a severe case of overtraining, causing a correspondingly longer recovery time, many months or longer.

On the other hand, if you've been racing sprint triathlons comfortably on only five hours per week of training, you will train longer hours to finish a half-Iron race comfortably. How much more is highly individual, but we will explore possible scenarios in our weekly planning.

Warm-up and Cool-down

I'm amazed at how many athletes understand the complexities of aerobic, anaerobic, VO_2max, aerodynamics, and so on, but have never learned how to warm up or cool down correctly. This habit is more important than stretching, can prevent injury, and reduces the risk of overtraining. Many athletes, especially those training for longer distances or over age 35, significantly reduce soreness and injury with disciplined warm-ups and cool-downs.

Again, we should counter the tendencies inherited from popular burst-mode sports, where a few quick stretches and a two-minute jog around the playing field constitute the "warm-up." Endurance sports, whose aim is to use slower-twitch aerobic muscle fibers and burn fat instead of sugar, require a longer warm-up. Since we emphasize aerobic threshold training, the warm-up produces intensities closer to the work interval. As volume increases for long-course preparation, a longer warm-up becomes more practical.

A word about stretching: though beneficial, stretching is best done *after* warm-up or after the entire workout and cool-down. The exception is a race situation where you simply cannot stretch until just before the competition, where it should be shortened to easy stretches of only a few minutes—or omitted entirely.

How long should you warm up? As a general rule, 15 minutes is a good average for most sessions in the three sports. Swimming may involve a shorter warm-up of 10 minutes, perhaps adding some stroke drills. Cycling may involve a longer warm-up, especially at the beginning of long rides over three hours. Hard anaerobic running or cycling sessions benefit from a 20-minute or longer warm-up. If you start at the edge of very steep terrain and must climb early, you should use your easiest gear on the bike or walk for a few minutes before starting to run.

Ideally, your heart rate should gradually rise during the warm-up and approach your work-interval heart rate by its end. If you had planned an aerobic threshold workout at 135bpm heart rate, you might start at 105bpm the first five minutes, move to 115–120bpm the second five minutes, and reach 130bpm after fifteen minutes. Heat, hills, or excesses in sugar or caffeine may cause your heart rate to rise more rapidly, so adjust for conditions. Also note that most HRMs take awhile to adjust in colder temperatures, and it may be five minutes or longer until you can trust the readings.

Cool-down strategies are diverse. For most cycling and running sessions, the same fifteen minutes accorded to warm-up is a good average, a bit longer for interval workouts or intensive climbing. Swimming may only require a 5- to 10-minute cool-down because of the cooler and softer liquid environment. Swimming is itself a recovery and flexibility exercise, relative to cycling and running, so you are closer to the rest state at the end of a swim. But if you are swimming 6,000 meters with 8–10×500m interval sets, you might take longer for cooling down.

Cooling down from a race is different from a workout: Either you have completed a hard anaerobic effort in a sprint- or Olympic-distance race or you have done a long-course race at a lower intensity, but with greater orthopedic and glandular stress. Many short-course racers benefit from an easy 10- to 15-minute jog or 20-minute easy bike after a hard anaerobic effort. These cool-down efforts may also be extended to maintain volume for an upcoming half-Iron race, since a one-hour race is probably less than a typical half-Iron weekend workout day.

For most half-Iron finishers, a formal cool-down may be unnecessary and perhaps impractical. Recovery benefits from easy walking, getting out of the sun, or returning to the swim area to cool the body with a few easy strokes for five to ten minutes. Many half-Iron races finish with high temperatures, sometimes over 100°F (38°C), so the primary concern is replenishing water, electrolytes, and a mixture of protein and carbohydrates. Running or cycling is not recommended, with the possible exception of riding back to the parking lot.

Work Interval

Experts stress that intervals are the fastest way to build speed. In fact, we can view all our training as interval workouts with three segments: warm-up, work interval, and cool-down. The only difference is that for some workouts, the work interval is itself split into smaller segments at higher intensity. Another advantage of warm-up and cool-down discipline is that you learn to change gears and economize different speeds in *every* workout. Many athletes report that a consistent warm-up promotes a speedier work interval without necessarily increasing heart rate or perceived exertion.

The work interval is the meat of the workout. We can boil down the work interval to three essential attributes:

- **Quality:** This is not so much good or bad quality, but rather the emphasis of the workout on one or more of the three energies—endurance, force, and speed.
- **Intensity:** Level of difficulty as measured by heart rate, power, or speed. We'll classify these with the training zones.
- **Duration:** Number of minutes or hours in the work interval.

There are countless combinations of these three factors. But the first filter we should employ is quality, asking the questions: What energy are we developing? What strength is maintained or limiter improved? If you can't answer these questions, you can't effectively plan a workout. Even if you plan the workout correctly, you must remind yourself of the underlying purpose or its effectiveness will wane.

Since this book focuses on fundamental training principles for long-course events, we will speak only briefly about the qualities of anaerobic endurance (the blending of endurance and speed) and power (the blending of force and speed in short bursts). Although a half-Iron race may have a few minutes at these higher levels of exertion, there is little or no need to train them specifically in workouts. The normal progression of speed from economy workouts, and the production of force from strength workouts both in and out of the weight room, will be enough for long-course races.

The central quality we'll develop for the half-Iron distance is muscular endurance, the blending of strength and endurance. We'll also need plenty of long-range endurance to finish a four- to seven-hour race comfortably, and some raw force to climb hills, swim in crowded open-water starts, and maintain running form in the final miles. Speed will develop by improving

TABLE 3.4 WORKOUT DESIGN QUALITIES

	INTENSITY (ZONE)	DURATION (MIN)	SAMPLE WORKOUTS
Endurance	1–2	60–240	2–4 hour bike 1–2 hour run
Muscular Endurance	2–3	20–120	1-hour run with 20min Zone 3 finish
			3-hour bike, last 20min of each hour in Zone 3
			6x400m swim intervals
			3min downhill running cadence repeats
			Drafting peloton ride without pulls
			1-hour flat ride in aero position in Zone 3
Muscular Endurance	4–5a	6–60	3x8–12min bike intervals
			8x800m run intervals
			3–4x1, 600m run intervals
			30–60min bike time trial
			8x200m swim intervals
			Hill climbing repeats
Force	2–5a HR less relevant	3–60	Steep hill or moderate grade in big gear, 65 rpm
			Pedal-stroke drills on bike
			Run steep hills or stair steps
			Swim paddles, fins, and drag devices
			Open-water and rough-water swims
			Strength training with weights
			Abdominal and core exercises
			Pilates, yoga
			Calisthenics

Note: Sleep and nutrition are an essential aspect of "speed work."

CONTINUED

TABLE 3.4 CONTINUED

	INTENSITY (ZONE)	DURATION (MIN)	SAMPLE WORKOUTS
Speed	1–5a	3–60	Pedal-stroke drills on bike
			SpinScan analysis on CompuTrainer
			Aero positioning and analysis
			Swim-stroke drills, underwater video analysis
			Evolution running method drills, run video analysis
			Faster cadence on bike or run
			Fewer strokes per length in pool
			Mental focus and meditation, yoga
			Increase frequency, shorten duration
			Lighter bike or shoes, faster swimsuit or wet suit
			Weight and/or percentage fat loss
			Improved nutrition
			More sleep, control of lifestyle stress

economy in all three sports, which means working on technique rather than by pushing top-end heart rates. Table 3.4 gives examples of quality, intensity, and duration in typical workouts for the half-Iron distance athlete.

Your work interval design task is now relatively easy:

1. Choose the quality you need to work on. Improve limiters first, then maintain strengths.
2. Select the intensity that bests develops that quality on that day. Obviously, the same quality benefits from variation of intensity: Alternate hard and easy days; save your highest-intensity workouts for only one session in each sport per week.
3. Make your duration the least number of minutes it takes to accomplish your purpose. If you cannot maintain the desired intensity for the duration of the work interval, you must shorten the duration or lower the intensity.

DESIGNING TESTS

Testing is a special type of workout, and racing can become a valid test. There are as many different tests as there are workouts, but for most of our half-Iron training we'll use basic tests that are easily repeatable for most athletes. With our emphasis on aerobic threshold training and muscular endurance, the most common tests will measure performance at lactate threshold or heart rates 10–20bpm below this level.

Testing Conflicts

The good news is that testing can be fun. That little spark of motivation, which even small improvements bring, can make your day and validate your training. If you are lucky enough to have a coach, please don't think he or she is testing you the way they do with the SAT or the Bar Exam. In fact, it's important to work less, relax more, and avoid cramming for sports testing. No one, including yourself, should judge your character based on a performance test. It's more like testing your vision or your blood sugar, a diagnostic tool to help you make more intelligent lifestyle decisions. Despite legendary test results attributed to some famous endurance athletes, many world champions have less-than-stellar test values, but they learned enough from tests to race to the finish line first. It's what you do with the test results that matters. If you never have a bad test, you probably aren't testing much or stretching your limits. Both positive and negative feedback are required for growth. Beginning, intermediate, and advanced athletes have conflicts about testing, often unspoken.

Beginning triathletes usually start by doing little or no formal testing, though they may be acutely aware of speed during a workout or a race. Giving a hard effort is generally not the problem, but controlled or consistent testing can be difficult. Yet these are the people who have the most to learn, and the most speed to gain, by testing.

Intermediate triathletes have usually done some tests, but may stop after initial baseline values are determined or when volume increases later in the season. Tests become less appealing and might be ditched in favor of longer workouts or racing. A way out of this dilemma is to use certain interval workouts to gather data or accurately monitor race performance. Make sure you are taking the recovery week seriously and reducing volume, so a challenging test toward the end of the rest week is valid. The opposite pole also requires caution: placing too much value on a single test, which may or may not provide valid performance clues. In any training year, you can expect to have a few bad tests in each sport, or a test invalidated by course conditions and technical problems.

Advanced or elite triathletes believe in testing and want detailed power data, heart rate, and perhaps even lab analysis. Some of the portable lactate measuring tools have become reasonably priced, and even expensive metabolic analyzers are used by more athletes every year. For an elite athlete, minor fluctuations in performance of just 1 or 2 percent can be the difference between winning and not making the podium at all. Consequently, it behooves them to use the most accurate tools. If you have the time, you can take advantage of as much technology as seems appropriate, but let's not forget the rule of simplicity. As with workouts, you must consider the investment of time and money, and how much you will actually learn about specific energies of endurance, force, and speed. Just because it's state-of-the-art technology does not mean it's the most valuable test for an athlete. Sometimes a simple time trial or race split with a heart rate graph will be more useful than a formal metabolic test.

Despite the tens of thousands of medical tests used in a modern hospital, doctors still rely on the stethoscope and hand-measured pulse. As with intermediate triathletes, race monitoring with a wattmeter, heart rate monitor, and chip-timed splits can be an invaluable gauge of training progress. Elite and intermediate triathletes can schedule specific C races just for this testing purpose at the end of a mesocycle or before a major race.

Testing Specific Attributes

A useful test should shine a spotlight on one or more of the main characters of the long-course triathlon drama: aerobic threshold, lactate threshold, and muscular endurance. Without specificity, your skills will wander in the shadows. Table 3.5 suggests tests for specific attributes.

Note that some of the tests are themselves based on a weekly interval workout. In those cases, choose the median or average value of the repetitions to compare with other tests. Also remember that environmental conditions severely affect testing:

- Nutrition and hydration: Higher blood sugar and caffeine levels significantly affect heart rate. Conversely, fatigue or low blood sugar will lower heart rates and possibly power output and speed.

TABLE 3.5 BASIC TESTS FOR LONG-COURSE TRIATHLETES

TEST	SPORT	ATTRIBUTE	ZONE
1,000m(yd) time trial	Swim	Muscular Endurance	3–5a
6x400m @ 30sec rest	Swim	Muscular Endurance	3
30min time trial	Bike	Muscular Endurance	4–5a
3x7–12min interval @ 2–3min rest	Bike	Muscular Endurance	4–5a
Bike graded exercise test, CompuTrainer	Bike	Muscular Endurance Maximum Power	1–5c
Olympic-distance race bike split	Bike	Muscular Endurance	5a
3–5 mile aerobic time trial	Run	Aerobic Threshold, Muscular Endurance, Economy	3

- Tests are best conducted after three to five days of active recovery, during a reduced-volume training week—yet another reason to treat rest weeks seriously. If regular weekly intervals or no-taper C races are used instead of formal tests after rest, you must intuitively interpret results based on level of fatigue. Only experienced athletes with a long history of test results can nudge this kind of data toward usefulness. Sometimes supremely fit athletes will be unable to reach lactate threshold heart rate in a bike or swim test despite no feelings of fatigue and plenty of power output. This result is itself a good indicator of muscular endurance and economy, though it unlinks heart rate from previous test results.

DESCRIPTION
Usually done all-out after warm-up and/or stroke drill. Zone varies with swimmer experience.
After warm-up and/or stroke drill with building effort last half of each interval. Measure decay between first and last split. HRM optional. Can be repeated weekly in training but testing validity usually requires lowering bike/run volume.
All-out after warm-up with minimal hills and wind. Measure average HR for last 20 minutes of test. Indoor or outdoor power meter very helpful.
Hold power at constant wattage and measure variation in HR and/or speed for each interval. OR: Hold HR constant at LT and measure power and/or speed decay between first and last interval.
Perform "Road Races/Courses Program 70" on CompuTrainer. Gradually increase power output to exhaustion, but do not attempt maximum heart rate.
Controlled 40km pace during race. Race at LT heart rate or steady power and measure time.
Heart rate held in very narrow range 9–11bpm under LT heart rate on running track. Measure time each 1,600m, including decay of pace for each mile at steady HR.

- Higher temperatures will raise heart rate. Running tests done over 85°F should be treated cautiously, even at aerobic threshold heart rates, and running tests should be avoided at temperatures over 90° to 95°F. Cycling heart rates are lowered by a headwind under most conditions, but may actually rise into a headwind at temperatures over 95°F over dark asphalt roads or near bodies of warm water. Water temperatures over 85°F can slow swim time trials and 100m(yd) pace averages in the pool, and very cool water under 78°F will lower heart rates. The body's response to heat or cold is greatly influenced by tolerance and accident of birth. For example, those riding in high temperatures all the time may be able to keep heart rates low on a bike test, whereas the average rider would soon become exhausted. If your latitude is less than 35°, semitropical or tropical, you need to develop a feel for how heat affects heart rates and tests. Obviously, early morning is the best testing time in the furnace locales, avoiding heat and wind.

- If you are training at altitude, it's best to test power and use perceived effort rather than rely upon heart rate. Ideally, you should be testing and training at a lower altitude anyway, and resting up above. From a practical standpoint you should postpone testing until you return from altitude training.
- Hard rain, severe wind, severe cold, and so on, are reasons to postpone a test or move it indoors. Athletes can learn to tolerate and even excel under these conditions, but consistent test results are almost impossible to obtain.

There are many other tests possible, but these have proven most useful for long-course athletes. If you are interested in tests using more technology, it's best to consult the specialist in these devices. Keep in mind that regular testing using simple, repeatable methods is better than infrequent use of high-tech equipment with volatile results. Elites may find time for both kinds of test. We review more complex testing in Chapter 10.

THE WEEKLY TRAINING CYCLE

In keeping with our inside-out approach to training design, we'll take our workout objects and use them as building blocks to erect a training week. Why do we design training around weeks? There is no such requirement in terms of physiology, but our seven-day scheduling of work and lifestyle has made weekly arrangements convenient. Many advanced and elite triathletes now use a longer cycle of perhaps ten days, which for lack of a better word we'll call a *megaweek*. This allows them to achieve adequate frequency and work on limiters with sufficient recovery. But since this book is about fundamental training for the half-Iron event, we'll focus on a weekly training cycle, understanding that it can be extended an extra one to five days for elite athletes or special circumstances.

For athletes coming from sprint distances or single endurance sports and training only four to seven hours per week, they may train only once a day. That's okay for long-course triathletes in the early preparation or transitional parts of the season, but long-course training usually requires some two-a-day workouts as athletes enter the Build periods. Weather, work, or transportation may require athletes to combine workouts in two sports into one workout, most commonly with a bike-to-run or brick workout.

How does physiology affect two workouts in a day? Remember that exercise by itself builds no fitness and breaks down bodily systems; only the recovery phase produces growth. Splitting the daily effort into two workouts provides two recovery cycles, two periods of nutritional replenishment, and two cycles of growth-hormone secretion. Studies show that about six to ten hours is optimal between daily workouts. This gap fits conveniently into most athletes' work, school, or family schedule.

Other benefits of two daily workouts include speed and economy. If workouts are strung together with little or no rest, speed usually slows in the second workout. Sometimes this is realistic preparation for racing, as with bricks where the ability to "run tired" is essential. But if all you do is run tired, swim tired, or bike tired, your speed will not improve optimally. Your technique will break down early, and you will be rehearsing less-than-ideal form in the secondary workout. This breakdown in technique is different in the three sports, and some are best done first, while others can be done later in the daily cycle.

We recommend two daily workouts when moving up to the half-Iron distance, because some try to cram all the daily training into one mega-session, often in a rush before going to work, or later in the day to finish before dark. Long, combined workouts do have their place in half-Iron training, but on a limited basis. For beginning long-course athletes and intermediates, alternating two-a-day workouts with a more restful single-workout day can work well.

This begs the question: If two workouts per day are better than forcing only one workout, wouldn't three daily workouts be even better? And for the elite athlete with fifteen waking hours to train each day, this practice is common. But for almost anyone who works for a living, goes to school, or raises children, three-a-day workouts are impractical. Shower, dress, nutrition, and recovery cannot catch up. Athletes report a feeling of always coming in or out of a workout, constantly changing into workout clothes. Keep this limitation in mind when mixing triathlon with social sports like golf, tennis, basketball, and so on. Treat these activities as full workout stress even though you may think they are shorter or have lower intensity.

About the only exception to this rule involves strength training or stretching such as yoga or Pilates. These shorter, low-intensity workouts can be done in conjunction with two other endurance workouts. But even here, scheduling is more effective when combining them after a swim workout or easy bike. Many triathletes swim near a weight room or stretching pads, so this combination can be a practical solution.

The Recovery Day

Since physiological systems can grow only during rest, this may be the most important day in your training week. Many people don't take it very seriously or find ways to fill it with lifestyle stress. I confess that in my first two years of endurance training I thought a rest day was something that only happened when my bike broke or a hurricane moved in from the Gulf Coast. As you might guess, injury and fatigue were my regular companions during this ignorant phase. As volume grows for long-course training, planned and executed recovery days are essential.

The simplest type of recovery day is the classic day off where you:

- stay off your legs all you can
- watch nutrition closely (healthy carbs, lean protein, and good fats)
- stretch
- drink plenty of fluids
- engage in massage, napping, elevating legs, floating in water, and listening to music

This is the best method for most beginning long-course athletes, and also for some intermediate athletes during periods of work, travel, or family stress. For elite triathletes, a complete day away from training may occur during a more intensive Build period. Inevitably, you will always find a circumstance where you can't train at all. It's better to plan for these, but even if they come unannounced, embrace them, do not regret them. Learn to revel in your day off!

For more experienced athletes, a more active recovery strategy is often employed. This means a low-intensity workout of relatively brief duration. Swimming may be the ideal active recovery workout for triathletes, as long as intensity is constrained. It can include work on stroke technique without raising heart rate. Swim progress depends on frequency, and the recovery day may well be the only time to maintain three or more sessions per week. It also combines well with certain strength training or stretching done afterward.

After swimming comes easy spins on the bike for recovery, perhaps of a social variety with slower family members or casual cycling groups off the road. Walking also makes a good recovery exercise, both planned sessions and random walks through parks, malls, or fascinating tours around diverse racing locales. Just make sure you don't spend too much time in the sun or extreme temperatures. Realize that some excursions can be more stressful than a planned workout. An easy jog of 20–30 minutes can be used for active recovery, but may still involve orthopedic stress. If your weekly active recovery day comes immediately after your longest or fastest run, running is probably not the best choice.

Experienced triathletes report reduced muscle soreness and faster return to normal training with active rest days. On the other hand, if you're having your toughest workday in months, taking a difficult written exam, or dealing with a sick child or spouse, less is more. When in doubt, leave it out.

The Breakthrough Workout

The simplest definition of a breakthrough workout is anything that requires thirty-six hours or more recovery time. This definition yields the broadest range of workouts, including weight training for the uninitiated. When we examine object relationships, the breakthrough workout is the pivotal point around which all other workouts and recovery revolve. There is a direct correlation between the effective experience of a triathlete to the quality and quantity of breakthrough workouts. Beginners should do very few with plenty of recovery, and experienced athletes should be specific and careful to allow sufficient recovery and maintain focus on limiters.

As Table 3.6 suggests, those who need the most improvement should do the least number of breakthrough workouts. Elites may be forced to a longer training week to provide for breakthrough workout recovery, or may stack multiple hard workouts on the same day. This practice is tricky at best, but risks are reduced when one of the same-day breakthrough workouts is a swim.

Our training philosophy is doubly true for breakthrough workouts: Less is more, quality is more important than quantity (Table 3.7). It's practically impossible for breakthrough workouts to maintain optimal intensity if there are too many of them. If you find yourself unable to get up to speed

TABLE 3.6 SUGGESTED WEEKLY FREQUENCY FOR BREAKTHROUGH WORKOUTS

EXPERIENCE	WORKOUTS	RECOVERY (HOURS)
Beginner	1–2	48
Intermediate	3	36
Advanced	3–4	6–48

TABLE 3.7 PREPARATION AND RECOVERY STRATEGIES FOR BREAKTHROUGH WORKOUTS

QUALITY	WORKOUT PREPARATION	IMMEDIATE RECOVERY
Timing	Afternoon for moderate or cool temperatures. Morning for hot weather.	Unhurried and complete.
Nutrition	Light but balanced between carbohydrates (80%) and protein (20%). Low to moderate caffeine use helpful.	Carbohydrates (70%) but even more protein (30%). Plenty of electrolytes and fluids. Omega-3 fatty acids (fish-oil pill) as anti-inflammatory.
Mental	Focus, focus, focus.	Relax and get extra rest when possible.
Pain	Allow for gradual increase in discomfort and fatigue, but avoid sharp pain.	Minimize with stretching, massage, and leg elevation.

DESCRIPTION (OTHER QUALITIES POSSIBLE)	EXAMPLE
Usually involves bike and run limiters, longer swims, and increasing endurance.	3-hour bike, Zone 2
One workout for each sport, increasing endurance and muscular endurance.	6x800m track intervals with 200m recovery, Zones 4–5a
One or two workouts in each sport, increasing muscular endurance and speed in longer workouts. May involve 8–12 day megaweeks to allow sufficient recovery. Varies with mesocycles.	4-hour brick: 3-hour ride plus 1-hour run, Zone 3

in a breakthrough workout, rest more and consider reducing breakthrough workout frequency. Some athletes maintain and improve running speed going to the track only once every two weeks, and many finish long-course races strongly while skipping a long run every other week. Some report that race personal records (PRs) occurred in seasons with fewer but higher quality breakthrough workouts. Weekly planning is convenient, but don't be a slave to the arbitrary calendar.

CHAPTER 4

Integrating Training and Lifestyle

It's been reported that Greece . . . may not be able to finish building all the event sites for this summer's Olympics. As a result, this year's triathlon combines running, swimming, and pouring concrete.

—Conan O'Brien

REALITY CHECK

Many endurance books plan training around the necessities of workouts, recovery, and resulting performance. This practice is good, but training lives in the larger ecology of lifestyle. Athletes who can plan everything around training are full-time professionals, the very rich, or those on a steady retirement income; even these lucky few have a life to live outside triathlon. The rest of us have to work for a living, go to school, or care for a family—or juggle all three together. Lifestyle often plays a larger role in physiological stress than actual workout time. We have twenty-four hours in a day, yet few athletes can train more than twenty-four hours in a week, and certainly this volume is not required to race well in a half-Iron race. Training is 5–15 percent of your life, but your physical and mental fitness is based mostly on the other 85 percent. How you blend training with the rest of your life is crucial to long-term success.

THE WEEKLY PLAN

You may be wondering why we have yet to introduce a sample weekly training plan. Most athletes want to jump into a concrete training plan without understanding individual workouts it relates to their lifestyle. Chapter 3 introduced the basic building block of planning, the individual workout. I then explained how individual workouts might interrelate within a training day, or over several days, building a whole fitness molecule. Now we'll build an organic structure into a full week. In order for any living organism to survive and flourish, it must harmonize with its environment. The blocks have to fit within your life structure.

I assume most of you have other life responsibilities that take up 25–60 hours of your week, and that these follow a fairly regular schedule. For professional or time-free athletes, all these principles can still apply and should probably be followed anyway. We'll save the discussion on extended training weeks for the free spirits until Chapter 10, which discusses "Advanced Concepts."

We'll determine the core weekly training hours before expanding this into the annual estimate. When I see a chart of "annual training hours," I wonder how the average athlete could predict so far into the future with any precision, anymore than professionals can determine how many hours they'll spend at their desk next year or how much study a college degree will require. Yes, there are statistical averages, but the range of actual hours in the real world is very broad. Most of us do understand what our schedule will be for the next week or two and can extrapolate demands on our time during certain seasons of the year. And it's simpler to add up the weekly training variations over a year than it is to deconstruct them from a single megacycle.

Despite globalization and technological advances, most athletes still have Saturday and Sunday off from work or school, and almost all racing takes place on these two days. Depending on their family obligations, most athletes have free weekend time, and group training over longer distances is most likely on the weekend. People get into the habit of doing their long ride and/or their long run on the weekend, and it's a difficult habit to break. With full Ironman training, there is merit in keeping the longest ride and longest run far apart for recovery, but since the longest run for half-Iron training requires only ninety minutes, the gap can be less. You could also complete the longest run on a weekday and still get to work or to sleep on time.

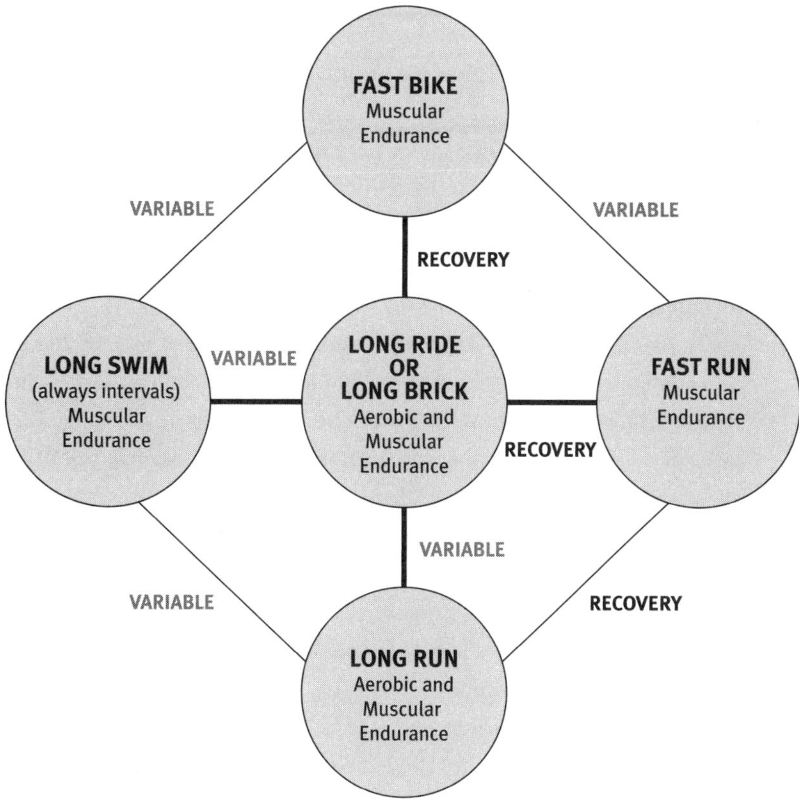

FIGURE 4.1
Relationship of breakthrough workouts to recovery in a training week

WEEKLY ENGINEERING

Building on Chapter 3, we can construct a diagram of breakthrough workouts and their links (Figure 4.1). Some workouts require an easier recovery day or days afterward, some allow variable workouts or even consecutive difficult days.

There are myriad possible links between workouts in a training week, but experience reveals a few simple rules of what does *not* work for most athletes. We hesitate to call any training rule universal, but expect great risks and little reward for violating these negatives:

- Do not combine your longest run and your fastest run on consecutive days or on the same day. You may run fast toward the end of a longer run, but give yourself recovery between track intervals near lactate threshold and the long road run.

- Avoid weight lifting on the same day as the fastest run or the longest run. The musculoskeletal stress of long or hard running and weight lifting are likely to produce injury over time, and will at the very least reduce the effectiveness of the run. It may require only twenty-four hours' recovery between the fast run and strength training, but often forty-eight hours or longer is better between the longest run and weight lifting.
- Avoid placing the fastest bike followed by the longest bike or brick on consecutive days. If you must combine two rides in two days, better the long ride first, then the faster, shorter ride on the next day. It's okay to combine the fastest ride with the weight lifting day, but usually not the longest ride or brick.
- You can lift weights after swimming but not immediately before. Improvement of swim technique requires fresh capacity. Since many athletes swim near a weight facility, it's natural to combine weight lifting after swimming, though with some reduction in total mass lifted. The same rule applies to core strength exercises like sit-ups, crunches, leg lifts, large ball, and so on: Do them after the swim, not before. Beginners are best advised to avoid combining swimming and weight lifting.
- Avoid doing the fastest run or the longest run in hot weather. The exact temperature is relative to your heat tolerance: In some climates, the summer predawn morning can be 83°F and 90 percent humidity. That makes it even more important to do your long run and track intervals early in the morning. If lifestyle forces you to miss the early start, opt for a slower or shorter run: Avoid intervals or long runs during the afternoon's when it's over 85°F. If your heat tolerance is good, however, you may attempt longer bikes or bike intervals in hotter weather, but hydration and electrolyte needs may in fact double for these workouts.
- One more tip for hot- or even warm-weather intervals: Use heart rate as a governor on effort. Allow for slower pacing and don't force the pace beyond your heat tolerance. Heat resistance can be a training tool, but excessive heat fatigue is not useful because it precludes recovery for many days.

- Reduce cycling in the winter cold. As with heat, extremes of cold are relative depending on your tolerance and your clothing. The modern wicking fabrics such as CoolMax and Lycra minimize moisture freezing in cold winds, and cycling outerwear is becoming lighter, more comfortable, and less bulky. Performance fabrics make winter cycling much more tolerable and are well worth the investment. But unless we live or can travel to warmer climates, most of us must reduce our winter volume. For triathletes this should be no great handicap since running can maintain your aerobic base in cold weather.

Okay, now that we're done with the negatives, we can move on to positive design.

Potential Training Week for Experienced, Working Triathlete

Let's examine one possible training week in Table 4.1. Remember, this athlete is not real, so don't rush to emulate.

This weekly plan might suit an experienced, intermediate triathlete in the late Base period. It could also work for a beginner with plenty of free time as a rare intensive Build week. Or an elite athlete might follow this plan in the early Preparation and Base periods, especially if he or she also were racing the full Iron distance. This variation implies training volume is the least universal factor, based on athlete experience and time available for recovery. It is difficult to generalize about annual training hours for this athlete. It could range anywhere from 350–1,000 hours per year depending on where they place this week in the season.

This plan maintains the structural design pattern in Figure 4.1. It includes breakthrough workouts in all three sports, provides for recovery from these workouts, and is flexible enough for balancing.

Days with two workouts can follow the vertical sequence of the table: top for morning and bottom for afternoon or evening. This sequence works well in moderate temperatures. You can reverse the sequence so that swim workouts come later if run workouts are done in the morning, but morning swimming usually has less effect on an afternoon run. Experienced athletes can turn two workouts into an aqua-run, useful for summer months when there is no good time for running in the afternoon

TABLE 4.1 SAMPLE WEEKLY TRAINING PLAN FOR HALF-IRON DISTANCE

DAY	WORKOUT	QUALITIES
Monday	Easy, technique swim	Active Recovery
Tuesday	Weight lifting, Core exercises	Strength
	Brick	Muscular Endurance, Transition Skill
Wednesday	Track intervals	Muscular Endurance, Speed
	Swim, short intervals	Muscular Endurance, Speed
Thursday	Weight lifting, Core exercises	Strength
	Bike intervals	Muscular Endurance, Speed
Friday	Swim, long intervals	Muscular Endurance
	Run	Muscular Endurance, Economy
Saturday	Long bike or brick	Endurance, Muscular Endurance
Sunday	Long run	Endurance
	Easy ride	Recovery
Total hours		

at temperatures from 95–105° F. Or you may have limited pool access with an early-morning masters swim group.

Reversing the sequence of weight training and cycling can work, but beginners may benefit from an earlier strength workout. Real-world cases with multisport athletes reveal they are more likely to skip an afternoon weight session or swim, but less likely to skip a late-day bike or run. If you find weight training or swim technique tedious, best to get them done

DURATION (MIN)	INTENSITY ZONE	DESCRIPTION
60	1	Stroke drills, limiters, loose interval structure
45–60	1–2	Leg press, leg limiter, lat pull-downs, bench press, sit-ups, leg raises, twists
60 bike, 30 run	2–3	Bike moderate, fast transition, run moderately hard
60	4–5a	4–6x800m at LTHR with 200m jogging recovery
60	3–5a	6x200@20sec rest, kick drills, paddles with pull buoy
45–60	1–2	Leg press, leg limiter, lat pull-downs, bench press, sit-ups, leg raises, twists
90	4–5a	3x8min intervals
65	3–5a	5–6x400m at T-Pace with 30sec recovery
60	2–3	15min warm-up, 1min Zone 2, 20min Zone 3, 10min cool-down
120–240	1–3	2–3 hour bike, 30–60min run. Beginners may omit the run.
60–120	1–3	Build pace, rolling hills
30–60	1	Optional
13.1–17.1		

early while your mind and body are fresh. We all have preferences, but in order to improve you must give limiters primary attention.

Some important questions to ask about any weekly plan:

- Can I realistically make it to these workouts? Should I limit some of them to only once every two weeks or longer?

- What are the logistical conflicts in the plan? High overhead for some sessions: travel time to training area, traffic on bike or run, lane availability in pool, weight machine availability in gym, extended commute to work or school, and so on. Most triathlon training has at least a 10 percent overhead beyond the workout, often longer. A 15-hour training week takes 17 to 20 hours to execute and merits extra sleep time.
- How many days or weeks can I "push hours" before my work, studies, or family life suffer? Be honest—relationships are important.
- Will I have sufficient time for recovery, rest, and sleep with this plan? Should I trim some hours to make sure? Most training plans can and should be trimmed by 10 percent or more after initial estimates. Less is more.
- Does this program effectively address my limiters and maintain my strengths? The answer here is moot if you haven't resolved the previous questions.
- How does planning change for different levels of athlete talent and experience: beginner, intermediate, and advanced? We explore the answer with the rest of the chapter.

Beginner's Weekly Focus

Stressing recovery first, let's examine Monday. For most beginners, it's better to take the rest day completely off. But since we want to continue to improve swimming skill, very common with beginners, we need to retain three swims per week. So we move this workout to Tuesday in place of strength training. We might preserve things like stretching and core exercises after the swim, but given a choice between swim improvement and weight training, let's remember we are primarily endurance athletes.

An exception to the beginner's day off might occur for someone new to biking and running, yet experienced in competitive swimming. They could swim Monday at lower intensity and still recover. Other activities for a rest day might include a casual walk, golf, yoga, or Pilates. But even with crosstraining, intensity should be kept low; omit entirely if tired. Keeping with the cultural norm, we place the recovery day on Monday after longer weekend workouts since this is when most of us ease back into work or school. It's a good day to gain momentum in your life outside of triathlon.

A true novice to all endurance sports with no prior racing would cut the rest of the week by 50–60 percent in the early season, and perhaps build to ten hours per week after six months of consistent training. Those without half-Iron experience but a few years racing at the Olympic-distance could attempt something closer to the full volume. Those athletes with prior competitive experience in one sport can use that experience to determine triathlon volume. If you ran 50–70 miles per week to run marathons or rode 200-plus weekly miles for bike racing, you can probably begin with ten hours per week of triathlon training spread across all three sports. But be especially cautious about increasing run mileage.

With brick workouts, the novice is still learning to deal with the pain and fatigue of running directly off the bike, so they may want to attempt only one, shorter brick per week. The long ride should be limited to cycling and perhaps a fifteen-minute cool-down walk with stretching afterward.

You can begin to learn the rhythm of intervals in the water, on the bike, and on the track, but these should be reduced in repetitions and intensity. Some beginners find they are better off with no hard interval training. This caution is best heeded by keeping most intervals 10bpm below lactate threshold heart rate on the bike or run, or below T-Pace in the pool. It's the variation in speed that makes intervals effective, not the maximum speed.

Intermediate Weekly Focus

It's difficult to define an exact date when we classify triathletes as intermediate or experienced. For most, you can draw a fuzzy line after one or two years of consistent training and racing at the sprint or Olympic distances. Some adventurous individuals, especially those who have competed in singular swimming, running, or cycling events, may jump right into long-course training, perhaps even doing a half-Iron as their first triathlon. Though we do not recommend it, we have to account for readers already registered for such a race in the near future.

We assume the athlete has good experience in at least one sport and perhaps a preference for it; he or she is gaining some familiarity with the other two. They have done a few shorter races with mixed success. They are probably using a heart rate monitor to gauge intensity and may have organized a training plan, perhaps using the principles of periodization. Many athletes moving into the middle ground employ mixed training in three sports but pay less attention to links between workouts or seasonal changes in volume and intensity. They usually alternate hard and easy days, understand the principle of rest, and know they should taper for a race. It's amazing how fast you can improve in the early stages with only these simple principles, but it's not true periodization.

Intermediate athletes training for long-course events should maintain a consistent structure. The absolute value of volume or intensity is of lesser importance than consistency. An athlete with a consistent periodization plan training ten hours per week may improve faster than one with an inconsistent mixed plan requiring fifteen hours per week. The consistent triathlete is less prone to injury and overtraining and is likely to maintain effective pacing for a longer race.

Relating to the plan in Table 4.1, many intermediate athletes could use this week in the later Base period. Modifications to the plan would be made based on limiters and experience. Some possible cases are given in Table 4.2.

TABLE 4.2 MODIFICATIONS TO WEEKLY PLAN FOR INTERMEDIATE TRIATHLETES BASED ON LIMITERS

SPORT	LIMITER	CHANGE
Swim	General	Increase to four weekly swims, or increase Friday swim by 50% with more long intervals. Address stroke limiters with drill and force limiters with equipment: paddles and buoy (upper), fins (lower).
Bike	Endurance	Increase length of long ride by 20%, increase shorter rides by 10%.
	Speed	Pedal-stroke drills before intervals, higher cadence, more intervals with less duration; reduce long ride by 25% every other week.
	Force	More hills, remain seated; increase weight lifting mass for leg press.
Run	Endurance	Increase length of long run by 10–20%
	Speed	Perform stride drills before track session, analyze running technique, midfoot or ball-of-foot strike; reduce long run by 25–30% every other week.
	Force	More hills, stair steps, consistent stretching

This lists only some of the possible changes; experience determines how effective they might be. For example, it's relatively easy for someone moving into triathlon from bike racing to increase cycling volume, but for someone with little cycling experience, even thirty minutes more on a ride can be stressful.

Experience can be a curse as well as a blessing. Veteran runners who have completed marathons or long races sometimes bring their big weekly running mileage into early triathlon training. Indeed, fast triathlon running requires much less volume, and run splits are determined as much by cycling endurance as foot speed. Runners need to learn the discipline of getting 50 percent or more of their training hours from cycling, using these to maintain aerobic base while focusing on economy in run workouts.

Those who began their endurance careers in shorter triathlons simply need to gradually turn up the volume. The key word here is gradual, about 10 percent per week maximum. Don't start full long-course volume the day you register for your first half-Iron race. Even with a measured increase, there should be weeks when you drop back to less volume. For those with well-balanced training for Olympic-distance events, you simply increase the longest ride and run workout, emphasize longer intervals in the pool, and perhaps moderate the pace of faster workouts.

Advanced Weekly Focus

As with intermediate triathletes, there's a fine line of separation. Some triathletes are content to reach the intermediate level and stay there for the rest of their careers, and that's fine if you're still having fun. But if you're reading these words, chances are you want to race faster and may even have a dream of moving into the advanced ranks. We'll loosely define advanced long-course athletes as those who can place in the top 10 percent of their age group or professionals. Advanced triathletes usually possess at least three years or more long-course experience and have probably done several half-Iron races. They often have Ironman racing experience and may augment their half-Iron training to prepare for a longer A race.

Although they have greater skill, advanced age-group triathletes would be well served by the weekly plan in Table 4.1. Provided they can gauge intensity correctly, it provides plenty of potential volume and variation in the three sports. But it would not be suitable for the entire season. Preparation periods might be shorter with more emphasis on skills, and Build periods might emphasize intensity with a pinch of anaerobic endurance intensity thrown into the mix.

Greater total volume would become necessary if training for a full Iron race, which might require winning your age group in the half-Iron event for a slot to the Ironman world championship. More time on one sport might be justified by experience: If you've been swimming five days a week in an organized group, you can continue, or if swimming is indeed your limiter, you should swim four to five days per week. If high bike volume has been with you for years, you can extend the length of the long ride accordingly, five hours or more for Iron-distance athletes. Increased running volume is less effective unless you're training for Iron distance, and even the best runners risk injury when intensity and/or volume rise too far or too fast.

Remember that volume and speed are like a seesaw: Too much emphasis on one is bound to decrease the other eventually (Figure 4.2).

Many coaches claim intensity is the key to endurance training and that is certainly true for advanced triathletes. They can tolerate higher intensities and produce higher speeds, but the margin for error between gaining speed and overtraining narrows. For most half-Iron distance athletes, development of anaerobic endurance has minimal effectiveness, and I recommend training at or below lactate threshold in muscular endurance sessions. Yet that 1- to 3-percent differential between winning and missing the podium may well involve those five extra heartbeats per minute between Zones 5a and 5b. If you want to win the overall championship or even the masters overall, you'll probably spend some time well above lactate threshold in a 3:55–4:30 half-Iron race effort. Training for that effort involves lactate threshold efforts (Zone 5a), and those may be all that you

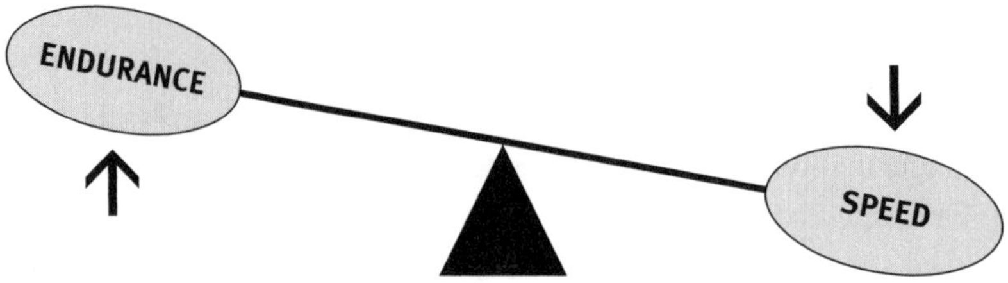

FIGURE 4.2
The endurance-speed seesaw

require. Or you may benefit from spending a small percentage of time on anaerobic endurance (Zone 5b), either in peloton bike rides, shorter swim intervals with little recovery, or VO_2max running efforts. Some athletes need to train at the race intensity, whereas many others will automatically raise their intensity by around five or ten beats per minute under racing conditions even if all training is slower. Advanced triathletes usually know which category describes them. One measure is how technique and economy survive into the anaerobic zones.

Other Considerations

For those who do not follow a Monday through Friday workweek, or who have variable schedules, the prime factor remains the rest day or at least active rest. You must choose one twenty-four-hour or longer period every five to ten days for recovery. This rest day should fall after a breakthrough workout. People in labor-intensive jobs with night and daytime schedules, child care issues, or those who travel extensively have special challenges. It's even more important for these people to avoid cramming workouts into a small period. More lifestyle variation means more bodily stress and a need for more rest. It's better to plan missing some workouts than to constantly rework frequency due to lifestyle issues.

You may be one of those fortunate athletes with much free time for training without the pressure of earning your living at triathlon. Or you may have a summer off from school or an extended vacation from work or time between jobs. Keep in mind, however, that endurance training is not like golf, fishing, or other more pedestrian pursuits. Just because triathlon is fun and you have time to train all day does not mean you should indulge, at least not if you want to improve.

Some time ago I saved up enough money to take a one-year sabbatical from consulting engineering to pursue writing, which ended up as a coaching career. I had more than enough time to train all I wanted for two Ironman events in one year, figuring I would nab PR times in both events, improving steadily all year. I quickly found, however, that there are implacable human limitations; extending volume indefinitely was not helping my racing. My ideal volume as a masters triathlete turned out to be not much more than I used before with a full-time job and family—maybe only 5 percent more. The largest benefit was more time to rest and less stress with nontriathlon pursuits. I did manage a podium finish in that first Ironman, but I credit that to more rest time, not more training. By the second Ironman I was burned out with training as the centerpiece in my life and racing slowed.

If you have a smaller window of free time, say a month or two, remember that crash training is seldom effective when pursued longer than two weeks, and even that long is only recommended for the most experienced athletes. Triathletes can indeed benefit from a weeklong bike tour or a camp for swimming or triathlon. It's not so much the training volume as the ability to focus mentally without distractions that breeds improvement.

Suffice to say that straying from well-balanced training for long periods will probably hurt your fitness and performance. If triathlon demands anything, it is balance.

CHAPTER 5

Building a Season in the Real World

The best thing about the future is that it only comes one day at a time.
—Abraham Lincoln

How do we define a "season" in triathlon? This term has several possible meanings:

- The traditional three-month periods of the calendar: winter, spring, summer, fall.
- The whole training year, culminating in a Peak racing period during one or two of the calendar seasons.
- The results of all your races of the year.

These all have valid uses in training design. The conflict occurs when we design the annual plan before planning for the race. If you know exactly what races you are doing in the next year (and sometimes these must be entered a full twelve months in advance), what your work, school, and/or family schedule will be, then your annual plan for the next twelve months and your race preparation plan are one and the same.

THE SEASONAL PROBLEM

Most working triathletes cannot achieve this ideal harmony with races. They have a good idea of what their racing goals are for the coming year, but lifestyle issues preclude exact planning for all four calendar seasons. In the real world, the driving factors of training and fitness are races and lifestyle—not the standard calendar year. Even the term "annual training plan" can be arbitrary; athletes may plan key races over eighteen months or longer. Multisport athletes may have seasons that emphasize shorter racing, even moving in and out of other individual sports. For example, an athlete might want to focus on balanced triathlon training for six months, mostly shorter races with one half-Iron event, and then do mostly running to qualify for Boston or a marathon PR. About the only people with fully organized, preplanned years are professional triathletes or amateurs with no other obligations.

We will plan a training season that grows organically out of race demands. For many athletes this cycle will be annual, but not necessarily so. Following our inside-out design pattern, we'll start with the A races and

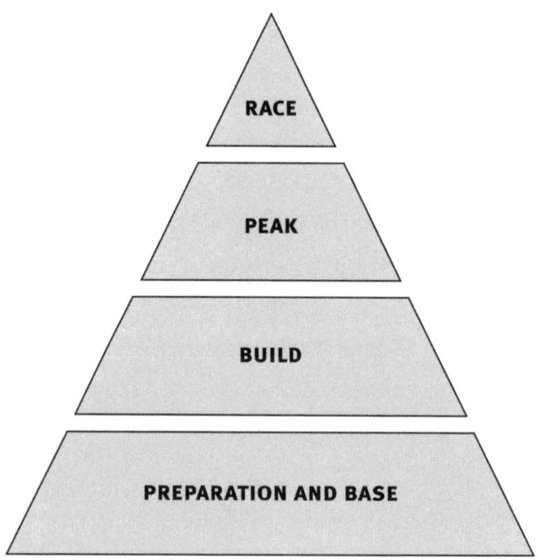

FIGURE 5.1
The seasonal pyramid driven by motivation to race faster

TABLE 5.1 COMMON PERIODIZATION TERMS

TERM	DEFINITION	ATTRIBUTES
A race	The most important races in the season, the fruition of other periods.	Only 2–4 of these are recommended per season. Four months between races is advised, or else only a few weeks during a single peak.
B race	Races not of primary importance but meriting up to one week of taper and peak.	There is no set number, but reality limits these to a few per season. The taper time is costly.
C race	Shorter races requiring no taper; done for testing or experimentation.	Best done locally without long travel. Should be significantly shorter than A race. Can include single-sport races.
Preparation	Weeks or months of training in very early season. Usually includes some cross-training.	4–12 weeks building skill, strength, and aerobic base. Deconstructing swim, bike, and run technique is best done here. Volume and intensity are low.
Base	Months of training following preparation period, or revisited between A races.	8–26 weeks of training, usually divided into 2–4 blocks of 3–4 weeks' duration.
Build	Weeks of training that specifically emphasize energies required in an upcoming A race.	3–8 weeks of training in one or two blocks. For the intermediate or advanced athlete, these often involve anaerobic work. For the beginner, base-period intensity continues with more specific application to race simulation.
Peak	Days or weeks that allow for tapering, absorbing prior training, and maintaining race sharpness.	May last only a few days up to several weeks for Iron-distance races. Determined by race distance and strategy.

CONTINUED

TABLE 5.1 CONTINUED

TERM	DEFINITION	ATTRIBUTES
Taper	The reduction of volume and/or intensity before an A or B race.	Often confused with peaking, the goal of pre-race training. Research shows volume reduction and intensity maintenance work best. Little or no taper is done for C races.
Race	Week prior to major race.	Based on race date, travel, check-in, and remaining peak fitness characteristics. With C races, similar to regular training week.
Transition	Week(s) following an A race. Characterized by rest and very light, unstructured activity.	Shorter in midseason, longer after last A race. Rest more, think about life outside triathlon.

move outward. Starting with a few simple race drivers, we'll expand our universe until it encompasses the whole year.

In terms of importance and time requirements, a season can be viewed as a simple pyramid (Figure 5.1). You could call this the motivational diagram.

When we try to actually design the training plan, we need something more object-oriented, and we use some new terms (Table 5.1).

With the terminology established, we can then build a diagram of object relationships. This design (Figure 5.2) is flexible enough to allow insertion or movement of other races and training blocks; it centers our thinking on racing so we become more intuitive when planning training weeks. The central objects of the system are the A races, which are fed by the training cycles of Base, Build, Peak, and Race. These cycles are in turn fed by the individual training weeks. Note that C races can also be "fed" by an individual training week, which also feeds into a training cycle. Given that we are having fun with triathlon as a lifestyle, the only real purpose of organized training is racing faster when it matters. The plan serves our racing—we are not slaves to the plan.

When we prepare for a half-Iron race, we strike a balance among the different periods, yet there is still significant variation for different athletes.

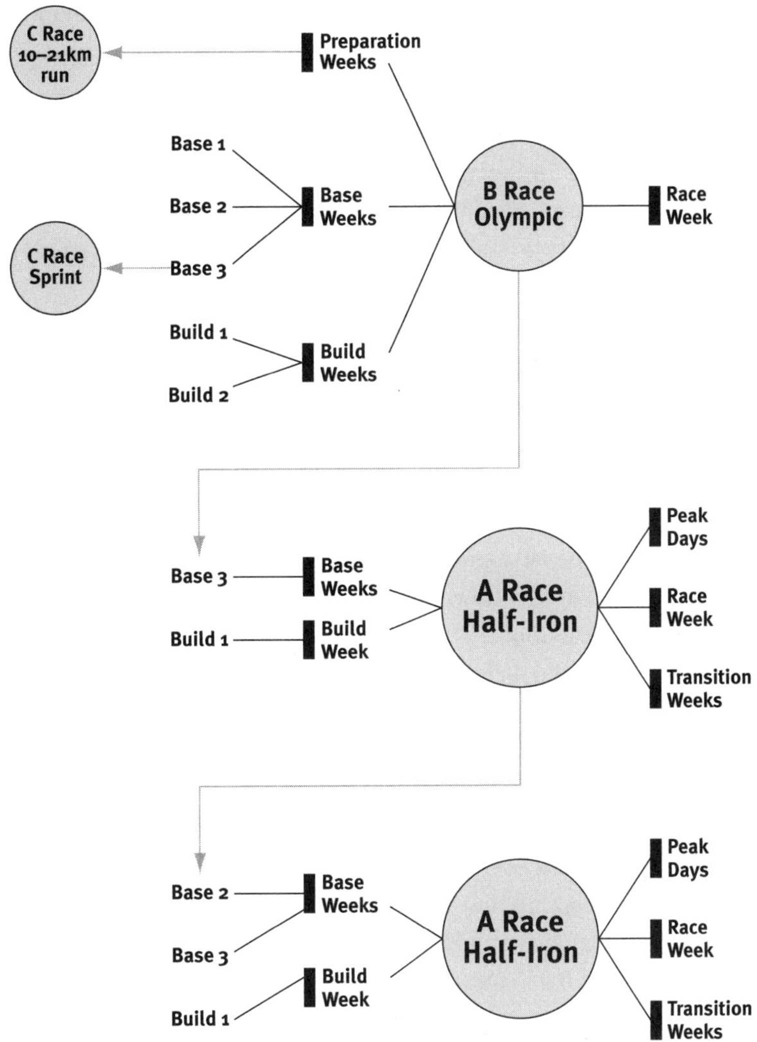

FIGURE 5.2
Objectives and how they relate in a potential training season

PREPARATION PERIOD

This period is best termed the "patience phase." You've gone through a period of active rest during the Transition phase after last season's final A race. You have an idea of when your big races are coming the next season. You miss structure and feel like getting serious again.

Most athletes spend from four to twelve weeks in the Preparation period. Those from colder winter climates or who have late-season A races will probably spend more than eight weeks. Those with earlier racing or who lost little fitness in the Transition period may be able to prepare in less time. But just about everyone takes four to six weeks to get back into the swing of structured training. Not only must you rebuild the fitness of your heart, lungs, and bloodstream, you are retraining your nervous system to guide your bones and muscles efficiently.

Even if you maintained off-season fitness through marathon running, cross-country skiing, rowing, or other extensive activity, your brain and peripheral nervous system have lost some sharpness for triathlon events. Athletes who push too hard on the Preparation period may feel good from an aerobic standpoint, but they still risk sudden injury from going too fast.

The Preparation phase is also a good time to deconstruct the mechanics of swim stroke, pedal technique, and running form—mostly neurological work. You must slow down the intensity and reduce the volume to make effective changes in technique. Everyone has at least a small weakness in some area of the three sports, and if you start out the year with full-speed workouts, you are likely to regroove bad habits. The goal of the previous racing phase was to move efficiently without thinking. Now you must think about everything and reengineer when necessary.

Some useful things to do during the Preparation phase are given in Table 5.2. Only full-time professionals are expected do most of these activities in one Preparation period. It's usually more productive to choose two or three items that truly address limiters and focus on these in one Preparation period. Limitations on training time and money for equipment exist for everyone. If you are patient and give yourself eight to twelve weeks for the Preparation phase, you have time to try more new skills.

Unfortunately, beginning athletes who might benefit most from the Preparation phase are the more likely to rush into longer or harder workouts. Many simply don't understand that skill building is just as important in triathlon as it is in sports like golf and tennis. You may read this book well into the season with no prior knowledge of Preparation methods. Once again we enjoin patience, gaining smoothness through relative slowness.

Other athletes who benefit from a longer Preparation phase include intermediate and advanced athletes training for longer races like Ironman. Since the Build period resembles the later Base periods, you have another

TABLE 5.2 PREPARATION ACTIVITIES

SPORT	ACTIVITY	BENEFITS
Swim	Underwater swim analysis video of your freestyle stroke. Solicit expert analysis from swim or triathlon coach. Watch swim videos like *Total Immersion* and *Swim Power* to learn more stroke drills. Compare form to your own video. Increase frequency, variety, and duration of stroke drills; decrease interval sets. Experiment with swim equipment: drag harness, stretch cords, paddles, short fins, etc.	Improved efficiency in the water. Fewer strokes per lap.
Bike	Perform SpinScan and LT power test on CompuTrainer. Experiment with different cleat positions, pedals, and bodily positions. Optimize fit factors for maximum power and efficient heart rate. Make videotape of fitting and session with advice from bike or triathlon coach. Employ fixed-gear bike, PowerCranks (limit 1–2 times weekly), and outdoor power meter (PowerTap, SRM, Ergomo). Increase usage if already experienced. Watch videotapes like *Wind Tunnel Magic* (John Cobb) on aerodynamic positioning. Employ workout-specific videos for indoor training, focusing on pedal-stroke technique and muscular endurance. Optimize aero position and time-trial equipment in wind tunnel (expensive) or perform qualitative aero positioning via motorpacing, including videotape from leading car.	Better right-left leg balance. Less aerodynamic drag. Better climbing smoothness. Accurate testing.

CONTINUED

month or longer to prepare. Remember "Preparation" does not mean easy. It means building speed through gradual aerobic improvement and enhanced skill building. Great champions often credit their victories in the Tour de France, Ironman races, or world championships to disciplined early-season preparation. You might say we race with our heart, but we prepare with our head, thinking more and acting less.

As you approach the end of the Preparation phase, you can gradually increase volume so that a training week resembles a Base 1 cycle. You may

TABLE 5.2 CONTINUED

SPORT	ACTIVITY	BENEFITS
Run	Make videotape of running form, including strides and other drills. Share with running or triathlon coach for analysis. Watch and learn from videotapes like *Evolution Running* and *The Pose Method*.	Fewer run-related injuries. Strike with mid-to-ball of foot. Higher cadence. Longer time to form breakdown.
	Happy with shoes and injury free: Buy several pairs for entire season. Unhappy with shoes and soreness or injury: Experiment with different shoes, orthotics, and solicit running store expert advice.	
	Increase frequency and duration of running form drills (strides, skipping, stair-stepping, stretching), outdoors or on indoor treadmill.	
Cross-train	Hike, mountain climb, mountain bike, cross-country ski, paddle (kayak, shell, etc.), rollerblade, etc.	Maintain aerobic capacity and strengthen large muscle groups.

take a recovery week in the middle of the Preparation period, and you certainly should take one in the final week before moving on to the Base period. This recovery is the ideal stop for "baseline testing" in all three sports.

BASE PERIOD

Base training is the core of the season for the long-course triathlete. In fact, some athletes do better with no Build period involving anaerobic intensity, but simply extending the Base period until it's time to peak for a major race with race simulations. This group includes:

- Beginning triathletes who will be racing their first half-Iron far below lactate threshold.
- Athletes over 60 who can still compete at a top level with reduced heart rates.

- Intermediate or advanced athletes focusing on one or more Iron-distance races in the season, using the half-Iron effort as a waypoint toward a higher goal.
- Athletes with an overriding propensity for slow-twitch muscle fiber or other compelling reasons to avoid anaerobic work.

Since Base building is the largest part of the pyramid, we spawn three Base phases. We can organize them in a variety of ways, but two methods have proven successful for many long-course athletes:

- Three weeks of hard training followed by one rest and recovery week, four weeks each for Base 1, 2, 3. This orthodox method has been useful to triathletes for several decades.
- Sixteen days of hard training followed by five days of rest and recovery, a three-week cycle for each Base period. This method could include repeating the Base 3 period a second time with only minor tweaking via race simulation. This pattern was developed more recently to help Iron-distance athletes undergo recovery more often and to assist older athletes with recovery from soreness and to avoid injury. This cycle also works for half-Iron distance training.

The method you choose has as much to do with lifestyle as your age and level of fitness. Most of us are stuck in a weekly schedule, with additional time on the weekend for longer workouts. Sometimes weekends are the only time for longer group workouts. Some athletes simply feel they are losing sharpness if they go seven days without a longer brick or run. Interestingly enough, if you compare the seasonal totals for the orthodox (21-work + 7-rest) cycle and the newer (16-work + 5-rest) cycle over all the Base periods, both plans offer about the same work-to-rest ratio (Table 5.3).

TABLE 5.3 COMPARISON OF BASE CYCLE METHODS

METHOD	CYCLES	WORK DAYS	REST DAYS
21/7	3	63	21
16/5	4	64	20

TABLE 5.4 POTENTIAL MIXTURE OF WORK AND REST DAYS

PERIOD	WORK DAYS	REST DAYS	TOTAL
Preparation 1–3	21	7	84
Base 1	21	7	28
Base 2–3	16	5	42
Build 1 only	16	5	21
Peak	4	3	7
Race	3	4	7

Most athletes would probably feel more comfortable with a longer four-week cycle during the Preparation period but could enjoy benefits of a three-week cycle as volume increases. Once you start race planning, it is rarely possible to time a four-week cycle in precise harmony with the upcoming races. With two useable ratios for the training cycle, it's easier to slot in B and C races and time our peaking for an A race. See Table 5.4 for some possible scenarios leading through the Base period.

In addition to dedicated rest blocks, we still follow the basic principles of alternating harder and easier days during the week and providing one day of active recovery every seven to ten days. For many working athletes, this recovery day is Monday and often involves an easy swim, weight lifting session, or bike spin.

You can change cycles during Base season. If you planned a 16/5 cycle and do not feel recovered by the fifth rest day, take one or two more. If you have trouble making it through all three challenging weeks of a 21/7 cycle, don't be afraid to shift to a 16/5 cycle. Your body has no Gregorian calendar inside; it simply responds to stress and rest over time. Remember the training plan is designed to serve your fitness—you are not the slave of the training plan.

The 16/5 cycle prevents a weekend C race from disturbing the work-to-rest ratio. By simply moving your longer bike and/or run to earlier in the week, the C race becomes your muscular or anaerobic endurance workout for that training week. The 16/5 cycle may leave enough time for a "Base 4" period, which could transition from aerobic base building to lactate threshold build efforts, and provide time for more testing or to do a B race.

If you do choose the 16/5 cycle for Base, it often means you must do longer workouts every weekend without a break. So make sure you are reducing weekday volume by a sizable amount, perhaps 50 percent or more. Use this time to get more sleep, catch up at the office, and spend quality time with family and friends. Revel in your rest days!

BUILD PERIOD

Perhaps the most perplexing period for long-course triathletes is the Build phase. It is commonly associated with increased speed work, anaerobic intensities, and so on. But for those attempting their first or even successive half-Iron races, it may differ very little from the Base period, certainly with similar intensity. For advanced athletes or those looking to do well in major Olympic-distance races, the Build period could involve significant work at lactate threshold intensity or even beyond. In any case, the Build period should be race-specific, involving race-pace simulations in all three sports. Muscular endurance is key for all triathletes, but beginners can best improve this attribute by high aerobic efforts. More advanced athletes also need these Zone 3 segments, but add Zone 4–5a workouts. Pros or age groupers trying to win the division at a world's qualifier may employ limited anaerobic endurance workouts.

Whatever your level of experience, the Build period will challenge your level of fitness and may send you beyond your comfort zone. These principles are paramount during Build: Keep it simple, keep it short, and closely monitor effects.

Keep It Simple

Although intervals should challenge you and involve variation, they should not strain your brain. Any interval sequence you cannot remember for at least the day you perform it is probably too complicated. Swimming fosters baroque interval patterns, and for those training for solo swim races under a kilometer, often involving a medley of strokes, this complex variation is effective. But the fitness required for racing in open water for 1,900 meters (1.2 miles) favors a simpler structure of short and long intervals, with a limited amount of work in other strokes like backstroke and breaststroke. Stroke drills should be done regularly, but intricate medley sets have limited use and should be minimized as race season approaches. Pyramid interval structures are good, but they should follow a simpler, linear progression such as 100-200-300-400-300-200-100 meters or yards of freestyle swimming.

This causes a dilemma for the masters swim group triathlete, who is often a minority in a pool full of fast swimmers training for shorter 50–400m swim meet races. You can participate in most of their training regimens for part of the year, but during race-specific Build and Peak for long-course events, you must focus on some simpler, longer interval workouts, perhaps reserving a half or full lane for long-course triathlete swimmers. Most good swim coaches are receptive to this approach, realizing these athletes are working as hard as or harder than the one-sport swimmers.

Cyclists can withstand a good deal of lactate threshold or even harder work without the risk of injury that runners face. The methods used to build muscular endurance for a 56-mile (90km) time trial involve longer intervals and longer power tests for time trials at lactate threshold.

A small dose of peloton rides or racing at anaerobic endurance speeds is allowable, but must be strictly governed. Triathletes are best advised to sit in with most groups in Zones 3–4, and do limited, fixed-time pulls in Zone 5a. Minimize sprinting and short jumping, and only go with breakaways where you know the escapees and reasonably expect a lactate threshold effort to stay with them. But your focus still remains on steady-state interval work in aero position at or below lactate threshold. No more than one peloton ride per week is advisable, and this for the intermediate or advanced triathlete who may have been a former road racer. Every two or three weeks is enough to improve handling skills and have some fun with your buddies. Avoid peloton work as long-course races approach: Overconfidence in bike intensity is likely to cause you to go out too fast in your long-course race, where you must still run a long way after your hard bike effort.

Runners who have a strong aerobic base, good biomechanics, and a near-clean injury history for the past three to six months can head to the track or a similar venue to work on speed at lactate threshold. As with swimming and cycling, longer intervals at lactate threshold heart rate are best for intermediate athletes. Beginners are better served by longer segments in high Zone 3, perhaps 20–30 minutes on a track or flat-to-rolling terrain. More experienced athletes can add a Zone 3 segment toward the end of a longer road run. You can do your track intervals with other triathletes or road runners, but as with cycling, avoid emulating complicated intervals or anaerobic endurance intensities.

Heed the motto, "Thou shalt not try to win an interval." Save your top-end performance for races. I can't count the times that I have passed my training partners in the last quarter of a long running race, even when they consistently beat me every week in 800–1,600m intervals, sometimes by 20–50m. Most athletes find it useful to gauge intervals by lactate threshold heart rate and measure lap speed as a secondary factor. The goal for long-course triathletes is to become more efficient at a given heart rate, not push harder and harder to "force" the speed higher. For beginners who have not done many solo run races, lactate threshold heart rate may be the only clue to correct pacing. For more experienced runners, lactate threshold pace on the track is usually 10–20 seconds per mile slower than your 10K race pace (5–10 seconds slower per 800 meters). You should be able to complete an entire interval set without much degradation in speed, perhaps running your last one or two intervals faster than the first.

Many runners also find "negative split" interval training helpful: You run the first half of the interval at a heart rate 5bpm below the target heart rate, then speed up gradually in the second half. This method also promotes the art of "neurological acceleration," where you naturally want to go faster and faster as a race progresses. In long-course triathlons, there is almost always a tendency to degrade speed toward the end of the race. If you can gradually increase perceived effort and maintain running form in the last six miles, you will likely pass many other competitors in half- or full Iron-distance races—one of the greatest joys in the sport.

Commonly used interval sets for running triathletes include 8–12×400m, 3–8×800m, and 3–6×1600m, and for lactate threshold intensities these usually involve a 200–400m jogging recovery. Sequences like 20×200m, which are popular with 5K and 10K road runners, are not as helpful for long-course triathletes who are unlikely to reach these speeds in a half-Iron race. Our experience shows that the 800m interval is the most versatile for experienced long-course triathletes, an ideal mix of strength, speed, and endurance. It can be expanded up to eight segments for a full Iron-distance race. It can be reduced to only three segments for beginners or those in a recovery week. It's easy to repeat even on a crowded track. The longer 1,600m intervals have been used successfully by Iron-distance triathletes and solo marathon runners, but some of these report faster recovery and higher racing speed with more frequent 800m intervals. The shorter 400m intervals are recommended for Olympic-distance triathletes, but are less effective for most long-course training. The only exception to this rule would be for those professional triathletes who've been racing short-course for a long time and are just moving up to the half-Iron race, or age-group division winners who want to trim down to higher speed and lower volume as a race approaches. Another 400m interval possibility is within the early Base period for those wishing to expand VO_2max with higher-intensity (Zone 5b) and long-recovery intervals.

Beginners can still do the 800m interval sets, but are best advised to learn their effectiveness in Zone 3, and then gradually increase intensity as experience and orthopedic resilience improves. They may indeed run intervals only slightly faster than jogging efforts, and that's okay for initial attempts.

If you don't have regular access to a track, or your regular venue is shut down for repairs or a meet, you can still do your intervals with your HRM on a relatively flat surface. For example, if you run 6×800m intervals in 3:20–3:25 at 158bpm with a 200m jogging recovery taking 80 seconds, you can use the heart rate monitor's interval feature to set up a 3:25 timer and perhaps a 1:20 timer, and set a heart rate zone between 153–161bpm for the intervals. If you're doing this on pavement instead of a tartan running track, you might want to reduce intensity or cut back on the number of intervals to avoid orthopedic stress. Or if you must run indoors during bad weather, know that speed will likely decrease and that running angles are more stressful on indoor tracks.

Intervals and racing are dangerous for all runners. Running too hard or too long is by far the most likely cause of injury to triathletes. If you are sore after a race or during excessive volume, if heat or humidity is very high, or if you're not getting enough sleep, it's best to avoid interval running and substitute a moderate Zone 2–3 effort. Or move the interval workout to a time when you are better rested. When in doubt, leave it out. Know that many runners have improved racing speed with little or no efforts beyond Zone 3.

Keep It Short

"Short" applies to the Build period itself and to the general strategy of interval workouts. Build periods for long-course athletes usually do not deviate much from Base 3 intensities, so you could just do another Base period, and dedicate only one Build period.

Another way to keep Build periods short is to reduce the number of weeks. Fourteen to sixteen days of high intensity, followed by five to seven days of rest, followed by another fourteen- to sixteen-day hard cycle is a good way to shorten the Build period from typical four-week cycles. Since interval training and variation is vital to the Build period, two short cycles can work better than one long cycle.

Each Build week should reduce volume compared to the Base period. In fact, the only way to ensure the quality and absorption of highly intense workouts is to reduce volume. For some experienced long-course athletes with years of high-volume training, this may be a slight reduction. For beginning triathletes or those new to long-course training volume, it may require a 30-percent or more decrease in volume. Some athletes try to increase intensity and volume together, usually with negative results. Injury and overtraining loom larger, but even if you can avoid these, speed increases are limited. Better to increase volume or intensity within separate periods.

You can, however, combine workout duration and intensity with gradual accelerations at the end of long workouts. If you have maintained long-course volume and done Base-period interval work at lactate threshold, you can attempt to accelerate for brief segments (five to fifteen minutes) toward the end of a longer ride or run. This kind of race simulation usually results in speeds closer to Zone 3 or 4 instead of Zone 5a. Even expert athletes can find it difficult to reach lactate threshold heart rate toward the end of a longer workout, minus any external race stimulation of "rabbits to chase." The distance fatigue of longer workouts acts as a governor on intensity. This experience is useful for racing: Starting out at a moderate, controlled pace allows you to increase to a harder perceived effort at the end of the bike or run segment with less risk of bonking or cramping. Many world records for pros and PRs for age groupers have even-paced timing between the first and last half of a race segment, though the athletes reported a steadily increasing challenge to maintain speed into the second half. In other words, if you start out feeling moderate, it's probably too fast. If it feels a bit easy, it's truly a steady, moderate pace.

For beginners or older athletes who wish to avoid anaerobic work altogether, these late-workout accelerations may be the best way to improve, limiting them to Zone 3 heart rate. Even top-ranked triathletes have had PR performances focusing on this type of Build period.

Monitor Effects

Although we favor regular testing throughout the season, athletes sometimes neglect it during the early Base periods. Workouts are easy to moderate, predictable, and there's plenty of time to recover. Heart rate zones are broad and easy to maintain. Speed changes are gradual and can be noted simply as "feeling fit." But once the Build period begins,

TABLE 5.5 COMMON INTERVAL WORKOUTS DURING BUILD PERIOD

SPORT	TYPE	INTENSITY	TIME OR QUALITY
Swim	4–6x400m/yd @ 40sec rest	Moderately hard Zone 3	Shorten recovery. Maintain speed and technique. May degrade due to bike/run fatigue during build period.
	6–8x200m/yd @ 20sec rest	Zone 4–5a	
	Pyramid 100-200-300-400-500-400-300-200-100m/yd @ 10–45sec rest	Zone 2–5a	
Bike	2–3x10min @ 3min rest 4–6x6min @ 2min rest	Zone 4–5a or CP 30	Variable due to course, wind. Power meter recommended.
	10x120sec climbing repeats with descending rest	Zone 4–5b (depends on grade)	Begin in easier gear, shift up in last half of climb.
Run	6–8x800m @ 200m jogging recovery	Zone 4–5a or 10K pace minus 10–20 seconds/mile	First interval holding back. Last interval higher perceived effort.
	3–5x1,000m @ 200m jogging recovery	Zone 3–5a or 10K pace minus 10–20 sec/mile	May be done in Zone 3 or 4 up to 1,600m interval.
Brick	In 90min ride: 2–3x10min @ 3min rest followed immediately by 30min run	Bike interval Zone 4–5a Run 15min Zone 4; 15min Zone 1–2	Build intensity on bike, fast on initial run, then recover last 15min on run.

radical changes will begin in the body and the mind. Think of the Build period as a "storm of training" where you need to pay more attention to weather instruments to stay on course and avoid "drowning" in your workouts.

There are two avenues of information: the interval workouts themselves and their resultant testing gains (or losses) conducted during a rest cycle. We'll classify a C race during the Build period as just another test with minimal rest. You should not be doing any long-course racing during the Build period.

Let's assume you've had a productive Base period, ending in high volume in Base 3, with consistent baseline values in your 1,000m/yd swim test, 30-minute bike time trial, and 3- to 5-mile high-aerobic run tests. You would repeat these or similar tests between two Build periods or at the end of one Build period. But within the Build cycle, pay closer attention to interval time and intensity. Some possible intervals and guidelines are listed in Table 5.5.

See the Swim, Bike, and Run Workout Appendices for possible Build-period workouts. Although I've spent considerable time explaining the Build period, it should represent very little of your actual season. As a final race-simulation workout for the half-Iron Build period, try this:

1. Ride 2–3 hours, starting at Zone 2 the first 30 minutes, then building to Zone 3.
2. Advanced triathletes should further accelerate to Zone 4 after 50 percent of the ride.
3. Transition quickly; run swiftly with high cadence for 2–3 miles.
4. Run steady in Zone 3 for 30 minutes, then beginners should stop.
5. Intermediates continue for a total of 60 minutes in Zone 3.
6. Advanced triathletes should accelerate to Zone 4 after 60 minutes, holding for 20 minutes, then cool down in Zone 1 for the last 10 minutes: 90 minutes total.

Summary of Important Build Principles

- Keep it simple, keep it short, monitor effects.
- The Build period should be race specific. For beginners this means more aerobic workouts, but aerobic does not mean "easy."
- Less is usually more.
- When in doubt, leave it out.

- More short intervals usually build speed better than a few longer ones.
- Save your fastest speeds for races, not workouts.
- Injury, excessive soreness, or life stress requires reducing Build-period intensities or scrapping it altogether in favor of Base 3 workouts of moderate intensity.
- Despite its risks, learn to go fast yet remain under control in the three sports during the Build period. If all you do is long, slow distance, you will simply remain a long, slow racer.

PEAK PERIOD

This period is brief but very important. What distinguishes true periodization from merely structured training is an effective peaking strategy. Peaking is also what separates the gold medal winners and world champions from other talented athletes who also work very hard. In long-course triathlons, peaking and race execution contribute more to speed than prior fitness or even talent. Long-course triathletes can have at most two Peak periods per racing season. It is possible to peak for two closely spaced half-Iron races, but this is only recommended for more experienced triathletes who have no other choice when trying to qualify for Ironman, national, or world championships. You can also schedule a C race during peaking, serving as a tune-up for a half-Iron race.

Tapering and peaking are sometimes used interchangeably, but this is not entirely correct. Tapering refers to the reduction in volume that helps produce a peak of fitness. But tapering volume is not enough to peak: You

TABLE 5.6 PEAK WEEK FOR HALF-IRON RACE

	MONDAY	TUESDAY	WEDNESDAY
PEAK WEEK	AM: Easy swim 40–60min	Breakthrough Brick: 60min ride Zone 2–3. <5min fast transition. 30min run Zone 3.	AM: Moderate swim: Warm-up 6x200 @ 20sec rest. Paddles, buoy, fins, drills. PM: 60min, last 20min Zone 3.

must continue to maintain intensity, simulate race conditions, and recover adequately. Most people find the concept of recovery boring, so it may help to think of it as "absorbing all the previous training." This analogy has a basis in physiology. You have been repeatedly depleting your glycogen and electrolyte stores and taxing your endocrine system. Your physiological sponge is almost dry. The Peak period allows the sponge to become supersaturated with these essential compounds, which are then released during your race.

How long should the Peak period be for the half-Iron race? We don't need the three- or four-week tapering of Iron-distance athletes. Usually, one peak week is sufficient (Table 5.6), followed by the race week. Experienced long-course athletes may only have five days of peaking before race week. If you are incorporating your half-Iron race to prepare for a full Iron event, then the half-Iron event becomes a B race and you will taper only five days before the event.

Breakthrough workouts are the key element in scheduling, and even more so during the Peak period. There are fewer breakthrough workouts requiring longer recovery: 72 hours or more for peaking, compared to 48 hours for the earlier periods.

This potential peak week leaves three days between the two brick workouts, but the swim breakthrough is only twenty-four hours before the longer brick on Saturday. This appears to violate the recovery rule of seventy-two hours, but it is only a swim, which should not affect the Saturday brick. Another option is to combine the swim into the Saturday brick, reducing the intervals by 30–50 percent, or doing an open-water

THURSDAY	**FRIDAY**	**SATURDAY**	**SUNDAY**
AM: Strength maintenance weightlifting PM: 90min ride Zone 1–2 with 3x5min Zone 3 pickups and long recoveries	AM: Breakthrough Swim: 4–6x400 @ 30sec rest PM: 60min Zone 2 run	Breakthrough Brick: 2:30 brick 90–120min ride Zone 2–3 <5min fast transition 30min run Zone 3–4	AM: Run 45min Zone 1–2

TABLE 5.7 USEFUL TIPS FOR PEAK WEEK

ISSUE	ACTION	RESULT
Endurance/ Speed Seesaw	Reduce volume, maintain intensity.	Trade endurance for more speed.
Running	Run short to moderate in Zone 3.	Allow healing of legs and feet, improve speed.
Cycling	Mostly aero position, avoid peloton riding.	Familiarize with solo riding, prevent going out too hard in early bike.
Swimming	High-speed, high-body position, fast start, buoy sighting drills. Open-water swim if possible.	Simulate early race stress, open-water conditions, feel of wet suit.
Bricks	Finish bike in Zone 3–4; start run fast in Zone 3.	Simulate "dead legs" at start of run; make fast running out of transition area automatic.
	Plan transitions similar to race.	Reduce stress, decrease time.
Hydration	Simulate race with your drink and the race drink.	Increase glycogen electrolyte stores, avoid gastric distress.
	Simulate drinking for race temperature.	Avoid dehydration.
Nutrition	Eat solid and gel foods as in race; salt tablets for hot racing.	Perfect tested products; use these in race.
Weather	Simulate race conditions, within reason: heat, wind.	Avoid heat fatigue but maintain heat tolerance. Avoid workouts over 95°F.
Travel	Compile and reconfirm all travel plans. Print copies of all schedules, maps, directions.	Avoid race week and race site stress.

swim before mounting the bike. The Saturday brick should also include identical race clothing, aero positioning, nutrition, and so on. If you have new race wheels, try them out for maneuverability. If you're confident from previous usage, you can stick with training wheels. If you're lucky enough to race a half-Iron event near home, do this final brick at the race site.

As with most of the examples in this book, Table 5.6 is only one of many possibilities. Everyone should work on limiters while maintaining strengths. If you are a bit slow on speed but have more than enough endurance, you can shorten and speed up the peak workouts. Unfortunately, the reverse is not true: It's too late to build more endurance ten days before a half-Iron race. Resist the temptation to go longer, which is easy to do since you are more rested and feel like you can do more.

Swim-stroke technique is deeply ingrained, so don't try to change your stroke now. Focus on things like crisp but fewer intervals, buoy navigation, pacing, and perhaps drafting behind other people in the water. Practice with your wet suit if practical and necessary for a cold-water race.

If you are ending most workouts feeling like you should do more, that's a good sign that everything is okay. Fatigue during peak week, including lifestyle stress, requires shortening a breakthrough workout or perhaps skipping a recovery workout. It's more important to show up for workouts and be crisp than to push through all the hours. You cannot make your engine any bigger during peak and race weeks. All you can do is fine-tune the performance, store fuel, and make your "vehicle" ready for racing. Common issues during Peak period are listed in Table 5.7.

RACE WEEK

All fitness aside, the key achievements of race week are confidence and joy. Now is the time to reap the benefits of all the training you have sown. Sometimes we get so caught up in the details of training, travel, and logistics that we forget the defining purpose—racing! Strive for harmony in all your relationships and be especially polite to friends, family, and coworkers. This practice will inoculate you against many pre-race jitters and encourage those near you to support your racing. Fortunately, many racers report a natural high on race week that radiates all around. Embrace the experience!

TABLE 5.8 POTENTIAL RACE WEEK PLAN

	MONDAY	TUESDAY	WEDNESDAY
RACE WEEK	Swim 45–60min 6x90sec @ 60sec rest, LT pace. 15min at race pace. Open water, if possible.	AM: Travel PM: Easy 40min run. Assemble and/or check bike. Note: Travel is variable and supersedes workouts. Rest more, if tired.	AM: 65–90min Brick. 45–60min bike, 20–30min run. both with 3x90sec LT intervals with very long recovery.

If you're one of those hyperactive personalities who becomes restless during reduced training—I think this covers at least half of all the triathletes, including pros—occupy your mind with mental work from your office, activities with family, or quiet reading. Reexperience inspirational books or videos about famous endurance athletes like Lance Armstrong, Steve Prefontaine, Natasha Badmann, or Dave Scott. Think big and think positive.

Study course maps and note any special scheduling or rules about the race. Most age-group athletes make at least one mental error during a long-course race; many make three or four. These often have little or nothing to do with fitness. What mistake are you most likely to make? Danger lurks where you least expect it. Write down possible scenarios and how to deal with them.

We include a first outline of potential race week planning here (Table 5.8), but this week is so important to the triathlete we've dedicated an entire chapter to "Racing the Perfect Distance" (Chapter 11).

THURSDAY	FRIDAY	SATURDAY	SUNDAY
AM: 30min run: 10min easy, 10min moderate, 10min easy. PM: optional 30min swim.	AM: Day off or 20min swim at race venue. PM: Check bike again, mount race tires.	AM: 45min Brick. 30min bike, 15min run, both with 3x30sec pickups. Midday: Finalize registration. PM: Check bike mechanics. Stay away from crowds, and think about the race.	RACE

CHAPTER 6

Swimming Skills

The water is your friend. . . . You don't have to fight with water, just share the same spirit as the water, and it will help you move.
—Alexandr Popov

THE LONELY SPORT

Swimmers are not necessarily lonely people; they usually have fulfilling social lives. But there is a veritable gulf between swimming and the other two sports. It stands alone. We learn to walk, to run, and to bike on the land, but we swim in the water. Although many think of cycling as the most modern triathlon sport, road bikes predate the modern freestyle technique, finally refined as the Australian crawl in 1950.

Europeans previously swam breaststroke, including military training back to Alexander the Great. This technique provided a "heads-up battle display," keeping track of friends and foes in the water and on the nearby coast. (This natural human tendency of lifting the head out of the water plagues open-water triathlete swimmers even today.) Speed was not very important to ancient swimmers—just making it across rivers, small lakes, or short coastlines with supplies and weapons was paramount. The Greeks recorded no swimming competition in their ancient Olympics, despite their seafaring culture along the Aegean Sea.

For Europeans, the front crawl was first seen in an 1844 London competition. Native Americans swam the front crawl, easily defeating the British breaststroke swimmers. Because of cultural prejudice and "vulgar splashing," it was not adopted by the British gentlemen, who preferred to keep their heads out of the water. So the British continued to swim only breaststroke until 1873.

In the 1870s John Arthur Trudgen learned the front crawl stroke from Native Americans during a trip to South America. Trudgen, however, mistakenly used the slower breaststroke kick instead of the native flutter kick.

The Trudgen stroke was improved by the British-born Australian swimming coach Richard Cavill. He studied natives from the Solomon Islands using the front crawl with a faster flutter kick. This modified Trudgen stroke became known as the Australian crawl until 1950, when it was shortened to crawl, technically known as the front crawl.

It's not surprising this New World stroke reached competitive heights on the continents of America and Australia. And these nations continue to dominate swimming competition. The birth of triathlon on the west coast of America would have been impossible without a preexisting culture of water sports. We owe the serendipitous structure of triathlon to swimming. Remember that bike racing and distance running had already existed for seventy-five years with no signs of merging. Although triathlon is now composed of talented athletes from all three disciplines, most top professionals have had some background in competitive swimming dating back to adolescence.

Why do swimmers transition to triathlon successfully? Perhaps it's related to the focus on technique and complex interval workouts, focusing on quality more than volume. Teenage swimmers become accustomed to training twice a day, and working on multiple stroke techniques, and they are made constantly aware of efficiency and speed. These principles apply very well to triathlon as a whole.

Another consideration is the swimmer's mental focus in handling solitude and sometimes drudgery. Much of the training requires staring at a straight line while moving across a standard rectangle in what is essentially a sensory-deprived environment of muted sounds, microgravity, and short-range vision. You are almost naked to the environment. You become like a monk staring at a stone wall for hours. These practices build self-reliance and develop an unselfconscious, uncomplaining attitude toward new and difficult skills.

It's no coincidence that Lance Armstrong, finding no athletic prowess in American team sports, first discovered his endurance talent in swim competition as a teenager, which led to triathlon racing and then to pro cycling. His cycling career was marked by the ardor of outsider, a lone wolf in the peloton with monomaniacal focus, doing many of his workouts alone.

SWIM VETERANS VERSUS DRYLANDERS

If you are a veteran swimmer, these facets are already familiar. We mention them primarily for the majority of age-group triathletes who did *not* have the privilege of early organized training in the water. These "drylanders" are prone to minimize the importance of the swim, which they justify for long-course racing where it accounts for only about 10 percent of the total race time. Since half- and full Ironman racing is nondrafting, the importance of being in the lead pack out of the water is less important. Strong cyclists and runners are accustomed to chasing down rivals after the swim, and this is true in a small local half-Iron race or the Ironman® Hawaii world championships. "Why spend more than 10 percent of my time (or worse, 10 percent of my brain) on swimming?" Not an uncommon protest, even if unspoken.

Experienced triathletes soon discover, however, that swimming progress is indirectly related to progress in the other three sports, and most of all to racing success. You want to get faster and want to "win," even if that just means beating your time goal for a race. Efficient swimming is essential to winning in triathlon. No, not as fast as an Olympic swimmer, but you should swim relatively faster than most triathletes. If you are new to fast swimming, realize that your times for distances from 100 to 1,500 meters are probably worse than competitive 9- to 12-year-olds in a large city. Even world-class marathon runners have experienced extreme distress trying to swim a fast 200–400 meters for the first time. But I know from personal experience and coached athletes that initial discomfort and inexperience can be overcome in reasonable time.

DIFFERENCES IN SWIM PRACTICE

Training for the swim is more like learning to swing a golf club or tennis racket, or playing the piano. Frequency of practices (a better description than "workout"), repetitive drills, and frequent intervals distinguish swimming from bike and run training. Physics and physiology show us why:

- Water is 1,000 times denser than air. You move ten times faster on a bike than in the water. Using a linear model, swimming fluid dynamics is 100 times more influential than bike aerodynamics. Think about all the triathletes spending thousands of dollars for aerobars, wheels, frames, helmets, skin-suits, and so on, and the countless hours tinkering with aero position. How much time and money do they spend reducing drag in the water?
- The drag factor makes buoyancy and body rotation essential to forward propulsion. Swimming even a calm-water course is three-dimensional. Running and cycling emphasize forward force with minimal up-down or rotational motion, "squared up" to the direction of travel; swimming requires continuous alternating rotation around the spinal axis.
- The multidimensional swim stroke requires greater balance, yet flotation in microgravity provides little feedback when we begin to "fall off." Imagine walking across the room and stumbling over something or gradually losing your balance. You immediately start to fall over and your body instinctively reacts to correct this imbalance. With swimming there is no feedback from gravity: You just keeping falling over repeatedly with unbalanced strokes, and the only effect you notice is slowing speed.

Swimming Advantages

- Your weight is fully supported by the water in a low-impact aerobic workout. Recovery time is less between workouts and between intervals than with running or cycling. You can train more often on successive days, including intervals. Injury is less frequent, and recovery from running injuries is often enhanced with water workouts.
- Swimmers usually do most of their training in a pool with constant temperature. Heat dissipates faster and intensity is maintained despite extreme outdoor temperatures.
- Indoor pools facilitate year-round training while cycling or running volume are shortened in the winter. Lighted pools encourage group or individual training in early-morning or evening hours, keeping it out of the way of work and other duties.

- Constant water conditions and standard pool lengths make it easier to measure progress. It is usually unnecessary to use a heart rate monitor to gauge intensity, relying instead on pace as determined in a 1,000m time trial.
- Technique drills at lower heart rates have little effect on weekly training load. Improving speed in the water for long-course triathlons requires less anaerobic work than the other two sports. For masters athletes, swim times can be maintained or even improved through age 50 and beyond.
- Women have little strength disadvantage, often posting faster swim splits than men.
- Those with strong visualization or conceptual skills may improve faster in swimming than in more talent-dependent sports. It may even become their best event despite starting late in life. Professional Ironman triathlete, coach, and co-author of *Going Long,* Gordo Byrn, managed a 49-minute Ironman® Canada swim despite no swim training before age 30, which he credited to "total commitment" to improvement.

TWO PATHS OF IMPROVEMENT

Swimmers Beginning with Triathlon

For less experienced swimmers who began racing in triathlons, the most important factors are weekly frequency and technique improvement. It's unrealistic to expect improvement from less than three sessions per week. You may have done well with only one or two weekly swims if you were only racing short-course, but to finish a half-Iron swim fresh and in reasonable time, three 45–60-minute sessions are recommended for beginners. You may need to build up to this if your volume was lower, but it should not take long. Remember that about 15–30 minutes per session involves warm-up and drills.

For those wishing to move up in the pack, to win their age division, qualify for Kona, or set a half-Iron PR, four or more 60-minute swims a week can make the difference. Even though swimming accounts for only 10 percent of the race time, our sliding scale shows optimal time at about 20–25 percent of weekly volume.

Experienced Swimmers

For swimmers with a competitive background or near the top of their triathlon division, long-course open-water skill depends on maintaining superior technique while extending endurance and pace to a 1,900m (1.2-mile) open-water venue. Many competitive swimmers are unfamiliar with racing beyond 1,500 meters or in open-water events—most race from 50 to 400 meters in a pool. This upward mobility is good for speed, but you must gauge pace so that you can exit the water fresh, move quickly through the transition area, and reach high cycling power in a matter of minutes. The intricacies of start position, drafting, and buoy navigation require special attention. Time saved from stroke building can be used by superior pool swimmers on these essentials.

Experienced swimmers will still benefit from reading the "Swim Technique" section, and should continue some drills. They should now work more on muscular endurance and endurance required for long-course, open-water swimming.

SWIM TECHNIQUE

One of the best ways to learn swim technique is to watch strong swimmers. As with a fluid golf swing or tennis stroke, fast swimmers follow certain basic fundamentals despite superficial differences. Spend some time watching Olympic or world-class swimming on television, or perhaps volunteer to work at a local age-group or collegiate swim meet—a good way for a beginner to "catch up" with more experienced swimmers. Once you know what to look for, you should have your own swim stroke videotaped from all angles, including underwater if possible. Some swim and triathlon coaches offer this service, including graphical stroke analysis. But you can still learn a lot from handheld video by a friend at poolside.

The foundation of strong swimming rests upon correct position and alignment. Before you think about moving your arms and legs in the water, you must achieve a streamlined body position that reduces drag: Balance, relaxation, and smoothness are essential. Only after considerable time investment and relative mastery of technique should you move on to increasing your propulsion with a bigger swim engine.

The Swimming Equation

A simple equation models swimming speed:

Speed = stroke length × stroke frequency

For example, if you can swim 50 meters or yards in 40 strokes, your stroke length is 1.25 meters or yards. If it takes you 90 seconds to swim 100 meters or yards, your stroke frequency is 0.889 strokes per second. Your overall speed is 1.11 meters or yards per second. The only way to improve this value is to increase the length or frequency of strokes. Note that world-class sprinters are swimming well over 2.1 meters per second.

Unlike running, where high cadence is paramount, swimming depends more on stroke length rather than frequency to improve speed. Swim authorities claim at least a two-to-one advantage stressing stroke length over frequency. Most triathletes need to limit stroke frequency and build efficiency by reducing drag, and only then try to speed up the stroke for faster interval sets and races. To measure progress, simply count the number of strokes it takes to cover one length of your standard training pool. If the count goes down, you are improving your stroke length. The "stroke-count drill," more fully explained in Table 6.2, is used to improve the athlete's stroke length by reducing drag.

Stroke-length emphasis does not mean you always swim at a slow cadence or with minimal effort. You must employ a reasonable stroke rate and speed to maintain an adequately high body position. The goal is to maintain a smooth pace while gradually building speed by extending stroke length. Swim training uses a higher ratio of interval training to encourage speed without degrading technique.

Swimming rewards visualization in design and practice, so we'll use an object diagram to describe its evolutionary flow (Figure 6.1).

The order of objects is important. Early swim training should involve body position, developing its attributes and performing related drills. Once a balanced alignment is achieved along the body's spinal axis, then stroke mechanics with the arms and hands are introduced and mastered. After increasing propulsion during the individual stroke, only then does the swimmer take this low-drag, forceful engine and "rev it up" to a higher rpm or stroke rate. Beginners may focus their efforts on body position and stroke mechanics for a year or longer before moving on to a faster stroke rate.

Experienced swimmers can also use this cycle. The sequence in Figure 6.1 describes the desired periodization for swim training in a season. We spend the Preparation and early Base periods focusing more on body position and balance using drills. Then we build stroke mechanics using the

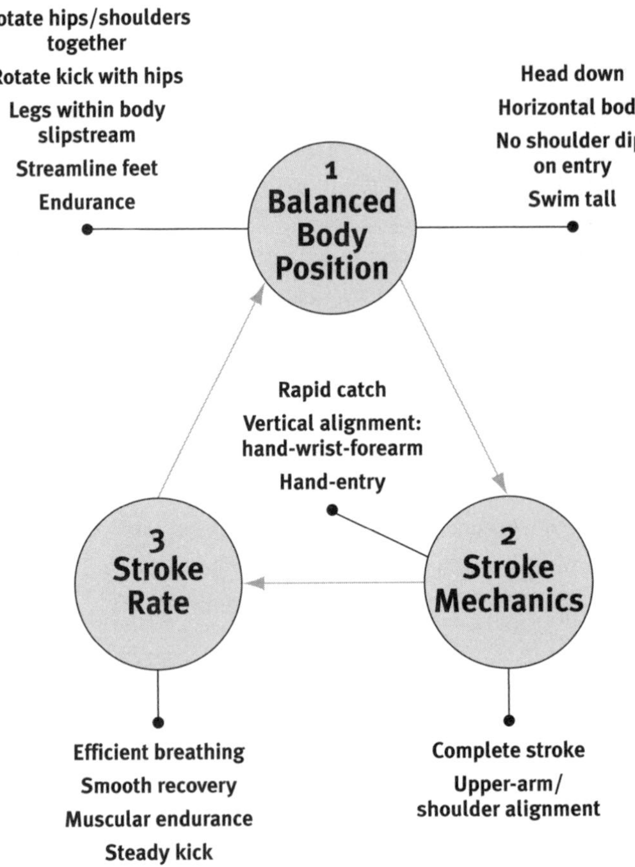

FIGURE 6.1
Evolution of swim performance

outer limbs. Once we near racing season, we prefer the technical aspects to fall below the level of consciousness so we can focus on building muscular endurance and pacing for interval sets and races.

Swim Terminology

Let's define some terms for our beginning swimmers (experienced swimmers may also benefit from review). It's surprising how many triathletes have done several races, perhaps even an Ironman, without clear knowledge about the "catch" or "pull" (Table 6.1).

TABLE 6.1 COMMON SWIMMING TERMS

TERM	DEFINITION	ROLE
Catch	After hand-entry into the water, the hand and forearm rotate at the elbow from facing down to facing rearward, "catching" the water.	Beginning of power stroke; can cause drag but provides no propulsion
Pull	After the initial catch, the pull movement follows a semicircle with the elbow higher than the hand and the hand-forearm paddle pointing toward the bottom of the pool. Ideally, the catch and pull are integrated into one smooth motion.	Middle of power stroke
Push	After the hand-forearm paddle crosses the front of the chest and the middle of the rib cage, they continue to push back facing the rear wall of the pool, reaching their greatest speed at the side of the body before exiting the water.	Peak of power stroke; provides most propulsion
Recovery	After completing the push, the hand is pulled out of the water with the small finger upward, as if removing it from the back pocket of a pair of pants. The forearm and hand are completely relaxed and hang down from the elbow close to the water surface and close to the swimmer's body. The recovering hand moves forward, with the fingers trailing downward just above the surface of the water.	Transition to next stroke
Flutter Kick	Preferred freestyle kick. The legs alternate, with one leg kicking downward while the other leg moves upward. While the legs provide only a small part of the overall speed, they are important to stabilize the body position. The leg in the initial position bends very slightly at the knees, and then kicks the lower leg and foot downward, similar to kicking a football. The legs may be bent inward slightly.	Raises body position, allows navigation, and provides mild propulsion; provides rhythm for entire stroke

CONTINUED

TABLE 6.1 CONTINUED

TERM	DEFINITION	ROLE
Dolphin Kick	Undulating kick with legs and feet held together used for butterfly.	Stroke variation; flip turns during freestyle
Whip or Frog Kick	Breaststroke kick with legs and feet spread apart and brought inward to create propulsion.	Stroke variation; resting or sighting during open-water swims
Bilateral Breathing	Alternating breathing to both the left and right sides during freestyle. For most triathletes, this means breathing every third stroke to alternate sides during training.	Improves stroke balance, CO_2 tolerance, and speed during training
Offside Breathing	Breathing on the opposite side of preferred breathing.	Improves stroke balance, open-water swimming with waves and sighting
Drill	Any swimming exercise that varies from the traditional freestyle crawl or complete stroke: catch-up, fist, single-arm, and side-kick are common examples.	Variation from ingrained habits allows for positive change
Medley	A mixture of swim strokes done in the same race or drill: butterfly-backstroke-breaststroke-freestyle is a common medley set order.	Stroke variation; recovery of opposing muscle groups in interval set
Stroke set	When a coach specifies a nonfreestyle set during training, often the swimmer's second-best stroke. Triathlete freestyle swimmers benefit most from backstroke.	Stroke variation, skill building
Total Immersion	A method of swim instruction advocated by Terry Laughlin (www.totalimmersion.net), widely used by triathlete swimmers.	Emphasizes body position and technique over strength and endurance

Overview of the Front Crawl

Arm movement

The arm movement in freestyle is alternating: While one arm is pulling and pushing, the other arm is recovering. The arm strokes provide most of the forward propulsion. The move can be separated into four parts: the catch, the pull, the push, and the recovery. Some authorities combine one or more of these, and indeed they are just aspects of one continuous flow, not discrete entities.

After hand entry, the arm drops slightly lower and the palm of the hand turns 45 degrees with the thumb-side of the palm toward the bottom. This is called *catching* the water and is in preparation for the *pull.* The pull movement follows a semicircle with the elbow higher than the hand, and the forearm-hand pointing and downward. Ideally, the hand and forearm together form a single, large paddle. The semicircle ends in front of the chest at the beginning of the rib cage.

The *push* phase moves the palm backward through the water underneath the body at the beginning and then by the side of the body at the end of the push. The movement increases speed throughout the pull-push phase until the hand is moving at its greatest speed shortly before the end of the push.

The *recovery* moves the elbow in a semicircle in a vertical plane in the swimming direction. The lower arm and hand are completely relaxed and hang down from the elbow close to the water surface and close to the swimmer's body. This gives the muscles a brief opportunity to rest. The beginning of the recovery feels like pulling the hand out of the back pocket of a pair of pants, with the small finger upward. Further into the recovery phase, the hand movement has been compared to pulling up a center zipper on a wet suit. The recovering hand moves forward, with the fingers trailing downward, just above the surface of the water.

Beginners often make the mistake of not relaxing the arm during the recovery, moving the hand too high and away from the body, a so-called "windmill recovery," perhaps higher than the elbow. This usually increases drag and incidental muscle effort at the expense of speed. (Some legendary swimmers have achieved great propulsion using a windmill recovery—Janet Evans the most noteworthy—but this is not recommended as ideal.) The hand should enter the water thumb first as far forward as possible, reducing drag through possible turbulence. After a brief rest the next cycle begins.

The leg movement in freestyle is called the flutter kick. The legs alternate motion, with one leg kicking downward while the other leg moves upward. While the legs contribute minimally to forward propulsion, they stabilize a high body position and maintain rhythm. For open-water swims using a buoyant wet suit, the kick is even less important, which explains why beginning or average swimmers benefit more from a wet suit than experts. Even if you are training for a cold- and open-water race, you should still spend most of your training time without a wet suit, since it masks bad stroke habits.

In the initial position the leg bends slightly at the knees, and then kicks the lower leg and the foot downward, similar to kicking a football. The legs may be bent inward slightly. After the kick the straight leg moves back up. A frequent mistake of beginners is to bend the legs too much or to kick too much out of the water. A tight flutter kick keeps your feet and legs within the body shadow.

Breathing

Ideally, the face is in the water during the front crawl, with the waterline above the eyes. Breaths are taken through the mouth by turning the head to the side of a recovering arm at the beginning of the recovery, breathing in the triangle between the upper arm, lower arm, and the waterline. The forward movement creates a bow wave with a trough in the surface near the ears. By turning the body along the spinal axis, the head will be lifted high enough within this trough to breathe without moving the entire mouth above the surface. Rough-water swims may require lifting the entire mouth above the water, but even then head-lift should be minimized.

The head is rotated back at the end of the recovery and points down and forward again when the recovered hand enters the water. Training should focus the eyes straight down at the lane-line. The swimmer breathes out through mouth and nose until the next breath. Exhaling with the mouth underwater ensures more time for inhalation when the mouth turns up. Breathing out through the nose avoids water entering the nose, especially in rough water or during a flip turn.

Bilateral breathing employs one breath every odd-numbered arm recovery, the third stroke for our triathlon training models. This sequence alternates the sides for breathing. Since breathing slightly reduces speed, competitive swimmers often breathe every third stroke or less. Bilateral breathing is very useful in swim workouts, but for long-course racing the large majority of triathletes will want to breathe mostly on their favored side, every second stroke. Beginners may need to build up minimum swim skill and aerobic capacity before attempting bilateral breathing.

Body movement

The body rolls along its long axis, from the neck, along the spine, and virtually extending through the rotating feet and legs. The shoulders rotate so that the shoulder of the recovering arm is higher than the shoulder of the pushing/pulling arm. This sidestroke makes the recovery much easier, reduces drag as one shoulder is out of the water, and reduces the need to turn the head to breathe. Swim as if you were rotating on a skewer through your spine, and visualize moving like a knife or a fish through the water. Side-to-side movement is kept to a minimum: One of the main functions of the leg kick is to maintain the line of the body.

Although the arms and hands act like large paddles and provide the necessary resistance to move forward, most of the propulsive force originates from the larger core muscles in the back, hips, and abdominals. As with a good golf swing, rotating along the core axis produces a smooth, powerful stroke, yet appears to be relaxed and effortless. Expert swimmers and good golfers often look as if they are not working very hard, while still demonstrating incredible power.

Key Thoughts for the Stroke

There are many stroke keys you can use to focus your mind on producing the proper technique, but you can only think about one or two of them at a time. Some are more important than others and should be mastered by beginners before moving on to the other keys. Some are useful for triathlete swimmers but may no longer be an issue for competitive swim veterans. The only way to know for sure where your own limiters lie is video evidence of your own stroke once or twice a year, regular timed testing using the keys, and race experience.

We'll arrange these in order of probability for triathlete swimmers, giving weight to the potential drag problems.

1. **Keep head down:** Lifting the head during the stroke, especially around breathing, could be called the "triathlete's disease" because it plagues 90 percent of us. Reasons include the natural human tendency to lift our chest and head as we breathe, lack of experience,

and the open-water habit of head-lifting for buoy navigation (Figure 6.2). To maintain balance, your head should be in line with your spine, level, and looking down at the bottom of the pool (Figure 6.3). The two most important aspects of floating body position are: (a) the weight of your head, and (b) the buoyancy provided by the air in your lungs acting as a fulcrum on a seesaw. Any lifting of the head causes an immediate drop of the hips and legs around the chest fulcrum. In other sports we keep our "eye on the ball" or face our direction of motion to steady the head. In swimming, there is nothing to look at but the bottom of the pool, and we are moving perpendicular to our visual direction. One other trick to keep your head down is to imagine the back of your neck as flat and exposed to the air above the water. A coach or friend can look for an exposed neck to indicate head position. When breathing, initiate head movement by rotating your hips and shoulders, not by directly turning the head from the neck, which usually tends to lift it. The hips should lead the chin.

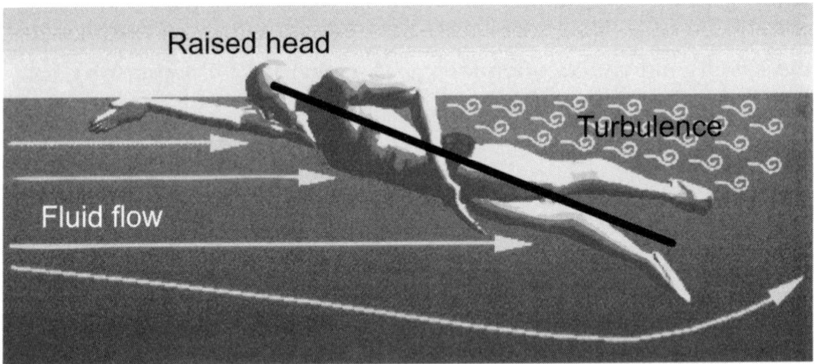

FIGURE 6.2
Sagging body position: A raised head increases turbulence and drag.

2. **Press the buoy or T:** To keep the body level (Figure 6.3), begin by feeling as if you are tilting it downhill. Consciously "press on the T" that represents the shoulders and chest midline down to the breastbone. The air in your lungs is a buoy, so pressing down here anchors your virtual center of gravity in the floating medium, causing your hips and legs to lift. Once you have achieved this "downhill level," your stroke will feel as if it is coasting quickly during the

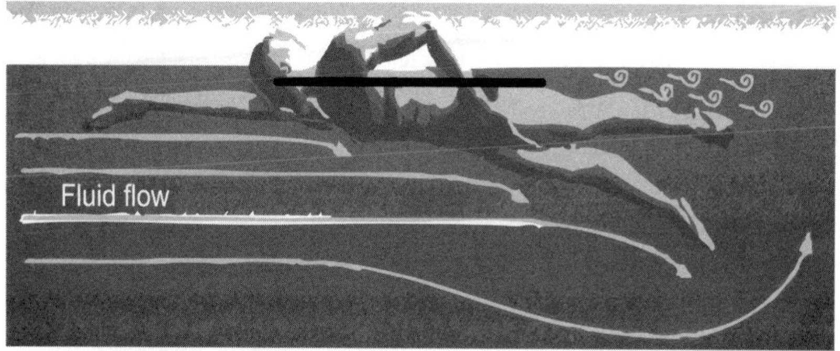

FIGURE 6.3
Level body position: Align head with spine to reduce turbulence and drag.

recovery phase while gliding with the forward arm. Many swimmers can actually hear and feel the water whizzing by faster. You will lose much less speed between arm strokes.

3. **Float the offside hand:** In addition to lifting the head, another way to throw the body off balance is to press down with the offside arm and hand while breathing. If you've been lifting your head for some time, you have probably ingrained this arm-pressing habit to compensate for the head-lift. When reaching with the offside arm, relax the hand and let it float, pointing in a straight, level line toward the wall.

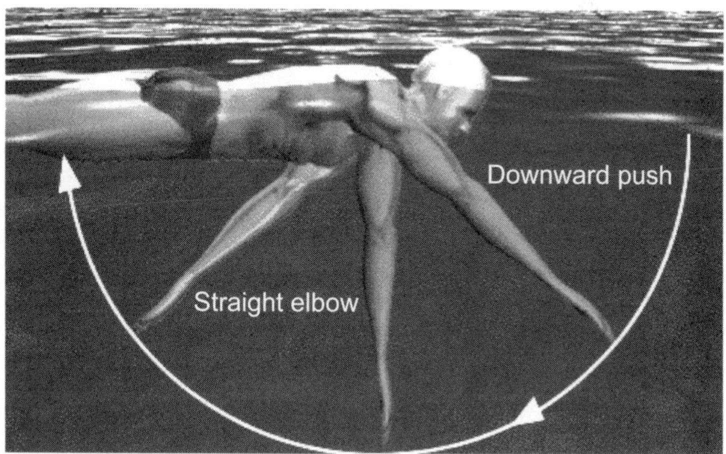

FIGURE 6.4
Incorrect paddlewheel motion: Extended arm presses downward.

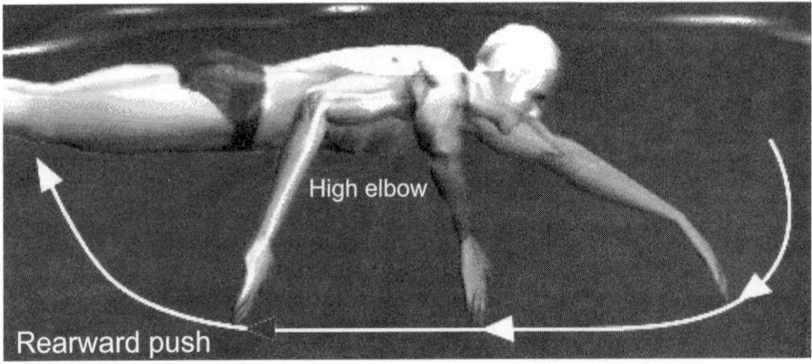

FIGURE 6.5
Correct caterpillar motion: Forearm and hand push rearward.

4. **Catch fast and light:** Once you have fully extended the stroke arm, straight and level, begin the catch immediately. Swimmers who have somewhat mastered keeping their head down, pressing the T, and level hand-entry may still leave the arm dangling too long. Even with perfect form, you are decelerating the moment you lift the rear arm for recovery, and you must begin the next stroke without delay. Although it begins quickly, the catch does not start forcefully. It begins with a light drop of the hand and forearm, which feels as if you are pulling down from the outer pinkie finger. If you try to press hard with the whole hand, you will inevitably press downward (Figure 6.4) instead of rotating the forearm-hand paddle from the elbow into a vertical position for pushing rearward (Figure 6.5).
5. **Rotate hips and shoulders together:** This one-piece rotation ensures you are using all of your core and torso muscles together as the center of force generation and presents the minimal drag profile to the water. You should feel as if your arms are connected to your torso by rubber bands, being led by the rotation around the spinal axis.
6. **Legs within the slipstream:** Sometimes called the "body shadow," the slipstream is the nonturbulent flow behind your broader arms and shoulders, where water moves faster around your legs. Splitting the legs or kicking too big up and down will move them into the turbulent flow, where drag increases. A quick, disciplined flutter kick is better than a big, hard, unruly kick. In

open-water swims, especially with a wet suit, efficiency may improve by kicking fewer beats per stroke, mostly for navigation, saving your legs for the bike.

7. **Rotate kick:** This could be presented in the negative as "don't kick flat." Your flutter-kicking legs and feet should be turning in response to your hips. This flattening starts when swimmers tire, and can be reinforced by too much kickboard drill, which encourages flat swimming. It is preferable for athletes to use side-kick drills, perhaps with fins, to become accustomed to kicking with feet turned near the vertical plane and rotating during the drill. Once your kick is coordinated with your rotation, its rhythmic beating will coordinate with arm stroke rhythm, reducing drag and building confidence.
8. **Streamlined feet:** Some beginning swimmers were taught to "point the toes" to achieve streamlining, but this method causes excessive leg stress and is not the optimal method for reducing drag. The feet should be extended horizontally, but relaxed, and allow for free flutter along the ankle hinge. This can be very difficult for triathletes with significant running volume, which breeds tighter ankles to resist pavement pounding. You can do yoga or other exercises to loosen the ankles, and drills with fins also promote flexibility.

We could extend this list indefinitely, or enumerate variations of each problem and key thought, but if you can master these keys you will be way ahead of the majority of triathlete swimmers. To further improve your swim split and save energy for the challenging bike to come, you will need to focus more on the muscular endurance required to swim 1,900 meters in a stressful open-water venue.

DRILLS TO IMPROVE SWIM TECHNIQUE

Think First, Drill Second

Swimmers quickly discover that regular drills accelerate improvement, and even veteran swimmers need to maintain some drill practice. In order for drills to be effective, however, they must directly address specific stroke limiters. And most important, you must maintain a conscious awareness of the purpose of the drill during execution. Simply doing drills with your mind turned off won't do much good. You must want to improve and to integrate the motions into your actual freestyle stroke and interval sets. Repetitive drilling without focus is like banging out hundreds of golf balls at a driving range with no plan for swing improvement: You will simply regroove bad habits. A good motto is "Think first, drill second."

Some swimmers find that taking a notebook with drills to the pool helps, or at least recording the results in their training logbooks. Fortunately, there are many prepackaged tools to help you do this, from online systems like TrainingPeaks.com to laminated drill documents from swim or triathlon coaches. Swimming with a masters group can be a good way for beginners to be exposed to a variety of drills, but they may not necessarily address your specific needs. Advanced swimmers doing power drills with paddles have little or nothing to do with beginners still trying to learn balance and keeping their head down. If you swim with a group, talk to your coach about developing a personalized drill set to address your limiters. They will often appreciate your conscientious effort and give you feedback on appropriate drills.

My advice for beginners or even intermediates without much swim training is to keep drills simple and consistent. Focus on no more than two or three easily remembered drills each week that address the common limiters of balance, head-body position, and breathing. Don't move on to more complex drills until you have achieved relative competence in fundamentals. Beginners should plan on doing drills in every swim workout, preferably three times per week. Don't be self-conscious if they seem awkward at first: It's easier and faster to improve for those with poor technique.

I recall a story about a coach who was forced to choose between two swimmers with the same time in a 200m team tryout. One had solid technique but only modest speed, and the other had poor technique but the same speed. He chose the second one, saying, "I can always teach technique to someone motivated and make them faster."

I've continued to perform drills in almost every swim practice well past the intermediate level, only reducing them near race taper or long-course race recovery. The only people I've seen do well with fewer drills are expert swimmers who competed at the major university level and with further experience in triathlon or masters swimming, but even they still do some drills.

TABLE 6.2 FUNDAMENTAL DRILL SETS AND STROKE KEYS

QUALITY	DRILL	DESCRIPTION
Balance	Back-kick	Kick on your back with hands at side. Shoulders should be down with hips lifted. This will place the head mostly underwater, with only the nose and mouth exposed.
	Back-kick, twist-down	Kick on back, then rotate onto side for a few kicks, then rotate chin so you are looking down at bottom of pool for a few kicks. Rotate chin back to the side-facing position, then return body to original position on back. Repeat for alternate side.
	Side-kick, arms down	Kick on side with arms at sides for one length. Rotate chin to breathe while keeping head-spinal alignment and firmness. Good balance requires less breathing, only an occasional chin rotation.
	Side-kick extended-arm	Extend bottom arm aligned with body about six inches under the water. Lifting the arm will lower the hips—not good.
	Side-kick, three-stroke transition	Start with extended-arm side-kick. After around ten kicks, do three freestyle strokes, ensuring full and straight arm extension on each stroke. Then resume side-kicking on the alternate side, taking a few breaths before repeating three strokes to transition to the other side. Once you are comfortable, time breathing during transition to achieve three-stroke bilateral breathing (see Bilateral drill in the Breathing section of this table).
Arm Stroke	Catch-up	The most common swimming drill. After pushing off with both arms extended, begin the freestyle stroke with one arm while leaving the other extended. Deliberately complete the one-arm stroke and after fully extending the stroke arm, begin the alternate sidestroke. Emphasizes glide, full extension, and correct catch, pull, and recovery. Begin drill slowly, and after experience, you can speed up to near normal stroke pace.

CONTINUED

TABLE 6.2 CONTINUED

QUALITY	DRILL	DESCRIPTION
	Fist	Clinch fingers and thumb in a moderately tight fist. Perform freestyle stroke by reaching over a barrel during hand-entry and catch. Feel forearm and fist as single unit for propulsion. Can be done by holding a tennis ball instead of clinching fist. Useful as active recovery lap between interval sets, feeling difference as full hand is added.
	Single-arm, extended (easy)	As with catch-up drill, start with both arms extended, perform one-arm stroke, and repeat with same arm for entire length. Switch arms for successive lengths. Can be combined with fins to work on fast hand-entry, but can be done without them after experience.
Arm Stroke CONTINUED	Single-arm, by side (difficult)	Keep alternate arm by side while stroking with other side. Breathe on offside of stroke. Requires steady kicking. Best done without fins. Beginners will find this tiring and difficult to balance, but improvement signifies improved strength and balance.
	Back skulling	On your back and looking beyond your feet, keep the arms at the sides while skulling with hands, the hands moving the body backward. Improves motion into water and balance.
	Stroke count	With a steady, deliberate stroke, count the strokes for one length of a 25–50m pool. Attempt to reduce strokes on successive lengths by streamlining and extending stroke. Maintain new stroke-count numbers on full-speed interval sets. Excellent for testing and as active recovery between interval sets.
Stroke Keys	Over the barrel	To ensure the proper catch, imagine reaching over a small barrel to carry it under your fore- and upper arm. Bend from elbow with forearm-hand facing down for catch and pull.

CONTINUED

TABLE 6.2 CONTINUED

QUALITY	DRILL	DESCRIPTION
Stroke Keys CONTINUED	Palm to the wall	During pull and push, imagine palm of hand facing and "eyeballing" the rear wall of pool. Maintain palm plane perpendicular to push direction until hand passes hip to begin recovery.
	Catch with pinkie	Begin catch by consciously pulling only the outer pinkie finger of the stroke hand. This will usually cause the hand to fall faster, at the correct angle, and facilitates skulling (propulsive slight hand oscillation) during pull and push.
	Brush the hip	To ensure completion of the whole stroke, feel or imagine the thumb of the stroke arm lightly brushing the hip before it exits the water for recovery.
	Twist on a skewer	Imagine the body constantly rotating around the spinal axis, as if on a skewer rod along the spine.
Breathing (used during regular sets)	Bilateral	For most triathletes, the ideal bilateral breathing occurs every third stroke. It can be combined with two breaths on the same side, followed by alternate breathing. Good practice between interval sets and for kicking drills. Racing should use mostly same-side breathing every second stroke.
	Offside	Repeat breathing opposite your stronger side on successive strokes: Left side is weaker for about 90 percent of swimmers. Breathe at least one length on the offside and then alternate. Practice breathing offside in the middle of longer interval sets or open-water swims.
	Buoy sighting	For pool practice, place a water bottle, buoy, start block, or chair on the middle of the lane wall and practice slightly lifting the head for sighting every 5–10 strokes. Find the ideal number of strokes between sightings. Only lift goggles slightly above waterline, preferably on a breath stroke. Combines well with bilateral breathing.

CONTINUED

TABLE **6.2** CONTINUED

QUALITY	DRILL	DESCRIPTION
Breathing (used during regular sets) CONTINUED	Drafting	Practice breathing and stroke pacing directly behind a leading swimmer's feet. Maintain focus on feet and avoid anything more than occasional light touching, yet keep head down for most strokes. Combine with buoy sighting drill to simulate race conditions. Note faster times for drafting sets, about 8 percent.
	Hypoxic	Deliberately avoid breathing for 3–6 strokes to simulate race starts, buoy turns, swimmer-bumping, and rough open water. These drills require some experience and endurance, and have limited usage for long-course events; not recommended for beginners.

There are an almost limitless number of swim drills and exercises, on both dry land and in the water. Some are baroque in complexity, and not all swim authorities agree on their efficacy. We have included the most fundamental, proven drills that have worked for thousands of triathlete swimmers (Table 6.2), but there may be others that work for you.

Tips and Tricks for Drills

As with just about everything else in training, your execution of the drill can be more important than what drill you select:

- Balance drills on both sides. Most swimmers have a preference for their favored hand side, the right side for 90 percent of the population. But you must work extra on your offside to balance your stroke. Starting the drill to the offside keeps you fresh when working on your more difficult side. Severe differences in right-left body strength may be corrected by occasionally doubling the drills for the weaker side.
- Quality and recovery outweigh speed and intensity, and even more so for drills. It's permissible for beginners to stop completely and rest a few seconds for each length while learning drills.

- One or two sets of drills done correctly with focus are preferable to many sets done hurriedly or with your brain turned off. Swim drills are a mind game.
- Watch your balance and avoid "falling off-line" into one direction or the other. Remember that in the water you may not sense when you are falling down—the lane-line or wave-divider is your only feedback. You may have to compensate more toward one side when starting: for example, turning to the left to go straight if you have a right-drifting tendency. Make sure your body itself is aligned in a straight line.
- Relax, relax, relax, especially the neck and facial muscles.

And don't forget to integrate drills with your regular freestyle sets. For many athletes, doing the majority of drills during the early swim warm-up is an effective use of time, since the drills are best done at a lower heart rate before fatigue sets in. After you become comfortable with drills, it pays to move some of them in between interval sets as reminders of correct form during active recovery. Some drills can be done toward the end of a workout immediately before some short sprints to groove the new stroke habits into intensive efforts. The stroke keys in Table 6.2 can be used during relevant drills, interval sets, or racing. Find the keys that address your limiters and produce faster interval splits in training and testing. Pick one or two keys to use during racing. The fewer keys you need, the better you are swimming, especially under stress.

TRIATHLETE LIMITERS

In addition to the classic problems of head-lifting and pushing down with the catch arm, there are certain other limiters that plague many triathletes. If you were already an experienced swimmer, they may not apply to you, but it's amazing how many triathletes are fit and racing well but still displaying common limiters.

Bilateral Breathing

Many triathletes have a standard breathing side that they use for almost all training and racing. For 90 percent of the swimmers, those that are right-handed, this is the right side. This is not unlike beginning or intermediate tennis players who still can't or won't hit a backhand: They can only play from one side of the court. For swimmers, it means you are developing most of your power from only one side of your body, and in open-water venues you can only see about half the course and competition. In fact, if you cannot breathe bilaterally without discomfort, this often indicates an inefficient stroke or poor fitness.

It's not difficult to learn the bilateral technique, requiring mostly patience and gradual progress. Beginners should first attempt bilateral breathing during slower warm-ups and Zone 1–2 interval sets. Although we don't recommend excessive use of a pull buoy, it can be useful for swimmers trying to learn stroke balance via bilateral breathing. As previously mentioned in Table 6.2, embedded bilateral breathing in a side-kick drill is a good way to start.

Once you've spent some time practicing bilateral breathing, there are immediate payoffs:

- **Increased rotation:** Many swimmers rotate twice as many degrees to their onside than to the offside. Bilateral breathing may be their first experience with full rotation on the offside. Once you've grooved a significant number of strokes with full rotation, you are likely to retain it even when not using bilateral breathing—when racing.
- **Rhythmic stroke:** As you balance the right and left angles of rotation, you improve the rhythm and timing of the stroke, including kicks. This is yet another reason to combine bilateral breathing with side-kick drills.
- **Flip turns:** Another beginning swimmer problem is timing the last breath before hitting the wall to turn. The ability to breathe from either side allows for more precise breath timing and comfortable turning.
- **Open-water navigation and mass starts:** In less predictable open-water racing, buoys can be on either side, and waves can make breathing from only one side very difficult. If you are drafting behind or being bumped by other swimmers, the ability to breathe for some strokes to the offside maintains the optimal distance from helpful or hurtful competitors.
- **Psychological:** Bilateral breathing doubles the size of your swimming universe. You no longer feel as isolated in the sensory-deprived aquatic environment. And it moves you over into that group of confident, skillful "good swimmers" who are smiling before the swim start of a triathlon.

Flip Turns

I'll start with a confession: In my first eighteen months as a triathlete, I raced two half-Ironmans, a full Iron-distance race, and an Ultraman triathlon of twenty-five hours with a 10,000m open-ocean swim—without knowing how to do a flip turn. Obviously, I was only self-coached. After doing well in the Ultraman Hawaii event, I decided it was downright embarrassing to still grab the wall before every turn. I had to hire a coach to come to the pool and show me how to do it properly. My big problem was keeping water from draining into my nose while inverted, even while exhaling. Fortunately, it only took a week or two to get pretty good at flip turns, and it immediately helped my swimming in terms of technique and fitness. Due to a sinus condition, I still wear a nose-clip when doing flip turns in a pool, but I can do without it in open-water racing or for a few turns without much problem. Beginners might benefit from the nose-clip until you learn to exhale properly in the turn.

So if you're not already doing them, you should learn flip turns even though most of your racing will be done in open water. Even if you are a rank beginner to triathlon and swimming, learning them early is the best path. Yes, it will slow you down at first, and every now and then you will hit a "bum turn" where you miss the wall or lose some momentum. This happens even to expert swimmers. But after some weeks of practice, the flip-turn motion can fall below the level of consciousness and become an automatic response to the approaching wall.

The best way to learn is to watch other swimmers doing them properly, in person or on video. Or better yet, get a coach or good swimmer to teach you in the pool. It doesn't take long to learn the basics, and you can refine technique as you perfect the mechanics of streamlining and bilateral breathing.

OTHER STROKES

Most triathletes will swim the entire half-Iron distance using the front crawl, but the other strokes are still useful in training. In order of usefulness for triathlon freestyle swimmers, they are backstroke, breaststroke, and butterfly.

Backstroke is useful because it reverses the sequence of the front crawl sidestroke. Muscles are used in the opposite direction, and flexibility around the joints is increased. This makes backstroke an excellent warm-up before practices and races, and a good active-recovery stroke between interval sets or the day after a hard race. The backstroke uses a straight-arm entry and straight-arm recovery. You push the water straight down toward your feet during the middle pull segment.

Breaststroke is useful for beginners who may have trouble finishing an entire half-Iron race using only freestyle, for occasional buoy sightings, and recovery after bumping or goggle displacement. For general stroke improvement, it improves hand-entry and the catch for all levels of swimmers.

Butterfly is the most difficult stroke for beginners to learn, and in fact can be bypassed by inexperienced swimmers preparing for their first or second half-Iron race. It's probably not worth the practice time to develop this stroke. But once you have achieved a half-Iron swim split around 30–33 minutes, additional power and muscular endurance can be promoted by butterfly practice. It also emphasizes "swimming from the core," focusing on the torso as the originator of power in the stroke.

How much time should you spend in non-crawl strokes during practice? Although many masters swim groups spend 50 percent of their time on medley or non-crawl intervals, most triathletes benefit from only about 25 percent of practice time in other strokes. Beginners should spend only 10–15 percent in other strokes, with more time on freestyle-specific drills.

If beginners or intermediates swim in group lanes with more experienced swimmers in other strokes, you probably will keep pace better by doing more freestyle in medley sets. Check with your coach to minimize conflict. If you are strapped for time and show up late for a practice or a race warm-up, better to skip other strokes and focus on freestyle.

SWIM EQUIPMENT

Even though racing is limited to goggles, swim cap, and wet suit, swimmers love to fill up the pool with lots of stuff. Some of it is useful to long-course triathletes. Some has limited effectiveness for all but the strongest swimmers. Some can actually be damaging to stroke technique and promote injury if misused. In keeping with our focus on fundamental principles for the half-Iron distance, we'll list the gear that has been proven most effective for beginning through expert swimmers. If you're a veteran swimmer with success using a wider variety of gear, don't let us stop you from your favorite equipment drills.

Kick Fins

Even though the kick's propulsive power has secondary importance in triathlons, it should be included as part of training and drills. A fundamentally sound and rhythmic kick promotes higher body position and straight-line navigation. Most triathletes have tight ankles from extensive running and can increase their flexibility by stretching and using kick fins. If you could purchase only one type of fins, we recommend the shorter variety because they promote body position, do not interfere with flip turns, and have little risk of causing knee or ankle stress. Longer fins have limited efficacy: They are useful in pure power sets and promote ankle flexibility, but they involve more risk.

Common fin drills for beginners involve the back- and side-kick drills listed in Table 6.2. They can also be used for some of the single-arm drills, but put aside the fins once you become comfortable with the drill. Do not attempt to combine fins with a pull buoy or paddles.

Swimmers as a whole have been able to improve their kick by using a standard kickboard, but fins are preferable as a kicking aid. Although kickboard practice improves leg strength and power, it promotes flat swimming and does little to augment balance. If your masters swim group regularly uses kickboards in practice, substitute fins or make kickboards only a small portion of your kick drills. If you swim alone, you can build a strong, rotating flutter kick without ever using a kickboard.

Pull Buoy

One of the most popular swim aids, the pull buoy has a mixed record for triathlete swimmers. On the positive side, it allows you to work on your arm stroke and breathing at a lower heart rate without any focus on your kick. And it mimics the feeling of a wet suit swim. On the other hand, it tends to cover up your balance and stroke limiters. Swimmers who go considerably faster using a pull buoy than with a strong kick probably have severe problems with body position and kick technique.

I recommend a limited use of the pull buoy for warm-up, recovery, and shorter drills, especially those involving paddles.

Paddles

These tools have perhaps the highest risk for injury if overused or misused. They also can cause swimmers to actually ingrain and increase their stroke mistakes, developing strength without balance. If you have sound arm-stroke technique, they can promote a stronger catch and greater propulsion for the push and pull. The best use of a pull buoy for many swimmers is in conjunction with paddle drills. There are many types of paddles on the market, all claiming to promote some specific stroke quality. We recommend a small- to medium-sized paddle with minimal "tricks" in construction.

I do not recommend paddles for beginning swimmers, people with shoulder problems, or anyone who is struggling with technique limiters. Once you have a sound stroke and are moving closer to racing season, paddles can be useful for adding force and building the right kind of muscular strength, but you must be even more careful about using good form. It only takes ten minutes of paddle-strokes in a swim session to improve strength, and this only once per week. As with the kickboard, you can develop a strong stroke and become a relatively fast triathlon swimmer without using them at all.

Stretch Cords

Stretch cords can be used on dry land to build swim-specific strength. Swimming uses muscles differently from land-based exercises such as weight lifting or calisthenics. Stretch cords allow the direction of force to more closely parallel the actual swim stroke. Once a basic facility with freestyle stroke is achieved, you can begin using stretch cords to improve the strength required for a fast catch, powerful pull-push, and full stroke. The detailed nature of stretch-cord exercises is beyond the scope of this book, but an excellent listing is available in the Ultrafit series book, *Going Long,* by Gordo Byrn and Joe Friel, published by VeloPress.

Other Resistance Gear

There are many exotic tools on the market to increase swim resistance and develop strength. These include drag-halters that pull an underwater parachute behind the swimmer, long-stretch rubber cords that allow for swimming a half or full pool length, drag-promoting swimsuits, and more. If your masters swim group experiments with these, it's probably okay to use them under the direction of an experienced coach. But they are superfluous for most age-group triathlon swimmers. Expert swimmers trying for 1–2 percent gains in speed might benefit from exotic usage, but these are beyond our fundamental emphasis.

OPEN-WATER SWIMMING AND WET SUITS

One of the most daunting experiences for beginners is their first open-water swim start. These can start on the beach, standing on a dock, or treading water behind a start line. Even in the best-managed races, there is an element of chaos to these starts. From year to year, the same race can differ for an individual. Those moving up to the half-Iron distance may have specialized in sprint races conducted in a lane-divided pool.

For others this wild and untamed venue can be fun and exciting. There's no need to worry about flip turns or lane dividers. Larger and stronger athletes have an advantage in rougher open water, jostling with other athletes. Competitive instincts, strategy, and muscular endurance rise to the level of stroke technique in promoting speed.

If the rules allow for it, you should use a wet suit for an open-water swim. This requirement is 78°F or less for age-group athletes. Some venues are very close to this temperature for the race schedule, so take your wet suit along if there is a chance you can use it. Wet suits are worth about 10 percent in faster times for beginning to intermediate swimmers, and about 5 percent for expert swimmers. The difference comes mostly from buoyancy and body position, where less-experienced swimmers suffer. The kick is further minimized, and you feel as if you are using a pull buoy.

For the open-water mass start, you must pull order out of chaos.

Modern wet suits are more comfortable, in both sleeveless and full-sleeved models. Expert swimmers often choose the sleeveless variety so as not to disturb their perfect arm stroke, but maximum gains come from the full-sleeved models. Many expert swimmers are having success with the less bouyant, full-body Lycra suits, which are legal in the pool or warmer waters, but their cost is high and their lifespan is low.

If you're a beginner doing your first half-Iron event, and your only goal is to finish the race, you can do without a wet suit. Just give yourself some extra minutes to finish the swim. If water temperature is below 73°F, the wet suit becomes more of a survival factor—you would be risking hypothermia without it. Keep your eye open for wet suit discounts: Manufacturers and retailers have large price reductions at different times of the season. You rarely have to spend full retail unless you are in a hurry.

Learn to don your wet suit and swim in it well *before* you travel to the race site. Cycling lubricants or cooking-oil spray can help in donning and removing the suit quickly. They do not operate like a scuba diving wet suit: the zipper goes in the back and they fit very snugly until you get into the water and loosen them up. You may well have to try a couple of suits until you get one that fits well, and most manufacturers will not accept returns once you swim in the water with the suit.

One more amusing story: In my first Iron-distance event, I purchased a wet suit and had done a few swims in our local pool, feeling it was a bit tight but not too bad. About ten minutes before the race start, another competitor told me I had it on the wrong way: "The zipper is supposed to be in the back!" he shouted. My wife and I struggled to remove it and drag it back on the right way, barely making it into the water before the gun went off. Fortunately, I had a good swim, five minutes faster than my race plan. The moral of the story: Think ahead!

Beginning swimmers are best advised to start toward the rear and off to the side of the main pack. Clear water without bumping into other swimmers is your best assurance of maximum speed and minimum stress. Staying back 10 meters and to the side another 20 meters will cost you less than 30 seconds in a 1,900m swim. What's important for this group is to understand the course layout and find the optimal line around the buoys. Beginners can misnavigate the course by 5 percent or more. If you've practiced sighting buoys in the pool and worked on balancing your stroke, this should not be a problem. You may need to stress one arm stroke or another to compensate for currents or weaknesses in your own technique. Beginners need to sight buoys at least every five full stroke cycles (five strokes with each arm).

Intermediate and advanced swimmers can move closer to the front and the optimal line depending on their estimated finish position. Know that swimming forward through slower swimmers is usually easier than having lots of swimmers coming over your back. Larger and stronger swimmers can endure more bumping, as can those with experience in other contact sports. If you freak out when touched in a pool lane, you might want to seed yourself farther back or to the side: Sometimes even expert swimmers will move off to the side to avoid trouble.

Once the initial pack breaks up, experienced swimmers can gain 8 percent or more advantage by drafting behind an equal or slightly faster swimmer. The best position is usually behind the swimmer's feet, but a position 45 degrees behind on either side also provides significant advantage. Make sure you do not bump into the swimmer. Some light touching of the feet may be inevitable, but if you are repeatedly disturbing the stroke of another swimmer, this is bad sportsmanship and may result in retaliation. If the swimmer is moving into you, fall backward or to the side. It's usually better to move around the drafting target at this point and find another, faster swimmer. It's not uncommon for swimmers to go out too hard in a half-Iron swim, and if you have superior endurance you may find yourself alone after the first half of the swim with no more draft targets in range. Make sure any drafting target is navigating buoys correctly: Any advantage you receive is quickly wiped out if the leader is taking you off course.

BEYOND TECHNIQUE—BUILDING SWIM FITNESS

Let's say you've been swimming competitively for many years before triathlon racing, or improved your swim in triathlons for a year or two. You are no longer in the middle of the swim pack, not the first out of the water but in the hunt on the bike and run in your division. Your Iron-distance swim split is down around 60–65 minutes and your half-Iron split is 29–33 minutes. Your 1,000m time trial is 17 minutes or less. You may well have reached a plateau where going faster is very difficult. You look good to other swimmers and coaches, and your videotape analysis has eliminated many weaknesses. What's left now is building more long-course endurance, muscular endurance, and speed into your practice and thereby your racing.

I reached this point after about two years in triathlon. I had watched several swim videos, conscientiously worked on rotation, hand-entry, head position, and building swim-specific strength. My Iron-distance splits were down around 62 minutes, now ranked just as high or higher than my bike or run splits within my masters age group. I attended a swim camp with Olympic swimming gold-medal winner, Olympic triathlete, and triathlon world champion Sheila Taormina. When I did some practice laps for analysis, I expected her to deconstruct my stroke and tell me what I was doing wrong with technique. What came back was something much simpler: "Your rotation is very good, your technique is fine. *Just swim harder.*" Sometimes we forget this with all our technique drills. If you ask an expert swimmer about the Total Immersion drills and practices, they usually say something like, "I already go faster than that now."

So we come full circle to the point where fitness is as important as it is in cycling and running. Once you achieve relative mastery of technique, you can't really swim faster unless you train faster and work harder in your interval sets. Once you are past the beginner's phase, you should be doing intervals in almost every workout, with the possible exception of the day after a long-course race. It's very difficult to maintain or improve speed by swimming continuously for thirty minutes or longer. Continuous swims should be limited to 1,000–1,500m (or yd.) time trials at top speed.

For most age-group swimmers practicing three or four times a week, one of these workouts should involve long intervals to promote endurance and another should use medium-distance intervals to build muscular endurance at or near lactate threshold. The remaining practice or two can be devoted to recovery and skills building. Whenever possible, triathlete swimmers should train in a 50m long-course pool. Unfortunately, these are becoming rare in the United States, and you should attempt more open-water swims in the spring and summer if you never get long-course pool training.

There are two possible workouts here and more in Appendix A.

Long interval workout

Warm-up: 100 drill, 100 kick, 100 drill, 100 kick

Main Set:

6×400 at T-Pace (i.e., 1,000m time-trial pace) with 40 seconds rest.

Try to negative split the second 200 with more perceived effort.

Cool-down: 100 drill, 50 kick easy, 500 swim good form

Total= 3,450

Medium interval workout

Warm-up: 3×100 descending times, 4×50 kick descending times

Main Set:

6×200 fast with 50 kick easy between 200s

200 kick steady

Cool-down: 200 easy swim

Total= 2,350

Note that the medium interval workout is considerably shorter. More experienced swimmers with established endurance can add additional drills to work on limiters after the main set.

CHAPTER 7

Cycling Skills

When I see an adult on a bicycle, I do not despair for the future of the human race. . . . Cycle tracks will abound in Utopia.

—H. G. Wells

THE LONG AND WINDING ROAD

For most age-group triathletes, cycling is the pivotal event. It accounts for 50 percent or more of the half-Iron race and composes at least half the weekly training volume. Strong cyclists have a tremendous advantage in the age-group divisions, and even the best runners must be competent at cycling to have a chance to win. Cycling endurance and strength often carry over to the other two events.

This large cycling contribution has led some triathletes to believe that volume is paramount to performance in long-course events. There is some truth in this: Most amateur triathletes struggle to find the time to put in the desired bike mileage. Lifestyle constraints, mechanical issues, early sunsets, and traffic all conspire to reduce the amount of time we can spend on the bike. The biggest change moving up to longer events is the bike commitment.

Fortunately, the half-Iron distance does not require or benefit from the gargantuan mileage done by Ironman specialists or long-distance road cyclists. In fact, the only compelling reason to ride over three hours in half-Iron training is for those planning longer bike segments in Ironman or long road races. If you can comfortably finish the typical weekend group ride, about 50–60 miles, you can finish the bike segment of a half-Iron race with enough left for the run.

The difference between finishing and competing in a division lies in the application of bike intensity. Road cyclists have known for decades that intensity is the key to cycling speed, and this knowledge has filtered down to triathletes. Add the modern principles of aerodynamic positioning, pedaling economy, and power measurement, and you have the tools for a respectable half-Iron bike split.

BEGINNING CONSIDERATIONS

For those new to cycling or moving up from only short-course racing, building sufficient endurance to bike 2.5–3.5 hours while conserving energy for a half-marathon run is essential. Even if you've been running solo marathons, cycling 56 miles (90km) is not the same kind of endurance as running three hours. It involves different muscle groups, pressure points, and heart rates. If you've never done any kind of endurance event over an hour or two, you'll find longer-distance cycling is much easier on the body than comparable hours running. Building endurance on longer rides takes mostly patience, attention to nutrition, and a comfortable bike fit.

Beginners should focus on building this endurance over a wide variety of terrain and course conditions, relegating speed to the background for the first six to twelve months of cycling.

BIKE FIT AND EQUIPMENT CHOICES

Unfortunately, most triathletes purchase a bike at the local shop without due consideration to aerodynamic body fit or triathlon needs. Despite a conscientious effort by most shops to fit the bike properly, only a tiny percentage have personnel with significant triathlon experience. The specialized shops will usually promote themselves as multisport retailers, sell aerodynamic frames, and perhaps other multisport clothing and equipment. Despite a market growth in triathlon gear and retailers, we find that most of our beginning or even intermediate triathletes come to us on road bikes, often ill-fitted, and definitely not set up aerodynamically. Simply throwing on some aerobars does not a tri-bike make. See Table 7.1

Perhaps this problem is unavoidable: Significant changes in body composition and bike-specific strength are common in the first year or two of cycling. The bike that fits well when just starting is likely to become substandard after you learn more about cycling strengths and limiters. It's preferable to look into a less-expensive model of road bike, triathlon bike, or perhaps even a used bike, provided you can find one within your fit parameters. Since cycling speed begins slowly, there is little advantage in seeking the lightest or most aerodynamic bike as a beginner.

A powerful aerodynamic position is essential.

One thing you should start with is an aerobar setup. Whether you purchase a standard road bike with clip-on aerobars added, or you choose a dedicated time-trial bike specifically for triathlon, learning to ride in aero position is essential for draft-free, long-course races. The faster you learn aerobars, the better you'll become at longer rides in a variety of wind conditions. You may come from hill country and have some experience on a road bike, but even hilly races require good triathletes to spend most of their time in aero position.

Many bike shops and some coaches will suggest that beginners first purchase a road bike, or perhaps continue spending most of their time riding a conventional road geometry setup. I'm going to move out of the mainstream here by suggesting you skip directly to a triathlon-specific bike if indeed triathlon is your main form of racing. Only those wishing to spend considerable time in draft-legal road racing or draft-legal triathlons (ITU and junior races), where aerobars and time-trial geometry are prohibited, should spend most of their time on a road frame. Most if not all half-Iron racing is draft-free and will likely remain so.

For myself and many coached beginners, early experience with a properly fit tri-bike promoted longer mileage with less soreness and a more positive attitude. I spent only two months on a road bike before moving to a triathlon bike—forced to change by a car crash that demolished the road bike. In some ways I'm thankful for that crash, because I upgraded to a more comfortable and faster time-trial bike. It only took a couple of weeks to learn the cowhorn handlebars and bar-end shifters, speeding up a full mile per hour in a month. I was able to spend all of my flat riding in aero position, whereas on a road bike I could only endure half the ride bent over. Some find a tri-bike daunting due to poor advice from road cyclists and bike shops, or the mistaken notion that a decent time-trial bike will cost hundreds if not thousands more than a road bike.

If you already have considerable investment in your road bike, you can race long-course simply by adding aerobars. But if you have a choice and are going to be spending over a thousand dollars anyway, why not start with something approaching the optimum setup? Fortunately, the triathlon bike niche has expanded to entry-level frames and component packages with prices comparable to a low-end road bike.

Triathletes are deluged with marketing materials and magazine articles about the hottest new frames, yet they often know little about the buzzwords and hype leveled at them. These manufacturers invest vast sums in research and development to design the fastest and most reliable frames. As with auto racing, they want to go fast and entice athletes who can win on their equipment. But once the marketing department starts placing ads in the magazines and Web sites, the data becomes more distorted. Lab test results may or may not apply in the real world of racing. What works for some professional triathletes may have little meaning for the average age grouper.

The range of terminology and technology used in modern cycling rivals that of space exploration. This book can include only a small fraction of them. We recommend dedicated works such as *The Cyclist's Training Bible* by Joe Friel and *Zinn and the Art of Road Bike Maintenance* by Lennard Zinn for more detailed descriptions of equipment and mechanics.

"If it does not fit, you will want to quit."

By "quitting," we don't necessarily mean giving up cycling or triathlon. But problems with bike fit will make you wish your long rides were short, or will make you "quit" on the harder pedal strokes and climbing required for intensive workouts. Riding a well-fit, reliable frame encourages you to

TABLE 7.1 COMMON TERMS ASSOCIATED WITH TRIATHLON CYCLING

TERM	DESCRIPTION	USES
Road bike frame	The traditional "double-diamond" frame geometry with curved ram bars and integrated brake/shifter levers. The seat tube angle to the crankset is around 73 degrees, farther back to facilitate sprinting and climbing. Usually made from steel, aluminum, titanium, or carbon. Can include aerobars for use in time trials and triathlons.	Comfort, climbing, price, availability, tradition
Time-trial/ triathlon frame	A frame specifically designed for riding in the aerobar position, often with aerodynamic tubing, custom wheel cutouts, and usually a forward saddle position relative to the crankset at 78–80 degrees. Usually made from aluminum, boron, titanium, or carbon. Handlebars are usually of cowhorn or integrated design with separate light brake levers and bar-end shifters on the aerobars.	Comfort in aero position, wind riding, speed, comfort for post-ride running
Boom-bike	A modern bike design used mostly in time trials, triathlons, or ultracycling that employs a flexible beam with no seat tube and direct airflow around the rear wheel. Most popular with triathletes and ultracyclists. Can facilitate a flexible seat angle of 73–81 degrees to optimize climbing or aero-position. Usually made from aluminum, titanium, or carbon, with beam composition often different from frame material.	Comfort in aero position, reduced road vibration, minimal drag, wind-riding, speed, comfort for post-ride running, ease of fit, improved performance for large riders

CONTINUED

TABLE 7.1 CONTINUED

TERM	DESCRIPTION	USES
Aerobar	The fastest aerodynamic upgrade you can make on your bike, since bodily wind drag exceeds drag on the wheels or frame. Available via inexpensive clip-on models or fully integrated handlebar sets. Essential for all triathletes, but not legal in most road races and unpopular on some road training rides.	Speed, comfort in long rides, windy riding, solo riding
Aero deep-rimmed wheel	A reduced-spoke wheel with a deeper rim of 30–70mm, made of carbon and/or metal in both clincher and tubular models. Promotes faster time trialing in a variety of wind conditions for most riders; the deeper the rim, the more unstable in a crosswind, especially for small riders.	Speed, windy rides, climbing
Tri-spoke or quad-spoke wheel	Solid composition wheel using 3–4 wide-bladed struts instead of conventional metal spokes to connect hub to rim. Usually faster than a low-spoke, deep-rimmed wheel, but marginally slower than a disc wheel (below). Legal in most conditions, but risky for the front wheel in windy conditions. Can be combined with a rear disc wheel to minimize drag.	Speed, straight headwinds, variety of courses
Disc wheel	Solid composite wheel without spokes. Legal only as the rear wheel in triathlons with moderate wind; illegal in Hawaii races. Lighter versions good for climbing and most triathlon courses.	Speed, light wind, or headwind riding

CONTINUED

TABLE 7.1 CONTINUED

TERM	DESCRIPTION	USES
Conventional wheel	Also known as a training wheel, with standard metal rim and usually 28–32 spokes. Can be used for racing for beginners or in C races where speed is not paramount. Usually uses clincher tires and tubes.	Inexpensive, durable, reliable, easy to maintain
Shimano components	The most popular mass-produced component vendor (Japanese), now including ten-speed varieties in various price ranges. Most wheels and components are "Shimano compatible."	Affordable, fast, durable, reliable, available
Campagnolo components	Also called "Campy components." The older, high-quality but less prolific component vendor (Italian), originator of ten-speed shifting and many innovations. Most wheels and components need special accessories to become "Campy compatible." Popular with traditional road cyclists.	Traditional, reliable, innovative, fast
Bar-end shifter	Placement of front and rear derailleur shifters at the end of the aerobars, rather than with integrated brake-shifters on the handlebar. The common configuration for most triathletes.	Light, convenient in aero position, simple
Integrated shifter	Commonly called STI shifters (from Shimano), they combine brake levers and shifters into one unit on the ram-bar of road bikes. Preferred by some triathletes and ultracyclists, even with a time-trial bike frame, especially in hillier venues.	Fast, convenient road position, available

CONTINUED

TABLE 7.1 CONTINUED

TERM	DESCRIPTION	USES
Clipless pedal	Modern binding connecting cycling shoe and pedal in solid, powerful connection with quick-release mechanism for exit. Recommended for all long-course triathletes.	Lightweight, powerful, safe
Toe-strap pedal	Older-style pedal connecting a running shoe via insertion in a strap. Useful for novice short-course triathletes or duathletes in shorter races. Not recommended for serious long-course triathletes.	Inexpensive, simple, fast in short duathlons
Aero helmet	A longer, rooster-style helmet with minimal holes for minimum drag in time trials and triathlons; now legal for triathlons. Not recommended for beginners, warmer weather, or training. Limited use in hot, long-course racing.	Aerodynamic, expensive, fast
Conventional helmet	A lighter, comfortable helmet with many ventilation holes for training and racing. Essential for hot-weather riding, but holes cause drag in racing.	Light, cool, inexpensive, available
Aero drink system	A special hydration system for triathlons mounted on the front aerobars or sometimes behind the rider, using a plastic straw for regular sipping. Useful in races involving regular bottle hand-ups, very useful in long-course, hotter races where hydration is essential. Causes some additional front drag and is rarer in shorter time trials or professional racing.	Available, ease of drinking in aero position

exceed limitations and remain optimistic about improvement. Those experiencing discomfort early in training will become discouraged on a poorly fit bike. If you cannot ride more than an hour on a moderate course without discomfort, your problems likely come from fitting. If you've been training consistently for six months or longer and have trouble riding 50 miles or more, you may need to optimize your current fit. There are five priorities in bike fitting and equipment choices, in order of importance:

1. **Safety:** If you crash, you lose, or at least suffer unnecessarily. Cycling is not an injury-prone sport, provided you are not stopped violently by pavement or another vehicle! And safety includes preventing repetitive-motion injuries to the knee and pressure points. Safety relies as much upon conscious awareness as physical equipment; overtrained or underrested athletes are more likely to crash.
2. **Comfort:** Minor irritations build up during long rides. Equipment that feels comfortable over a short distance can become intolerable in longer training and racing. Imagine tapping two fingers on your forearm a few times: no pain or discomfort. Now imagine tapping 50,000 times, and it becomes excruciating. This number approximates the sum of right and left pedal strokes in a half-Iron race.
3. **Aerodynamics:** In draft-free half-Iron and Iron-distance races, drag is more important than weight in determining speed. The human body is the biggest drag factor, followed by wheels, and then the frame. Fitting is critical to reducing drag.
4. **Power:** Once you are able to finish a long ride safely, comfortably, and efficiently, you want to pour all the power you can into the pedal strokes. Expert cyclists have mastered the first three factors and focus mostly on increasing power, which for long time trials requires improving muscular endurance. Modern technology allows us to measure power directly at a reasonable cost.

It's easy to forget bike fit numbers or methods. Bikes ridden on bumpy roads, in the rain and in hard racing have a tendency to shift gradually without conscious awareness. We recommend keeping a notebook (or computer log) of all fitting values and inspecting your bike every month or two for fit consistency, structural integrity, and loosened bolts.

The high-tech aerodynamic frames require more attention to detailed measurement than a traditional road bike. Lance Armstrong, former triathlete and master of the time trial, was nicknamed "Mr. Millimeter" in his obsession with precise bike fit and mechanical adjustment.

This caution is very important for athletes disassembling time-trial bikes for air transport to events and usually reassembling them under pressure before race check-in. Many race horror stories involve these travel-and-assembly scenarios. If you prefer not to mess with bike shipping and reassembly, check with bike shops that offer this service for a fee. As with automobiles or anything mechanical, higher-mileage riders will spend more time and money on maintenance. Murphy's Law is alive and well for cycling: "If anything can go wrong, it will—and at the worst possible moment!"

Feet and Pedals

Bike fitting starts from the bottom up, or if you view the pedal stroke as a circle drawn by the feet, from the inside out as you move away from the center of the crank-arm. We start by fitting the pedal-cleat to the cycling shoe before considering anything else. As with running, cycling power is generated via contact with the mid- to ball-of-foot, rotating on top of the pedal.

For most riders, the optimal position is with the pedal spindle directly under the ball of the foot, the so-called neutral position, and we recommend this as a good starting point for most beginners. You can find the ball of the foot on a bare foot by feeling with your hands on the bottom and seeing the slight extrusion of bone on the inner foot. After donning your cycling

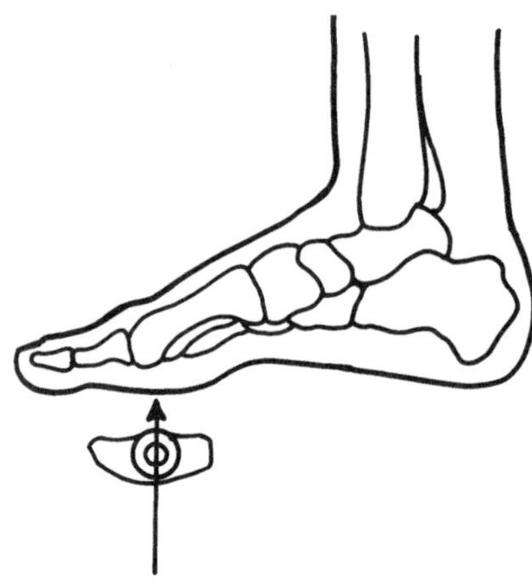

FIGURE 7.1
Cleat fit

shoes, mark this point on the shoe's outer rim. Many modern shoes have graduated scales around the cleats to assist with marking this point.

After clipping into your pedals, check your marked shoe position over the spindle in a mirror or have a friend look at it while mounted squarely on an indoor trainer. Repeat the procedure for the other foot, but don't expect the same cleat position for the right and left foot: Size and strength varies considerably.

Once you have some experience and start tackling steeper hills and longer rides, many triathletes find that moving the pedal slightly rearward toward the midfoot can help with climbing or pushing a big gear in aero position. This cleat position may alleviate symptoms of "hot feet" that many riders experience on longer rides or on hotter days. When making cleat-position changes, move gradually in 1–3mm increments, doing a test ride before moving farther. This gradual shift-and-test pattern holds for all cycling changes: Any drastic change is likely to feel unbalanced and increase the risk of soreness or injury.

Saddle Position and Knees

Done correctly, the saddle forward-rearward (fore-aft) position and height can prevent knee, back, and foot pain in longer rides; done incorrectly they can rob you of power, cause discomfort, and lead to injury over time.

Saddle forward-rearward (fore-aft) position

There are two aspects to consider: the strictly horizontal placement of the seat relative to crank-arm and handlebars and the slight tilt of the saddle nose up or down. Most riders should begin with a level saddle as measured with a bubble-level on a conventional frame with seat post. Boom-bike riders (Softride, Titanflex, Zipp, etc.) will need to start with an additional 3–6 degrees of forward tilt to offset the drop of the flexible boom. Investing in a magnetic angle locator, more precise and easier to use than a carpenter's level, is ideal for checking frame geometry, knee angle, saddle angle, and other factors.

For those fitting a saddle to a time-trial/triathlon style frame, it will already be farther forward relative to the handlebars. Those modifying a road bike for triathlon should consider the purchase of an angled seat post to move the saddle into a steeper, aero-friendly position. Boom-bike riders can choose a range somewhere between 75–81 degrees for the saddle-to-crank-bolt angle, depending on their beam size and riding preferences.

Frame geometry affects the optimal pedal-cleat position. For a more conventional road frame around 72–73 degrees, the seat's position should place the kneecap above the pedal-cleat position. After warming up on a trainer, rotate the crank arm to the "flat" nine o'clock/three o'clock position and drop a plumb line from just under the kneecap (the head of the tibia) down to the pedal, where it should cross the spindle near the ball of the foot. Be careful not to distort the angle by leaning toward the measurement side.

For a forward-positioned triathlon frame of 75–81 degrees, boom-bike, or road bike with angled-forward seat post, dropping a plumb line from the kneecap may place the line considerably ahead of the spindle, toward the toes (Figure 7.2). The exact distance forward is determined by the steepness of the seat position angle. Riders may need to experiment with several pedal-cleat and saddle fore-aft positions to find the one that works best for long-course racing. Do not, however, move the pedal-cleat far forward in order to line up with the plumb line. These extreme forward cleat positions may suit track cyclists and road-racing sprinters, but not long-course triathletes.

Although a level seat works for many riders, those using a steeper-angled aero position can benefit from a *slight* tilt of the nose downward. Note that a severe tilt may feel good in the parking lot but is bound to cause discomfort on longer rides. Flexible riders used to road bikes in hilly terrain may be able to tolerate a *slight* tilt backward.

Apart from leg strength, most riders favor the left or right side when pedaling in the aero position, getting the anatomy out of the way of the nose of the saddle. You can assist this process by a *slight* right or left nudge of the saddle nose (less than 5 degrees) away from the leaning side. Anything more may disrupt your stroke balance. This left or right nudge seems to work for both male and female cyclists.

Seat height

Most experts consider seat height the critical factor in bike fit, and there are various formulas to measure it. These rely on statistical averages for the general population, but individual rider characteristics vary, especially when leaning over aerobars. We recommend using bodily feedback and real-world measurements instead of theoretical formulas.

Once you have achieved a workable, comfortable bike fit and spent some time with it, you should not change seat height very often. It is the most volatile of all bike measurements. You can reexamine seat height each season and implement gradual changes (2–3mm) if your flexibility, equipment, or riding conditions warrant it.

There is a simple method to establish seat height that may work well for beginners or as a quick starting point before attempting more precise measurement.

1. Warm up briefly on an indoor trainer.
2. Unclip the shoes from the binding and place your heel on the pedal at the bottom of the pedal stroke, the point farthest from the seat.
3. The leg should be fully extended, without leaning, with the heel just touching the pedal.
4. Record the distance between the center of the crank bolt to the smaller bolt used to connect the saddle to the post or beam assembly. Variations in shoe and pedal design reduce the precision of this measurement, but it's a good starting value.

A more precise method employs a goniometer, a device for measuring joint angles—in this case, the knee. These are available from most medical supply stores or you can make your own with rulers and a protractor.

1. Warm up briefly on an indoor trainer.
2. With feet clipped into the pedals, have someone measure the angle of the upper and lower leg at the knee (without leaning on the pedal) when fully extended on the downstroke. For most riders, 30 degrees is the optimal angle at the bottom of the pedal stroke. Note that this angle is affected by forward-rearward saddle and pedal-cleat positions, so subsequent slight adjustments may be necessary.
3. Record the distance between the center of the crank bolt to the seat-post-to-saddle connector or rail. This height becomes a reference point for future changes and should only be changed gradually.

Fitting stem, handlebars, and aerobars

While most bike shops can fit a triathlete reasonably well from the waist down, the specifics of aerodynamic positioning are what distinguishes expert fitters. For one thing, it's a relatively new discipline, reaching maturity in the 1990s and still undergoing periodic revolutions in wind-tunnel testing and equipment. Even renowned authorities like John Cobb, who fit

FIGURE 7.2
Conservative aero position for long-course racing

Lance Armstrong for his Tour de France time trials, are refining their theories and employ different methods than they did only a few years ago. As Cobb has emphasized, aerodynamic positioning is as much an art as a science, and in some ways you are never really "done" with fitting. Since athlete fitness, flexibility, and race distances vary throughout the season, so does the optimal aero position.

With this variability in mind, we recommend employing an adjustable stem, such as the Look Ergo model, or experimenting with easily installable stems of varying lengths. It's unlikely that a beginner will purchase an off-the-shelf, prebuilt stem and handlebar setup with optimal fit. Spend the time to experiment before finalizing your purchase, and insist on presale cooperation from the retailer. Purchasing an adjustable stem is ideal for beginners who are likely to change body composition and flexibility during the first year of training.

Modern aerobar setups include systems where stem, handlebars, and aerobars are combined into one adjustable unit. These reduce weight and drag but are not the best choice for beginners. You should have experience with your optimal measurements before choosing the integrated model. Experienced triathletes can upgrade later.

Most bikes now use threadless steerer tubes (carbon or metal) and ring spacers to determine stem height. You may need to start with a steerer tube cut with extra space above and below the stem connection to find the optimal height.

The neutral position for most triathletes places the handlebars about one inch (25mm) below the level saddle. Find the level position using a large yardstick and leveler, and then measure the drop from that level. Beginners with no previous aerobar experience, those with back inflexibility, or those moving up in distance to longer rides may be more comfortable up to one inch higher. More experienced and more flexible triathletes may be more comfortable up to one inch lower. Long-course athletes may also go slightly lower than normal for short-course races done well before or after their longer course races. Note that lower aerobar positions usually require more forward seat positions to provide sufficient breathing room for the chest and diaphragm.

Generally, lower is more aerodynamic and faster, and higher is more comfortable and more powerful. Trying to force yourself into an uncomfortable position to resemble elite time trialists or triathletes is counterproductive in the long run. If you find yourself coming out of aero position frequently (not just for climbing), you are losing the speed gains of a lower position. Figure 7.2 shows a conservative position for long-course racing. More flexible and elite athletes might lower the handlebars/aerobars by one inch (25mm) or more.

Once you determine handlebar and aerobar height, you must adjust the length of the aerobar to facilitate comfortable hand and head position. This should place the ear-hole over the crook of the bent arm on the aerobar pad. Choosing adjustable-length aerobars is recommended for finding optimal length. Most athletes will achieve good aerodynamics and comfort with the forearms parallel to the ground, or nearly so. You will see some experienced riders with a higher or lower hand angle to the elbow, perhaps to compensate for other fitting factors.

Aerodynamics and Power

Yet another seesaw in triathlon training comes when we optimize aerodynamics and power output. Once a basic, comfortable aero position has

TABLE 7.2 REAL-WORLD EFFECTS OF AEROPOSITION ON 40KM TIME TRIAL FOR AN AVERAGE TRIATHLETE

POSITIONING	DRAG (LBS)	SPEED (MPH)	TIME
Original position, hands on hoods	9.38	17.6	1:24:32
Adding aerobars	8.05	18.4	1:20:49
Rider-initiated position changes	7.61	18.7	1:19:31
Expert coach positioning	6.58	19.5	1:16:14

been achieved as outlined in the previous section, further reductions in body drag will likely cause reductions in power. It's a complex set of trade-offs between watts applied to the rear wheel while pedaling and watts subtracted due to frictional forces of airflow along the body. Since drag increases with the square of the velocity, an expert triathlete moving at 25.5mph has twice as much drag as someone going only 18.0mph, and the expert produces around twice as much power, perhaps 300 watts compared to only 150 watts required to go 18.0mph.

Extremely elongated aero position will likely reduce wattage, reducing the powerful force of core and torso muscles. If you are not flexible enough to maintain an aero position comfortably for a 56-mile bike segment, you will likely run slower in the race. For the longer half-Iron distance, you will need to eat and drink more during the bike segment, and digestion can be compromised by extreme upper-body position.

We have seen elite triathletes in a completely level position with a flat back (A-type), and sometimes age groupers try to mimic this as their own ideal. Remember that many top time trialists have generated great power with a slightly curved back (B-type): Lance Armstrong and Miguel Indurain in cycling, plus Jürgen Zack in triathlon. These athletes chose a position that maximized power while still incorporating aerodynamic fundamentals.

Many drag reduction techniques don't require pretzel-like body positions:

Aerodynamic wheels reduce drag and increase speed.

- Choose the most aerodynamic wheels that your budget and race rules will allow: These range from disc wheels and tri-spokes (see photo on the next page) to deeper-rimmed, reduced-spoke wheels. Wheels account for about half the drag-watts involved in body position.
- Aero helmets have become legal and affordable for triathletes, but beware of using them on hotter courses, because aero means few if any holes for ventilation.
- Water bottles can be mounted on the frame or behind the seat to reduce drag, and the optimal choice depends on frame geometry. If you're used to carrying a lot of bottles for longer training rides, try reducing the number to only what you need to make it to the first aid station on the half-Iron course. Or experiment with backpack hydration systems, also available in aerodynamic models.
- Mounting food or hydration items near the aerobars causes more drag, but one exception might be an aerobar drinking system on hot courses. The straw reminds you to drink—dehydration power loss trumps aerodynamics in longer races.
- Some races do not require the race number on the body during the bike leg, saving you another 5 watts. If you must use a race-number belt on the bike, tuck the flapping bottom into your tri shorts.
- Choosing a one-piece triathlon suit or unflappable two-piece setup reduces drag, as does eliminating gloves.

Whatever choices you make, experiment with them well before the race date. People changing position, equipment, or just about anything on race week usually meet with a sad fate, maybe even a DNF. These tales of woe include veteran world champions who should have known better. Familiar is faster on race day.

TABLE 7.3 USEFUL DRIVETRAIN TERMS

TERM	DESCRIPTION	VALUES	USAGE
Big chainring	Larger-radius gear on outer crankset	53 teeth	Suitable for most triathletes, combines with 39-tooth small ring, called the "53/39"
		54, 55, or 56 teeth	Increases power for stronger riders and/or 650c wheels
Small chainring	Smaller-radius gear on inner crankset	39 teeth	Used for climbing and warm-up, combines with 53-tooth big ring; does not combine well with 55- or 56-tooth large chainrings
		42 teeth	Used for climbing and warm-up, combines with 54–56-tooth big chain ring, termed "55/42" "56/42," etc.
Front derailleur	Moves chain between big and small chainring	2 positions with frictional (variable) shifting	Shifts before climbing to small ring, back up to big ring for flatter terrain
Rear derailleur	Moves chain between 9 or 10 variable-radius cogs on rear wheel	9 or 10 positions with indexed (fixed) shifting	Adjusts rear cog for optimal cadence and power output in varying terrain
Cogset	A set of 9 or 10 toothed gears on rear hub, placed in decreasing size from inside-out on the wheel	11–23 teeth	Common gear found on most bikes and suitable for flat to rolling courses
		12–25 teeth	Useful gear for hillier courses and weaker riders
		11–21 teeth	Preferred gear for very strong riders up to moderately hilly courses
		12–27 teeth	Extreme gear for mountainous terrain and/or weaker riders

CONTINUED

TABLE 7.3 CONTINUED

TERM	DESCRIPTION	VALUES	USAGE
700c wheel	The standard diameter wheel used in road cycling	27 inches diameter	Medium to large triathletes
650c wheel	A smaller diameter wheel popular for time trials and triathlons	26 inches diameter	Small to medium triathletes, or those optimizing aerodynamics
Bigger gear	More difficult, faster gear	Fewer teeth and smaller diameter than previous gear	Increase speed or reduce cadence on flat or downhill terrain, or when cresting hill
Smaller gear	Easier, slower gear	More teeth and diameter than previous gear	Decrease speed or increase cadence on uphill terrain
Gearing up	Shifting into a bigger gear to the outside of the cogset	Decreasing tension on right shifter cable, moves chain to right	Increase speed or reduce cadence on flat or downhill terrain, or when cresting hill
Gearing down	Shifting into a smaller gear to the inside of the rear cogset	Increasing tension on right shifter cable, moves chain to left	Decrease speed or increase cadence on uphill terrain
Shifter Cable	Thin metal cable connecting shifters to front and rear derailleurs	Long on rear and short on front derailleur	Allows shifter control of derailleurs. Can be externally routed or hidden to reduce drag. Can corrode and break; requires periodic replacement

CONTINUED

TABLE 7.3 CONTINUED

TERM	DESCRIPTION	VALUES	USAGE
Shifter cable housing	Outer fixed-length shell composed of plastic and metal surrounding shifter cable	Longer housing connected to bar-end shifters and shorter housing along chain stay to rear derailleur	Provides protection and fixed distance for shifter cable. Can corrode and shred; equires periodic replacement

DRIVETRAIN

The drivetrain includes your cranks, small and big chainrings, chain, and rear cogset (Table 7.3). These tools are the sole instrument of power transmission from your body to the rear wheel. Choices made here can significantly improve economy. Long-course racing usually involves more varied and difficult terrain than shorter events, often requiring "all the gears" to finish comfortably. Since you are likely to be shifting more, you need to do so quickly and efficiently.

Beginners often have trouble with effective shifting: Most use fewer gears than they should, both with the front and rear derailleur. This lack of confidence is often caused by poorly maintained bikes with bad derailleur adjustments, worn cables, and occasionally less-than-reliable component models. Although many entry-level bikes come equipped with lesser components, if you have a choice, it's usually worth the extra money to invest in Ultegra or Dura-Ace model lines from Shimano, or the Campagnolo models of Chorus or Record. Both manufacturers now feature ten-speed cogsets, and the extra middle gear can be very useful in a steady-paced time trial.

Those with no maintenance experience must rely on bike shops and mechanics to perform even minor cable tension adjustments, and this becomes costly and time consuming as cycling volume grows. Learning to perform the simpler maintenance tasks yourself will save time in the long run: changing tires, cogsets, chains, brake pads, and cables are minimal skills all triathletes should have, but many do not. You don't have to be an innately gifted "mechanical type" to learn these basic tasks—bikes are amazingly simple machines compared to cars and computers. Anyone of reasonable patience and average dexterity can teach themselves the basics using books such as Lennard Zinn's classic, *Zinn and the Art of Road Bike Maintenance* (VeloPress).

Gears and Ratios

Applying the principles of mechanical advantage, a bigger-sized ring with more teeth on the front is harder to push and delivers more power, whereas a bigger-sized cog with more teeth on the rear wheel is easier to push and delivers less power. On a standard drivetrain using a 53/39 front ring combination and typical rear cogset of 11–23, the easiest gear used for the steepest hills would be a combination of 39×23, which would move your rear wheel around 1.70 revolutions for each complete turn of the cranks. As you crested that hill and continued along a steep descent of 10 percent or greater, you might well use your biggest gear combination of 53×11, the big front chainring with the smallest rear cog

TABLE 7.4 TYPICAL GEAR RATIO FOR 53/39 CHAINRINGS AND 11–23 TEN-SPEED COGSET

REAR COG TEETH	GEAR RATIO (WHEEL REVOLUTIONS PER CRANK CYCLE)	
	Small Ring Teeth = 39	Big Ring Teeth = 53
23	1.70	2.30
21	1.86	2.52
19	2.05	2.79
17	2.29	3.12
16	2.44	3.31
15	2.60	3.53
14	2.79	3.79
13	3.00	4.08
12	3.25	4.42
11	3.55	4.82

of only eleven teeth, which moves your wheel 4.82 revolutions for each turn of the cranks. This tremendous range of power is shown in Table 7.4.

Even though certain front-rear gear combinations appear to have similar or equal ratio, they do not necessarily output the same power. The chain angle itself makes shifting and power transfer less efficient for lower gears (inner cogs) employing the big front chainring (outer ring). Likewise, gearing up to higher gears and more speed is more efficiently performed using the big chainring. It's rarely if ever advisable to stay in a combination like 53×23 for very long, and the same can be said for 39×11.

Expert triathletes may choose a larger front ring size that enables them to employ mostly the middle gears where smoothness and power transfer are optimal. Beginning to intermediate riders will likely do well with a standard 53/39 ring setup and an 11–23 or 12–25 cogset using standard 700c (27-inch) wheels, or perhaps a 55/42 for 650c (26-inch) wheels.

Cadence is Key

Some riders obsess on technical aspects like gear inches and the power potential of bigger chainrings and cranks. The more consistently successful triathletes, however, the ones with balanced splits on the bike and the run in long-course racing, are seeking a more intuitive feel for the correct gear, instinctively maintaining a steady cadence while allowing gears to fall below the level of consciousness.

Correct gearing is intertwined with optimal cadence. We encourage beginning to intermediate riders to install a cadence meter, since it is often more useful than a speedometer for training and racing. Even expert riders need periodic cadence checkups to avoid extremes. The underlying purpose of gear shifting enables a cadence of around 90rpm for most triathlon courses in flat to rolling terrain. Cadence will inevitably go down for climbing or fighting a headwind and rise for downhill or downwind riding, but most aerobic training should be done with steady cadence. Many cyclists believe they have a relatively high cadence around 90rpm, but observations by expert coaches in half- and full Ironman races often find athletes are closer to 80rpm. Some decay in cadence may be inevitable, but if you've been training mostly around 85–95rpm you'll stay near the optimal value under stress. In fact, if you are training on a moderate course at 90rpm, it's likely you will instinctively choose the right gears and achieve optimal heart rate in Zone 2 or 3.

Cadence has a profound effect on leg fatigue and the resulting run pace after the bike segment. Athletes forcing a bigger gear at a lower cadence, especially in hilly courses, will experience stiffer legs in the early run even if their aerobic capacity supports higher bike intensity. Disciplined riders who spin in an easier gear are likely to feel fresh and ready to race hard as they exit the bike-to-run transition. If you find yourself stiff or cramping on the run in long-course races or intensive training bricks, try easing up a gear into the wind, uphill, or in the final miles of the bike.

My own larger body frame makes it difficult to compete with the best climbers in my division. But it's amazing how many of these I catch later on the flat sections or on the run, and the reason is a disciplined use of the small chainring, easier gear, and higher cadence on difficult courses.

BIKE TRAINING

Bike training epitomizes the fundamental principles of long-course training and periodization. Endurance is the most important skill, followed by strength, which is blended with endurance to create muscular endurance for climbing and pushing a relatively big gear over a 2.0–3.5-hour time trial. As with the other two sports, beginners should patiently focus on skills and endurance before moving on to the other two factors. Experienced

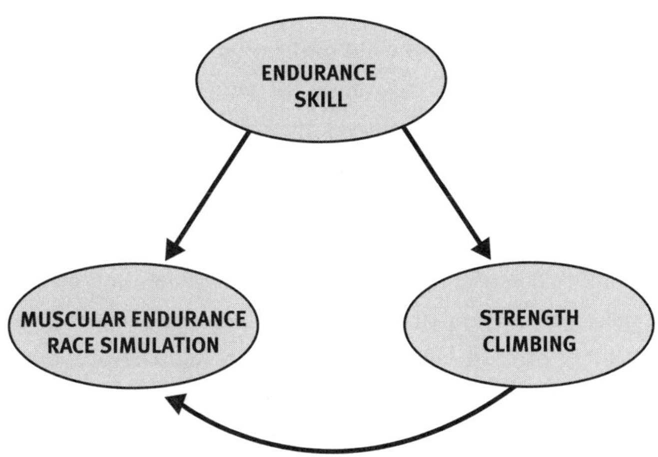

FIGURE 7.3
Progression of bike training

athletes should speed up the progression within each season, moving from early base-building to strength enhancement in the hills to faster intervals and race simulations later in the year.

Endurance and Skill Building

Cycling endurance may well be the prevailing quality for triathlon success, since its aerobic base benefits the other two sports. The keys to building this endurance are not glamorous, requiring mostly patience and disciplined work habits. More than swimming or running, cycling is something that beginners can improve simply by doing lots of it. It is a natural, noneccentric motion in a fixed circle of pedal strokes. Excessive volume in swimming can degrade technique, and too much running can lead to injury. But you can ride your bike for long, slow distances (LSD) and improve aerobic capacity and even economy, provided you are comfortable. For this reason, triathletes may see the most rapid progress in cycling, especially those coming from a long-distance running background. The main limiter for many age-group athletes is simply finding more time to ride in a busy life schedule. Fortunately, the half-Iron distance can be successfully completed with only moderate mileage—the ability to complete a 2–3 hour ride without undue fatigue.

Once you have achieved a comfortable and effective fit, the development of bike skills grows naturally during workouts in Zone 1 or 2. Since heart rates are low and lactic acid minimal, your mind is free to focus on economy with the pedal stroke, aero position, and efficient climbing. Most of us loved riding a bike as a child for its own sake and would spend all day riding with no outside motivation to "train" for anything. The biggest motivator for beginners to improve their cycling is the fun factor: enthusiasm will lead you to longer mileage, and longer mileage will lead you to better fitness and faster riding.

Progress in bike volume should be gradual and consistent, with minimal discomfort. If you've done nothing but 60–90-minute rides before in short-course preparation, don't suddenly start riding centuries for long-course training. Increase volume by about 10 percent per week, especially the longest ride, until you can ride 2.5–3.0 hours without discomfort. For beginners, this may well take three to six months, and that's okay. Avoid the temptation to go out with hammerheads and "race" against stronger riders. You need an established base of perhaps 1,000 cycling miles before attempting higher intensity.

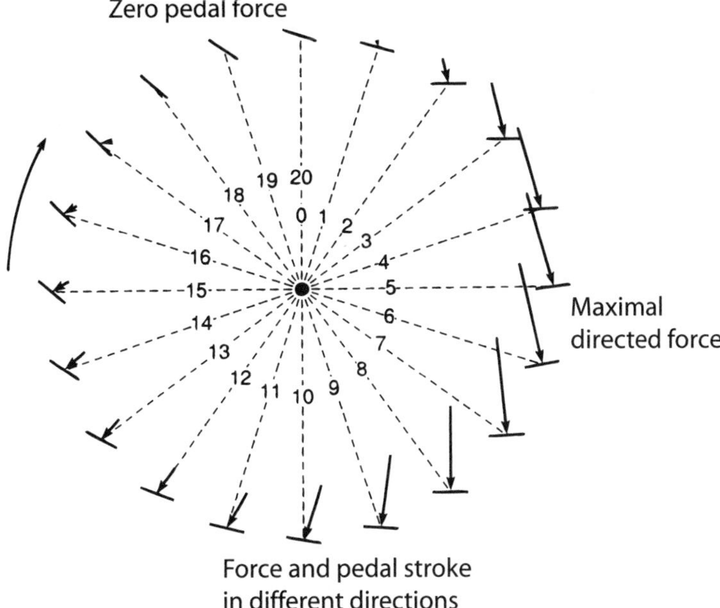

FIGURE 7.4

Conscious effort can be used to push and pull through the "dead spots" at the top and bottom of the pedal stroke.

Skill building starts with pedal-stroke fundamentals (Figure 7.4) and maintaining a steady cadence. Some mental keys for your internal dialogue include:

- Draw two parallel circles with your feet when pedaling, imagining the pedal flowing all the way around the circle, using the whole leg musculature. Avoid a pistonlike emphasis of up and down only.
- Feel as if you are scraping mud off your shoe at the bottom of the pedal stroke, moving backward, and that you are smoothly pushing "over the barrel" at the top of the stroke. These are the weaker areas of the circle where force is minimal or degrading.
- Relax the face, mouth, hands, and upper body so that blood flow and force generation will proceed from the core to the lower extremities.
- Some mental dissociation is inevitable in longer rides, and sometimes it's okay to let your mind wander a little. But pay attention to safety and realize that for stronger riders, even short gaps in focus usually result in rapid drops in heart rate and cadence.

- The mental difference between novice and expert riders is that beginners use dissociation to remove their consciousness from riding discomfort, while experts tend to focus even harder on riding as pain increases, veritably bathing themselves in the experience. Lance Armstrong was once asked what he thought about during a grueling seven-hour stage, and he said simply, "I think about cycling."

Skill-building tools

Modern technology has given cyclists a smorgasbord of tools to improve pedal-stroke technique, ranging from the traditional to the baroque (Table 7.5). Some work for just about all cyclists, others have more limited application during certain periods, and most require hard budgeting choices. Beginners may well do better by riding steadily for a year or longer before using anything other than their regular bike. Those wishing to move into the intermediate ranks can benefit from a more conscious evolution of skill, while experts usually employ several tools to improve performance. Some athletes become very strong riders at the top of their division with no special equipment beyond training and racing bikes.

Note that I do not list a heart rate monitor as an optional skill-building device. We consider its use mandatory for periodic training on both the bike and run.

Developing Bike-specific Strength

The traditional method for building bike strength is simple: Just go out and climb some hills. I had the misfortune of beginning my triathlon and cycling career in one of the flattest areas in the United States, at sea level around Galveston Bay near Houston, Texas. Finding hills to climb was not so simple. There was only one bridge that allowed for a 7-percent climb of merely 90 seconds, and we had to repeat that climb 10–15 times for significant effect. But we had steady winds of 15–25mph most days with gusts up to 35mph, so strength could be augmented by pressing a harder gear into the wind.

If you find yourself stuck in "flatland," you can schedule periodic "climbing expeditions" where you drive to a hillier area to work on climbing. Combined with consistent weight training, you can still become a competent climber within your division.

For beginners, climbing is especially helpful, not only for hillier racecourses but to develop the strength required for all types of terrain. It's much easier for a good rider residing in the mountains to reengineer their fitness for an occasional flatland race than for a flatlander to adapt to hilly courses.

Always warm up before significant climbing, at least 15 minutes and preferably 20–30 minutes for beginning riders or those who've been away from climbing. You don't have to climb the steepest hills to get the best results: Starting with gentle rollers under 5 percent grade is sufficient. Although cadence will naturally slow when climbing, keeping the rate from 65–75rpm will develop a smoother stroke in the hills. Low-cadence drills of 55rpm are useful only for experienced cyclists requiring severe leg tension to build more strength.

Experienced riders will look for longer climbs with grades up to around 7–8 percent. The severe mountainous grades aren't found very often in large half-Iron competitions, so grades over 10 percent are best kept short and infrequent. A good rule is to be able to climb a grade 1 percent higher than the one you'll be racing for at least the same distance. You should train on most of these grades in Zone 3 or Zone 4, with perhaps some cresting near Zone 5a.

Note that climbing in hot weather will perturb heart rates beyond actual wattage output: It's easy to go five to ten beats higher than normal in a longer climb. If you'll be climbing steep hills with hot weather in your target race (Buffalo Springs in Texas or St. Croix in the Virgin Islands are good examples), be prepared for potentially doubled hydration requirements. It's quite possible to down two liters an hour while climbing these courses.

Another target for experienced riders is the ability to climb lesser grades into a headwind without coming out of aero position. This technique is useful only when you can maintain adequate power in a lower gear, combined with a strong headwind that rewards staying down. There aren't many places on the planet where the wind blows hard in steep terrain, but regions of Texas, Hawaii, and coastal mountain areas reward this odd skill. If you find yourself tightening up, it's best to rise on the handlebars even if it slows you down. Remember you still have to run after climbing.

Strength is better developed by staying in the saddle for most of your hill training. Even though it may feel more comfortable to stand up in a long climb, you are usually more efficient and faster while seated. To become an all-around climber, however, you must also become efficient at

Climbing is a primary skill.

standing up on the pedals. This will happen more often for smaller riders, while large cyclists may only stand up infrequently to stretch. Most riders will stand more during the faster pace and pressure of racing, requiring skill and upper-body strength.

Despite the importance of force in ascending, climbing is as much an art as it is a powerfest. The great climbers possess a dexterity and balance similar to ballet dancers. And they have the iron will to stay with the climb despite considerable suffering. To gain this perseverence requires lots of climbing, including competition with other riders. It's not something that can be quantified or completely described in words.

There is one strategy that seems universal: Size up the hill early, decide on gearing, and begin the climb with high cadence and at least one gear easier than is required to complete it. Less experienced climbers will often attack the hill at the base and pump themselves out of gas well before the crest. Both the laws of gravity and of physiology reward those who show discipline in gradually increasing effort up the climb, with enough energy left to gear up near the crest and increase speed immediately thereafter.

Training to Race

The key to longer time trialing is muscular endurance. If you've been doing long rides, climbing, and working into headwinds during your early career (or early season for experienced cyclists), you've already built a modicum of muscular endurance. Now is the time to fine-tune this quality for maximum speed over a 56-mile half-Iron bike course, remembering there are still 13.1 miles (21.1km) to run afterward.

The key to building the specific speed for long time trials is disciplined intervals at or below lactate threshold. Fortunately, cycling involves a low-impact, noneccentric motion that promotes longer intervals without much risk of injury. Athletes who have troubled recovery from running on a track can usually endure bike intervals without difficulty. In fact, many age-group triathletes do well at the half-Iron distance with only swim and bike intervals and little run training beyond Zone 3.

If you've been cycling over varied terrain with the proper warm-up and cool-down, you have already been doing intervals of a sort: increasing power, recovering, then increasing power again. Now we add more precise time controls to the variation of intensity, tailoring the effort to meet our specific needs. To gauge the optimal intensity and length for intervals, we test heart rate and power output at lactate threshold, easily done via a 30-minute time trial. The easiest version of this test requires only a heart rate monitor and stopwatch over a relatively flat, nonstop course.

After 48 hours of active recovery, warm up for 15–30 minutes and start riding hard; measure average heart rate from 10–30 minutes into the time trial. If you have a CompuTrainer, PowerTap, SRM, Ergomo, or similar device, you can add critical power (CP30) to your testing as outlined later in this section.

If we look at the wide spectrum of long-course triathletes, most will benefit from longer-duration intervals around lactate threshold (Zone 5a). Beginners preparing for their first half-Iron race may only be able to tolerate intervals in Zone 3 or low Zone 4, and thereby gain sufficient muscular endurance to finish the ride comfortably. Table 7.5 details useful long-course intervals.

Experts trying to win their division or the overall race may need to do a small amount of work above lactate threshold to build anaerobic endurance. But experienced athletes using the half-Iron race as a stepping stone to full Iron events should maintain the same constraints they would use for Ironman training intervals: that is, at or below lactate threshold.

There are complex variations of these intervals, including pyramid sets and sets based mostly on power output. You can also mix shorter

TABLE 7.5 USEFUL LONG-COURSE BIKE INTERVALS

TYPE	INTENSITY (ZONE)	QTY	DURATION (MIN)
Prep, Base 1	3	3–6	3–6
Base 2–3, Build	4–5a	2–3	5–12
Force-building	3–4	2–3	3–8
Long-ride	3–5a	1–3	5–20
Economy	4–5a	2–3	5–12
Hill	3–5a	2–9	1–12
Mental Focus	3–5a	10–20	3–5
Anaerobic Endurance	5a–b	3–4	2–5

intervals into longer tempo segments in Zone 3. If you have an outdoor power meter, you will find it a more reliable measure of interval pace and progress than your heart rate monitor. Maintaining target power output through the end of the last interval is usually harder than keeping your heart rate up, since power decreases over time using a steady heart rate. Conversely, as your fitness improves it will become harder to raise your heart rate to lactate threshold despite solid power output; high Zone 3 intervals may well serve the same purpose as lactate threshold intervals. This is good news: You are now generating race-ready power while conserving energy for the run.

Interval Tips and Tricks

Fundamental principles for bike interval training include:

- Prefer solitude for interval training, away from cyclists, other vehicles, and traffic stops. It is rare to find training partners doing intervals at the same speed on the same day. Triathlon intervals are best done on your time-trial bike in aero position as you will race. If you do join a partner or small group, prior agreement on pull-length and recovery is desirable.
- Start the interval slower than you think you should, especially the first one. Gradually build your effort throughout each interval, main-

REST (MIN)	QUALITY
1–2	Moderate effort, normal cadence
2–3	Popular long-course interval, 80–90rpm
2–3	Low cadence, big gear, smooth pedaling
3–5	Second half of longest ride or brick
2–3	High-cadence, easier gear, rapidly smooth pedaling
.5–3	Hill repeats with recovery descending same hill
1–5	Maintain steady cadence, awareness within ride
1–3	Limited use for half-Iron experts only

taining focus through the halfway point and going a little harder the last minute or so. You'll find this effect is instinctive if you gauge power output precisely.

- More or harder is not necessarily better. Physiology dictates a narrow range of effective interval training, well below the maximum output possible on a given day. Never try to "win" an interval—save it for the race. Consistently doing controlled-pace intervals with sufficient recovery is more productive to long-term racing success. If you finish your intervals thinking you could do one more without discomfort, don't do it. You have already achieved the optimal effect.
- Avoid intervals when tired, recovering from injury, or experiencing extreme lifestyle stress. The recovery required for bike intervals is less than running but still necessary. Don't be afraid to shorten intervals or substitute a moderate aerobic workout if your body or spirit is not ready.
- As your long-course race approaches, your intervals should closely resemble the muscular endurance required for that race. It is possible to build too much speed on the bike before a long-course race, which will encourage you to go out too hard on the bike. Beginners usually benefit from aerobic intervals in high Zone 3 as race simulation; advanced athletes should stay at or below lactate threshold. Remember that you are training for a triathlon, not a bike race.

Group Rides

Although half-Iron triathlons don't allow drafting, some group riding is helpful to triathletes. Most age groupers have substandard handling skills: I've watched triathletes fall down at even the slightest touch from another rider in the wind, something most roadies would barely notice. The in-close work required for peloton (pace-line) riding requires precise wheel alignment and attention to fast-changing conditions, which is useful on race day. The key for triathletes is to control the structure and amount of peloton riding just as they do interval training.

Peloton riding itself is a form of interval training. The more it resembles the useful heart rates, intensity durations, and recovery periods of intervals, the more beneficial it will be to triathletes. The ideal triathlete group is composed of three to five riders all doing fixed-length pulls at a high, steady speed in aero position, but this kind of group is very rare. The more chaotic or jumpy the pace, the less useful it becomes for triathletes.

The best thing about group rides is the fun factor. In some ways, road cycling is a more social sport than triathlon because of this group or team element. If you're a beginner doing nothing but solo rides, it's easy to get bored without a reference frame for improvement. Joining other riders of similar or somewhat stronger skills gives you feedback to your progress. As with any human endeavor, you learn a tremendous amount by watching a skilled practitioner.

This group fun and intensity is not without risks. A rider is more likely to fall in a hard-charging peloton than on a solo ride, though there is no evidence of more serious injury overall for group riders. Therefore, start conservative and join a smaller group riding at or slightly faster than your best speed. A beginning triathlete won't benefit much from riding with a Category 1–2 road cycling peloton, at least not for very long. Once you have a modicum of fitness and can ride for over two hours without undue fatigue, you can probably join most of the recreational group rides in your location.

Use the heart rate monitor as a governor of intensity during group workouts. It's easy for your heart rate to shoot sky-high in peloton accelerations, and you need to plan your strategy to allow for sufficient recovery while drafting. Beginners should indeed do very little pulling at the front and draft most of the ride. If and when you do start pulling, pick a specific time or distance that will raise your heart rate no higher than your lactate threshold, and then fall back to the rear once that's been achieved.

Different riding groups have different rules in the peloton, many unspoken. Just because riders are fast and experienced does not always mean they will be polite or safe in their peloton techniques. It's best to ask specific questions before the ride start and during the early warm-up, such as who the strongest riders are, when sprinting is likely, and when people might get dropped. Finding someone around your level and shadowing their behavior is a good way to learn the ropes.

The "cruel world" factor

If you start cycling as a triathlete and move to riding in a peloton later on, you'll eventually find out that life in the pack can be cruel. Road cyclists sometimes use cutthroat tactics to wear out other riders and leave the weaker behind—"survival of the fittest" is the law of the competitive peloton. Although it's rare for someone to be deliberately unsafe, the stronger, faster riders may appear to behave recklessly. Realize these tactics are probably legal in their racing universe, even if prohibited in triathlons.

Keep your eyes open and maintain a healthy distance between your front wheel and the rear wheel of the rider in front. Avoid "crossing wheels," which can quickly lead to disaster if someone swerves into you. Your front wheel is no match for the rigid and weighted rear wheel ahead of you. Conversely, be careful about your own changes in speed and direction while leading other riders; mistakes can start a domino effect, bringing several riders down.

Strong road cyclists are likely to frown upon using aerobars and perhaps time-trial frames when riding in the peloton. As a minimum safety factor, keep your hands on the handlebars or brake hoods and don't use your aerobars when drafting. You may be able to use them judiciously when in the lead position or catching up after being dropped with more than a 10m gap. Many roadies would prefer you not have aerobars at all, but it's not always practical to remove them for every weekend group ride. Fortunately, there are now more triathlete-oriented riding groups available, and nowadays triathletes meet with more tolerance from road cyclists.

If riding with a certain group appears unsafe or is just too hairy for your nerves, don't ride with them. Likewise, if you are not willing to follow their rules, find another group or ride alone. If you're having a really bad day, don't be ashamed to fall back or turn around and go home—it happens to the best of us sometimes.

TABLE 7.6 COMMON SKILL- AND POWER-BUILDING DEVICES

TOOL	DESCRIPTION	STRENGTHS	LIMITERS
CompuTrainer	Sophisticated indoor trainer with power measurement, computerized courses, and SpinScan analysis of left-right pedal stroke.	Accurate, durable, useful for testing. Useful for skillbuilding. Relatively portable.	More expensive than simple indoor trainers. Indoor training can become boring.
Fixed-Gear Bike	Modified frame without derailleurs and only one cogset on the wheel. The traditional method for improving pedal stroke smoothness and strength.	Promotes smooth pedal stroke. Forces focus on technique rather than speed. Simplified riding and maintenance.	Risky for beginners unable to control leg rotation. Not practical in hilly terrain. Extensive modification required.
Power Cranks	Sophisticated crankset that uncouples right and left cranks so that they turn independently. Available in fixed or variable-length cranks.	Promotes balanced pedal stroke by inflating any differences in right-left leg strength. Encourages smoothness and consistency.	Causes leg fatigue. Can cause injury with excessive use. Requires semi-permanent installation on training frame. Fairly expensive.
Power Tap	Measures power as with CompuTrainer, but is mounted in wheel for outdoor use.	Measures critical power outdoors in actual training and/or racing conditions.	Requires special wheel building with hub. Expensive in lighter models.
SRM	Measures power, installed in crank	Measures critical power outdoors in actual training and/or racing conditions.	Expensive, not easily moved to other bikes. Very expensive in ten-speed solid-axle models.

CONTINUED

TABLE 7.6 CONTINUED

TOOL	DESCRIPTION	STRENGTHS	LIMITERS
Ergomo	Similar to SRM, installed in crank.	Measures critical power outdoors in actual training and/or racing conditions. Less expensive than SRM.	Expensive and currently unavailable for ten-speed solid-axle crank systems.

The good news is that if you survive the suffering of the road peloton, you will be a stronger and mentally tougher rider in triathlons. Peloton riding was the driving force for improvement in my first two years of triathlon, and it gave me an enduring love for the sport. Getting dropped by stronger riders was one of the most miserable—yet motivating—experiences of my life. I resolved not to let this happen again, and by the end of the season I could stay with the best riders in the group.

The time to avoid peloton riding is in the weeks immediately preceding your long-course A race. The anaerobic endurance and speed used in the peloton may falsely program you to go out too hard in the longer time trial, leaving little for the run afterward.

The Power Revolution

The most significant development in cycling for the new millennium has been the rapid expansion of power training. Reliable, lightweight power meters began trickling in by the mid-1990s, and they caused nothing short of a revolution. Lance Armstrong credited his first Tour de France victory in 1999 to his use of the power meter to develop a new style of training, and European racers quickly followed suit. As prices fell, amateur cyclists and triathletes began using the tools effectively.

Beginning triathletes are advised to focus on heart rate monitoring to establish pace on their thoroughly aerobic rides. After a certain facility and fitness is achieved, testing of power output can guide bike fitting and establishing lactate threshold intensity. Initial testing can be conducted by a coach on a CompuTrainer to measure watts without necessarily investing in an expensive outdoor power meter (see Table 7.6). Intermediate and

TABLE 7.7 USE OF POWER VERSUS HEART RATE AND PERCEIVED EXERTION

ISSUE	HEART RATE	PERCEIVED EXERTION	POWER	POWER METER ADVANTAGE
Time	Lags 20–120 seconds behind effort	Subjective, depending upon rate of change	Immediate, objective feedback	Intensity changes immediately display, directly revealing cause and effect.
Steady-state (aerobic)	Very low at start, may go up or down for longer rides	Too easy for useful, steady pacing	Held moderately low through workout	Allows objective and accurate measurement aerobic threshold (AeT) workouts.
Intervals	Low at start, rises toward end	Low at start, steadily rises	High at start, steady average throughout	Prevents starting intervals too hard. Encourages build in effort while holding power steady. Pushes final interval segment to maintain power.
Climbing	Low at start, rises throughout	Depends on body mass and fitness	Novice: spikes at start, decays at crest Expert: steady from start to finish	Trains climbers to steadily release energy for the whole climb, instead of attacking at the bottom.
Training Load	May rise or fall with overtraining	Subjective, less accurate for long-course fatigue	Falls rapidly with overtraining or insufficient recovery	Cleary indicates training plateaus and emphasizes the need for sufficient rest and recovery.

advanced riders should consider investment in one of the lightweight road models if they are serious about moving to the next level. The specific time-trial fitness required for triathlon is well served by the power meter.

Most modern power devices integrate heart rate, speed, and cadence into one monitor, so you can easily combine these measurements. Although wattage is a useful value, that does not mean we stop using our HRMs. In fact, for long-course training and especially during the race itself, the HRM can provide the "master number" for determining pace and energy usage. No matter how many watts you generate, you still must consume enough calories to finish the 56-mile ride comfortably, with some left over for the run. Athletes who can blow away the competition in an Olympic-distance race often find they run out of gas in the half-Iron venue. Calorie and fluid consumption are closely tied to heart rate. Some of the advantages of power meters are listed in Table 7.7.

Power-based Testing

We've repeatedly emphasized the importance of regular testing for all three sports, but the power meter makes cycling the most precisely measured discipline. Someday we may have similar microelectronic devices implanted in shoes or perhaps underwater, but for now cycling technology leads the way.

The original form of power testing required a stationary ergometer such as the CompuTrainer. As with running treadmills, results were not always comparable to real-world training and racing conditions on the road. Fortunately, devices like the wheel-based PowerTap and crank-based SRM allow us to conduct a simple thirty-minute time trial on the road. In fact, when you budget which device to buy first, go with the outdoor power meter before the indoor power trainer. You're more likely to test regularly if you can do it on a regular outdoor ride, and these devices can still be used indoors on a basic wind, magnetic, or fluid trainer.

I recommend the thirty-minute time trial as the ideal long-course triathlete test for determining lactate threshold and muscular endurance on the bike. The natural pace that most athletes will employ for this period is likely to produce lactate threshold heart rate and power output. Anything shorter is likely to result in values more valid for anaerobic endurance. Anything longer (such as the popular 40km distance) is likely to cause fatigue and degradation of power in all but the strongest time trialists. You can go hard for thirty minutes within a training week without adversely affecting other workouts. Note that it closely resembles the effort required for long-course interval sets like 3×10 minutes at LT, omitting the rest periods. It can even substitute for your weekly interval workout.

There should be at least forty-eight hours of active recovery before attempting the thirty-minute time trial; that is, no breakthrough workouts. It's easier to schedule this rest within your recovery week, which jibes with our goal of monthly time-trial testing. Try to eat normally the night before and the day of the test, allowing three hours or more for digestion. Avoid caffeine before the test since it raises heart rate.

Ideally, you should find a relatively flat piece of road without traffic lights, excessive traffic, high wind, or difficult turns. Practically, this may be difficult to find. If you train in a relatively windy or hilly locale, you may want to balance their effect with an out-and-back course. Once you find the best course available, use the same one for successive tests. In the real outdoor world, there are no perfectly precise tests.

For optimum performance, you need to warm up at least fifteen minutes, but we recommend a longer warm-up of thirty minutes, including a few accelerations to test-pace with long recoveries. Testing on hot days requires extensive fluid and electrolytes on hand; testing on cold days can mean taking a bathroom break before the test. Some riders like to get off the bike for a few minutes before a time trial, while others like to roll up and just start pedaling hard.

Use the lap start button on your power meter to begin the session and quickly select optimal gearing and cadence. As with intervals and other muscular endurance efforts, it's better to start slower than you think and slowly build effort. Since we're trying to achieve a fairly steady power value for lactate threshold, early spikes followed by late-session decay will not provide a useful baseline. Once you begin the test and get a few minutes into the time trial, it's better to continue it to completion even if there are some "ringers" thrown in, such as traffic or equipment variances. If you have to come to a long stop for something like a flat, then abort the test.

As you hit the 30-minute mark, hit the lap button again to record the time, average heart rate, and average power for the 30-minute interval. If you have the computer interface for your power meter (recommended), continue your ride home and load the values into your computer for analysis. If not, record them manually in your logbook.

The name for the average power in your 30-minute time trial is the *critical power* over 30 minutes, and we write this as CP30. You can test for similar values such as CP12 for a shorter time trial or CP180 for a long ride. But it's the CP30 figure that is closest to lactate threshold power. We combine it with the lactate threshold heart rate (LTHR), which is the average heart rate from minutes 10–30 of the time trial. These two numbers provide the key to all our other training zones and goals in the near future.

As we created target heart rate zones of 5–15bpm based on tested values, we create a range of plus or minus 5 percent around the CP30 value for threshold training zone. If your CP30 value was 250 watts, your range for lactate threshold training would be about 238–262 watts. When performing muscular-endurance intervals such as 3×10 minutes, we would target our power in this range for the entire interval.

Most half-Iron competitors can prepare for racing knowing only the CP30 value; however, those wishing to win their division or the overall

TABLE 7.8 CORRELATION BETWEEN HEART RATE, POWER, EXERTION, AND RACE TRAINING

HEART RATE ZONE	CRITICAL POWER (MIN)	PERCEIVED EXERTION	TYPICAL USAGE (AVERAGED)
5c	0.2–1	Maximal	Road and track cycling
5b	6–12	Very hard	Road cycling
5c	30	Hard	Sprint- and Olympic-distance triathlon
4	60	Moderately hard to hard	Olympic-distance triathlon, expert half-Iron
3	90	Moderately hard	Half-Iron, expert Ironman
2	180–240	Steady	Ironman, beginner half-Iron, ultracycling
1	12	Easy	Beginner Ironman, ultracycling

race may benefit from knowing their anaerobic endurance value as determined by CP12. Experts don't necessarily need to be training at CP12 intensity; however, some time may well be spent there during the race.

We can tabulate a rough correlation among critical power, heart rate zones, and race intensities (Table 7.8). Understand that heart rate and power output are physically dissociated, however useful it may be for us to conceptually relate them. Your heart does not know or care about the exact power output from your legs. Nor are races necessarily won by the athlete with the best critical power. Beginners and experts will exhibit a very wide range of zones in the same event, and even experts riding close together may be doing so with significantly different intensity plans. As with triathlon in general, real-world experience trumps theory. You have to go out, do the testing, and then race to find your own correlation.

Racing with Power

There is a trend toward racing with a power meter that's now affecting triathlon. It began with road cyclists without much concern for aerodynamics. More recently, triathletes in Iron-distance races have been using the SRM or Ergomo in combination with their aero wheel setups to ride that "razor's edge" between a top bike split and overpacing. Current availability of lighter wheel-based units like the PowerTap SL are bringing age-group cyclists into the race-with-power group. There are pros and cons for racing with a power meter:

- Beginners and many intermediate triathletes should stick to their HRM to gauge pace, and in fact most intermediate half-Iron racers will be able to race strong and conserve energy based on judicious gearing, cadence, and heart rate considerations.
- If you are a top age grouper or professional triathlete using a disc wheel, it's probably not worth the loss in speed to use a spoked rear wheel just to measure power, unless the half-Iron distance is a B race to prepare for a full-Iron race later on. If you use a crank-based power meter (SRM or Ergomo), then aerodynamics are not an issue.
- You can race several times a year in half-Iron races without recovery problems, so using a power meter in earlier races may give you clues for the optimum pace in "big-time" long-course events such as national championships or worlds qualifiers.

- The power meter will not necessarily tell you about fuel consumption, hydration, or nutrition. Strong cyclists can generate steadily high watts without much leg fatigue, yet may be overreaching their ability to process calories for the whole race distance. You still need a heart rate monitor to discern inner physiology.
- A rough guideline for veterans with half-Iron experience is to target power at around 80–87 percent of CP30. Elites trying to win the race may indeed go higher, while masters athletes may win their age group using considerably lower bike power, but saving for a fast run.
- Most riders should avoid going more than 10 percent over CP30 watts when climbing grades at or below 10 percent. Some heavier riders who can also climb well, however, are an exception to this rule, requiring more power to maintain adequate cadence uphill.
- Use gearing, cadence, and the power meter to constrain intensity, aiming for maximum climbing power at the crest, not the bottom, of the hill.
- Start with slightly less power and gradually increase in the second half of the ride. Remember that steady-state power is not like steady-state heart rate: It's increasingly difficult to maintain power on a 56-mile ride.
- Watch for power and heart rate spikes right out of the swim transition, especially when there are early hills (common in top half-Iron events). Changes in blood flow, adrenaline, and psychology make hearts beat faster and muscles burn more calories, yet you do not feel the fatigue until much later in the ride and run, when it's too late to recover that lost energy.

CHAPTER 8

Running Skills

No, no . . . I was not very talented. My basic speed was low. Only with will-power was I able to reach this world best standard in long-distance running.

—Emil Zatopek, who won the Olympic triple crown of distance running: the marathon, 5,000m, and 10,000m races in the same year (Helsinki 1952)

RUNNING: THE NATURAL SPORT

If swimming depends on technique and cycling favors power, some would say running is based on talent. It's something we naturally learn as toddlers, and we remember our first experiences in school when we ran 20–50 meters or so against the other kids. We noticed one or two children were considerably faster than the others, and if you tracked these children through secondary school, they would probably be among the fastest sprinters when reaching adulthood.

Sometime around adolescence the endurance runners came forth, usually smaller than the sprinters, and they formed a select group who were willing to suffer more through longer workouts and excelled in running the mile, 1,500 meters, or cross-country races. If you were lucky enough to be in this group, you may have been told you were a "talented distance runner," and were probably coached in the basics of interval training for races from 800 through 5,000 meters. Luckier still, you might even have had a skillful endurance coach who taught you about heart rate monitoring or nutrition. But most runners were motivated by their early talent and often succeeded in spite of mediocre or absent coaching in technique. They just followed their heart on to bigger venues in college and beyond, where competition brought them good teachers.

Then come the rest of us: the ones who never ran distance as kids, though perhaps we had some experience in team sports where sprinting 40–100 meters was valuable. This group forms the majority of age-group triathletes worldwide. Most of these do not view themselves as "talented runners," yet many excel in triathlons, can win their division, and have strong run splits compared to other triathlete runners. They often do well in age-group road running races. If you spot them at your local race, they do not necessarily look like the runner type.

What's going on here? If running were based mostly on talent, how would these athletes develop the skill and the will to race with the talented folks? The classic answer from many veterans would be: "They did lots of intervals and speed work. They learned to run fast by training fast." If these triathletes were specializing in sprint- and Olympic-distance racing, there may be some truth here. Many time-restricted amateur athletes do well in national short-course championships simply by training fast through brief weekly volumes.

Yet when we come to half- and full Iron-distance races, we find these speedy runners are sometimes caught by athletes who have less foot speed. It's not an uncommon story for the slower athlete at the track interval training session to pass his training partners in a half- or full marathon run during a race. What's going on here?

- The running speed required for a competitive half-Ironman time is not that fast, certainly not compared to national- or world-class runners, or even compared to the winners of a local half-marathon running race. Raw foot speed is a powerful weapon, especially for pros, but it is not as overpowering as in stand-alone running.
- Running after a hard 56-mile (90km) bike is not the same thing as only running. Great marathoners like Frank Shorter quickly found this out when they attempted triathlons. Indeed, the typical age grouper's run split may indicate bike muscular endurance as much as running ability.
- Technique can be learned considerably beyond innate ability. Good running form through the end of a half-Iron race rewards the

efficient runner while others may tire. As Coach Rich Strauss once said, "He who slows down the least finishes first."

Even if you were born talented, these factors are still important for stretching your limits and avoiding injury. Since talented runners are starting out closer to the limits of human performance, attention to small details in technique can make the difference in elite placement. As with the other two sports, research and practical experience have shown that working on economy pays the biggest dividends in the long run.

The Plague of Running Injuries

Medical researchers at the Centers for Disease Control define an epidemic as an illness that affects 10 percent or more of the population. Even the worst urban breakouts of the Black Plague in Europe infected only about 50 percent of the population. Yet when we study the modern running population, we find that 55–70 percent experience serious injury during their running careers, and a significant number of these are forced to stop running entirely. Add lesser, unreported problems like tendinitis, which reduces training volume and intensity, and some sports doctors claim the running injury rate over time is nearly 100 percent. We do not exaggerate when we claim that running injuries are a plague, and they affect the fast and slow alike.

This is a shame, since running is the most natural of the three sports, requiring little equipment and no special skills. Our Paleolithic ancestors were running most of their lives, averaging a slow jog of about 10 miles per day with occasional bursts of speed to chase down (or run away from) other mammals. They ate a natural diet of wild game and unprocessed nuts, fruits, and vegetables, requiring only about thirty-five hours per week "working" to maintain their food and shelter—the rest of the time was free with clean air, pure water, peace and quiet, and none of the "lifestyle diseases" of our civilization. They were born endurance athletes, and indeed we retain in our genes the highest long-range endurance of any land mammal. How did modern life turn running sour?

The first factor is simple: Our ancestors ran and walked barefoot. They learned the most efficient, lowest-impact method of propulsion from an early age and never had to "unlearn it" to wear shoes. We usually fit shoes on our infants as soon as possible, to "train" them to walk properly. The second factor is the rigid paved surface that most of us train and race upon. We unlearn our natural instincts of minimizing foot impact via barefoot running, and then we go out and run on the hardest substance possible. It's no wonder we get hurt. The real miracle is that some are able to run fast and long and *not* get injured very often.

The Kenyan Parable

One of the only places left on earth where humans have not unlearned natural running efficiency is the African continent, especially the central and eastern regions. When Kenyan runners burst on the endurance running scene, first at Olympic middle distances and later in the marathon, they dominated these events as no other nation had done. And they show no signs of slacking off.

Coaches wondered how they did it and made some initial assumptions that it must have something to do with their aerobic capacity (VO_2max), lactate tolerance, or special training methods. Some speculated that East Africans were just "born distance runners" similar to the way West African descendants dominated sprinting in the Western Hemisphere. But these teleological theories were not proven by the scientific evidence. Kenyan runners did not have aerobic capacity or lactate threshold levels any greater than trained distance runners from other continents. Their body composition was comparable to other competitive runners. When their training habits were studied in the 1970s and 1980s, they were found to be less structured than Western methods. It's only in the last decade or two that they began to train under expert coaches.

The answer to the riddle of Kenyan speed was surprisingly simple: They ran barefoot on natural trails most of their lives, and they ran at naturally high cadence. Without any external prodding or training, this turned many of them into fast runners in childhood, and even faster racers as adults. The Kenyans were not necessarily stronger, nor did they have bigger hearts or lungs, but they ran more efficiently, able to maintain a higher rate of speed with less energy expenditure. In races like the marathon, or in our case running after a long bike in a half-Iron race, this is the most important factor.

The Running Triangle

We assume that you want to run faster. There are only three ways to do this:

- **Increase aerobic capacity (VO_2max):** This factor is greatly influenced by genetics and body composition. It is difficult to change

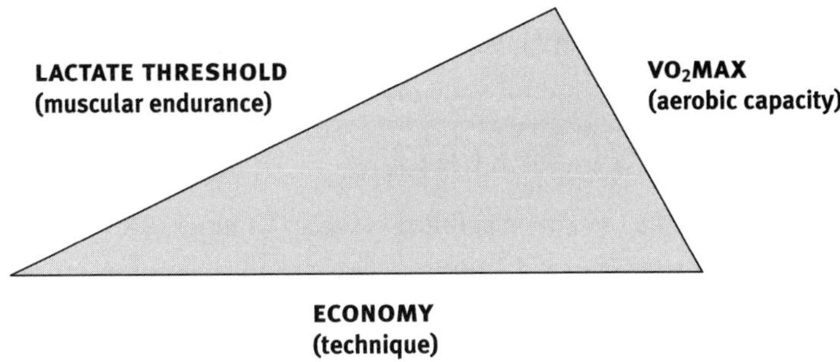

FIGURE **8.1**
Relative importance of three running attributes

once a point of general fitness is achieved. For most age groupers, good nutrition and weight control affect this number as much as training. Workouts to improve VO$_2$max are stressful to bones and joints and often require extensive recovery.

- **Raise lactate threshold:** The ability to tolerate lactate (which we now better understand as the ability to process positive hydrogen ions) can be trained by specific muscular endurance (ME) training. For the long-course athlete, running near LT accounts for a small percentage of volume.
- **Improve economy:** For age groupers and pros alike, this is the most productive side of the triangle. Relatively small changes in running technique can amplify improvements in running times, reduce the probability of injury, and promote faster recovery.

Efficient Running Systems

We'll focus on improving economy in this chapter, since it resists injury for beginning runners and promotes speed for intermediate to advanced athletes. Fortunately, there have been several systems developed in the past decade to help achieve an economical style of running, and triathletes have led the way in adopting and promoting them. As with cycling and periodization, some of these changes moved westward from Eastern Europe, notably by Nicholas Romanov, Ph.D., a former Russian university professor who developed the "Pose" method of running. He has drawn on previous classical methods from other sports and ballet. These techniques have been further refined in the United States by coaches like Ken Mierke and his method of "Evolution Running." We'll rely on Mierke's work, and you can learn more about his method at www.EvolutionRunning.com.

THE RUNNING MATRIX

Stripped to the bare essentials, running is the art of moving forward as fast and as long as possible with minimal waste and maximum efficiency. The only equipment required is a pair of running shoes, and this only because we usually train and race on a hard surface. The five forces that affect this forward motion are propulsion, vertical lift, impact, acceleration, balance, and limb movement:

- **Propulsion:** the force moving the runner forward, the most important force to maximize. The greater the forward propulsion, the faster the speed.
- **Vertical lift:** the force causing upward movement of the head and body, perpendicular to the direction of travel. Vertical motion does nothing to help the runner move forward, and wastes energy that could be used to move forward. It also increases the total space the body must travel to cover a given ground. Note that bicycles have zero vertical displacement (stump-jumping mountain bikes excepted) and therefore have a much faster speed than runners. All the force is directed forward. As with swimming, head-bobbing is discouraged.
- **Impact:** the force generated when the foot strikes the ground, including energy expended by the legs, hips, and back muscles to support the upper body. On pavement, this is actually 375–400 pounds per foot strike for a 150-pound runner, up to 72,000 pounds per minute of stress on the body.
- **Acceleration:** the force required to restart the foot back up and forward. It must absorb all of the prior impact forces and then add more energy to overcome gravity and keep moving forward.
- **Balance:** the ability to keep the center of mass above the feet (on flat terrain) and steadily moving forward.
- **Limb movement:** Moving the limbs requires energy, and anything that does not provide propulsion should be minimized. This includes eccentric movement of the legs in the stride and the extraneous motion of the arms, head, and so on.

Science of Running Speed

As with the swim stroke, there are two determinants of running speed: stride length and stride frequency. But the value of length and frequency are inverted from sprinting. Whereas sprinting up to 200 meters may rely on longer strides to produce speeds nearing 30mph, distance running depends on higher cadence and shorter stride length. One of the distinguishing characteristics of the champion Kenyan marathoners is the ability to maintain high cadence of 90–95rpm even in the last grueling marathon miles (one "revolution" includes both right and left foot strikes). Unfortunately, many of us who ran sprints or played team sports in high school learned the long-stride sprinting techniques that are in fact the enemy of fast and injury-free distance running.

A longer stride involves more vertical displacement, which requires covering more distance and increases the impact stress of foot striking. It often involves straightening the knee and landing toward the heel, which transmits greater shock up the leg and to the rest of the body. A shorter stride, however, takes advantage of the springlike nature of the forefoot, Achilles tendon, and calf, which form an elastic band to absorb the shock of impact and recoil for acceleration toward the next step. If you learn to gradually increase your cadence, you will naturally shorten your stride. Do not attempt a sudden increase in cadence—develop it over time with drills.

These world-class marathon runners display the correct method of striking the ground with the ball of foot. As you might guess, they are leading the race.

You can test cadence by counting right foot strikes up to 90 and see if this takes more or less than 60 seconds, or you can use a wristwatch lap-counter to measure the number of right foot strikes per minute. Some coaches encourage the use of a musical metronome set to 90 beats per minute to encourage proper cadence.

Foot Strike

Linked to the skills of short stride and rapid cadence is the foot strike. At impact a tremendous amount of stored energy is compressed into the foot against the ground, much the same way as a golf or tennis ball deforms when bouncing. The faster the bounce, the greater the rebound, which is a why a golf ball bounces higher or flies off the face of a club much faster than a tennis ball. The tennis ball dissipates much of the stored up energy while flattening against the striking surface. The faster your feet can rebound from the ground, the less energy is wasted in useless frictional heat.

Many runners incorrectly strike the ground first with the heel, then roll forward and off the front of the foot. The initial impact shocks the entire leg, and energy is lost while the foot rolls forward, maintaining contact with the ground. A considerable force must be exerted to reaccelerate the foot back up again. Heel striking is in fact a good way to put on the brakes when you're running too fast. Imagine running down a hill and into a wall: You would start to lean back on your heels to slow down. Many runners are doing this unconsciously with every step.

The optimal foot strike touches the ground first with the forefoot, which includes the mid- to ball-of-foot region. This does not mean stretching to run on your toes, but lifting the leg straight up and putting it straight down in a relaxed fashion. Not only does this minimize the time the foot is in contact with the ground, but it also allows the stride to more closely follow the slope of the terrain, moving forward instead of digging

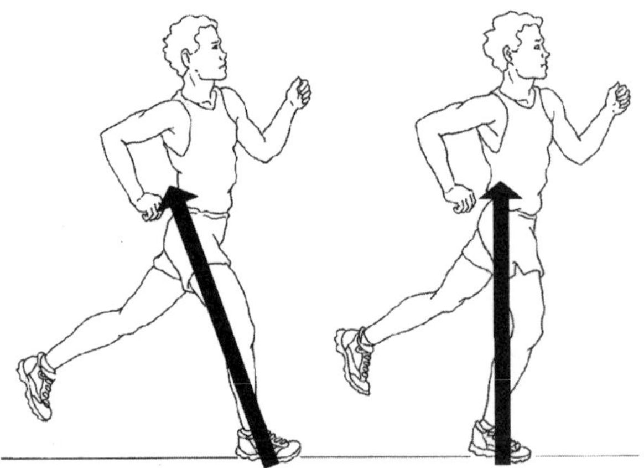

FIGURE 8.2

Incorrect (L) and correct (R) foot-strike speed

down and hopping back up with every stride. The stress on key injury areas like the knees, shins, and lower back is reduced.

One of the easiest drills to prevent heel striking is one of the most simple: running in place. Keeping your center of mass over the feet and simply lifting them up and down in place naturally requires you to stay on the forefoot to maintain balance. Another good practice is to simply hop with both feet at the same time, focusing on keeping weight on the forefoot. If you try to strike toward your heels, you will probably start moving backward! Not only does this drill give you the "feel" of striking the forefoot, it builds essential strength in the muscles and tendons involved in a good foot strike.

Propulsion

Propelling the body forward is the goal of running, but there are more and less efficient methods. A method some runners use is the "toe-off," where the knee is straightened to propel off the toes. This motion causes vertical lift and excessive use of the quadriceps muscles. The smaller quadriceps fatigue more rapidly than larger muscle groups like the hips and are less efficient in generating propulsion. For triathletes, using muscle groups other than the quadriceps for running is important because they are already fatigued from the hard bike of long-course events. One sign displayed by fans at an Ironman race jokingly offered "New Quads for Sale!" on the run course, and I'm sure many would have paid dearly at that point.

Another pitfall can quickly fatigue the other side of the thigh, the hamstrings. In this case the knee is overflexed at the foot strike in a pulling-through motion initiated by the hamstring. Although the hamstrings are useful to efficient running, they should not bear the load alone. Combining them with the larger hips and gluteus maximus (glutes) allows for stronger running while using less energy.

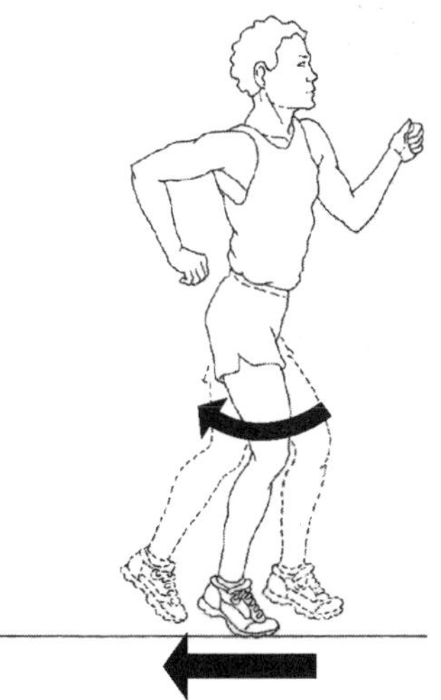

FIGURE 8.3
Preferred method of propulsion. Note slightly bent knee with foot-drag movement.

To achieve this combination of large muscle groups, the preferred method of propulsion uses a constant, slightly bent knee in a foot-drag motion, not unlike the mud-scrape sensation at the bottom of a bike pedal stroke. This method will correctly employ the glutes and prevent bouncing and undue thigh fatigue (Figure 8.3).

One drill to promote this ability is the hip extension. Stand on one leg while extending the other leg rearward, knee slightly bent. Hold this position and maintain balance over the feet without leaning forward. This drill is harder than you might think and will take some time before you can effectively hold the position and maintain balance. Gradually increase the length of the hold and the number of repetitions.

No matter how efficiently we strike with the forefoot, there is still an aspect of deceleration when we touch the ground. We are traveling forward at 6–10mph, and suddenly our foot slows down. If our foot is still moving forward when it hits, we are in fact moving at a negative velocity relative to the ground passing by, increasing the shock to the feet and the legs. If we begin to accelerate the foot backward *before* the ground impact, we minimize this velocity differential, and our stride more closely resembles a bicycle wheel rolling out of the way of the pavement underneath.

Limb Movement

Both the legs and arms contribute to forward running motion. When we expend energy to propel forward, it is energy well spent. When we use excessive energy to move the legs in the air, we are wasting energy. After the foot strike, we want the lower leg to naturally swing back and up toward the buttocks without having to "pull through" with our hamstrings. If we drive forward with the knee, allowing our foot to lag behind a bit, strike with the forefoot, and then simply lift the foot up, it will naturally swing back. Do not pause at the rear of the pendulum swing; simply let the foot start to swing forward. This pendulum motion is most efficient when the thigh muscles are relaxed, initiating the motion from the hips.

Another issue for runners is the arm swing, and again we are burdened with misconceptions derived from sprinting. When running 100 meters all out, the arms become an active blood pump to facilitate a brief anaerobic effort and a counterbalance against an explosive, long stride. Their swing is pronounced and definite, and great sprinters usually have large biceps. Distance runners also swing their arms, but they provide minimal blood flow. They are simply pendulums that complement the swinging legs below. Their motion should be relaxed and economical, and a shorter pendulum (arms bent 90 degrees or more) is faster and requires less energy than a longer pendulum with arms sticking farther out. There is a tendency for runners to stretch their arms out farther when climbing or trying to kick at the end of a race to compensate for fatigue and a degrading running style.

Crossing the arms is another common problem, often caused by excessive rotation of the shoulders and torso—yet another symptom of overstriding. Shoulders should be squared up with minimal rotation, and the arms should swing front-to-rear with minimal side-to-side deviation. Hands are best kept relaxed and slightly contracted by curling the fingers gently in the thumb.

The Earth is Not Flat

As with cycling, it's unlikely that all your races will be in flatland. Although climbing is not as critical in terms of speed as it is in cycling, the ability of hills to stress the musculoskeletal system is greater. Ask anyone who has raced what they thought would be an "easy" downhill marathon, and they will tell you that running down hills is indeed more difficult and painful than climbing or pacing the flats. We can use what we learned about propulsion and foot strike to optimize running in all three dimensions.

Up the hill

I suggested a shorter stride and higher cadence for faster running, and can only double that advice for uphill running. Facing a steep hill causes some runners to struggle upward with longer strides—less effective because the airborne portion of the stride moves even slower as gravity's effects increase. It's faster and requires less energy to shorten the stride and maintain steady cadence as you move up the hill.

The body will naturally lean into the slope of the hill, so that it becomes impossible to heel strike up a steep grade. If you've been drilling and practicing to strike with the forefoot in the flats, then doing so in the hills will not shock the legs. Drive the knee upward and then pull the foot into the ground, maintaining an acute angle with the slope. As with flat running, minimize contact time with the ground; springing forward is even more important running up hills.

Down the hill

One of the potentially painful possibilities for a runner is a steep downhill toward the end of a long race. There are many long-distance courses with these downhill sections toward the end (Buffalo Springs in Texas or the "hot corner" as you approach Ali'i Drive in Kona, for example). But if you plan and execute effectively, you can lay down some fast mile splits and beat your goal at the finish.

Lean forward slightly down the hill, with the foot strike coming slightly behind the center of gravity. Roll down the hill parallel to the slope, much as a bike wheel descends effortlessly. Gravity will aid your propulsion, and your main job is to "get out of the way" of the forward momentum. Many runners have an unconscious fear of falling (or perhaps not so unconscious) and instinctively try to brake the speed. Optimal descending on the run should leave you feeling as if you are about to fall over, but not quite. The feet squirt forward at a high cadence down the hill, yet another reason to practice cadence drills in training and to run the flats at 90rpm or higher.

Shoes

Before we leave our discussion on running technique, I'd like to say a few words about shoes. The modern running shoe has done more to promote distance running than any other factor. Bad shoe choices, however, have probably caused more injuries than anything else. Before running shoes, people ran marathons in basketball sneakers, and only the hearty few were willing to endure that kind of pain. We do recommend barefoot running on a grassy field for training drills, but it's unlikely you can run barefoot very far on pavement. You will have to buy some running shoes to cushion the impact.

As with triathlon bikes, there are several good brands, and the choice between them is anatomical and largely personal. There is no absolute rule to fit a shoe, but your chances of getting one properly fit increase if you go to a dedicated running store to purchase them. As with bike purchases, very few runners choose the right shoe on the first try, so don't feel awkward if you have to bring some back to the store the next day or switch to another brand after some races.

If you're relatively new to running, or are moving up into longer distance training for the half-Iron distance, it's probably better to buy your shoes at retail prices at a local shop you can trust. Check their return policy, and don't be afraid to ask questions. Once you've found a working brand and model, you can buy two to three pairs together for most of the season. Shoe models change every year, and many people lament that their favorite model was altered.

When Bill Bowerman and Phil Knight created the first waffle trainer, it was a revolution in cushioning and stability. Shoe manufacturers continued to increase the cushioning, thinking that more shock absorption was better. Like padded bike saddles, there is a limit to cushioning effectiveness over longer run distances. Some running coaches have even advocated the least amount of cushioning possible, suggesting running flats or cheap running shoes are better for all training than the full-featured expensive models.

I'm going to come out somewhere in the middle of this spectrum, advocating a firmer shoe, but with the possibility of stabilizers or motion control for larger or injury-prone runners. I'm a larger runner racing in marathon and double-marathon runs and definitely prefer the large stabilizer shoes for high-volume training. But I'm sure I would do well with a simpler, lighter, and cheaper shoe if I trained shorter than the half-marathon, and in fact that is what I use for most long-course races.

Racing flats are recommended only for runs up to 5–10K; only elite marathoners (weighing 30–40 pounds less than most age-group triathletes) can endure them in longer races. Beginners should avoid racing flats entirely.

Some runners need special orthotics, and the trend in modern high-end shoes is to incorporate many orthotic benefits right out of the box. If you have specialized medical problems, you need advice from a physician, kinesiologist, or similar professional who also has experience running distances around your longest race. Some of the classic problems requiring orthotics are caused by deficient running technique. If you become a more efficient runner and strike with the midfoot to forefoot, following other drills and techniques in this chapter, you may find you no longer need orthotics or shoes with thicker padding.

RUN TRAINING

Triathlon is growing faster than any other endurance event, including its component sports, so it's no wonder that many athletes are beginning without much running experience. Running has been a prolific feeder into triathlon, but you may set a half-Iron race as your first goal without much running experience. Longer running races are a good platform for moving into triathlon, but the volume required for long-course triathlons does not demand high-volume running. An athlete training for a half-Iron triathlon can do quite well running no more than someone training for a 10K run.

The reason for reduced running volume lies in the source of aerobic base or long-range endurance. For solo runners, most of their training time is spent maintaining this aerobic base, pounding out the mileage. For long-course triathletes, most of their aerobic base comes from cycling, narrowing the focus of running to economy (technique), muscular endurance, and race-specific training off the bike. Many strong runners who raced in stand-alone half- and full marathons are able to cut their run volume by 50 percent or more and still race well in long-course triathlons. This is good news for beginning runners who sometimes develop injuries due to increases in volume or intensity. A study on beginners preparing for their first marathon showed that subjects who spent their first five months walking on half their training days were only half as likely to become injured as those who did all their training on the run. A balanced triathlon training schedule encourages ample recovery and requires no large volume, even for the half-Iron distance.

Beginning to Run

If you studied the previous section on run technique, you are well on your way to learning to run properly and avoid injury—the reason we included technique first. The following story illustrates the power of learning technique as a beginning runner: One of my athletes began his career in triathlon and running with a four-hour marathon, which wasn't bad for a beginning college student. He began studying run technique (very similar to the methods outlined in this chapter), learning the right way from the start. Within only two years he was running a 3:15 marathon in a full Ironman after a sub-five-hour bike, and the following year he had the best American amateur time at the Ironman world championship in Hawaii, passing some good pros on the run segment.

The goal for beginners is to start with lower volume and gradually build. It's better to think in terms of minutes running in a heart rate training zone rather than mileage or minutes per mile. And the run zones for beginners are 1 and 2 only. Runs of 20–45 minutes three or four times a week are enough to start, with one of these coming immediately after a medium bike (also known as a *brick, combination,* or *transition* workout). There is no need to run fast, provided you are focusing on the fundamentals of technique—speed will come naturally. If you find you cannot maintain the proper running form, you are running too far or too fast. As with the other two sports, it's better to start more slowly than you think you should and gradually build intensity to a moderate level.

Don't underestimate the value of walking, including hiking, backpacking, or even golf if you walk and carry your own clubs. Separate walks can be used on nonrunning days, or longer runs can be interspersed by short 30–60-second walks every mile or so. I've used this latter technique in marathon and ultramarathon training to maintain intensity, avoid injury, and maintain good running form for many hours. And it's the method I recommend for athletes racing their first half- or full Ironman event: walking each mile-marker aid station for around 20–30 seconds.

How long do you remain a beginning runner? Even if you came from cycling or swimming with excellent fitness, you should constrain volume and intensity on the run. Lance Armstrong (with his legendary VO_2max numbers) complained that returning to running after winning seven Tour de France titles was agonizing, just three miles. Your aerobic base from another endurance sport should speed you through the learning process in around three to six months.

Beginners coming from no endurance experience whatsoever, or those who have significant weight-loss goals, may take a year or two before moving to the next level.

Long-range Endurance

To finish a four- to seven-hour half-Iron event takes prodigious long-range endurance, and the evidence of this stamina (or lack of it) will show up dramatically on the run. The most important factor in long-range run endurance is the length of the longest run, followed by the total weekly volume. You should increase the time of your longest run by no more than 10 percent each week, and this is usually not the same as increasing the distance by 10 percent. If you are keeping your long runs at Zone 2 or below, there will be a "cardiac creep" factor that reduces pace for a steady heart rate on longer runs, at least until you have well-developed strength and endurance.

For the half-Iron distance, you should gradually increase the length of the long run to around 90 minutes. Anything more than this is only necessary for those planning a full-Iron race or marathon later on. A beginner could probably complete a half-Iron race standing up with a long run of only 60–75 minutes, provided he or she had sufficient bike volume. Runs over 90 minutes for beginners require more recovery and increase the risk of injury. If you find yourself with extra time on your hands, you would do better to extend your longest bike than attempt to run beyond 90 minutes for a half-Iron race. Veteran and expert runners can begin to increase the intensity of the 90-minute long run into Zone 3 or occasionally run up to 120 minutes.

Once you've reached that 90-minute plateau, you have sufficient endurance to consider lengthening other runs. You can extend the length of the brick run after a medium bike to 30 minutes and increase another stand-alone run to 45–60 minutes. Resist the temptation to start running faster than Zone 1 or 2 during the endurance-building phase. If you continue to work on economy and the appropriate drills, your speed should gradually improve even at the same heart rate. If you find you are running the same speed with a significantly reduced heart rate and good recovery, that's a good sign that you are training properly. There will be plenty of time to raise your heart rate in future muscular endurance workouts.

When do you graduate from the school of long-range endurance? You can stay in this phase for a couple of years and probably do quite well without ever exceeding it. I ran my first marathon in 3:32 and finished my first half-Iron race with a 1:55 run split only six months later without any interval training whatsoever, just medium to long runs in Zones 1 and 2. First-time half-Iron athletes can be confident in finishing the run okay by focusing only on economy and endurance. Once you decide you want to move up in the division rankings, however, you will have to consider some muscular endurance workouts.

Running Muscular Endurance

If you've been doing some of the recommended running drills and brick workouts off the bike for a few months, you've already built some muscular endurance without much conscious effort. The stiff-legged, burning sensation that we all felt in those first attempts at running off the bike should have begun to subside, indicating the muscular ability to tolerate the transition from cycling (quadriceps) to running (hamstrings and glutes). Even modest cycling volume will build considerable leg strength beyond that attained by most runners. Short-course triathlons themselves are great muscular-endurance workouts, which is why we encourage novices to attempt a good number of C sprint triathlons or duathlons.

Races from 10K to the half-marathon (21.1km) are useful in building muscular endurance for triathletes. Beginning to intermediate long-course triathletes should consider racing these as "heart zone tests," where pace is determined first by heart rate, and minutes-per-mile pace is only secondary. The goal with heart-zone racing is to go out at a lower-than-optimal heart rate of Zone 3–4 and gradually build to a full muscular endurance heart rate of 5a or higher in the second half of the race, perhaps moving to Zone 5b in the last mile. Athletes can learn much about pacing variations when fresh and tired, and extrapolate an effective pace for an upcoming half-Iron event. Some even find they can beat their PR running times when employing this conservative approach.

Racing distances longer than the half-marathon have little efficacy for the half-Iron triathlete. But if you simply love marathons or ultraruns, and it's part of your lifestyle (I empathize with you here, starting as a marathon runner), try to complete them in the winter so they do not interfere with later Base and Build periods of the triathlon season. Given a choice between finishing a marathon or a half-Iron race as your first-ever ultraevent, choose the half-Iron race. It requires more endurance, but the training and racing is less likely to cause injury.

Climbing on the Run

As with cycling, running in the hills builds strength and varies heart rate, two key elements in muscular endurance. Hill running also builds economy because it requires fundamentals like balance, forefoot strike, and high cadence to succeed. Gently rolling terrain works best for beginning to intermediate runners, and steep grades have utility only for elites or those preparing for run courses with similarly difficult climbs. A good rule of thumb is to practice climbing a grade 1 percent higher than you will race. If you live or will race in flatland, you should still try to do some hill running, even if that only means running up and down bridge/highway ramps or perhaps the stair-steps at a local stadium.

One of the best ways to climb is on trails, where the softer surface reduces impact and the variable terrain builds neuromuscular skills. It's a great way to break the monotony both physically and mentally of pounding the same pavement every day. The best surface from an impact perspective is packed cinder. After that, dirt trails without too many tree roots or rocks are acceptable. Interestingly enough, grass is not the ideal unpaved long-distance surface since it often has unseen indentations and fatigues the ankles for long runs. Grass is useful, however, for barefoot running drills of 50–100 yards—such as in the infield of a running track.

Tempo, High-Aerobic, or Zone 3 Running

Strictly speaking, these all refer to the same intensity, but you will hear the word "tempo" used by some coaches and athletes as somewhere closer to lactate threshold pace. We mean an intensity of about ten to eleven beats below LT, which can be inserted at the finish of a medium to long run or included as longer intervals with proportionate recovery. Once your long run is comfortable for 90 minutes in Zone 2, you can insert 5- to 20-minute segments in the middle or end of the run to more closely simulate race pace. Experienced runners who have a strong aerobic base can schedule an entire 90-minute run at tempo pace after warm-up.

Although Zone 3 is classified as an aerobic training zone, realize that significant amounts of lactate are generated, and musculoskeletal stress is approaching the same level as lactate threshold running. What experienced runners should avoid running is a gray zone where all of your runs end up averaging Zone 3, leaving you too tired to recover but too slow to increase speed. Zone 3 is very important for long-course athletes in training and racing, but you have to continue base work in Zones 1 and 2 for it to be safe and effective.

Interval Training for Experienced and Elite Runners

It merits repeating that many long-course triathletes are quite happy and productive training for the run only in Zones 1 and 2. Some masters athletes have won world championships in half- or full Iron races without training above Zone 3, saving all higher efforts for racing. Athletes of all levels have raced well never going to a track, doing all the intensity work on the road. But there comes a time when interval training becomes worth the risk for runners, and indeed hard intervals cause more injuries on the run than in the pool or on the bike. Before engaging in this high-risk, speculative investment in time and energy, ask yourself:

1. Are you especially prone to running injuries? Have moderately long runs in Zones 1 and 2 caused excessive soreness or forced you to stop running in the last six to twelve months?
2. Do you have weight-loss issues, biomechanical weakness, or physiological problems that make hard running more stressful? Best to address and eliminate these before attempting fast training, and the adjunct solution to these problems requires training in Zones 1 and 2.
3. Can you tolerate tempo runs and bike rides up to forty minutes in Zone 3 without undue soreness or unreasonable recovery time? Long-course racing requires relative mastery of Zone 3 before attempting a faster pace.
4. Are you racing well in your division in short-course races, without problems finishing or recovering from an Olympic-distance triathlon or half-marathon run? Although competition varies, we mean finishing in the top five or six in a smaller local triathlon or the top ten to fifteen in a national or worlds qualifier. You are in the hunt and have reasonable expectation of moving up in place.
5. Are you at a point in your career or season where strictly aerobic training gets boring?

If answers to 1 and 2 are negative and 3, 4, and 5 are positive, you may be a candidate for run interval training.

As with bike intervals, you'll need to test your running lactate threshold pace to determine your interval running pace. You'll need a friend with a stopwatch to help with timing and heart rates. As with all LT tests, avoid eating or drinking caffeine for three hours before the test. Wear a heart rate monitor you can trust on this track—school tracks sometimes have electromagnetic sources that can perturb heart rate readings on parts of the track. Avoid testing during illness, lifestyle stress, or without sufficient rest and recovery.

1. Warm up thoroughly for 15–20 minutes, and use the same warm-up procedure for successive tests.
2. On a 400m running track, find the starting point and the 200m halfway marker.
3. Start running very slowly, jogging barely faster than a walk.

4. Increase pace gradually every 200 meters, with your partner calling out the time and you calling out the heart rate. He or she must run across the track infield to meet you at the 200m half-laps and record the time and heart rate values.
5. Continue to increase pace by three to five seconds each lap until you cannot go any faster. This may take ten full laps (4km) so don't attempt this test until you are fit and rested.
6. Note breathing for each 200m segment until exhaustion. When breathing becomes labored, with inhaling more pronounced, note the heart rate on the sheet. This is the ventilatory threshold (VT), very close to the actual lactate threshold (LT). It should come well *before* exhaustion. Most athletes will feel they could have gone one more lap a little faster.

A typical table of values is shown in Table 8.1

The ventilatory threshold is observed at 159bpm at a pace of 52 seconds per 200 meters. This could indicate lactate threshold intervals of perhaps 3–6 repetitions of 800 meters at 3:28 as a possible weekly track workout. Other possible run interval workouts are described in Table 8.2.

There are myriad combinations of the different intervals, such as 2×800m plus 1×1,600m repeated twice or 2×400 plus 1×800m repeated

TABLE 8.1 RESULTS FOR RUN GRADED EXERCISE TEST

TIME (SEC)	HEART RATE (BPM)
78	127
75	132
70	137
66	143
61	149
57	153
52	159 (VT)
48	162

four times. Until you have considerable experience running intervals and judging pace, we recommend sticking with simpler, linear formulas that you can execute without thinking too much. Sometimes beginners show up at a club workout only to find themselves torn apart by people going all out or varying distance and pace beyond comprehension. It may be more productive to trust intervals to a stopwatch and HRM by yourself until you are confident in your approach and can resist the temptation to overintensify.

Even if you are cautious, some days you will be too sore or tired to go to the track, and you should allow yourself more rest on those days. Either

TABLE 8.2 COMMON INTERVAL WORKOUTS FOR TRIATHLETES AND RUNNERS

INTERVALS	INTENSITY	QUALITY	USES
3–8x800m with 200m jogging recovery	4–5a (LT ± 3bpm)	Muscular endurance, lactate threshold speed	Versatile intervals for long-course athletes
3–5x1 600m (1mi) with 200–400m jogging recovery	4–5a (LT ± 3bpm)	Muscular endurance	Marathon and full Iron-distance training
10–12x400m	5a–b	Muscular endurance, anaerobic endurance	Short-course triathletes, 10K runners, elite half-Iron triathletes
8–10x400m	3–5a	Muscular endurance	Intermediate triathletes (shortened version of 800m intevals) early-season intervals
20x200m	5b	Anaerobic endurance	5–10K runners, sprint-distance triathletes. Not recommended for long-course triathletes

reduce the number of intervals and/or intensity, or better still, switch to a steady Zone 2 run over the same time, saving the intervals for a more productive day. Other solid reasons to cancel an interval workout include very cold days (likely muscle pulls) or very hot days (dehydration and inevitably slower running), countering the speed benefits of interval training.

Some athletes don't mind running fast, but dislike the repetitive nature of track workouts or have limited track access. You can transform most of the interval workouts by basing them on time and heart rate instead of distance. For example, instead of doing 6×800 meters at LTHR (158bpm, for example) around 3:15 per interval with 200 meters recovery, you can use your lap-counter (or interval programmable HRM) to run set-time intervals at 3:15 with 1:15 recovery each interval, trying to stay within 155–161bpm for each work interval. Even if you have access to a track, beginning to intermediate triathletes are often better off using heart rate as a primary intensity tool, not time per lap. You need some experience racing various distances, both stand-alone and in a triathlon, to gauge time-based intervals.

Some of the newer GPS wrist units will allow you to program precise half- or full-mile intervals with quarter- or half-mile recoveries. Taking one of these on the trail for interval training can be a lot of fun. Remember, however, that the purpose of intervals is to teach you to run fast, and if conditions are extremely hilly or trail conditions poor, you will have difficulty making consistent speed gains.

If you get tired of the track or will be racing on an unusual course (Xterra, mixed pavement and trails, etc.), it's a good idea to do at least one or two nontrack interval sessions to simulate race surfaces.

Interval Caveats

Given the potential for overtraining and injury with run interval training, you should keep these factors in mind:

- Don't combine weight lifting on the same day as a running interval workout. Some athletes will need 48 hours between heavy lifting and fast running. Avoid running entirely right after a weight workout.
- Give yourself 48–72 hours between fast interval running and your longest run. It's also recommended to take a day off from running after intervals, or at least limit the next day to 30 minutes or less at Zone 1–2 pace. The same applies to racing: Never schedule an interval

workout the day before or after a race; in fact, you can probably reduce or skip intervals, using the race as your weekly speed workout.

- Interval workouts more than once a week are unnecessary for long-course triathletes. One lactate threshold interval session and one tempo run each week are all that is required to gain the muscular endurance required for the half-Iron run.
- Don't start track intervals too early in the season, and don't wait until it's too late to benefit from them. An ideal time to start is about 12–14 weeks before your first major races, perhaps toward the end of the Base 3 period. The training time of about four to six weeks before a race has the greatest effect on actual race performance—you can't suddenly "get fast" two weeks before a race. Better to do some tempo runs or short pickups rather than start intervals.
- For most athletes, "less is more" is the best strategy for intervals. Keep it short; keep it simple. If you finish your planned interval set thinking you could do one more, don't. That's a good sign you are training properly.
- Competing on the track with training partners can be fun, but be aware of your relative training goals. Unless you are training for the same race distance on the same day, it is unlikely they will be pacing at your optimal level. Even similar athletes with identical race schedules will have different beneficial training zones. Remember the interval-training commandment: "Thou shalt not try to win an interval." Save your best efforts for race day.
- There is a direct correlation among body fat composition, VO_2max, and the ability to run intervals without risk of injury. If you've been struggling with weight loss or recently had some nutritional lapses, it's better to correct these while running Zones 1 or 2 than going to the track to try to compensate. Anaerobic running burns sugar more than fat and can actually increase the craving for sweets and unhealthy foods. Conquer your nutritional issues before tackling the track. Dropping five pounds will immediately increase your speed without any extra running effort.
- Run intervals are not for everyone or may only be appropriate in limited fashion. Many champion masters athletes race quite well without any interval run training. Some elite long-course athletes have turned in strong running splits doing all their fast running at tempo pace on the road.

CHAPTER 9

Feeding the Mind and Body

It is easier to read ten volumes on philosophy than to put even one principle into practice.

—Leo Tolstoy

INTEGRATION OF MIND AND BODY

You cannot master nutrition without control of your mind, and your thinking will remain clouded without the proper amount of fuel and optimal body composition. From birth we become attached, even addicted, to the so-called "norms" of our culture, especially eating habits. The first thing we crave after taking our first breath is the milk from our mother's breast. As the Native American saying goes, "Life eats life."

The Niagara of Words

Today, the endurance athlete rides in the wake of a tidal wave of so-called "healthy energy foods" that are now a multibillion-dollar industry. Athletes are deluged with information on television, at race expos, training camps, the Internet—everywhere a veritable Niagara of words about special foods we can eat to make our bodies leaner, stronger, faster. Experts line up on many sides of this issue, promoting more or less protein, more or fewer carbohydrates, and the evil or good of certain fats, some of these experts paid in cash or research grants by the same companies manufacturing sports products.

The underlying truth is that there are few if any magical foods or pills you can take that will consistently make you faster. The substances that do—EPO, steroids, and amphetamines—have been banned in all amateur and professional competition, rightly so because of their dangerous side effects. But there are thousands of things you can ingest or overingest to make you gain body fat, lose strength, recover slowly, or race poorly. The foods that work best for most athletes in endurance sports have been around for 100,000 years: lean meats and fish from wild sources, milk, vegetable protein sources, whole carbohydrates found in fruits and vegetables, and natural unsaturated fats found in nuts and vegetables. Natural foods promote body fat reduction and optimal weight management as well as fueling race performance. There's not as much profit in marketing these foods, since they came along in our hunter-gatherer stage before civilization and before the notion of monetary gain.

Most of the foods that cause athletes problems have been developed in the last 150 years or so, products of the Industrial Revolution. They built upon the older culture of refined grains that came out of the Neolithic period, where centralized populations in cities required a concentrated, storable source of calories for citizens. The human brain grew a considerable volume in this period, and it runs totally on sugar (glucose).

Which brings us back full circle: The nutritional problems of most if not all endurance athletes are centered in the brain and in our culture, not the muscles or stomach. How we think about food, how food interweaves with modern culture, and how our lifestyle uses fuel—these are the essential issues.

For many age-group athletes, body composition and nutrition are indeed the greatest limiters to performance. I have yet to meet any triathletes who do not know something about the relative proportions of protein, carbohydrates, and fat they should eat. But I would venture to say that only about 10 percent of age groupers are happy with their body composition and race at optimal weight.

Desire is the Key

The legendary track coach Bill Bowerman told his most famous disciple, Steve Prefontaine, "You can't coach desire, Pre." And that is true: As coaches we cannot make our athletes want to improve or win—they have to bring that to the table themselves. I've learned there is no way to make someone eat right, no matter how much we plead for a healthy diet of unprocessed, natural foods. People have to want to change, and change can be harder for humans than other mammals. If you force an animal to miss a meal, or you change the food supply, it will quickly adapt. Move the cheese in a maze and a mouse will soon figure out a new route to dinner. Humans are perhaps the only creatures that will continue to go down an obsolete path for years or decades, even though the "cheese" (positive outcome) is no longer there.

The reason it's difficult for humans to change behavior is because our desires are influenced by more than just the five senses of the animal, which adapts quickly to changes in environment without thinking. Our mind acts as an overriding sixth sense that reinforces our desires, and our mind is programmed from birth by society. We are trained to fit into our social culture, to codify our desires into useful channels. I think we can agree our culture has taken us into some unhealthy areas lately, too much of a good thing. Words can also be used to deceive and manipulate. It's no coincidence that as air and water quality decline, so does the availability of natural, unprocessed foods.

Eating is a normal and natural desire, as is the desire to train and compete. The problem arises when we lose control of our desires. Our vices are merely our virtues taken to a negative extreme. In order to control desire, you must first control your thoughts, and most thinking is done via internal dialogue. Since a dialogue is composed of two entities, the question arises: To whom are we speaking? Is there a "Higher Self" that we aspire to be?

The key to athletic performance (or lifestyle success) is using your mind to control your desires. Desires are like the polar opposites of a magnet: One pole attracts you to positive behaviors to achieve your larger goal, while the other pole attracts you toward short-term gratification of bodily desires. Neither one of these poles is good or bad in and of itself. The goal is to walk a noble middle path between the polar opposites, to harmonize your higher goals with the needs of the body. Fanaticism is rarely successful in training or dieting, though steadfast dedication and commitment may appear obsessive to the nonathlete. Calm, persistent effort pays the greatest dividends on the path to achievement.

The Illusion of Self

Successful endurance athletes are usually people who know what they are about. They appear to have a strong sense of "self," and that is not the same thing as merely being selfish. But if you were to ask them what this "self" truly encompasses, they would state a simple set of values and goals. They have identified themselves with the goal of being a champion. Once a goal is achieved (or not), you will find that most of them have already moved on to the next vista.

Athletes having problems with nutrition have internal obstacles that prevent this self-identification with otherwise laudable goals. Despite externally directed statements about "bad foods," most of the time these problems are traced back to life stress, not any particular dietary element. Most of this stress stems from relationships: to family, to coworkers, to financial conditions.

Training is secondary to this life stress, merely amplifying imbalances in other areas. The cause of overtraining is just as likely to come from lifestyle stress as actual training stress. If you ask yourself why you eat less-than-optimal foods, it is likely in response to stress. Food, especially the refined sugar in most processed foods, acts as a short-term tranquilizer to relieve stress. Statistically speaking, addictions to sugar and unhealthy foods are more common than addictions to nicotine, drugs, or alcohol—often they overlap. The problem with food is that our society permits and even encourages food disorders with massive ad campaigns and distorted pseudoscience regarding mass-marketed products.

Another strong motivation in modern culture is guilt. Since we no longer advocate violence to control behavior (we hope), and natural dangers have been largely brought under our control, society controls negative behavior with guilt. When we act badly, we feel bad. This may be a useful tool for children or the immature, but we carry over these guilt complexes when we eat the wrong foods. If guilt about eating really worked, we would not eat bad foods and would have no need to feel guilty anymore. But guilt and the neurohormones it releases become as addictive as cigarettes or doughnuts for breakfast. We must begin to see food as our friend, a good and necessary source of fuel for our racing passion.

It helps to sit down and write (or type on a computer) the pros and cons of your internal dialogue, with special consideration to your attitudes toward food and daily meals. Carry your training logbook for the entire day. Pay attention to your internal dialogue. Whenever you think or say

something about yourself, write it down. At the end of the day, c
the statements you recorded. Label each one as positive (P) or
(N), and total each group. This gives you an estimate of how self-talk is working for or against you. You might also note how your eating patterns flowed that day during this conversation with yourself.

If you had many negative statements, try to come up with a positive alternative. For example, instead of saying, "I'm still too heavy for that hilly bike course," you might substitute, "I've lost many pounds since becoming a triathlete, and those upcoming hills are a great motivation to lose a few more." The next time you approach the negative situation, try to use the alternative positive statement.

STEPS TOWARD OPTIMAL NUTRITION

Designing a nutrition plan is similar to designing a good training plan: You first observe your baseline values via testing. Simply write down everything you eat and drink for a week (two weeks is even better). Do not try to alter your eating patterns during this period—simply eat as usual. Deliberately reducing calories during the test is like "cheating" by going over your lactate threshold on a bike power test.

Do write *everything* down, including approximately how much water, minerals, and vitamins you ingest. While you're at home, you may need to weigh your food or measure its volume. You will definitely need to read labels. Imagine taking a medication with side effects or bad interactions: the prescription data sheet is your only clue. Not reading food labels is like taking powerful drugs without following the prescription. Many foods with attractive logos saying "healthy," "natural," "low-fat," or "low in carbs" are in fact loaded with useless calories, additives, sugar, and trans fats.

Essential items for your log that can be found on most labels include:

- Total calories
- Grams of carbohydrates, protein, and fat, and their relative caloric percentage in each food item. Fat has more than double the calorie contribution (9 calories per gram) of protein or carbs (4 calories per gram).
- Vitamin and mineral levels. The recommend daily allowances, originally created to avoid severe deficiencies, have limited applicability to the needs of optimally performing athletes, sometimes by a factor

of ten or more. Vitamin C is a good example: With an RDA of only 60mg, it is better supplemented at 500–1,000mg per day.
- Grams and percentages of monounsaturated, polyunsaturated, and saturated fats
- Grams of fiber

There are other details that are not legally mandated for food labels, but are sometimes included with health-food labels or can be estimated:

- **Essential fatty acids (EFAs):** These include omega-3 and omega-6, which are found in nuts, vegetables, fish, and oils like flaxseed (linseed) and also in supplements like fish-oil pills. The balance of these two varieties with a third type, saturated fat, is very important, and the imbalance of fatty acids is estimated to affect 50 million Americans. Fortunately, taking only three fish-oil pills a day (or eating more wild salmon, walnuts, or other omega-3–rich foods) will balance the omega-3 levels for most people.
- **Amino acids:** not all proteins are alike. Some are complete (eggs) while others are not (soy, beef, whey). A variety of amino acids is needed for recovery and rebuilding tissue during endurance training.

As you can see, logging and analyzing all this information is not easy. If you want to do it yourself, you'll need to take a small notebook or PDA with you all day long and could make use of something like a computer spreadsheet to categorize and add up the information. Fortunately, there are online services and freely downloadable software available to assist. Check your Internet search engine for the latest software.

Once you've logged your dietary habits over a week, the first issue to address is the macronutrient (large volume foods) consumption. Foods and beverages fall along a spectrum of nutrient-rich or calorie-rich foods (Figure 9.1). The nutrient-rich choices allow us to build or rebuild our bodies after the destructive aspects of training. The calorie-rich foods give us the energy required to finish the current workout and fuel for the next one. Both types of foods can be good and useful for endurance athletes at certain times. The key to optimal weight for racing is to balance the two groups.

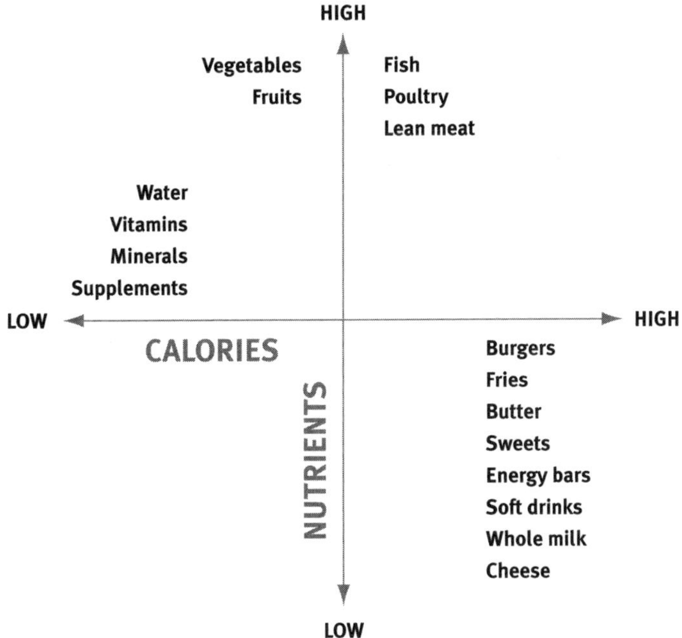

FIGURE 9.1
Value of nutrient- and calorie-rich food

Endurance athletes benefit from focusing on these three fundamentals:

1. **Eliminate processed foods from your diet.** Most modern food processing strips away nutrients while packing in calories, a "lose-lose" scenario. The only compelling reason for processed foods is when traveling long distances to minimize load: that is, when training and racing. Unfortunately, the reason we consume processed foods is low price, lack of time, and massive profits for the food industry. The packaging and taste are deliberately designed to be addictive and increase sales. Once we form the processed-food habit, it's very hard to break. As simple as this sounds, it's difficult for athletes to actually accomplish, including myself.
2. **The majority of calories should come from whole fruits (not refined juices), vegetables, and lean protein sources.** How many television commercials have you ever seen about buying raw apples or snacking on raw carrots?

3. **Carbohydrate-intensive foods, the starches and refined sugars, should be limited to immediately before, during, and after longer workouts.** Even here you should be careful to read labels and time their ingestion. The tradition of "carbo-loading" for endurance events, even long-course events like the half- and full Ironman, has become exaggerated and can do more harm than good.

THE MACRONUTRIENTS

The Water of Life

Maybe you thought there were only three macronutrients? You may have omitted the most important macronutrient: water. It composes two-thirds of the earth's surface, 75 percent of human body mass, and most of the nutrient consumed during a race—its proper use or misuse is critical. You can go for days or perhaps weeks without solid food, but too much or too little water can cause death in a single day. Fortunately, enough has been said about the importance of hydration, so most triathletes are aware of the need to keep drinking. Many of triathlon's major events are conducted in warm to hot conditions on the final run, further enforcing good hydration.

We may have become too paranoid about dehydration in recent decades, leading to the common problem of hyponatremia: too much water without enough sodium. Ingesting massive amounts of water before, during, and after competition, without complementary amounts of sodium and/or potassium, quickly strips the body of electrolytes. Many of the early symptoms of dehydration resemble the effects of hyponatremia. In hot races like Ironman® Hawaii and the Buffalo Springs Lake Ironman 70.3 event, ingesting enough sodium can make the difference between the podium and a DNF.

Most athletes still need to pay attention to water intake during the training week, however. The mass-marketing of soft drinks and caffeinated beverages have us drinking less pure water. Even if you're drinking a diet soft drink without caffeine, thinking you are eliminating damaging substances, it is not as good for you as drinking springwater or distilled water. Artificial sweeteners like aspartame and saccharine can put an extra load on the kidneys and have been associated with subtle neurological effects. For example, I get a small twitch in my hand during a golf swing or swim stroke when I drink aspartame diet beverages.

The solution is simple: Drink the purest water you can get. Filtered or bottled water or springwater is best, but tap water is still preferable to most processed beverages. Distilled water is okay provided you are also taking in sodium and potassium. Other sources of pure, filtered water include fruits like bananas, oranges, and apples, all composed mostly of water and naturally containing the right electrolyte mix.

Avoid drinking large quantities of water all at once, which can lead to a bloated feeling and can deplete the body of electrolytes. Sip slowly and naturally, about 4–6 ounces at a time throughout the day. If you are going to drink some other beverage with meals, try to include straight water before or during the meal and reduce the intake of the other beverage. If you use caffeine in a hardworking, hard-training day, realize that fresh-brewed coffee or tea are healthier sources than most soft drinks with other additives. The caffeine in sports gels and bars is relatively low in concentration and often derived from natural sources like green tea.

Protein

Protein has a yo-yo history on the scale of athletic research, some decades up and some down. Up through the nineteenth century, myths about absorbing the power of animals persisted, and meat was the primary fuel of athletes. In the twentieth century, scientists discovered that most of the energy used by athletes came from carbohydrates and fat, culminating in the Krebs cycle describing glycolysis in 1957. In the next few decades, carbohydrate intake became paramount and protein relatively ignored by endurance athletes. The so-called carbo-loading regimens became the staple of marathon runners and tour cyclists. Only the bodybuilders and strength athletes worried about protein.

Scientific breakthroughs regarding cell structure and studies on competitive athletes resurrected protein's importance. Many long-distance endurance athletes tested as protein deficient. While only 10–15 percent of the calories required for exercise can come directly from burning protein, the cells and processes that surround them are dependent on the amino acids in protein. To recover from the catabolic (destructive) physiology of endurance events, especially high-volume training for longer events, triathletes require as much or more protein per kilogram of body weight as strength athletes from American football or bodybuilding.

Readers should be aware that there is still controversy about the ideal amount of protein for endurance athletes. If you fill a room full of registered dieticians, high-performance coaches, and elite athletes, you will likely see a lively debate about exactly how much protein is required, and when it should be ingested. The conflict can be traced to comparing studies of average or moderately active exercisers with long-course athletes training 15–35 hours per week. The bottom line is we simply don't have a definitive study on the nutrition of athletes training specifically for races of 5–25 hours or even longer. These people are too busy training to spend much time in a university lab.

Within this milieu is a growing consensus among researchers, experienced long-course athletes, and their coaches that more protein is required than the recommended daily allowance (RDA) provided by government agencies, and perhaps more than recommended by older sports nutrition models. The possible detrimental effects of excessive protein intake are outweighed by the extensive calorie burning and rebuilding required in high-volume training, much the same way that adverse effects of sodium have little meaning to triathletes training in 90–95°F temperatures for a long-course race in Hawaii. More recent protein research indicates:

- Daily protein intake of 2 grams per kilogram (2.2 pounds) of body weight may be required for athletes training at 65 percent of their VO_2max (that's only Zone 1 or 2 intensity). The recommended daily allowance of protein from the USDA is only 0.8 grams per kilogram. Both registered dieticians (RDs) and elites would agree the USDA figure is too low for endurance athletes, with many RDs recommending something around 1.2 grams of protein per kilogram of body mass, and elite coaches and athletes advocating 1.8–2.2 grams per kilogram.
- Endurance athletes may require protein intakes higher than bodybuilders. The increased use of amino acids and high concentration of mitochondria (energy-producing cell components) in aerobic muscle fibers require additional protein.
- Low protein intake results in a loss of lean body mass and decreased power. It's no coincidence that the most power-oriented of the three sports—cycling—supports the highest protein intake.
- Women eating too little protein experience significant losses in lean tissue, poor immune response, and muscle dysfunction.

- Athletes at greatest risk for protein deficiency include those on calorie-restricted diets, vegetarians, and younger athletes. These groups should pay particular attention to maintaining adequate protein.
- After a low-protein meal, amino acids in the blood and muscle decrease continuously for up to five to seven hours. To counteract this effect, post-exercise drinks and meals should be especially high in protein, from 25–33 percent of total calories, to speed muscle rebuilding and recovery.

How much more protein is beneficial and realistic? That depends on the athlete, the event, and the period of training. There is little evidence of protein effectiveness over 2 grams per kilogram of body weight, and the side effects increase. Many athletes find it difficult to maintain a protein intake of 1.8–2.0 grams per kilogram of body mass. They may think their diets are high in protein, but when balanced against all the carbohydrates they ingest, it composes only 15 percent or less of total calories.

Please understand we are *not* advocating the high-protein, low-carbohydrate diets espoused by Dr. Atkins. Extreme restrictions on carbohydrate intake, especially before, during, and after racing, are detrimental to the endurance athlete. A balanced approach with periodization of carbohydrate intake, both daily and within the training season, have proven effective for most of our athletes.

All proteins are not created equal

Many athletes agree that they need more protein for hard training. So they eat some protein-rich foods or add some powdered protein supplement, considering only total protein grams. But as with carbohydrates and fats, there are different classes of proteins required for optimal health. Not all protein sources supply a complete collection of amino acids. In relation to human metabolism, proteins come in two groups (Table 9.1).

- **Essential proteins:** which cannot be synthesized by the body on its own. They must be consumed from dietary sources. They also require additional vitamins and minerals for conversion into active compounds used by the brain and nervous system.
- **Nonessential proteins:** which can be manufactured by the human body. This label can be deceiving since external dietary supplementation may still be necessary for endurance athletes. Producing these

TABLE 9.1 ESSENTIAL AND NONESSENTIAL PROTEINS

ESSENTIAL	COMMENTS	NONESSENTIAL	COMMENTS
Arginine	Inadequate synthesis in children	Alanine	
Histidine	Inadequate synthesis in children	Asparagine	
Isoleucine		Aspartate	
Leucine		Cysteine	
Lysine		Glutamate	
Methionine		Glutamine	Conditionally essential under stress
Phenylalanine		Glycine	
Theonine		Proline	
Tryptophan		Serine	
Valine		Tyrosine	

amino acids depends on adequate levels of other compounds; otherwise a nonessential amino-acid deficiency can result. For example, glutamine requires magnesium, serine requires niacin, and glycine requires choline. Some nonessential amino acids require essential ones for production.

Unless you are buying health food or a sport-specific nutritional product, you won't find these listed on labels. It's not necessary to micromanage each amino acid, but you should be aware of some general rules about foods and their protein:

- Eggs are the ideal protein, complete and easily digestible. Although many athletes favor only the egg white because of fears about fat and cholesterol, the yolk has also been found to contain endurance-promoting substances. A good compromise is to consume only one yolk per day out of every two or three egg whites. I find that a three-egg veggie omelet tastes just as good with only one yolk as with three.

- Whey (milk-derived) protein and beef are also excellent sources, but are not as digestible in some athletes. Some experts recommend whey protein after workouts for recovery but claim that during or immediately before workouts it can cause ammonia production and muscle fatigue. In my own case, I find excessive whey mixed with carbohydrates during a workout encourages frequent urination, so I use soy protein and carbohydrates immediately before and during workouts and save whey for recovery. Other athletes digest whey during workouts and races without issue.
- Although beef, chicken, and pork are good protein sources, their mass production in places such as the United States results in many questionable additives, including trace amounts of growth hormone (a banned substance) and harmful chemicals like chlorine. The overcrowded, grain-fed lifestyle of feedlot cattle, chickens, and swine promote fat instead of lean protein in many supermarket cuts. Wild game like venison, bison, or fowl are preferable to mass-produced grain-fed cattle. You can also search out free-roaming poultry and egg sources.
- Fish and seafood are excellent protein sources, but sometimes have similar problems as mass-produced cattle. Prefer wild-caught fish like salmon to farm-fed varieties, which have fewer nutrients and less "good fat." You must read labels carefully since "Atlantic Salmon" does not necessarily mean it was caught in the Atlantic Ocean—it may still be farm-fed. You have to see the label "wild" or "wild caught" to be sure. Environmental studies find that increasing amounts of mercury are being found in tuna and salmon, but most experts agree that eating these once or twice a week poses no danger for healthy adults.

Protein Supplements

Many time-limited triathletes have found it difficult or impossible to maintain adequate protein through natural sources alone, so they use powdered supplementation in drinks before, during, and after workouts (see Table 9.2 for potentially high protein ratios with natural foods). Quality protein is one of the most expensive additives to put in a sports drink, so you'll find these cost more than carbohydrate- and electrolyte-only mixtures (see the sports drink tables at the end of this chapter).

There is a wide variation in the type and quality of protein, so it's important to read labels to ensure you are getting the right grams of protein, the right variety (usually whey, soy, or egg), and good production quality with a minimum of additives. Most protein supplements contain trace amounts of monosodium glutamate (the MSG commonly found in Asian foods) as a by-product of the protein synthesis, though it is not required for this to be on the label. Those with MSG reactions should exercise caution. Some popular commercial brands even have trans fats (labeled as "partially hydrolyzed" or "hydrogenated" followed by some oil), high-fructose corn syrup, and other things that may taste good but actually subtract from health and athletic performance. As with everything you consume, read labels carefully.

Another consideration for elite athletes is the potential for micro-particles of banned substances finding their way into the protein powder. Overseas factories that package protein often manufacture other substances not permitted in triathlon competition but legally sold in that country. If you are an elite triathlete who is likely to be tested for banned substances, you should test supplements before ingesting or test yourself after ingestion but well before competition. Some recent brands are becoming certified as free from banned substances, certainly a desirable trend.

Ideally, you should ingest as much natural protein as possible from lean sources, but in the real world it's difficult. If you train in high volume and ingest many calories, try to get some of your protein immediately before/during/after workouts by using a protein sports drink with a carbohydrate-to-protein ratio of 3–5 to 1. Different athletes respond to greater or lesser concentrations of protein in workout drinks, somewhere up to 25 percent of total calories. For recovery, you can try mixing protein powders with lots of whole fruit (not fruit juices), which adds fiber, healthy carbohydrates, and essential phytonutrients to your overall diet.

Fats and Oils

Many endurance athletes believe that carbohydrates are the key to endurance. While it's true they compose a larger portion of calories than proteins and fats, the goal of endurance athletes is to teach the body to burn more fat and less sugar. The high-carbohydrate diets advocated in the seventies, eighties, and early nineties have been found suspect in providing a steady source of energy during training and racing, and allowing for

TABLE 9.2 PROTEIN INTAKE FOR A 70-KILOGRAM (154-POUND) ATHLETE FROM NATURAL SOURCES

GRAMS OF PROTEIN PER KILOGRAM BODY MASS	TOTAL PROTEIN (G)	FOODS (PROTEIN, G)
0.8	56	2 eggs (12) 1 serving roast beef (30) 3 oz cheese (14)
1.0	70	2 eggs (12) 1 serving roast beef (30) 1.5 oz cheese (7) shrimp cocktail (21)
1.2	84	2 eggs (12) 3 slices bacon (6) 1 serving roast beef (30) 3 oz cheese (14) shrimp cocktail (21)
1.4	95	3 eggs (18) 2 slices Canadian bacon (12) 1 serving roast beef (30) 3 oz cheese (14) shrimp cocktail (21)
1.6	112	2 eggs (12) 3 slices bacon (6) 1 serving roast beef (30) 4 oz cottage cheese (17) shrimp cocktail (22) 1 serving salmon (25)
1.8	126	3 eggs (18) 2 slices Canadian bacon (12) 1 roast beef (30) 5 oz cottage cheese (20) shrimp cocktail (21) 1 serving salmon (25)
2.0	140	3 eggs (18) 2 slices Canadian bacon (12) 1 serving roast beef (30) 5 oz cottage cheese (20) shrimp cocktail (21) 1 serving salmon (25) 3 slices turkey (14)

proper recovery. For the human body to reach optimum health and fitness, a balance of fats is required.

As with proteins there are different kinds of fats, some that require proportioning and some that are downright destructive to bodily functions. In addition to their energy-producing attributes, good fats can reduce inflammation, prevent injury, and provide immunity to disease.

All fats are composed of lipids that are not soluble in water. Common products like olive oil and almond butter are examples of useful water-insoluble fats. Fat is the most energy-dense substance at 9 calories per gram versus only 4 calories per protein or carbohydrate gram. It's the richest source of internal energy in the body itself: glycogen (carbohydrate) stores provide enough energy for about 90 minutes of exercise, but even lean athletes have up to 119 hours of stored fat for use during exercise. A small amount of carbohydrate is still required to jump-start the fat-burning process, which is why we recommend consuming carbohydrates during longer workouts and races.

The use of diets higher in fat has been shown to improve performance in numerous studies. Increasing dietary fat improved VO_2max and endurance, while reducing fatigue and the rate of carbohydrate burning. While most studies show that fat burning is optimal at 60 percent of VO_2max, athletes consuming higher-fat diets were able to raise this range up to 80 percent of aerobic capacity. This intensity turns out to be near the race pace of veteran half-Iron distance athletes. Tested athletes were also able to maintain anaerobic power for shorter-distance efforts.

The World Health Organization wrote that athletes may take in as much as 35 percent of calories as fat. Contrary to popular opinion, this does not cause additional cardiovascular stress or weight gain if calories are kept constant. Many of the deleterious effects associated with fat and cholesterol do not take place in a vacuum and are usually accompanied by high carbohydrate and/or trans-fat ingestion.

Please understand that these modest fat increases are not the same thing as the high-fat, low-carbohydrate plans advocated in the mass culture—they are simply more balanced in terms of fats versus carbohydrates.

Women's issues

Triathlon is perhaps the most progressive endurance sport, where men and women train comparable hours and compete side by side in the same race, especially at long-course venues. Yet female endurance athletes have a distinctive metabolism, using more fat and fewer carbohydrates than men and storing less glycogen from dietary carbohydrates. Since the goal of long-range endurance is more fat burning, women are inherently more efficient. Specific problems such as menstrual termination and a higher risk of cardiovascular disease have been found in women eating higher-carbohydrate, lower-fat diets. Our modern cultural matrix, unfortunately, still encourages women to follow low-fat diets.

Other issues related to fat include healthy skin, which requires fat on the inside to insulate against water-soluble pollutants and provide a soft, smooth, and unwrinkled appearance. A similar benefit is provided for healthy hair. Hormones related to pregnancy require a suitable fat balance. Progesterone, produced from fats, allows a newly conceived embryo to absorb nutrients necessary for survival. Estrogen, useful to both women and men during endurance training, is also dependent on fat. Some of the recently studied problems with estrogen supplementation in post-menopausal women may be related to deficiencies aggravated by a fatty-acid imbalance in the diet.

Fatty-acid balance

As with macronutrients in general, balance is the key to healthy consumption of fat. Fats are split into three groups (A, B, and C), none of which are necessarily good or bad in and of themselves. But in balance with each other and with carbohydrates and protein, they have dramatic effects on health and fitness. Essential fatty acids, such as linoleic acid, are similar to essential amino acids in that they cannot be produced by the body; they must be consumed to ensure health. Fats have been called by different names and combine in various ways, but we can summarize their relationship to the endurance performance in Table 9.3.

As endurance athletes, we are acutely aware of inflammation and trying to prevent it. Yet some inflammation and coagulation is necessary for muscular growth and repair. It is only in extreme cases where we add the suffix "-itis" to indicate injury. We want to balance and shorten the inflammatory cycle, not completely eradicate it. Therefore, we still need a small proportion of B (saturated) fats. When ingested directly from natural sources (such as eggs) as part of a balanced fat intake, they do not have the feared negative effects on the cardiovascular system. These problems are much more likely when we manufacture the Series 2 ecosanoids from other unnatural sources, namely from ingestion of trans fats and in

TABLE 9.3 CLASSES OF FATTY ACIDS

TYPE	BODY CONVERTS TO	EFFECTS	FOODS
A (Omega-6)	Series 1 ecosanoids	Anti-inflammatory, unsaturated	Vegetables, safflower oil, corn
B	Series 2 ecosanoids	Inflammatory, saturated	Whole milk, butter, meat, egg yolks. Includes trans fats and margarine, which convert to Series 2 in the body.
C (Omega-3)	Series 3 ecosanoids	Anti-inflammatory, unsaturated	Fish, beans, walnuts, flaxseed oil

the presence of highly processed carbohydrates such as high-fructose corn syrup.

The double whammy of processed sugar and trans fats is precisely what we are most likely to encounter in foods like cupcakes, cookies, doughnuts, chips, and so forth, which we easily recognize as "junk food." Without reading labels, you may not realize that many foods labeled "low-fat" or "encourages health" may also contain high concentrations of high-fructose corn syrup and trans fats. Popular cereal brands are an example, despite their "healthy food" or "zero cholesterol" labels. Even some energy bars derive many of their calories from high-fructose corn syrup and partially hydrogenated oils (trans fats). Although trans fats do not begin as saturated fats, they are converted into the most damaging substances within the body.

Other oils that begin healthy, such as olive oil, can be turned into bad fats by heating or improper storage. The problem with many fried foods is not the oil itself, but the heating process—yet another reason to focus on raw, steamed, and relatively unprocessed vegetables. About the only oil that stands up well to moderate heating is grape seed oil, which has proven a useful alternative for my own love of stir-fried vegetables. It is thin and almost tasteless, so does not disturb other herbs and spices added to the veggies.

It has been estimated that the average American has a 40 to 1 fatty-acid imbalance in his or her diet, where the B fats overwhelm the A (omega-6) and C (omega-3) varieties. You don't have to be eating steak and eggs every day to achieve this imbalance; endurance athletes relying on high-carbohydrate regimens can easily become deficient in omega-3 fatty acids. Fortunately, the imbalance itself can be easily countered by moderate intake of wild salmon, walnuts, or an omega-3 fatty-acid supplement (3–5 grams/day) and reliance on fruits and vegetables for carbs.

The goal should be to achieve a 2 to 1 ratio of A- and C-type fats over the B type. Interestingly enough, if you are a vegetarian absent of meat sources, you will still achieve a balance in B-type fats by ingesting equal amounts of A and C fats, since some of the A fats from vegetable sources will be converted to Series 2 ecosanoids. There really is no such thing as a "no-fat" diet, even for vegetarians, nor is such a state desirable for optimum endurance performance. On the other hand, if you eat too much red meat and not enough vegetables, beans, or fish, you may experience excessive inflammation and longer recovery time between breakthrough workouts.

Carbohydrates

We've reserved carbohydrates for last to balance its premier position in endurance lore. It's impossible to train optimally for long-course triathlons without ingesting a good deal of carbohydrates, yet it's safe to say that most triathletes are getting plenty of carbs relative to protein and fat. Only severe carbohydrate restriction, such as that proposed by the Atkins diet, would likely lead an athlete into chronic carbohydrate deficiency or ketosis, where the liver is completely depleted of glycogen. The ingestion of sports drinks, gels, and bars alone has made this condition rare in athletes, and add to that the popularity of bread, pasta, and other high-glycemic foods. Temporary lapses in carbohydrates and blood sugar may occur when obsessing over calories, especially during the highest-volume training. Natural, unprocessed sources and balance are preferred to calorie counting for endurance athletes.

If most of you are getting a sufficient volume of carbohydrates, that leaves us with these questions: (1) Where do these carbohydrates come from? (2) When are they consumed? (3) What is the optimal dose of simple and complex sugars to enable superior performance? To answer these questions, we must strike a balance between blood sugar and its regulator, insulin.

The sugar versus insulin roller coaster

If burning fat and protein is like a cruise on a gentle sea, burning sugar is more like riding a roller coaster for many athletes. They consume large amounts of carbohydrates, creating a correspondingly intense insulin reaction to regulate the serum glucose levels. Then they train long and hard, depleting glycogen, then ingest more sugar to recover, followed again by a strong insulin response. It's no wonder that these athletes are prone to fatigue and slow to recover.

The body reacts very rapidly to sugar ingestion, more quickly than with almost any other substance. Insulin is a necessary hormone to regulate blood sugar, and its absence has dire consequences such as diabetes. But once secreted by the pancreas, it does other things such as converting carbohydrates and protein to fat, preventing the burning of fat, and transferring fat already in the blood to more permanent storage—the opposite of what we need for optimal performance and weight regulation. The consequence of strong insulin response is repeated craving caused by lowered blood sugar. The sugar high is quickly replaced by the sugar crash and then craving for more sugar.

The degree of insulin response is directly related to the Glycemic Index (GI) of the food. The higher-glycemic foods produce a more dramatic rise in blood sugar and hence a stronger insulin response. Lower glycemic foods are processed into the bloodstream more slowly and produce a milder insulin response. High GI foods are a relatively recent development in human history, and our ancient ancestors evolved to digest lower glycemic carbohydrates found in fruits, plus wild grains, nuts, and vegetables. Some high, low, and moderately glycemic foods are listed in Table 9.4.

People who are not physically active should avoid high-glycemic foods. They do have a necessary role, however, for the endurance athlete, since the prodigious calorie requirements of longer workouts require dense carbohydrate sources. Sports drinks, gels, and energy bars with a mixture of protein and complex and simple sugars can provide the extra calories to jump-start the fat-burning process required for efforts over ninety minutes. The dangers of excess insulin response are prevented by the rapid burning of ingested calories.

This caloric need does not mean going on a sugar binge. Recent studies show that a mixture of simple and complex carbohydrates with 15–25 percent protein provides the steadiest flow of energy for longer sessions.

TABLE 9.4 GLYCEMIC INDEX (GI) OF SELECTED FOODS

The GI ranks carbohydrate-containing foods according to their immediate effect on blood-sugar levels. High-GI foods elicit a fast blood-glucose response, low-GI foods a slow and sustained response. Low-GI foods are beneficial before training and competition and throughout most of your day. Medium- and high-GI foods help speed recovery during and after exercise. Total carbohydrate intake, combined with a high GI, is the most important factor in speeding recovery.

LOW GI (LESS THAN 50)	**MEDIUM GI (FROM 50–79)**	**HIGH GI (GREATER THAN 80)**
	GRAIN-BASED FOODS	
27 Rice bran	51 Vermicelli	80 Muesli cereal
38 Pasta, spaghetti	58 Rice, parboiled	81 Wild rice, Saskatchewan
45 Barley (pearl)	60 All-bran cereal	82 Semolina bread
45 Spaghetti, white, boiled 15 minutes	61 Spaghetti, brown	87 Oatmeal
46 Fettuccine	63 Wheat kernels	89 Rye bread, whole-meal
48 Rye	65 Bulgur	93 Couscous
	68 Rye or pumpernickel bread	95 Gnocchi
	68 Oat-bran bread	95 Barley-flour bread
	69 Multigrain bread	95 Rye crispbread
	74 Buckwheat	96 Muesli
	75 Bulgur bread	100 Whole-meal wheat bread
	79 Brown rice	103 Millet
	DAIRY PRODUCTS/SUBSTITUTES	
43 Soy milk	52 Yogurt	
46 Skim milk		
	SIMPLE SUGARS	
31 Fructose	65 Lactose	92 Sucrose
		138 Glucose
		152 Maltose

CONTINUED

TABLE 9.4 CONTINUED

VEGETABLES

12 Bengal gram dal
20 Soybeans
32 Dried peas
37 Red lentils
43 Black beans
45 Kidney beans, dried
46 Black-eyed peas
46 Butter beans
46 Baby lima beans
47 Rye kernels
49 Chickpeas (garbanzo beans)
Most green vegetables

50 Green peas, dried
50 Lima beans
54 Brown beans
55 Pinto beans
57 Haricot (navy) beans
59 Black-eyed beans
60 Baked beans (canned)
65 Green peas, frozen
65 Romano beans
68 Green peas
70 Potato, sweet
74 Yam
74 Kidney beans (canned)

80 Potato, new, boiled
80 Sweet corn
88 Beet
99 Rutabaga
100 Potato, mashed
107 Pumpkin
108 Broad beans (fava)
117 Cooked carrots
118 Potato, instant
128 Potato, russet, baked
139 Cooked parsnips

FRUITS

10 Nopal (prickly pear)
32 Cherries
34 Plum
36 Grapefruit
40 Peach
44 Apricot
49 Strawberries

53 Apple
55 Plum
58 Pear
59 Apple juice
63 Orange
63 Pears, canned
66 Pineapple juice
66 Grapes
69 Grapefruit juice
74 Orange juice
74 Peaches, canned
75 Kiwi
79 Fruit cocktail

80 Mango
84 Banana
91 Raisins
91 Apricots, canned
93 Cantaloupe
94 Pineapple
103 Watermelon

The longer the race, the more popular additional protein and complex carbohydrates have become. The exact proportion varies with the individual's own insulin response. Some athletes have trouble digesting protein during lactate threshold efforts and prefer only liquid or gel-based carbohydrates when racing a half-Iron event at elite speeds. Others prefer ingestion of solid bars with protein and/or a protein-laden sports drink. Athletes who regularly eat bars and use protein in longer training may still opt for a carb-only drink in a one-hour sprint triathlon.

Competing sports drink and gel vendors go to great lengths to promote their kind of sugar. Whether you are drinking complex or simple carbohydrates, they are still sugar. There have been studies that show maltodextrin, a complex carbohydrate, still classified by some as a sugar, is absorbed more rapidly in the intestine during workouts. Other experts claim that it is unnatural and overly glycemic, and they prefer more natural sources like fructose or brown rice syrup. Some nutritionists claim fructose causes intestinal distress and should be avoided. Many drink manufacturers mix it up with both simple and complex carbohydrates, trying to please a wide audience who want steady burn yet an appealing taste. Other vendors go with the plainest, unflavored drinks.

Since we've seen athletes at both ends of this simple-to-complex carbohydrate spectrum racing well, it's hard to suggest a universally applicable product. There is definitely a trend in longer races to more complex carbohydrates with varying protein concentrations. In ultradistance races lasting ten to twenty-five hours or longer, you will rarely see simple-sugar-only products. In sprint triathlons, you will see more simple carbs ingested. We recommend you experiment with a balance of simple and complex sugars and protein for longer workouts and then tweak the exact proportions to see what works best. Establish a firm pattern well *before* your important long-course race, and never change products during A-race week. Chances are you will have to use a carb-only drink or gel supplied by a half-Iron aid station, so practice with that brand as well.

Post-workout nutrition

After workout or race completion, muscle glycogen is depleted and ingesting a relatively large proportion of carbohydrates hastens recovery. This effect is maximized when combined with a protein mixture of 20–35 percent. The easiest method for most athletes is a recovery drink combining these with electrolytes and water. After that, the body can tolerate a sizable meal for two hours without excessive insulin response. For example, if you drink a high-glycemic recovery drink and eat a pasta dinner within ninety minutes of a four-hour brick once per week, you are less likely to gain weight than if it becomes your regular dinner.

Most athletes have favorite foods they are loath to relinquish, so permitting them after long workouts or races is a practical compromise. Note that truly toxic substances in food like trans fats or potentially carcinogenic additives have no "safe period" for usage: They should be avoided at all times, and in fact their negative effects are enhanced when rapidly absorbed after a workout. Even if you occasionally eat big, stay natural.

Once you are back to your normal life, what kind of foods should you eat? In addition to the balance of proteins and fats previously listed, low- to moderate-glycemic carbohydrates include brown rice, beans, fresh fruits, and berries. Bananas, oranges, and grapes are the highest-glycemic fruits; though healthy, they should be consumed in moderation with other fruits when trying to lose weight.

In the past, many endurance athletes consumed ostensibly healthy carbohydrates like enriched bread, bagels, and pasta as an alternative to "junk food" containing sucrose. Yet the net effect of these high-glycemic, processed grains is very similar to sugar. For example, a typical dark chocolate bar (so-called junk food) may have a lower GI than enriched pasta (so-called endurance food). You can moderate the effect of these products by sticking with 100-percent whole wheat bread (it has to say "100-percent" on the label, or else it's probably enriched white flour), 100-percent whole wheat pasta or the newer protein-laden pastas cooked al dente (firm), or whole-grain brown rice. You still need to moderate these grains, even with the healthy variety. Remember they are relatively recent to the human diet, and unless you are very active immediately before or after ingesting them, they are likely to be stored as additional fat.

PRACTICAL APPLICATION FOR ENDURANCE ATHLETES

As we stated earlier, most endurance athletes are aware of the theoretical relationship of macronutrients to performance. Fewer are able to put them into practical use, maintaining optimal weight while providing energy for hard training. Many diet systems are too complex or too radical to maintain during the racing season. As with the foods themselves, the simpler our approach the better: Our lean ancestors had no diet foods or books on nutrition, just natural, unprocessed sources of energy.

Review of Fundamentals

The six simple rules merit review:

1. Eat lots of fruits and vegetables: When not training or racing, they should compose most of your carbohydrates.
2. Eat lean protein with every meal: It will encourage a steadier blood sugar, promote recovery, and discourage overeating of carbohydrates.
3. Eat high-glycemic foods and drinks immediately before, during, and after workouts or races. The amount varies depending on a workout duration of 90–180 minutes and the experience of the athlete. Veteran long-course athletes have learned to burn fat and conserve glycogen, so may require high GI foods only after their longest workouts or races. Larger athletes require more calories than leaner, smaller-framed ones.
4. Limit saturated fats, and avoid trans fats (hydrogenated or hydrolyzed oils) entirely.
5. Eat fats from groups A (omega-6) and C (omega-3) as described in the previous section.
6. Eat smaller meals more frequently: This habit follows the practice of our ancestors and the animal kingdom, and promotes better digestion and steadier blood sugar for training and racing.

Even though we do not recommend severe calorie restriction, you may find yourself becoming hungrier when moving to a more balanced diet despite no change in total calories. The common Western diet has created an epidemic of "carbohydrate addiction." It's not unusual to go through a two- to four-week withdrawal period as the body adjusts to burning more fat and protein, but less sugar, even when not training. Much of this is psychological. You can usually deal with these cravings by eating whole fruits frequently in moderate portions and drinking plenty of water. If you find yourself not able to eat any more fruit, but you still have a craving for sweets, that's a good sign you are experiencing more of a psychological addiction than true blood sugar or low-calorie problems.

Long workouts are not the time for calorie restriction

Remember to eat plenty of carbohydrates before, during, and after longer workouts. Don't try to restrict calories while training by using diluted sports drinks or fewer gels and bars. For every 3–4 extra grams of carbohydrate ingested, try to add 1 gram of protein to the mix.

On average, athletes will burn about 700 calories per hour on the bike and over 1,000 calories per hour on the run: Larger athletes burn more, smaller athletes less. Cyclists can usually ingest 400 calories per hour for longer bikes via drinks, gels, and bars without issue. It's difficult for runners to ingest more than 350 calories per hour. For swim sessions of only one hour, or shorter bike and run sessions up to 60 minutes, no additional calories are required, only water. Adding a little electrolyte powder for shorter, hot workouts over 95°F is the only needed supplementation. Anaerobic training will usually reduce the amount of carbohydrates that can be processed by the intestine, so you may need to fuel earlier before or during the warm-up. It's also very easy to forget to eat when hammering in a bike peloton or running intervals on a track. If you do ingest a high-glycemic drink or gel before a workout or race, try to time it about 15 minutes before the start. Anything earlier and you will invoke an insulin response; anything later and the calories may not become available until well into the session.

Periodization of Diet

As with the training itself, the volume (total calories) and intensity (caloric density and GI) of foods varies at different times of the season (Table 9.5). The best time to experiment with diet variation and attempting weight loss (or gain) is during the early season when training volume and intensity are low. Many triathletes wait for the high-volume sessions during the long-course racing period to burn off excess body fat. By then it's often too late to change habits or measure response. If nutrition is a unique skill set, it is best started during the skill-building part of the season.

If you were going to change your swim stroke or bike crank length, you would expect a transition period of a few weeks or longer before measuring improvement, moving out of the comfort zone. The same thing can happen with dietary change, which is the reason it should be done gradually within a long-range plan and preferably with the help of a nutritionist or coach who shares your "food philosophy."

TABLE 9.5 PERIODIZATION OF MACRONUTRIENTS OVER TRAINING YEAR

PERIOD	FAT %	CARBS %	PROTEIN %
PREPARATION	35	40	25
BASE Low intensity requires fat-burning capacity; consume good fats (omega 3 and 6) and limit saturated and hydrogenated oils. Maintain protein and derive carbohydrates mostly from fruits and vegetables.			
BUILD Increase proportion of carbs from natural sources, limiting sugars and starches to workout and recovery.	32	43	25
PEAK Time carbs for breakthrough workouts and reduce during longer recovery intervals.	28	47	25
RACE Increase carbs, but reduce overall calories on race week; "carbo-loading" is automatically caused by taper without gorging. Consume only good, easily digestible fats.	25	50	25

The pH Factor

The relative measure of acidic hydrogen ions (H^+) to alkaline hydroxide ions (OH^-) is called pH, a negative base-ten logarithm ranging from 0 (highly acidic) to 14 (highly alkaline). The higher the pH, the lower the concentration of hydrogen ions, or the more alkaline the substance. The human body works well in a narrow range of balanced pH around 6.4. Go much above or below this number, and you dramatically change biochemical reaction rates. Most cells cannot survive outside this narrow range.

Aerobic training produces energy by burning fat and carbohydrates, and as with all "fires" this requires oxygen. The resulting oxidation reactions cause a buildup of positive hydrogen ions, making the tissues more acidic. The so-called "burn" and fatigue caused by hard training, traditionally attributed to lactate buildup, is now considered just a symptom of excess hydrogen ions. Just as spicy (acidic) food makes your tongue burn, acid-producing exercise makes your muscles burn and requires recovery time for the body to reestablish the pH balance in the bloodstream and affected tissues. There are added effects of acidity that progress with aging, so that hard training requires longer recovery time. Some aging effects like loss of muscle mass can never be completely stalled, but they can be postponed by raising the alkalinity of diet.

Muscle protein is composed of nitrogen, which reacts with the positive hydrogen ion and is then processed out of the body as urea in urine. Along with it goes calcium, essential for strong bones. As we age, we are in fact peeing away our muscles and bones. In addition to the oxidation effects of training, the other way we increase acidity is by eating certain foods. In fact, most modern foods are quite acidic, though we would not know this from tasting them. A net acidic effect on the body does not mean the food itself has a lower pH, just that it lowers the body's pH after absorption. In fact, foods that taste sweet or neutral can raise blood acidity, while foods composed of mild acids (lemons and oranges, for example) promote a more alkaline (higher pH) blood response.

About the only natural foods that have a net alkaline effect are fruits and vegetables, and you should already be eating plenty of these as your main source of carbohydrates. Although some of the foods on the acidic side of the equation are healthy sources of protein, without the balance of negative ions from the fruits and vegetables, you cannot achieve optimal health. Table 9.6 shows the relative acidity (positive number) and alkalinity (negative value) of foods. This is not the same thing as pH, but it is a relative ranking developed (by T. Remer and F. Manz) to measure the body's likely response to these foods.

An interesting sidenote to the recent studies on oxidation, muscle-bone loss, and acid/alkaline levels can be found in an unlikely place. Two thousand or more years before the ranking described above, Vedic texts from India were recommending the foods on the alkaline list as encouraging *prana* or energy and preserving the body frame for a long life. Exposed to the British colonial education system, these yoga systems were easily modified to incorporate the scientific notion of pH balance in the late nineteenth century. Many yoga instructors have encouraged their students to test their pH via litmus paper on the tongue for over a century, with higher pH indicating greater harmony of the physical vehicle.

As with other lessons learned from Paleolithic research, we find the natural approach analyzed by modern science following the ancient

TABLE 9.6 ACIDIC VERSUS ALKALINE FOODS

Food	Value
ACID FOODS (+)	
Grains	
Brown rice	+12.5
Rolled oats	+10.7
Whole-wheat bread	+8.2
Spaghetti	+7.3
Corn flakes	+6.0
White rice	+4.6
Dairy	
Parmesan cheese	+34.2
Processed cheese	+28.7
Hard cheese	+19.2
Cottage cheese	+8.7
Whole milk	+0.7
Legumes	
Peanuts	+8.3
Meats, Fish, Eggs	
Trout	+10.8
Turkey	+9.9
Chicken	+8.7
Eggs	+8.1
Beef	+7.8
ALKALINE FOODS (–)	
Fruits	
Raisins	–21.0
Black currants	–6.5
Bananas	–5.5
Apricots	–4.8
Vegetables	
Spinach	–14.0
Carrots	–4.9
Celery	–5.2
Lettuce	–2.5

practices. As Yogi Berra (the baseball player, not a Hindu yogi) put it, "It's déjà vu all over again."

A Word for Vegetarians

Vegetarian lifestyles are becoming more prevalent in Western cultures after a long facility in Asia and India. Most of these newer vegetarians still consume milk and eggs (ovo-lacto vegetarians), and some consume fish (pisco-vegetarians). Our experience finds few if any pure "vegans" (no animal products whatsoever) in endurance sports. Some vegetarians pursue this lifestyle as part of a religious heritage or environmental consciousness that comes before their love of triathlon. How does this relate to the principles of the Paleo diet as discussed?

From a formal perspective, the Paleo diet recommends wilder meats and eggs as the best source of protein. It also proposes that the foods eaten by your ancestors 30,000 years ago are probably best for you today. Since many coastal cultures (the Inuit and Asian cultures along the Pacific Rim, for example) relied on fish as the only source of animal flesh, we can agree that some Paleolithic cultures ate no beef, pork, or poultry, yet consumed plenty of protein and good fats. The endurance and physical vitality of these Pacific Rim cultures is without question.

Critical to the endurance athlete is the availability and use of quality protein with every meal. It is possible to maintain 25 percent of total calories from protein by ingesting only egg, soy, and whey protein with occasional fish meals, though it requires more discipline in the beginning. Although many have assumed that vegetarians are routinely protein deficient, studies have found this not to be the case. In fact, vegetarian athletes are often acutely aware of maintaining a high volume and high quality of protein, just as athletes who live and train in the hottest regions are more acutely aware of hydration and sodium needs. Vegetarians can also bypass the health hazards of growth-hormone-infused and grain-fed beef and pork, chlorine-laden poultry, and other symptoms of our mass-production food culture. It's often easier and cheaper to find healthy eggs or natural whey sources than it is to find wild chicken meat, venison, or bison in urban areas.

It is not my purpose to advocate a vegetarian lifestyle, but I do confirm it's possible to follow the nutritional precepts of optimal endurance performance without eating meat. World champions in varying endurance events have proven this. It does take discipline and may require the use of additional powdered drink supplements before/during/after workouts. Many small and varied protein doses can add up to significant total grams and all the favored amino acids: for example, eating a small handful of nuts two to three times a day, mushrooms mixed into salad, skim milk, a hard-boiled egg snack, and so on.

SPORT-SPECIFIC CALORIES AND SUPPLEMENTS

Unfortunately, most of our media exposure to nutrition involves sports drinks, gels, bars, and seemingly magical powders and pills to improve performance. There has indeed been a revolution in sports nutrition, but none of these extras will be effective without the foundation of a balanced, natural diet. Beginners can probably train and race okay up to the half-Iron distance with only a sports drink and some gel-packs for longer workouts or races. You should not attempt to experiment with anything beyond the basics until you've achieved some stability with weight and reliable, energy-producing natural sources.

This field is changing so rapidly that it's impossible to describe all the vendors in this book. I'll stick to sources I've used myself or with my coached athletes, but don't consider any reference here as an endorsement—you must find your ideal product yourself. Keep in mind that many pros choose products based on sponsorship dollars, and that we all have to drink brand names in long-course races beyond what we can carry. For the most part, the sports nutrition industry is honest and does its best to make a reliable product, but as with any mass-produced commodity, there are imperfections and variations on how humans will respond under stress. To paraphrase Edison, choosing a sports drink is literally "90 percent perspiration."

We could fill the pages of an entire book on nothing but sports nutrition products, but we'll restrict our discussion to a brief tabular summary. There are more products coming to market every month, and athletes from beginner to elite have used and been successful with most of the listed products. As with bike frame and running shoe brands, the final decision should include word-of-mouth advice from a friend or coach and real-world experimentation with the products. Don't rely exclusively on advertising data or magazine articles.

TABLE 9.7 CLASSES OF SPORT-SPECIFIC NUTRITIONAL PRODUCTS

TYPE	USAGE	COMPOSITION	COMMENTS
Sports drinks	During training and racing over 1 hour. Shorter workouts need only water.	Carbohydrates, sodium, potassium, other supplements; some include 15–30 percent protein	Most common endurance product. Athletes must choose protein and electrolyte balance with carbs.
Pre-workout and recovery drinks	Before and after longer workouts and races	Carbohydrates, electrolytes, protein, easily digestible fats	Helpful for long workouts and races; may replace with balanced meal if available.
Gels	During training and racing over 90 minutes	Carbohydrates, electrolytes, caffeine, other supplements	Useful in longer workouts and races, in addition to sports drink calories.
Bars	During training and racing over 2 hours	Carbohydrates, electrolytes, protein, other supplements	Useful for longer cycling and cold-weather training and races. Can be used for pre- and post-workout.
Vitamins, minerals, and antioxidants	Daily during all training, recovery, and rest	Standard vitamins, minerals, trace elements, and special supplements such as omega-3 and coenzyme Q10	Necessary for all endurance athletes. Ideal mixture varies with athlete and training.
Ergogenics	Before, during, and after intensive or high-volume training and racing	Highly variable	Recent cutting-edge, legal supplements for experienced athletes.

TABLE 9.8 SPORTS DRINK

BRAND	CARBS	ELECTROLYTES	PROTEIN
Gatorade	Yes	Yes	No
Powerade	Yes	Yes	No
Accelerade	Yes	Yes	20%
Sustained Energy	Yes	Yes	16%
Hammer Gel	Yes	Yes	No
InfinIT	Yes	Yes	Varies

The trend is toward varying protein concentrations for long-course, but races usually supply carb-only drinks at aid stations.

TABLE 9.9 RECOVERY DRINKS

BRAND	CARBS	ELECTROLYTES	PROTEIN	FAT
Endurox R4	Yes	Yes	25%	1g
Recoverite	Yes	Yes	30%	1g
Metabolol Endurance	Yes	Yes	25%	20%
Ensure	Yes	Yes	30%	30%

Recovery drinks are used after workouts and sometimes before or during longer races. These products contain some fat and are harder to digest in high heat and at anaerobic intensity.

TABLE 9.10 SPORTS BARS

BRAND	CARBS	ELECTROLYTES	PROTEIN	FAT
Clif Bar	40–50%	Yes	15–30%	10–20%
PowerBar	40–50%	Yes	15–30%	10–20%
TwinLab Ironman	40%	Yes	30%	30%
Balance	40%	Yes	30%	30%
Boulder	50–60%	Yes	15–25%	10–15%

Sports bars take longer to digest than drinks or gels but give some solid foundation in the stomach during rides or races over two hours. They provide additional protein if none is available in liquid form. Require additional fluid to digest.

TABLE 9.11 SPORTS GELS

BRAND	CARBS	ELECTROLYTES	PROTEIN
Clif Shot	Yes	Yes	No
GU	Yes	Yes	No
JogMate	Yes	Yes	Yes
Hammer Gel (dissolves in water bottle)	Yes	Yes	No
PowerGel	Yes	Yes	No

Sports gels require immediate addition of fluids to digest; most are around 100 calories per package or 600 calories in a larger flask.

TABLE 9.12 VITAMINS, MINERALS, AND ANTIOXIDANTS

TYPE	USAGE	BENEFIT
Multivitamin	3–5 times a day for most endurance athletes	Balanced nutrition, prevents deficiency
B group	1–5 times a day, depending on previous multivitamin concentration	Immune response, mental clarity, fatigue prevention, antioxidant
C	3–5 times a day, 500–1,000mg per day	Antioxidant, immune response
E	3 times, 800IU per day	Antioxidant, virility, cardiac response
Omega-3 (fish-oil pill)	3–5 times daily, more when injured or sore	Antioxidant, anti-inflammatory, cardiac response
Iron	Mostly from food, supplement only with doctor's supervision	Aerobic capacity, fatigue prevention, circulatory health
Calcium	Unnecessary with balanced alkaline diet	Promotes bone density, but studies show dairy products can actually reduce the overall calcium in some women, since it increases acidity. Eat alkaline foods to increase calcium levels.
Sodium	Mixed with beverage or via 100–200mg tablets during hot or long training	Prevents dehydration and hyponatremia, prevents cramping. Essential for human life. Dangerous to omit in high heat.
Potassium	Mixed with beverage or via 25mg tablets during hot or long training	Prevents cramping, dehydration, and fatigue
Magnesium	Useful in hot training in small doses, 25mg	Overall mineral balance, cramping, fatigue prevention
Manganese	Useful in hot training in small doses, 25mg	Overall mineral balance, cramping, fatigue prevention

All athletes should take a multivitamin and mineral supplement several times each day. Additional minerals and antioxidants are very helpful during high-volume, high-intensity, or high-temperature training.

TABLE 9.13 ERGOGENIC AIDS

NAME	USAGE
Glycerol	Mixed with four parts water or sports drink before long and hot events
Caffeine	Coffee, tea, sports drinks, or gels. Up to 200mg every 2 hours, or 50mg per 100 calorie gel.
Choline	Egg yolks, organ meat, spinach, soybeans, lettuce, wheat germ. Or 1g supplement pill.
Galactose	Specialized "supersugar"
Creatine	Best when mixed with carbohydrate, 1–5g before or during session
Sodium Phosphate	Up to 6g before competition, or 10g/day for race-week loading
Coenzyme Q10	200mg daily or before races
Glutamine	2g per day or more
Glucosamine	750mg, 2–4 times daily with meals
Chondritin Sulfate	600mg, 2–4 times daily with meals
Methylsulfonylmethane (MSM)	500mg, 2–4 times daily with meals

Note: Ergogenic aids are growing in popularity but have mixed results in different athletes. Beginners should focus on fundamental natural diet and multivitamin, mineral, and antioxidant products. Advanced athletes must experiment before racing with product.

BENEFITS	POSSIBLE SIDE EFFECTS
Retains fluids, delays dehydration.	Dizziness, "icky" feeling, increased thirst. Finish drinking 30 minutes before race start.
Most popular ergogenic. Works best when dosage limited before race. Improves fat burning, alertness, competitive finish.	Diuretic, stomach upset, elevated heart rate, nervousness, headaches, addiction.
Useful in workouts or races over 2 hours.	Diarrhea, flatulence. Contraindicated with ibuprofen or aspirin.
Ease of digestion. Avoids insulin response, low GI.	None reported.
Improves muscular strength and power, promotes lean muscle mass gain. Good for bike peloton, strength sessions. Use by endurance athletes should be only 20% of recommended dosage for strength athletes. Less effective in long-course, aerobic efforts.	Diuretic, gastric distress, mood alteration. High dosage (>25mg) side effects in strength athletes.
Promotes LT and VO_2max efforts, less effective for aerobic, long-course events.	Not for sodium supplementation. Limited race usage due to rapid tolerance. Ineffective for beginners.
Cardiovascular health, energy production. Counteracts free radicals and cell degeneration with aging.	Limit usage to once daily or before races.
Conditionally essential amino acid, becomes necessary with longer training.	Full benefits not yet confirmed.
Maintains joint cartilage. Useful for longer workouts, especially running.	Contraindicated for pregnant or lactating women. Aggravates shellfish allergies.
Promotes cartilage formation.	
Promotes formation of collagen, connective tissue, joint cartilage.	

CHAPTER 10

Advanced Concepts

If we are going to the moon and back in this decade, we must have rapid decisions. . . . There is such a thing as cluttering up your mind with too much trivial information.

—Wernher von Braun, founding director of NASA Manned Space Exploration

"TRIATHLON AIN'T ROCKET SCIENCE"—OR IS IT?

Triathletes are some of the most technically advanced people I have met, even though I've spent decades working for advanced technology companies and NASA's Manned Space Center—hence the above quotation. In my early days of triathlon racing, I noticed how closely it resembled planning a manned space mission. The quality of minds that coach and the athletes who win triathlon championships are among the best in the field of physiology. It attracts a disproportionate number of participants from medicine, life science, and various engineering disciplines. Where other popular sports typically have athletes who drop out of school due to academic deficiencies or forgo college to turn pro, triathlon champions often have advanced degrees up to the doctoral level. As you read this book, I safely assume you are an intelligent and perceptive individual simply because you are a triathlete.

There are so many variables, so much technology, so many things to go right or wrong with training and racing. You need to have a working knowledge of many theories and be willing to apply those principles in myriad variations. As physically demanding as triathlon is, a big reason for its growing popularity is the mental challenge. About the only physical sport I've played that compares to triathlon's technical complexity is golf, and certainly racing at the highest levels is a kind of aerobic chess.

That being said, it is possible to overthink the sport of triathlon. Training is limited by time, and thoughts should not be crowded during an actual race. If you must think of three or more things, you might race okay; think about only two things, and you will have a better day; but if you can focus on one concept, those are the days you win races, break records, or have your own personal record. Paradoxically, the reason for training and paying attention to countless details is to be able to forget about them on race day, focusing only on pacing and the moment at hand.

Although we intend this book to be useful to first-time long-course athletes, we know that a good number of more experienced and elite triathletes will read it. And some triathlon beginners will come from technical backgrounds involving physiology or related disciplines, or have advanced knowledge of one of the three individual sports. To quench the thirst of these advanced students, we reveal some of the more advanced concepts in this chapter.

I must confess my own life as a "techno-geek," absorbing the arcana of triathlon like a sponge in my initial years of training. As I've matured in racing and as a human being, however, I think less about technical details related to my own training, having fused them into a more intuitive appreciation of the whole. Most of the technical challenge now lies in coaching others, teaching them about the details, and writing for the serious triathlete.

One should be careful not to project technicality onto all racers. Many champion and veteran athletes do very well without thinking much about technical details. Others obsess over every millimeter, gram, and kilocalorie—Lance Armstrong and Dave Scott are good examples of this type. If you were to take a poll, I think you'd find most champion triathletes lean more toward the obsessive side of the spectrum, but even these will admit there's a negative side to detail orientation. Their best races are credited more to heart and passion than to the accumulation of mere rational knowledge.

Some of this chapter will review topics initiated in others, but with more detail. Complex concepts do bear repeating. We know some experienced readers will skip quickly to this chapter for the shinier nuggets to be found.

MASTERY OF THE WILD WATER

As we noted in Chapter 6 on swimming, technique is more important in the water than with the other two sports, but there comes a point when it is not enough. Once you have mastered stroke technique, you will have to learn to swim harder to go faster. Those with prior competitive swimming experience may have reached that point before entering triathlon. They already have become used to swimming hard intervals in most of their workouts. But if you're a more recent graduate of the preparatory school of technique improvement, this transition can be challenging.

I have emphasized repeatedly in this book that muscular endurance is the key to success in triathlon, especially in the long-course events where excessive intensity is counterproductive. Still, swimming often involves a higher perceived effort for training at a certain heart rate. A workout that would feel like anaerobic endurance (Zone 5b–c) in cycling or running may indeed only produce muscular endurance (Zone 4–5a) heart rates in swimming. If you want to swim at the top of your division in the half-Iron distance, which is not much farther than the Olympic-distance swim of 1,500 meters, you will likely have to swim quite hard, probably above your lactate threshold. The good news is that hard swim training is easier to recover from than it would be with the bike or run.

The other factor requiring anaerobic endurance in long-course swimming is the competitive open-water venue. You might well turn in a top bike or run split with completely even pacing at or below lactate threshold, but swimming will likely involve significant variations in breathing and heart rate, even in a calm-water swim. The start itself is an adrenaline rush for beginner and expert alike, and unless you can catch the strongest swimmers easily on the bike, most top age groupers and pros want to go out with the lead pack on the swim, and if you want to win an elite division it may indeed be necessary.

Drafting on the swim is legal and worth around 10 percent of your energy. Finding a swift drafting target can take a minute or two off your half-Iron swim split while still using less energy. Once the swim-start chaos has cleared, finding the right drafting partners is the first thing an advanced triathlete should do. Some experts like to begin right in the melee and stick behind the fastest feet all the time; other strong swimmers have been known to start slightly to the side and angle in on the lead pack after 100–300 meters. And then there's that one lucky guy or girl who set swim records in college and knows nothing but is leading the whole way (they have already skipped to the advanced cycling section of this chapter). If you know you have one of those "ringers" in the swim, you might want to relegate yourself to the chase pack and maintain a relative gap to the leader that you know you can close on the bike.

Those wishing to keep up with the elite triathlon swimmers will have to train specifically for this kind of effort. Instead of the typical "build" efforts in intervals, where speed is moderate and then increases toward the latter intervals, you will need to practice going out quite hard, then easing into a draft, then speeding up again at the finish. For example, after warm-up you might do 6×50-yard or meter intervals all out with only five seconds' rest, followed by 3×300 at T-Pace (1,000yd/m time-trial pace), and then 6×100 fast. Or you could swim a 300yd/m time trial followed by your regular medium interval session.

Other tricks include running 50–100 meters to the pool or along the beach to simulate a running start. The USA Triathlon training center in Clermont, Florida, even has a special downhill entry into its 70m pool just to practice these kinds of starts and exits from the water.

If you are going to swim with the triathlon elites, you may need to spend four, five, or even six days a week in the pool or open water, unless you came to the sport already with the highest level of swimmers. Use that extra day or two to focus on open-water swimming and/or anaerobic endurance through short-to-medium intervals above threshold. This is contrary to the advice we give to the broad majority of triathlon swimmers, but it becomes necessary to improve after a certain point.

Another way to save some swim minutes is reconsideration of equipment. Most advanced swimmers have already chosen goggles that are reliable and effective in keeping out water, but you might want to reexamine the quality of vision you achieve. Are you sighting buoys and navigating as well as possible? Just a one-degree deviation over half the course can cost fifteen seconds or more on the final result, the difference between winning the swim (or your division split) or not. Sometimes fast pool swimmers have chosen hydrodynamic, comfortable goggles that work well in the pool, but that may lack the peripheral and long-range vision needed for open water. The visual range for open-water swimming can be ten times greater than indoor swimming, so it pays to review your practices. And, of course, get your eyes checked regularly by an optometrist and consider contacts or prescription goggles if indicated.

Wet suits have done more than any one piece of equipment to improve swim splits, but veteran swimmers may still be using a suit a few years behind the technology. Comfort and streamlining have improved in recent years, as has variation in styles and sizing. If you're one of those fast swimmers who think a wet suit doesn't really matter for a strong fish like yourself, think again. Also consider the full-body Lycra suits from pool racing for the warmer days: The half-Iron swimmer of 1,900m can definitely benefit, since it only takes a few seconds to remove them in the transition area.

Speeds have also improved using the recent tri-suits, with swim manufacturers incorporating some of the same sharklike material found in the full-body suits. Some excellent swimmers are now reporting times almost as good with a neoprene wet suit using the newer fabrics legal in all water temperatures. Unfortunately, the only way to know for sure is to actually do a time trial in the suit, which precludes returning it. You might borrow a fellow competitor's suit in your size to try, or look for Internet discounts on used suits or discards from sponsored teams. Many elite pool swimmers discard a full-body Lycra suit after only one or two races, which is still useful for most triathletes. Some manufacturers are wisely allowing swimmers to try out a suit at the actual race site without obligation, which definitely worked for me in one Ironman race, and I bought the suit.

The concepts involving stroke mechanics were covered in our basic swim section, Chapter 6. What's left for the advanced triathlete is a focus on racing strategy in the open water and specialized training for this venue. Only elite swimmers can go "all out" for the entire half-Iron swim, but veterans can definitely push harder than an Ironman swim, considerably above lactate threshold.

The 1,500m Standard

One of the best predictors of half-Iron swim performance is a 1,500m time trial in a long-course pool without drafting. This is close enough to the actual race distance to serve as a race simulation and is a classic "distance test" for most elite swimmers, the metric mile. You can also use the

1,650-yard short-course version of this test, but it's less realistic. If you've previously been measuring your threshold pace with 1,000-yard/meter time trials, increase this to 1,500 meters or 1,650 yards. Conduct this test every three to four weeks as you move into the latter Base periods and during the race season. You can substitute a race effort 1,500–1,900 meters for the test, but remember that few triathlon open-water courses are measured precisely and that weather greatly influences speed. If you find yourself beating known rivals or consistently moving higher in swim place rankings in your region or larger competitions, you have evidence of significant improvement.

We can start with the elite swimmers, who can usually do this test in twenty minutes or less. If you can swim 1,500 meters long-course in twenty minutes, you can stay with just about any lead pack at a half-Iron race, unless there happen to be ITU Olympic-distance pros involved. Unless you are in a smaller, regional long-course race, you probably cannot lead the swim with slower ability, certainly not in an Ironman qualifier or Ironman 70.3 championship.

Once you have the technique and fitness to meet this twenty-minute goal, you can also work on your 300–400m start capability. You will probably have to swim this initial distance very hard to join the lead pack. If it's a smaller group and you know the other elite swimmers, you may be able to lessen this shock by drafting behind the acknowledged best swimmer. You can develop specific training sets that mimic this all-out start, followed by a steady-state effort for the rest of the swim.

If you are not close to the elite standard of twenty minutes, it's rather pointless to try to go out with the leader, though many will attempt this. In a half-Iron race, you might even recover and go on to have a decent overall race, but it's usually counterproductive and not good strategy.

For the rest of us who call ourselves "advanced" at long-course, the age groupers who are strong cyclists/runners but know they cannot lead in the swim, a more realistic goal is to reduce the 1,500m time trial to 22–23 minutes. Most veteran triathletes with good all-around fitness and body composition can bring their 1,500m time down from 25–26 minutes to 23 minutes in a reasonable time, perhaps one season with diligence. You may need to add more pool time, moving from three to four or even five swims per week, with some of these sessions going well beyond one hour.

After that, it gets increasingly difficult and requires micromanagement of stroke technique and perhaps additional practice time. If you chose the half-

Iron distance as a time compromise between short-course and Ironman training, the extra time may not be worth the investment, and definitely is not if it means reducing bike or run training or cutting into precious rest.

Controlled Chaos of Open Water

Just as road racing in a peloton is different from cycling on a track or in a time trial, so open-water swimming differs radically from pool swimming. Some people find this daunting, and many fine pool swimmers with competitive experience don't like to be touched in the water. Or they have strokes that degrade in rough water. Fortunately, experience and the intrepid spirit of triathletes can solve these problems.

Others relish the relative chaos of an open-water mass start. Stronger, larger athletes and those who played contact sports readily understand the bump and grind. Those with strategic minds relish the large "chessboard" of a lake, river, or ocean in which to start their attack on the race. Sometimes people with no previous swim experience eventually become dangerous in the open water, consistently coming out of the water in a higher place than their pool splits would indicate.

If you can adopt this wild-water mind-set, you will definitely become a better overall long-course racer. The ability to exit with stronger swimmers maximizes your bike skills, giving you stronger athletes to chase and pass on the bike. Remember that triathlon is one unified event in three phases, and any improvement in one area usually benefits the other phases as well.

Advanced Muscular Endurance Swims

These workouts are not recommended for beginners or for intermediates very often. If you only swim three times per week, you can only do one of these. If you swim five or more times per week, it is possible to fit in two, which is typical for pros. They can build the essential qualities needed to move ahead in the pack during a 1,900m swim. Before you tackle the specific problems of a fast start, you need to bolster your ME workouts to get your 1,500m time to the lowest reasonable value. You will likely reach a plateau within a macrocycle or season, and at this point you can consider adding some fast-start medicine to your prescribed training. We highly recommend using the 6×400m workout in Chapter 6 on swimming as your basic ME swim. It's the classic method of improving your 1,500m or half-Iron swim split.

Below are some more ME swims that are geared specifically to open water, and one pool swim that you can use to build fast start speed.

Open-water Swim A

Warm-up: Easy swimming out and back for 10 minutes.

Initial Set:

Swim ten times easy out 50 meters; then build up back to shore and run up to the beach.

Main Set:

Swim 5 minutes at threshold (out and back to shore); then five times easy out for 25 meters and fast back to shore and run up to the beach. Repeat this four times.

Pull Set:

Continuous swim for 15 minutes. Mix parallel-to-shore and out-and-back swimming

Cool-down: Your choice, about 10 minutes.

Open-water Swim B

Warm-up: Your choice

Initial Set:

Swim ten times easy out 50 meters, build up back to shore, and run up to the beach.

Main Set:

Swim 3×1,000 meters (or on estimated time), including a beach/shore run of 5 minutes between each rep.

Cool-down: Your choice, about 10 minutes.

Open-water Swim C

Warm-up: Easy swimming out and back for 10 minutes.

Initial Set:

From the shore, swim 8×40 seconds build, then 40 seconds easy.

Main Set:

Swim 6×5 minutes. For first and last 90 seconds go hard, then settle into threshold pace.

- Swim thirty easy backstrokes between reps.
- Can be done out and back or parallel to shore.

Pull Set:

Continuous swim for 15 minutes, but mix it up with out-and-back and parallel-to-the-shore swimming.

Fast Start:

Repeat ten grand prix starts (running from shore to water) with thirty strokes hard and fast, then swim back easy to the shore.

Cool-down: 15 minutes mixed/choice work

Training for a Fast Open-water Start in the Pool

Warm-up: 300 freestyle, easy to steady

Pull Set:

Swim 8×50, followed by 800 with pull buoy and paddles

- Swim 50 meters very hard on 3 seconds recovery. Expect your speed to degrade as you fatigue.
- At the end of the 50 meters repeats, take 30 seconds rest then swim 800 at T-Pace; check your splits every 200 meters (very briefly).
- This should feel extremely difficult, like a tough race start. If you want to see if you can take it out hard in a race, this will show you the impact and let you know your ability as well as the risks.
- This set is done early so that you can feel the impact of only a short warm-up—deep warm-ups are essential when you want to drill the start of a swim.

Kick Set with Fins:

3×(3×100), first set is kick with board, second is kick, third is kick/swim by 25 (you can mix strokes).

- Within each set, descend 1–3.
- Send-off interval by set is 2:00, 1:50, 1:40.

Speed Set (Facilitates Drafting):

9×50 on 1:20 recovery

- Get three people in your lane, leave three seconds apart, trailing swimmers sprint up to the feet of leading swimmer and then hang on—it will teach the difficulty of bridging. After leading *one* swim, leader drops to end of group, so each person leads one out of every three swims. Leader goes all-out.

Main Set:

8×100 free, threshold pace with 10 seconds recovery

- Rest 60 seconds.

4×100 free on 2:00 (allow at least 30-second recovery interval).

- Start at 95 percent effort and aim to swim 0.5–1.0 seconds faster per 100.
- Hold form!

Cool-down: 200 very easy mix of strokes, pause 5–10 seconds at each 25.

HANGING WITH THE HAMMERHEADS ON THE BIKE

There's nothing quite like the feel of going fast on a bike. I often think of that line from Tom Cruise in the movie *Top Gun.* As he's walking to the cockpit of his F-14 Tomcat fighter, he exclaims to his fellow test pilots, "I feel the *need* for *speed.*" There is something about fast cycling that goes beyond mere fitness or technique: You have to *want to, love to,* ***will*** *to* go fast. It's something we have in common with the auto-racers, downhill skiers, test pilots, and astronauts—the sheer passion for speed. On a bike, speed is quite palpable: You feel and hear the wind on your face, the rolling of the wheels, the scenery rushing by.

To be classified as a top triathlon cyclist, you must be a fast cyclist, period. There are few if any triathletes who could ride for a team in the Tour de France or even win a national amateur championship. There is simply not enough time for bike training with all the swimming and running (the latter which inevitably lowers cycling speed). But many top triathletes have the aerobic capacity to train with pro cyclists, and many top age-group triathletes can win their local road-cycling time trial or train with the Cat. 1–3 cyclists in their area. If you marvel at the top bike splits in your region, those athletes are likely riding with the fastest people they can find in their area every week or two, including fast road racers. They love speed and have no fear of hills, wind, tight corners, close passes—or most road racers. Many are the tales of triathletes initially scorned at road rides or races, only to quickly silence the critics with their mental toughness and muscular endurance. The best cyclist of our generation, Lance Armstrong, began as a triathlete.

We spent many pages in Chapter 7 on cycling emphasizing the importance of good aero position on the bike as essential for comfort and speed. As with the swim equipment, the finer points become even more important at higher speed. The effects of drag at an elite 25–26mph are considerably higher than those of the average triathlete at 20mph.

Things like aero helmets, one-piece tri-suits, internally routed cables, gloveless hands—even the exact position of thumbs on the aerobars—become obsessions for those wishing to win the bike segment. But in the last analysis, the person with the fastest bike split in a long-course triathlon is usually the strongest cyclist, period. You can't fake a time trial for 56 miles.

First Improve Power, Then Equipment

How do you achieve these higher cycling speeds and still have something left for the run? You will end up training with more attention to quality, which often means a higher heart rate and definitely higher and more consistent power output. For today's best cyclists in road and triathlon events, that means using a power meter for training and perhaps for racing. These devices are not cheap, especially the more accurate ones, but if you are already a competent cyclist with good endurance, they can do more than any device to move you into the top ranks. Given a choice between a disc wheel or a good power meter, both costing around $1,000, the investment in power measurement will pay bigger dividends in the long run.

Once you have improved power output at lactate threshold, and this consistently over a season, the aerodynamic benefits of racing wheels will be even greater. But since aero wheels hit the market before good power equipment, most triathletes have reversed this investment advice. Fortunately, the price of power measurement continues to go down or remain reasonable, while disc wheel prices go up.

Frame design used to be split into two distinct groups: those frames that were light and allowed the rider to generate power over varying terrain, and frames that stressed aerodynamics at the expense of comfort, speed, or climbing. Although these two categories still exist, the comfort and power potential of time-trial bikes has improved dramatically in the past decades. There are also many more manufacturers of strong time-trial/triathlon bikes in the market, and some models definitely favor different types of bodies and athletes. Some athletes will perform better on a softer boom-bike design, others on a stiffer conventional frame. Some benefit from an aggressive forward position of 78–80 degrees; others generate more power in aero position farther back toward the conventional position of 73 degrees; others are in between the two extremes. There are as many optimal bike frame setups as there are human body types.

What you want to avoid is having "blind faith" in any one brand or marketing data presented about a certain frame. Just because your training buddy looks good and rides fast on a certain brand does not mean it's right for you. Yet people purchase bike frames like automobiles, because they've seen someone else looking good driving an attractive model. If you examine the course records for many half- and full Iron-distance courses, you'll find they were achieved on rather unremarkable frames, at least in superficial appearance. What you will see, however, is that the top riders fit almost perfectly upon their frames, both in terms of static position geometry and dynamic quality of pedaling. The frame that puts you in the best position with highest pedaling economy is the frame that's right for you, whether it costs $1,000 or $5,000.

Wheels have also taken great leaps in evolution, but they also have increased radically in price. Manufacturers have found that riders will pay almost anything for a newfangled feature, and wheels bear a higher profit margin than frames, which require more of a dealer network and attached components.

Most of the new wheel features are helpful, but there is no linear relationship between price and speed. Wheels costing $1,600 will not save twice as many minutes as those costing $800, but some people are willing to pay another thousand dollars for one more minute. The wide majority of age-group triathletes would probably receive the best value from deep-rimmed or tri-spoke wheels that can be ridden on all courses and in almost all conditions. Those who could win their age group probably could benefit from a disc wheel or even finer refinement of the front wheel. Beginners can go with a medium-rimmed, low-spoke wheel and do quite well in the first few years of competition, and this for only a few hundred dollars, not a few thousand.

Although most of the top-of-the-line wheels are available in clincher models now, and clincher tires are faster than they've ever been, taking the time to invest in and learn to manage tubular (sew-up) tires is still worth it for the advanced triathlete. There are considerable savings in weight, drag, and improved handling with tubulars. And if you're racing long-course, the time will eventually come when you will have to change a tire in a race, and this is potentially much faster with a tubular. You will see just about all pros riding tubulars, despite the popularity of racing clinchers. I would still, however, recommend training on clinchers for cost and convenience reasons. Learning to glue on a tubular is one thing; having to continue gluing them and replacing tires two to three times in a long training ride gets pretty old.

Aerobars have moved more and more toward an integration of the handlebar, aerobar, brake lever, and sometimes the stem. But if you look at the true wind-tunnel tests, weight, and feel, there's not much more to do once everything has become carbon, light, and perhaps integrated. Since your body's position still has more to do with speed, comfort, and power generation than the static configuration of the aerobar and related components, spending a lot of money to save a few grams for something that looks carbon and cool may not be worth it. The front-end setup that works for you over long hours of training and racing will produce the best times. For some this is best done with a newer, integrated carbon system; for others, it involves a clip-on bar and adjustable stem. Don't spend more money on aerobars unless you are uncomfortable or lack aerodynamic quality—or you have spent all that you can to improve wheels and drivetrain. I'm amazed at how many strong riders will post the best bike split in a race using the most simple, draft-legal clip-on bars with traditional ram handlebar and shifter.

Quality and Intensity Are the Keys

Now we have come full circle. To reach the highest ends of cycling, you must be able to apply more force to the pedals over a longer period of time. The only way to do this is to improve strength and fine-tune the intensity of workouts. If you've never taken weight training seriously, you skip a lot of gym workouts, or you just mull your way through, it's unlikely you'll ever reach your full cycling potential. With running and swimming, you can race well with little or no strength training. Cycling, however, may be the only sport in triathlon that truly benefits from raw power, the kind you find in the legs of football players or shot-putters.

If you are already a strong cyclist looking to become the best in your region, you'll have to ride faster with stronger riders, yet avoid overtraining. This means riding along a "razor's edge" of intensity, pushing hard but with plenty of recovery. All cyclists, especially steady-state long-course triathletes, have a tendency to fall into what road racers call "gray zone" cycling. For beginning or intermediate triathletes, this is not such a bad thing, since they are cautious in saving energy for the run. But for the elites and top age groupers, you must be able to suffer some on the bike and still have plenty left for the run. The only way to achieve this

1–3-percent difference between "very good" and "great" is by putting in a lot of muscular-endurance miles on the bike, and for the half-Ironman athlete, a little anaerobic endurance as well.

If you beat most triathletes without a problem, you may have to seek out Category 1 or 2 road cycling groups to get that sprinkling of anaerobic endurance riding (Zone 5b), joining their wild and woolly group rides. If you choose this path, don't overdo it, and stay away from cutthroat peloton riding a few weeks before an A race. The tendency to hammer in the early miles or draft (illegal in half-Iron racing) is easy to ingrain, and you must "deprogram" before a nondrafting, steady-paced triathlon.

In all your bike training, as you get closer to your A race, go slow on recovery days and hard on your quality days. Avoid the gray zone of low Zone 3 when you should be riding steady in Zone 2. And as we said in the previous bike chapter, the best way to make sure you are riding at the right intensity is to use a power meter. Very fit athletes have a flattened heart rate profile during intense training that does not reflect their true intensity. And power meters are now light enough and built into wheels fit for racing, so you can take your intensity data with you to the racecourse to manage pacing there as well.

Advanced Power Training

We introduced the concept of power training in Chapter 7, and we want to expand upon it. No other factor has changed cycling more in the last decade. There are few if any top road racers or triathletes who still do not use power measurement in some phase of training or racing. You can become a strong cyclist and finish triathlons well without ever using a power meter, but you will develop bike speed and learn to preserve energy for a long-course run more effectively if you know exactly how much energy you are developing and expending. Cycling is currently the only triathlon sport that allows measurement of energy usage directly; swimmers and runners can only guess at power based on speed and heart rate.

You might want to review the basics of power training in Chapter 7, "Cycling Skills." In this chapter, we'll break away into the advanced concepts. Despite its wide acceptance in the cycling and triathlon community, power training is so new that its foundational theory is still evolving. Since power varies greatly in real time, the use of computer software and analytical methods become necessary. When you first start using power, there is an initial "Aha!" experience when you see how much energy it takes to go steady, fight the wind, or climb a hill. After a few workouts, however, you need to examine detailed graphs and tables and have some comparable framework with which to compare your performance. The use of power analysis software, usually provided by manufacturers like PowerTap, Polar, or SRM is the minimum requirement. Pushing the envelope on power software are systems like TrainingPeaks.com and CyclingPeaks.com, which allow you to examine almost every relevant perspective. We'll try to skim the treetops of this new science, with thanks to power experts like Andrew Coggan, Ph.D., and Hunter Allen for their pioneering work.

Just as there are standard heart rate ranges for training intensity zones, there are comparable power zones that can be developed. As with heart rate training, the critical value involves lactate threshold power. When training with power, we regularly measure threshold power output just as we measured threshold heart rate. For the wide majority of triathletes, the effective and simple way to do this is by a 30-minute time trial performed every three to four weeks.

If you followed our recommendations in Chapter 7 on cycling skills, you already know your lactate threshold heart rate. Now measure average power you are generating over this period, which we initially called "critical power over 30 minutes" (CP30). Other writers use terms like functional threshold (FT) power, but for the long-course triathletes and time trialists, they are essentially the same thing. If you come from a road-racing or long time-trialing background, you may be able to maintain FT for up to 60 minutes, but this kind of power would be mostly limited to professional triathletes.

It is possible for elite triathletes to maintain lactate threshold heart rate for an entire half-Iron bike segment and still have enough for a speedy run. But it is not likely that they are also maintaining the same power output, since "cardiac creep" causes heart rate to gradually rise after a few hours for the same power output.

The goal for triathletes is to test and train for a relatively level power curve over the 30-minute time trial. If you find you are generating considerable variations or spikes that are *not* due to the terrain or weather, it may indicate fruitful areas for improvement in muscular endurance or pedaling economy. To achieve the performance enhancement you want for a half-Iron race, you must extend this ability to a 56-mile ride over variable terrain and do this with the economy that will allow for a speedy half-marathon run.

We start by creating our advanced power zones using Dr. Coggan's scale. You can purchase software or create your own spreadsheet to calculate these values (Table 10.1).

Note the difference in percentages of lactate threshold power and heart rate for each zone. They are not linear, and they create individual progression curves. Power ranges provide higher resolution and the ability to fine-tune intensity.

To use Table 10.1, simply plug in the values from your most recent 30-minute time-trial test (or other valid performance). For example, a strong 40-year-old age-group triathlete was tested at 300 watts (average over the entire 30-minute outdoor time trial) and 155bpm threshold heart rate (the average heart rate starting at minute 10 and ending at minute 30 of the time trial) and produced these values (Table 10.2).

TABLE 10.1 COGGAN POWER ZONES RELATIONSHIP TO HEART RATE INTENSITY

TRAINING ZONE	POWER RANGE (WATTS)		HEART RATE RANGE (BPM)	
	Lower (%)	Upper (%)	Lower (%)	Upper (%)
Active recovery (Zone 1)	Less than 55		Less than 68	
Endurance (Zone 2)	56	75	69	83
Tempo (Zone 3)	76	90	84	94
Threshold (Zone 4–5a)	91	105	95	105
Aerobic power (Zone 5b)	106	120	More than 106	
Anaerobic capacity (Zone 5c)	More than 121		Not applicable	

TABLE 10.2 SAMPLE AGE-GROUP TRIATHLETE POWER ZONES

TRAINING ZONE	POWER RANGE (WATTS)		HEART RATE RANGE (BPM)	
	Lower (%)	Upper (%)	Lower (%)	Upper (%)
Active recovery	Less than 165		Less than 105	
Endurance	168	225	107	129
Tempo	228	270	130	146
Threshold	273	315	147	163
Aerobic power	318	360	More than 163	
Anaerobic capacity	More than 363		Not applicable	

You might ask: "What do aerobic power (also known as VO_2max power) and anaerobic capacity have to do with my training?" If you are a long-course triathlete, the answer is "little, if anything." You simply do not access this kind of power more than 1–2 percent of the ride, nor do you need to train specifically to achieve it. That's not to say this sample athlete never has a heart rate over 163bpm when climbing a steep hill, or that the athlete should never participate in a group ride with a sprint finish, just that training time is better spent focused on zones that are likely and desirable in the half-Iron race.

In fact, one of the most important things to learn from the power zones is where to sit during a typical "steady" ride, the kind of power that should result during 80–90 percent of your training time on the bike. Note that an endurance ride for this athlete (typically 2.5–4 hours for half-Iron training) does not exceed 225 watts, except perhaps in the occasional steep climb. Go out on your typical long group ride of the week and see how easy it is to go well *over* this prescribed wattage, especially early into the ride. If you have experience at riding 100 miles or longer, see how difficult it is to maintain this wattage after five hours or so if you went out hard—unless you have other riders to push you.

Also note just how easily you should be riding on a more restful recovery ride, such as those after a weekend C race or the evening after a morning long run. As one pro cyclist described it, recovery rides should be done at a pace that is "guilt-provokingly slow." It's rare indeed to find a group of your racing buddies who ride this slowly together on their so-called "easy day."

The flip side of this table shows that rides in the Tempo power zone can get quite challenging after only one hour. For the veteran half-Iron athlete, this power output is critical for race performance: If you do your long rides in the Endurance power zone and one other ride in the Tempo power zone, that is all the intensity you need to do quite well in a half-Iron race. As you get closer to race season, however, you want to avoid turning your Endurance rides into Tempo power sessions; this mistake is common with triathletes.

Add to the Tempo ride some Threshold rides with moderate intervals of 6–10 minutes, and you can move your bike split up near the top of the rankings in most races.

The finer points of aerobic threshold (AeT)

Even within the important Endurance zone, we can make fine distinctions between what is called "aerobic threshold" (AeT) and other types of steady riding:

- **Aerobic threshold (AeT):** This is the first opening of breath. Not breathing hard, just opening of breath. See if you can breathe through your nose only; if not, you are probably over AeT. This could be related to the top of Friel's Zone 1.
- **Steady:** Add another five beats per minute of heart rate, or 60–70 percent of your threshold power. You should be able to do your longest ride completely at this pace without much difficulty, and indeed most of your long rides in a training year would be completely steady. As race season approaches, simply throw in a few 10–20-minute accelerations to tempo every hour, and you have enough intensity to become a strong long-course rider. But remember "steady" is not recovery: It still requires mental focus and is not merely slow.
- **Upper steady:** Add yet another five beats per minute, or 75 percent of your threshold power. Now you must stay mentally focused to

maintain wattage. But this is still not "hard" or "tempo" riding at all. You may not want to converse with fellow riders anymore, though if you did, it would not make you breathe much harder. This would compose a big chunk of longer rides when you are very fit, as well as being the midpoint of shorter bike workouts not involving threshold intervals or recovery.

We'll say it again: The most important way to build long-course triathlon bike fitness is to spend the large majority of your bike time in steady and upper-steady states. The biggest problem with veteran athletes trying to move up in rank is spending too much time in Tempo (Zone 3), which hurts recovery and the ability to absorb other harder training at lactate threshold.

The problem with heart rate monitoring is that once athletes reach a point approaching peak fitness, there is a flattening of heart rate that makes gauging the desired training intensity difficult. With a power meter, 225 watts is still 225 watts, whether it's early or late in the season, or at the beginning or end of your long ride. You have a direct line to reality.

RUNNING WITH THE GAZELLES

When I first started distance running rather late in life, I always called the top runners in our club *gazelles*. They looked so relaxed and built for speed. How did they get that way?

Controllable Factors

We have to admit that running does have something to do with genetics, or perhaps better said, less to do with things we can practice. The reason is simple: We are born with a natural ability to walk and run as bipeds, but this is not so with swimming or cycling, which we must consciously learn. But when we get to distance running, innate body composition must combine with cardiorespiratory fitness and mechanical execution to produce good speed over longer distances like the half-marathon. The last two factors are within our control: fitness via our training plan and mechanics via mental focus and the nervous system. We can indeed learn to run fast, just as we can learn to speak a foreign language almost as well as a native, given patience and intelligent application.

We covered the running mechanics thoroughly in Chapter 8, and we refer you to those pages. Although they can be classified as "advanced concepts," we found them so fundamental to running and injury prevention that we placed them in the primary running chapter. If you have not achieved optimal running technique, simply trying to run harder or faster can produce injury or overpacing in a race. Even if you are already advanced, you must consistently review and maintain running technique.

That leaves us with genetics (body composition) and training. About the only genetic factor we can control, albeit with difficulty, is our body composition. And this requires controlling our eating (see Chapter 9, "Feeding the Mind and Body"). For most age groupers, this factor may indeed be the greatest limiter, and it shows up most pronouncedly on the run. A well-trained veteran can be ten pounds overweight yet still swim fast and bike strongly on a flat course, but you will see a dramatic drop-off in the relative ranking on the run. Just look at the splits for the winner of the Clydesdale or Athena division and you will see the drop-off in running placement.

On a smaller scale, even two or three pounds of extra weight can cost minutes in a hilly half-Iron race, the difference between finishing on the podium or getting a slot for Kona. Like technique flaws, excess body mass increases your risk of injury, especially during harder or long runs. So you need to master this factor before increasing your run intensity. Indeed, many large athletes would be better served with little or no anaerobic running except on race day.

Training for Speed

Once you have paid due attention to the technique and body composition factors, what's left is fine-tuning the intensity and recovery. This balance is a delicate matter for long-course athletes, since the things that lead to elite running can easily go over the edge into overtraining and overpacing in a race. Fortunately, these risks are much less with the half-Iron distance than for marathon runners or Ironman racers.

As we did with the technique, we can learn something from the Kenyan runners who dominate the world in long-distance running. You might think their training plans are complex, but they are rather simple. About 90–120 minutes of running each day, split into two workouts. Surprisingly, they rate only about 23 minutes per day as "quality running." Before you think that's too little, you should know that quality for them involves a pace of around 4 minutes per mile. I doubt readers of this triathlon book will be doing their intensity work at this speed, but learn that in order to run fast, you must train very fast for relatively brief periods.

In our previous running chapter, we emphasized lactate threshold intervals on the track or road as the breakthrough intensity workouts in the training week. We discouraged most triathletes from going harder because of the injury and overtraining risk. For those who now run relatively fast and want to move to the higher levels of long-course racing, we modify that advice and say that some brief work considerably above lactate threshold (Zones 4–5a), done at or near VO_2max (Zone 5b), can be helpful. You might think of VO_2max training as analogous to handling a radioactive substance: potentially very powerful, but quite dangerous if mishandled or allowed to overaccumulate.

Determining VO_2max pace

The most accurate method to determine VO_2max (aerobic capacity) is to go to an accurate testing lab. Even then, reputable labs have shown wide variation in tests results for the same athlete, or the same lab will show differences for the same athlete over a brief period. Although knowing your aerobic capacity is a useful rule of thumb, you still need to discover what your outdoor running pace is at this effort. Fortunately, you can conduct this test on your own without fancy equipment.

1. Warm up in Zones 1–2 for 15 minutes.
2. Do some technique drills such as six to eight strides.
3. Run another 5 minutes easy, with a buildup to testing pace.
4. Recover 3–5 minutes. Wear your heart rate monitor.
5. Run 6 minutes on a running track at the fastest pace possible. Aim for even splits or slightly negative splits in the final laps.
6. Note your heart rate in the final minute. This value is useful *if* it is relatively steady for the final laps. If it is continuing to rise more than three beats or so, the value may be invalid as a future guide.
7. At the end of six minutes, stop and note the exact distance of the final lap (a tape measure can be helpful here, or pace off the distance from the last turn), and add that to the number of previous laps × 400 meters for the total distance in meters.
8. Divide 142,000 by the total number of meters covered. If you ran 1,578 meters in six minutes, your VO_2max pace is about 90 seconds per 400 meters.

With this value you can plan your high-intensity workouts. The 400m pacing value is more useful than heart rate for VO_2max workouts, since high-intensity intervals can be too brief to register effectively on an HRM. It's a safe bet, however, that if you find yourself going way over your tested VO_2max heart rate in several intervals, your pacing is too hard.

VO_2max intervals

These workouts are best done 8–15 weeks before your first A race of the season. They should not be attempted more than once per week. For some athletes, once every 10–14 days is plenty. You only need 10–15 minutes of VO_2max-paced work to achieve results. More than this is counterproductive.

- **Workout 1:** Warm up well and then, on a track, or with a GPS device on a soft surface such as grass, run 20–24×200 meters at VO_2max pace (about 20 seconds per mile faster than your 5K race pace per mile). Jogging recovery for 100 meters after each, taking the same amount of time as the preceding 200 meters. Stop when you can no longer maintain the targeted pace.
- **Workout 2:** Warm up well and then (preferably on a track) run 15–20×30 seconds at a VO_2max pace. Recover by jogging easily for 30 seconds after each. You should cover half of the fast rep distance during your jog (for example, run 150 meters in 30 seconds, jog 75 meters in 30 seconds). Stop when you can no longer maintain the targeted pace.
- **Workout 3:** Warm up with four or more strides. Then 5×1,000 meters (recover for 500 meters) at VO_2max. Maintain quick cadence of 90 right-foot strikes per minute or higher.
- **Workout 4:** Warm up with four or more strides. Then run 200, 400, 600, 800, 1,000, 800, 600, 400, 200 at VO_2max pace, recovering for half the interval distance before the next one.

After you've done your preplanned period of VO_2max interval training, you should progress toward lactate-threshold intervals at a lower intensity as described in the running chapter.

Unless you are a veteran triathlete approaching division-winning speeds, LT intervals are probably all you need. Note that many renowned masters athletes win their age group regularly without ever doing VO_2max intervals, saving those efforts only for race day. On a personal note, I have won my masters age group regularly in regional races and qualified for Kona many times doing no VO_2max work in training, only reaching this intensity in short-course B and C races and stand-alone marathons. If you really have a hankering to push yourself hard, it's usually better to put this extra intensity into muscular-endurance intervals or more climbing on the bike.

CHAPTER 11

Racing the Perfect Distance

If God invented marathons to keep people from doing anything more stupid, the triathlon must have taken Him completely by surprise.
—P. Z. Pearce

WINNING AND LOSING

Most of this book is dedicated to building fitness and helping you to organize your training. But if you've been in the sport long enough to try a half-Iron race, you are seeking more than casual fitness. You want to race longer or faster or probably both. Training for races is unique: Much time is spent preparing for a brief payoff at the end. Long-course training and racing have an even larger disparity. Whereas fitness is built gradually, and patiently, with predictable scheduling, racing tends toward the sudden, the urgent, and the unknown.

Some character types are ideally suited to the racing mind-set, inclined to perform above and beyond good fitness. Others start the race well prepared but fall short in execution. Veteran athletes have tasted both kinds of experience, but those who we call "winners" have learned to make effective race-day execution a regular habit. Even when fitness is suspect, luck is bad, or strategy misfires, they still find a way to come out on top—or very close to the top. As Joe Friel says, if race results were determined by things like VO_2max, we would just compare our test results at the starting line and avoid a whole lot of suffering.

The good news is that so-called "losing" is self-corrective. We actually learn more from loss than from victory, and if you are wise enough to apply the lessons learned to future training and racing, chances are you will accomplish your goals more often. Much of the difference is purely semantic: How do you define *winning* in multisport—or in life?

Finishing a long race brings forth a spiritual joy.

Winning is not the same thing for a beginner or a masters age grouper as it is for a professional trying to win the world championship. A good rule of thumb is that we all want to race better than we did the last time at that distance, or finish a longer distance than ever before. Even a PR performance will have gaps in it that you wish were better. Finishing times that appear only average can still show moments of courage and skill overcoming obstacles or bad luck. Triathlon gives you three ways to show your courage and ability, and in the half-Iron venue you have considerable time to recover from limiters.

Some of my most gratifying days on a racecourse did not involve the fastest times, but were based on qualities of courage, suffering, loved ones, and an immeasurable spiritual joy. They are as likely for the first-time finisher as for a pro winning the world championship. They are as intense at age 80 as age 30.

Even with this flexible definition of success, you are more likely to achieve it if you have a good race plan, which includes the time leading up to the event. The real secret to effective racing is confidence, and knowing you have planned the details beforehand enables them to fall below the level of consciousness. You can focus on higher motivations and fully enjoy the experience.

Choosing the Right Race

This chapter will focus on the A race, which we previously defined as one to four of your most important races of the season. For the long-course athlete, this means only two peaking periods for the year, with possibly two A races close together forming one peak. One error common to amateur and pro alike is attempting to peak more often in one year, leading to burnout. This happens even with famous champions who have an incredible season or two, lots of long-course and even short-course championships, followed by an extended period of poor performance or injury. Sometimes they never return to the sport, or at least not at their previous level.

With professional athletes we can understand their dilemma, since triathlon racing is not yet a high-paying profession, and they feel they have to take advantage of fast years for sponsorships and income. About the only pro triathletes who can afford *not* to race most of the year are Ironman world champions and Olympic gold medalists.

Your race planning begins with choosing the right event. As you move to longer courses, this choice becomes even more important. There once were only a few half-Iron events to choose from, but now we have almost too many to choose from. You can now find long-course races as often as you would short-course events a few years ago.

For many age groupers who race a sprint triathlon every few weeks, it's hard to learn the discipline of saying "no" to short regional races that interfere with their long-course preparation. Fortunately, this problem is not so acute for the half-Iron distance, which usually requires no more than eight to ten days of quality taper and similar days of race recovery.

One strategy that has worked for some is to choose liberally from races you'd like to do early in the year, calculate costs and examine travel plans, but delay actual race registration and airline reservations until the latest opportunity. That makes it easier to drop races if you're tired or life has dealt you a difficult schedule. Note that the half-Iron national championships, Ironman® Hawaii qualifiers, and the Ironman 70.3 championships may fill up early, forcing you to register well in advance.

I usually find myself dropping a couple of planned shorter races every year to ensure proper recovery and time to peak for a full or half-Ironman. Yes, it would be great to see old friends and win the age group at the state or regional short-course championship, but one must set a priority, because the half-Iron event could lead to a national or world championship qualification. With the steady growth in triathlon, there will always be more racing opportunities in the future.

The problem with some athletes is that they reach a high level of fitness in their long-course training and then believe they can "spend their fortune" on several shorter races, often too close to the long race. On the other hand, many veteran triathletes choose the half-Iron distance because it allows them to still have fun in shorter races close to home. The key is timing, balance, and leaving enough empty space in your schedule.

TAPER AND PEAK

This topic is one of the most controversial in all of triathlon, even more for the half- and full Ironman-distance races. If you had to pick information that pros treat as "top secret," it would be their taper-and-peak plan before an A race. Most will be glad to talk about key workouts during regular training, but the period leading up to the race is sacred. This attitude is justified: Like politics or warfare, what you do the days right before a battle can make all the difference.

The optimal pre-race period varies for different people and for the same athlete from year to year. Learning from your superiors is useful, but one of the biggest mistakes a new half-Iron competitor can make is trying to follow the taper routine of their favorite pro listed in a magazine, or blindly follow last-minute anecdotes overheard at the race expo or Web site. Yes, you can learn from others, but that does not mean you should copy them.

Definition of Taper and Peak

First, let's define what we mean by *taper* and *peak,* terms that are sometimes interchanged but do not necessarily mean the same thing. For our purposes, we'll define taper as any reduction in volume and/or intensity at any point in training. A rest and recovery week is a kind of mini-taper that we undertake to prepare for another two- to four-week block of hard training. Even a Monday rest day each week could be called a micro-taper between weekly segments. But this kind of taper does not involve peaking for a race, which is much more specific.

We define peaking as a programmed sequence of workouts that maximize performance (which is really speed) for a specific race venue. Part of this peaking process may include tapering intensity and/or volume, but that is not the whole of it. It is possible to follow a peaking procedure without much taper at all. For example, a person planning for an Ironman chooses a half-Iron event to test fitness and perhaps to qualify for the Ironman event. They may choose *little or no taper* and craft simulation workouts that will improve speed without reducing volume or intensity.

Taper-and-peak scenarios have opposing polarity. One end of the spectrum involves minor weekly training change: simply train through the event with perhaps some simulation workouts. This is not likely to produce a PR performance but is useful for elites or top age groupers who know they can place well without reducing volume. Unfortunately, this method is also used by intermediate and advanced triathletes who are nervous or unwilling to cut back, fearing loss of fitness. Many are the woeful tales of Olympic-grade athletes doing long runs or bikes only a few days before their medal event, unable to cope with all the nervous energy, exhibiting a psychological state that might be characterized as obsessive-compulsive.

The other polarity says to do as little as possible, to maximize rest and allow nature to do her work with little conscious interference from the athlete's mind. Many beginners try this route, and it usually will improve performance, but is unlikely to produce *maximal* performance for a particular athlete. About the only time we recommended it is in dire circumstances where injury, infectious illness, overtraining, or all three leave the athlete no other alternative—except withdrawing from the event.

Interestingly enough, some legendary performances have come from sick athletes who were *forced* to rest more than they would have liked before an Olympic gold medal, Super Bowl victory, or Ironman triumph. Given a choice between too much or too little before an event, we'd rather see an athlete go with all rest than too much work.

Rarely, however, should the intelligent athlete choose either extreme. There is a path between these two polarities that produces the razor's edge of fitness that we crave at the starting line. If you followed the fundamental principles we've taught in the earlier chapters, peaking for a race should be hassle-free and fun. Athletes pounding out miles for many months discover that a well-planned, balanced taper can produce feelings of joy and confidence—even enhancing relationships that were perhaps neglected during previous training weeks.

How Long Should I Taper?

This question is the most common for long-course athletes. The half-Iron distance does not require the same period as the full-Iron taper, either for beginners, age groupers, or pros. The factors that determine the period for different types tend to converge around an eight- to ten-day taper-and-peak period. Pro triathletes have won half-Iron national championships on eight days' taper, sometimes only five, and even beginners rarely benefit from more than ten days' reduction for all three sports. The new half-Iron racer is often still building long-course endurance two weeks out with relatively low volume, and the elite does not require as much taper to recover.

In fact, the ideal length of taper is slightly different for three events: running recovery takes longer than cycling, and cycling takes longer than swimming. The classic full Iron-distance period of three weeks, including two peak weeks and the race week itself, is compressed to a period of 8–10 days, which we could term an oversized race week. The length of travel and interval between location arrival and the race start is usually brief for half-Iron races, so indeed much of the race week is spent at home.

Keep the half-Iron taper-and-peak as simple as possible. Many beginners might choose a ten-day taper because it allows for more recovery time between breakthrough workouts and less rushing about with scheduling and travel. The veteran may choose an eight-day or shorter taper to remain sharp and perhaps minimize interference with other preparation, perhaps a full Ironman coming up later. In fact, if a half-Iron event is only a B race for you, five days may be all it takes to adequately tune the body for racing.

There are two ways to handle this peaking period before a race:

- The linear taper, where volume is reduced in a straight-line decay over time. For example, runs descend from 90 minutes to 45 minutes to 30 minutes to 15 minutes, and so on for cycling and swimming. This method is effective and may indeed be simpler for a first-time long-course triathlete to execute.
- The breakthrough-and-long-recovery taper, where workout intensity is kept high, but a period of 72 hours of active recovery intervenes between hard efforts, instead of the typical 48-hour period in normal training. This method pays higher dividends for the more experienced long-course athlete and is common for elites. They continue to build speed for as long as possible, sacrificing a little endurance in the trade by reducing volume. That being said, remember that no *real and lasting* changes to fitness or speed can occur less than two

weeks before an event. You cannot forge a bigger sword right before the race; only sharpen the blade you already have.

Our approach will be to teach the more advanced method but give alternate scenarios for different classes of athletes.

Your overall mental attitude and confidence have as much to do with "absorbing" the effects of the oversized pre-race week as the actual workouts. Factors like nutrition, travel stress, and relationships with loved ones and the race staff also play a big role. Some people become nervous during taper or when attempting an event for the first time, leading to irritability and social friction. This kind of stress is just as costly as overdoing your workouts. Now is a good time to use your visualization and calming inner voice to control your mind and emotions. You can often tell when veteran triathletes are ready to have a good race by their attitude and tone of conversation.

Sample Peaking Schedule

Although it's impossible to come up with a universal pre-race schedule for all athletes, we will include a good example that can work for many half-Iron athletes. The values are based on someone training around 15 hours in the regular training weeks, with the longest run of 2 hours, longest brick of 4 hours (3-hour ride and 1-hour run), and longest swim of 65 minutes. Athletes tapering from less volume need to reduce these values proportionally. Those with higher volume should still adhere to time limits since they must taper more rapidly from larger volume. The motto for the tapering athlete should be "Less is more."

Before beginning the taper-and-peak regimen, take an additional 24–48 hours of complete or active rest (Wednesday and Thursday relative to Table 11.1). This pre-peak rest promotes fresh and spirited workouts at the peaking intensity.

Some days in Table 11.1 are "swim only." These should be considered active recovery days, with very little activity other than the brief swim. Also note that there are only two workouts that could be termed moderately hard, the brick workouts on Saturday and Tuesday, with 72 hours in between. This does not mean going slow, but reducing intense periods and extending recovery so that the overall mood is crisp but not taxing.

The most important day for sleep is two days before the race, Friday night before a Sunday race. Many studies have shown that athletes who

TABLE 11.1 SAMPLE PEAKING SCHEDULE FOR HALF-IRON RACE

DAYS OUT	WEEKDAY	WORKOUT	COMMENTS
9	Friday	AM: Swim (Muscular Endurance) 6x400@40-second rest PM: Run 75 minutes (up to 75% of longest run)	Last hard swim, long run. Can move two days earlier for longer taper.
8	Saturday	AM: (Brick) Bike 90 minutes (up to 50% of longest ride), start Zone 2–3, finish last 10 minutes Zone 4 to simulate race fatigue. Practice fast transition. 30-minute run (up to 50% of longest brick run).	Race-pace simulation at end of ride, first half of run.
7	Sunday	AM: Run 60 minutes (up to 50% of longest run), Zone 2.	Can reduce time if fatigued.
6	Monday	AM: 45-minute continuous swim (preferably open water); may add fartlek intervals.	Active recovery day, emphasize rest.
5	Tuesday	Brick: Bike 60 minutes Zone 2–3, with last 10 minutes Zone 4 to simulate race fatigue. Practice fast transition. Run 15–20 minutes, Zone 3.	Crisp, but not stressful.
4	Wednesday	Swim only 40 minutes: Warm-up: 2x100 descending times (30sec); 3x50 kick descending times (30sec); Main Set: 4x200 fast with 50 kick easy between 200s. Cool-down: 200 easy swim.	Swim only: crisp but short.
3	Thursday	AM: Run 30 minutes. Warm up including four pickups. Then two 90-second intervals (recover 3 minutes) slightly faster than race pace. PM: Bike 45–60 minutes with four 90-second intervals at race effort (three-minute recoveries). Cool down and stretch.	Easy except for pickups. Shorten if long travel.

CONTINUED

TABLE 11.1 CONTINUED

DAYS OUT	WEEKDAY	WORKOUT	COMMENTS
2	Friday	Swim 25 minutes on race course with several short accelerations to race pace. Work on sighting and swimming straight. If open water unavailable, sight "buoys" every 4–6 strokes using an object on pool deck.	Beginners can omit workout, especially if traveling. Sleep important. Last large dinner.
1	Saturday	Pre-race brick: Bike 30 minutes, fast transition, then run 15 minutes, practicing in or near race transition. Include 3–4 short, race efforts on each segment. Absorb course layout. Check out swim start, perhaps brief 10–15 minute swim practice if no Friday access to course.	Real-world course conditions more important than speed. Eat significant calories, minimal fiber.
0	Sunday	RACE DAY: Awake and eat 2.5–4 hours before race start (400–800 calories). 10–15 minute warm-up in all three sports, depending on bike racking and convenience. Bike 15 minutes with 2x60-second pickups, rack bike, run 10–15 minutes with 2x30-second pickups; prepare transition space, swim 5–10 minutes and stretch. Try to finish swim warm-up 10–15 minutes before start, 30 minutes maximum. Arrive at start in plenty of time!	Sleep, nutrition, and unrushed morning are paramount.

have trouble sleeping the night before the race can still perform at a high level, but 36 hours before the start, sleep is more important. Along with quality sleep, it's important to do as little as possible two days before the race: brief swimming for veterans and perhaps nothing at all for beginners. Do not attempt to run, but you might try a 15–30-minute relaxed walk if swimming is not practical.

For those driving the day before the race—not recommended for the half-Iron distance unless you live nearby—you may be better off doing the short brick at home in the cool morning before driving. It's preferable to practice at the race site if you can arrive not long after noon and it's not too hot.

Remember that excessive walking, socializing, and exploring at the expo can become more taxing than workouts, especially if you are in the sun. Stay off your feet and in the shade as much as possible. Books, television, or inspiring videos are good ways to pass the time.

The race venue determines the schedule the day before and morning of the race. Some races are very strict about bike racking and discourage swim warm-ups on race morning. Hint: You can sometimes creep way down the course and enter the water well away from the other swimmers to warm up before your wave start. Given a choice between an ideal warm-up and getting your gear arranged and your body to the starting line in plenty of time, you should shorten the warm-up. Just try to do *something* for fifteen minutes or so before the race. Warm-up is not as critical for half-Iron athletes as it is for shorter distances, especially if you are a beginner—advised to start each race segment in Zone 1–2 and gradually build pace. But if you are a pro or a division-winning age grouper planning to go out in Zone 4 or 5 in each sport, the warm-up becomes important.

RACE STRATEGY

Although we place this section after race-week scheduling, you should begin planning your race strategy well before arriving at the event, several weeks earlier as you proceed with training tests. Part of the testing process should have included interval sessions slightly above race pace, time trials, and race-simulation workouts. You should use the data collected from these breakthrough workouts and tests to determine a realistic time goal. The more experience you have, the better chance you have of predicting actual performance on race day.

I believe that even a first-timer should have a flexible time goal, even if it's seven hours or more. Simply saying your goal is to "finish the race" gives you specious excuses to slow down or make other mental errors that could prevent your safe and healthy finish. Sticking to a flexible, realistic plan is likely to make the first experience more pleasurable, building your confidence as you pass relatively easy milestones for each segment (Table 11.2). Using easy gears on the bike and walking the aid stations are perfectly acceptable for the beginner (usually recommended), but even then you should have a time limit for walking, something like 20–30 seconds each mile. You may happily discover halfway through the run that you feel good and no longer need them.

Race planning is where the assistance of an experienced coach can really help. Few age-group racers have a realistic appraisal of their own potential and tend to go out too fast or expect too little of themselves.

TABLE 11.2 SAMPLE RACING PLAN FOR ADVANCED TRIATHLETE

MILE	RACE TIME	PACE/ MILE	SPLIT TIME	HEART RATE	COMMENTS
1.2					Hard swim
Swim	**0:31:00**	**0:25:50**	**0:31:00**	**140–150**	
0	0:33:50	0:02:50			Transition 1
1	0:36:40	0:02:50	0:02:50	140–150	Hold back slightly
10	1:02:10	0:02:50	0:28:20	140–150	
20	1:30:30	0:02:50	0:56:40	140–150	
30	1:58:45	0:02:45	1:24:55	144–154	Check 30-mile split; steadily increase effort
40	2:26:15	0:02:45	1:52:25	144–154	
50	2:53:45	0:02:45	2:19:55	144–154	
55	3:07:37	0:02:52	2:33:47	135–144	Spin easier last 2 miles
56					
Bike	**3:10:29**	**0:02:52**	**2:36:39**	**135–144**	

CONTINUED

TABLE 11.2 CONTINUED

MILE	RACE TIME	PACE	SPLIT TIME	HEART RATE	COMMENTS
0	3:11:59	0:01:30			Transition 2 (faster than first)
1	3:19:44	0:07:45	0:07:45	145–150	Smooth and easy start
2	3:27:14	0:07:30	0:15:15	145–150	
3	3:34:44	0:07:30	0:22:45	145–150	
4	3:42:14	0:07:30	0:30:15	145–150	Steady pace
5	3:49:44	0:07:30	0:37:45	145–150	
6	3:57:14	0:07:30	0:45:15	145–150	
7	4:04:59	0:07:45	0:53:00	145–150	Check 7-mile split; steadily increase effort, heart rate
8	4:12:44	0:07:45	1:00:45	150–155	
9	4:20:29	0:07:45	1:08:30	150–155	
10	4:28:14	0:07:45	1:16:15	150–155	
11	4:35:59	0:07:45	1:24:00	150–155	
12	4:43:44	0:07:45	1:31:45	150–155	
13	4:51:14	0:07:30	1:39:15	155–160	All you have left
13.1					
Run	**4:51:59**	**0:07:45**	**1:40:00**	**155–160**	**Finish**

Even if you cannot afford full-time coaching, you might consider a one-hour consultation with a coach who can analyze your current test results and predict a realistic pace for the half-Iron distance. Such predictions are best made around four to six weeks before the race. Anything closer makes it difficult to improve racing speed, although it's easier for the newcomer with a lower starting point than those for with a more established aerobic capacity.

As with training, the key to determining race intensity is performance at lactate threshold (Zone 4–5a). Depending on your fitness and level of experience, you can set race goals based on this value. You should have been doing tests and/or intervals at this intensity on the bike (30-minute time trial), run (800m or 1,600m track intervals), or swim (1,000–1,650-yard/meter time trial). Your speed for these efforts can

TABLE 11.3 TYPICAL RACING ZONES FOR HALF-IRON RACE BASED ON EXPERIENCE

RACE SEGMENT	ZONE BASED ON EXPERIENCE		
	Beginner	Intermediate	Advanced
Swim	2	3–4	4–5a
Early Bike	1–2	2–3	3–4
Latter Bike	2–3	3–4	4–5a
Early Run	2	3	4–5a
Latter Run	3	4	5a–b

be used to estimate your speed in other zones that you will use at different points in the half-Iron race.

The values in Table 11.2 are based on average heart rate on relatively flat portions of a course during nominal conditions. Extremes of heat, wind, or climbing grade can dramatically affect the actual heart rate and speed. Some half-Iron courses can be as difficult as the Ironman® Hawaii race, albeit for a shorter distance. You should treat these as "two-thirds-Ironman" courses and plan accordingly.

Be aware that *optimal* or *target* heart rate is not the same thing as the *average* heart rate you see in race simulations using your HRM with lap timer. We all have heart rate "dropouts" caused by downhill cycling or running, turns, aid stations, mental dissociation, and so on, and these bring the average measured heart rate about five beats per minute lower than the target heart rate you are consciously aiming for. For example, someone wants to do the bike with a heart rate in the middle of Zone 3, which for them is around 135–144bpm. They consciously aim for seeing "140" on their HRM for the flat portions of the bike and are reasonably successful. Later analysis of the heart rate file shows their *average* heart rate was only 134bpm for the ride. This is a normal indicator of correct heart rate pacing.

Those pacing the bike with a power meter do not have to worry so much about dropouts, since these are offset by uphill sections, post-turn accelerations, and aggressive passes, which are correctly recorded by a good power meter. A power meter shows real-time, real-world measurement, whereas heart rate is a secondary, time-lagged value.

What we are advocating for most athletes is a pacing approach that is based more on heart rate, power, and/or perceived effort than speed. About the only people who should be racing based solely on position and speed are the elite athletes who have a chance of winning the race or at least their age group. Even then, the real "racing" may not start until halfway through the bike or the later stages of the run. For just about everyone else, the best finish time is usually achieved by conservative pacing in the first half of the race.

When to go for it

The half-Iron distance is different from its full-blown cousin in that you can sometimes "go for it" by exceeding planned race intensity and survive to the finish with a decent time. This gamble rarely if ever works for the full Iron-distance event. If you've previously excelled at Olympic-distance racing but have never completed a half-Iron event, the only way this might work is if you have taken in enough calories and electrolytes on the bike to fuel the overpacing; otherwise, you may well end up walking toward the end of the run, whatever your athletic prowess.

Most veteran half-Iron competitors should go out relatively hard on the swim but remain at what seems like more of a full-Iron or aerobic pace during the initial stages of the bike. This is also a good strategy for athletes using the half-Iron distance as a "tune-up" for a more important full Iron race: It serves as a pacing test for the longer distance without fear of bonking or being unable to finish.

Racing the Swim

About 10–15 minutes before the bike start, drink 10 ounces of sports drink or a cup of water and a 100-calorie gel-pack. These calories provide an extra energy spark for the stressful swim start.

As in any triathlon swim, athletes should self-seed based on ability. Those expecting to finish in less than 29 minutes toward the front, those over 35 minutes toward the back, with others positioned relative to their time. It's easier to pass people ahead of you than it is to have other swimmers climbing over your back to get by, which is likely if you start too far forward. Starting in the wrong place may also cause you to go all out in the first 200–300 meters of the swim, wasting precious fuel early and leading to an inevitable breakdown in technique before the swim finish.

One way to avoid the crowd is to start wide as well as a little back. The actual time difference starting 20 meters wide and using a "banana line" to the first buoy is around five to ten seconds on most courses. If you start with the main pack on your breathing side, you can clearly see where to enter the main line for the best draft.

Excitement and adrenaline at the start is a double-edged sword: It will enable you to swim faster than you think, but if you go out too hard, it will burn fuel at an incredible rate. Only the strongest triathlon swimmers should be starting all out to join the lead pack; everyone else should be on "cruise control" for most of the swim.

In the first 1,000 meters, focus more on technique, drafting, and good buoy navigation. You will find this leads to optimal speed. After the halfway point, you can pick up the pace a little, but remember, in swimming this does not necessarily mean increasing cadence, but maintaining a full rotation and body position, and finishing the stroke.

Advanced swimmers can and probably should go out with the lead pack, but unless there is some cash or other incentive to "win the swim" outright, it is often better to be drafting a little behind the first swimmer out of the water, keeping them in your sights. If you can beat them through the transition area and onto the bike course, so much the better. But don't underestimate the value of stalking your elite rival through much of the race. This strategy is used often by the best half-Iron racers to measure out their energy and pass the leader at a strategic point in the later bike or on the run. It can also be used by age groupers to stay with known division winners when fighting for a qualifying slot.

All other swimmers should strive to maintain economy and a good pace but leave the water feeling like they could have gone harder. A little muscle soreness and disorientation is normal at the swim finish, but if you stand up feeling exhausted before you even get on the bike, you went out too hard.

Swim-to-Bike Transition

The key thought for transitions comes from Coach Rich Strauss: "Slow is smooth and smooth is fast." That means having everything planned and positioned in advance, yet not being rushed in execution. You have been horizontal for a long time in a sensory-deprived environment, and suddenly you are upright in the daylight. Attempting to sprint at full speed through the transition is the last thing you want to do.

For wet suit swims, the first thing to locate is the zipper strap, which you steadily begin to pull down upon exiting the water. Remove your goggles and swim cap, but do not throw the cap aside as this may result in an "abandoning equipment" penalty. While jogging at a moderate pace, you can begin to pull your wet suit off your upper body before getting to your bike's rack position, so that upon arrival all you need to do is remove the bottom legs. Hint: A little cooking spray applied throughout the inside of the suit *and the outside of the ankles* helps it slip off the feet quickly. Many half-Iron races do not have a mandatory transition bagging area, so just leave the suit near your racked position, out of the way of other gear and not impeding anyone else. Those races with "clean" bike rack areas (no items allowed on the ground) require you to stow the suit in your marked transition bag before heading out to the bike. Volunteers can and will often do this for you, so listen for their advice as you are moving through.

Although you should plan for regular eating and drinking on the bike, avoid doing it in the stressful transition area. Perhaps a sip or two of water handed up, but don't waste time or digestive stress in transition. After you have exited the transition and are out on the open road with a good cycling rhythm, then you can start drinking and eating gels or solid food. The most important transition key about food is not to forget or drop your gel flask and/or bar for the bike segment.

We do recommend experienced triathletes learn how to start the ride with shoes already clipped into the pedals, which is still allowed in most half-Iron races (though becoming forbidden in many full Ironman events), leaving the transition area with feet atop the shoes and then pulling them on during the first 200 meters of the bike. If you don't have triathlon-specific cycling shoes, don't attempt this without a pull-on strap. And don't try it on race day unless you have successfully practiced it many times before. Most beginners choose to go with an easier shoe donning before walking the bike more slowly to the mount line.

Racing the Bike

For the beginning to intermediate triathlete, the first 15–28 miles of the bike involves holding back and maintaining a steady rhythm, staying in Zones 1–3. Many courses have deliberately tough hills in the first few miles, and it's easy to blow up and waste energy. It is likely that some will pass you in the early stages, but that's okay—let them go.

Advanced triathletes with strong riding skills, especially those who have been training for longer century or Ironman events, may have the capability of doing the entire bike at or near lactate threshold. If you are lucky enough to be one of these, you still need to hold back a little and make sure you are in Zone 4–5a, and not Zone 5b dueling with other strong cyclists as if this were a bike race, which it is not.

Even for the elite athlete, the half-Iron distance bike is about the higher end of muscular endurance, not anaerobic endurance. A power meter can be of great assistance here, and if you're using this race to prepare for a more important full Iron race, you'll get data on what "overpacing" could be like in an Ironman.

Strong cycling ability does not require all advanced triathletes or those wishing to win their age group to go out hard, even though they might get away with it. Many will do very well with a more conservative Zone 3 strategy to start the bike, building intensity in the second half of the ride. Some elite riders have become so efficient in Zone 3 there is no need to exceed it, saving more anaerobic work for the run. A lot depends on who shows up for your race. Unlike the Ironman, however, even elites are likely to undergo suffering during the bike to win the race.

Bike nutrition

After the halfway point on the bike, the body has usually switched over to optimal fat-burning mode, provided you have not gone out too hard. At this point, attempting to accelerate into the higher-end or next heart rate zone is relatively safe for all athletes, because the body is unlikely to allow high sugar burning once fat burning is established.

Most athletes should probably stick to gels or liquid calories if pacing closer to LT during the latter bike, finishing any solid food earlier in the ride. Many elites want no solid food at all on a half-Iron bike, but they still ensure they are taking in plenty of calories.

Modern research has shown a fraction of protein, anywhere from 15–25 percent of the total calories, facilitates steady fuel burning and delays fatigue in longer events. As we noted in the nutrition chapter (see listing of products), there is wide variation in an individual's ability to digest protein during a race and in what form of protein works best. In any case, do not attempt any nutritional changes from previous long rides and race simulations. About the only thing that can change is the specific brand of sports drinks or gel-packs available at aid stations, and these are usually carbohydrate-only.

Start drinking after five or ten minutes into the ride, well before you start consuming gels or bars 30–40 minutes into the ride. This initial liquid settles your stomach and makes sure the thicker calories will be absorbed. The rate the stomach and intestines can process food is directly related to the amount of water available. Because there is so much difference in athlete size and digestion, we cannot generalize about the exact number of calories. On average, a half-Iron athlete will burn 700–800 calories per hour on the bike and perhaps 1,000 or more per hour on the run. You need to be replacing about half of these calories on the bike, about 400 per hour, and preferably more than one quarter of them on the run, about 250–350 per hour. These are average figures: Some athletes can and do consume much more, and some simply cannot process that many. The trick is to find the best way to get your body to absorb the most calories and electrolytes possible without causing distress. As with other factors, what you've been doing regularly in training is what your body will likely tolerate on race day.

A good rule of thumb is to eat *something* every 30–45 minutes during the bike, a 100-calorie gel-pack with perhaps one 250-calorie bar for the entire ride. If you are taking three hours or more for the ride, you need to eat more than someone taking 2:15. Some experienced athletes keep a double- or triple-strength sports drink bottle on their bike and use it intermittently for the same amount of calories as a gel-pack, mixing it with straight water hand-ups on the course.

Salt tablets and potassium supplementation are common elements seen at races like Ironman® Hawaii, but what about half-Iron races? If you are racing somewhere like Buffalo Springs Lake in Texas, St. Croix, or in Cancun, Mexico, you probably want to add extra sodium beyond that normally found in drinks, gels, and bars.

Some prefer the standard salt/potassium tablets; others prefer an electrolyte powder that can be mixed in their sports drink bottles. Those doing an ocean swim should avoid sodium supplementation until an hour or so into the bike, since the swim itself will involve some incidental sodium ingestion. Using a more dilute mixture of sports drink the first 30–60 minutes can help even out this high-concentration sodium. Ocean water, especially in tropical regions, is many more times salty than a typical sports drink—one unintentional swallow may exceed the sodium in an entire liter of sports drink.

Cooler half-Iron venues may require no additional sodium supplementation beyond sports drinks and gels. Do not, however, attempt the whole bike segment on water only, risking a bonk or even more dangerous hyponatremia (sodium depletion). Perform simulations in climactic conditions close to the actual race to know for sure. You can easily carry salt tablets "just in case." You do not have to ingest them during a cooler overcast day, or you can delay using them until the hotter run.

I prefer a completely steady flow of calories, electrolytes, and water throughout the ride, with evenly mixed water bottles spiked with electrolyte powder, regular gel-pack ingestion every 40 minutes, and one sports bar around the middle of the bike. I get about 70 percent of the ride done on my own fluids, two large bottles, and then need maybe one or two hand-ups of the race-sponsor fluid. Temperatures over 85°F may require additional sodium tablets on the run as well as the bike.

The latter bike

The second half of the bike should have you feeling like you can push a little harder but not fatigued enough to slow down. If you are a beginner who has done few rides over two to three hours, you may experience decay in bike form even if pacing correctly. Don't be afraid to come out of the saddle, stretch, and occasionally ride out of your aerobars if this is your first half-Iron race. It's more important to relax your body for the run than to have a fast bike split.

If you are more advanced, pushing a harder pace from the start, watch out for "cardiac creep" where your heart rate may be edging up significantly over lactate threshold. Your stronger legs may indeed be able to output high power for the entire 56 miles, but if your power output exceeds your ability to absorb fluid and calories, you could bonk before the run is over.

If you thought you could ride the entire bike leg at LT and find that you are now falling back, you need to rethink your strategy, conserving energy for the run. It is possible to recover from bike overpacing and still make it through a half-marathon run at a decent speed, something quite unlikely in the full Iron race.

If you did not eat or carry enough food, try to get some gel-packs or other calories provided by the race. Always carry one or two more gel-packs than you think you need for the bike or the run in case you burn fuel faster. I've had some of my best long-course races where I rode fast and comfortably but needed more calories than expected. Race day is not the time to limit calories—save dieting for later.

Pacing decisions for the latter bike are affected by the difficulty of the run. A hilly 13.1-mile run at 95–100°F dictates a different cycling strategy than a flatter run in cool weather. Your body composition and experience running tired are also important. If you trained with many "heater bricks" near home, you probably can handle a hot run on race day. If all your training was at or below 75°F and you find yourself in much hotter conditions, you may have to back off the bike pace to run strongly.

Whatever your bike strength, all athletes need to back off the last 2–4 miles of the bike, spinning in an easier gear to set their legs up for a steady run start. Most courses naturally require slowing as you come back into town or a waterside park. Letting another cyclist pass in these final miles is no sign of weakness, since you are likely to catch them in or just out of the transition area with your fresher legs. Begin visualization and positive self-talk about the transition, remembering rack location, equipment setup, and run strategy. By the time you dismount, the physical actions will become smooth and automatic.

Bike-to-Run Transition

Your second transition should be considerably faster than your first. There is less gear to fiddle with, and you should have practiced many times with your training bricks. Top triathletes are consistently able to pull this off much faster than the average racer. That being said, you should no more rush the second transition than the first. If you did not don socks for the bike segment, you should wear them for the run. It's not worth the blisters, which start to form around 5–10K into a run without socks, enough time for an Olympic-distance finish but not enough for the half-marathon run.

We also recommend something more substantial than racing flats for all but the lightest and fastest runners—even elites. There are good lightweight training shoes that strike a balance between speed and support, averaging around 10 ounces (281 grams). These are worth having for your half- and full-marathon run courses. Beginners, larger, or older triathletes may well need a fully cushioned, heavier shoe.

If you previously did only shorter races that finish by midmorning, note that sunglasses are good for the half-Iron run finishing at noon or later, as are a ventilated cap or visor, and a racing top to avoid sunburn. You should have applied sunscreen before the swim and perhaps a little more if it's handy at the start of the run. Sun protection should be essentially the same as in the full Ironman.

And don't forget your gel-packs or perhaps a hydration fuel belt for the run. If you are depending on the race staff for extra running calories, make sure you tried the sponsor's product in training. I try to leave with two to three gel-packs of my own for the run, finding the caffeinated brands very helpful for the second half. Running nutrition is not as critical as bike calories, but you are likely to need something more than the sports drink provided. An average value is 250 calories per hour. Runners taking two or more hours over 13.1 miles need more than elites taking under 1:35. Few athletes can easily digest solids on the run; these should be eaten well before the bike finish.

Racing the Run

Whether you are a beginner who started the bike slowly or an elite who hammered the whole 56 miles, your legs will feel funny at the start of the run. The ability to transition the legs from post-bike pain or numbness to smooth running is perhaps the fundamental skill of triathlon and duathlon, something you practice regularly in bricks. During the race, the key to managing this discomfort is to discount leg pain and focus instead on heart rate and breathing in the early miles. As the discomfort subsides, begin thinking about good running form.

You should have a well-defined limit for heart rate and/or mile pace at the start of the run and stay within it. Set your watch so that lap time is easily readable and begin clicking off the times for each mile, keeping in mind that most triathlon courses have at least one mismeasured mile. Even if you are a beginner planning to walk the aid stations each mile or two, the lap timer will keep your walks disciplined and pace respectable. Experienced athletes running harder can use the mile pace to break the course into shorter frames with definite time goals.

You can dispense with mile pacing and heart rate *if* you are chasing the race leaders or are pacing with a quality runner (note that pacing with a non-racer on foot or bike is illegal). Drafting can be worth 5–8 percent on the run and is recommended for headwind sections. But don't let someone pull you along so fast that you greatly exceed heart rate pacing in the early miles. After mile 3, you can begin to accelerate as your running transforms to a normal gait.

Use the 10K or 7-mile marker to gauge your progress and make decisions for the rest of the race. If you've been meeting mile pacing and heart rate goals the first half of the run without distress, it's an easy decision to run harder the second half, perhaps finding a slightly better runner to pace beside. Gradually increase the intensity so that heart rate rises perhaps five beats per minute and pace is maintained or improves by 5–10 seconds per mile (3–8 seconds per kilometer). If your hydration, nutrition, and heart rate are nominal, but your legs are tired and form is degrading, be content with simply maintaining pace while increasing perceived effort.

If mile pace has been steady but heart rate a little high, you may well be able to increase pace without negative consequences. Some racers just exhibit a higher heart rate on race day than during tests, but the question becomes, "How much higher than training can I go?" Taper and nutritional loading can raise blood sugar and heart rate, as can caffeine-based gels and bars. If you've seen this before in a race and dealt with it successfully, you can probably go for it. But if you are 10–15bpm too high for the bike and run, you are risking a major bonk. Remember that most racers misjudge what they can "get away with" in a long-course event.

Beginning triathletes who have been walking aid stations the first half of the run probably should continue to do so, but some may be able to skip a few walks, or skip them after mile 10. Note that judicious 20–30-second walk breaks at aid stations do not affect your overall pace very much, so if you want to continue them, do so. Just avoid turning a 30-second walk into a 60-second walk unless you absolutely have to. Avoid sitting or standing still, because that just makes it harder to get moving again.

There is little or no need for beginners or intermediates to raise heart rate or pacing the second half of the run, unless heat and fatigue are naturally nudging them higher. In that case, you should probably drink more. If heart rate is falling without discernible cause, you should probably eat more.

Another trick for "heater runs" is to put ice in your cap every couple of aid stations, something you can do with a cap but not with a visor. Alert the aid-station volunteers you need ice 10–15 meters before you pass them and have your cap off and ready. Avoid cold water sprays directly to the legs and hips, since the sudden temperature change can cause cramps. Cold water or ice should be applied to the head, neck, and shoulders and allowed to drip gradually to the legs.

Dousing with ice water is an effective way to cool the core temperature during a hot run.

The last 3 miles (5K) is a time when many racers can begin to run measurably harder. Elites should focus on winning the race or their division—now is the time to pursue those up ahead, duel with rivals, and fight with all your spirit. Those with less experience can focus on making pre-race time goals or looking good in the final mile. Maintaining good running form and optimal cadence is important. Move your thoughts away from the pain and keep reciting the mottoes of good form: relaxed upper body, quick foot turnover, mid-to-ball-of-foot strike, steady arm motion, and best effort to the finish line. Catching and passing someone in the last 200 meters is always fun, especially your division rival.

Don't forget to look around and enjoy the finish line crowd. If this is your first time or a PR, relish the experience for all the joy you take from it. Anytime you finish a half-Iron race standing up, it's a good day to be alive. When I finish a long-course race, I usually say to myself, "I must be the luckiest guy on earth to get to do this!"

A few days after the race, experienced athletes will likely conduct a "postmortem" on how they performed, analyzing heart rate, power, and pacing information. An HRM and power meter that download to your computer is very good for this. If you have a coach, this data is invaluable to them in helping you improve. You might make a few notes about course conditions, and attach a file or Web site address with race results. Qualitative impressions can be as important as hard data. Remember that you often learn more from a so-called "bad" race than a good one. As Lance Armstrong said, there really are no bad days: just good days and great days. If you had a great race, you have confirmed that your strategy and prior training is working.

CHAPTER 12

Case Studies

Experience is a mean school, but fools will learn from no other.
—Benjamin Franklin

LEARNING FROM OTHERS

Reading this book demonstrates one of the primary benefits of civilization: We don't have to learn how to do everything from scratch. Someone has come before us and written down how *they* did it. That being said, there is no way to copy what another person has done, even when they set a fine example and wish to teach it.

The only common denominator is our individuality. All men and women may be created equal, but once the race starts they spread out quickly on the course of life. Two triathletes racing together for an entire long-course race is about as likely as a no-hitter in baseball or a hole in one in golf. It happens, but don't count on it.

Case studies have become primary tools in everything from law to medicine to psychology. Real-world examples are often worth volumes of theory. If you find some commonality with our three types, give it a try. But don't try to "become" someone else or their training. In the end, you have to work things out for yourself and that necessarily takes more time.

On a personal note, I took a fairly simple approach to my first Ironman race attempt. I read Mark Allen's training plan and figured if I could do even half of it, I would probably finish standing up in a reasonable time. Now that I've met Mark Allen and raced in Kona, I realize that back then I had no idea of how he was training or what "doing half his workload" really meant. Yet the weekly numbers and relative proportion of three sports served as a useful guideline. I trained reasonably well for a beginner and finished ahead of my goal, though it was nowhere near the quality of training presented in this book or by a good coach. Numbers are just symbols on paper, and there is much behind them we don't know until we've been down that road ourselves.

BEGINNER BOBBIE

Bobbie attended her first triathlon camp in the winter after a sporadic season of three sprint triathlons and a couple of 5K running events. Her goal was to move to the Olympic distance the following year, but after attending the camp and conferring with coaches there, she felt confident she could finish a half-Iron race sometime the following year, provided her work schedule did not conflict with the additional training involved.

Before competing in triathlons, she had no endurance experience except jogging a few 5K races with friends. She competed in typical high school sports like volleyball and has good muscular strength and adequate endurance. Her primary limiter is swimming, especially in the open water where she still feels uncomfortable with large stars and rough-water conditions. Her cycling is improving, and she will upgrade to a full-featured triathlon bike as suggested by the camp coaches. Her running is steady, but tends to fall off after six miles of continuous effort. She learned some of the techniques of "Evolution Running" (as developed by Ken Mierke; see www.evolutionrunning.com) at the camp, and will continue these drills to improve running. She switched running shoe brands at the end of last season, and this has helped alleviate tendinitis problems on longer runs.

For her first half-Iron attempt, she has chosen a relatively easy course with mildly rolling terrain within 100 miles of home. She's planning on driving to the course for the race and will do a course simulation workout four weeks out. Two of her beginner triathlete friends have registered for the same race. She also plans some B- and C-priority races in her home state leading up to the half-Iron event, and then a 5K "fun run" to finish off her season.

Bobbie's training will focus on extending her short-course endurance to the long-range variety required for the half-Iron venue. She will gradually build up to the weekend easy group ride of three hours in the spring, sitting in and doing little or no pulls. To work on her swimming limiter, she has enlisted a local swim coach to make an underwater video for analysis and to prescribe drills to help correct her stroke technique. She plans follow-up sessions with the coach on a monthly basis and will swim in his masters group.

Her early-season bike training will emphasize the proper aero position on the new bike, smooth pedal stroke, and correct gearing choices for flat to rolling terrain and strong winds. None of her races in the next season have steep climbs, but she will train on grades slightly harder than the racecourses.

VETERAN VINCE

Vince is an age-group veteran in the masters division. Before competing in triathlons, he had been a regular runner for many years, finishing two marathons and numerous shorter runs. He has finished over a dozen triathlons, including two half-Iron events. His goal for next season is to improve his overall finishing time and to break into the top ten age-group finishers, gaining a slot to the USAT half-Iron national championship in the fall.

His strongest asset is running endurance garnered from over a decade of long-distance running, though he needs to work on improving speed after a hard bike. His swimming is adequate, but could be improved by further refinement of technique and development of muscular endurance. His biggest problem with swimming is mental discipline: making it to the pool for early-morning workouts three times per week and finishing the necessary stroke drills and hard intervals as prescribed. When tired he tends to "blow off" swim workouts or reduce them to easy, gray-zone efforts.

Although he can finish long rides without undue fatigue, his power output at lactate threshold is a bit low and needs refinement via strength training and muscular-endurance intervals. He trains and often races on flat-as-a-pancake coastal roads and has trouble with steeper or longer

TABLE 12.1 BEGINNER BOBBIE'S TRAINING PLAN AND GOALS

WEEK	DATE	RACES	PRIORITY	PERIOD
50	4-Dec.			Preparation
51	11-Dec.			Preparation
52	18-Dec.			Preparation
53	25-Dec.			Preparation
1	1-Jan.			Preparation
2	8-Jan.			Preparation
3	15-Jan.			Preparation
4	22-Jan.			Preparation
5	29-Jan.			Base 1
6	5-Feb.	10K run	C	Base 1
7	12-Feb.			Base 1
8	19-Feb.			Base 1
9	26-Feb.			Base 1
10	5-Mar.			Base 1
11	12-Mar.			Base 1
12	19-Mar.			Base 1
13	26-Mar.			Base 2
14	2-Apr.			Base 2
15	9-Apr.	Sprint Duathlon	C	Base 2
16	16-Apr.			Base 2
17	23-Apr.			Base 3
18	30-Apr.			Base 3
19	7-May			Base 3
20	14-May			Base 3
21	21-May	Sprint Triathlon	C	Base 3
22	28-May			Base 3
23	4-Jun.			Base 3
24	11-Jun.			Base 3
25	18-Jun.			Peak
26	25-Jun.	International Triathlon	A	Race
27	2-Jul.			Transition
28	9-Jul.			Transition
29	16-Jul.			Base 2
30	23-Jul.			Base 2
31	30-Jul.			Base 2
32	6-Aug.			Base 2

HOURS	STRENGTH	GOALS/METHODS
5.6	AA	Acclimate to training. Improve swim technique with underwater video and prescribed stroke drills. Purchase and custom fit aerodynamic bike. Video analysis of running form, implement drills to improve.
6.4	AA	
7.2	AA	
8.0	AA	
6.4	AA	
7.2	AA	
8.0	AA	
8.8	AA	
5.6	MT	Use 10K race to baseline running threshold heart rate. Gradually increase mass lifted, focusing on hip and leg strength. Analyze pedal stroke technique with CompuTrainer, prescribed drills. Baseline bike LTHR with 30-minute time trial. Long run at 60–70 minutes; long bike at 90–120 minutes.
9.6	MT	
10.4	MT	
11.2	MT	
6.4	MT	
10.4	MT	
11.2	SM	
12.0	SM	
7.2	SM	Practice transitions for upcoming duathlon. Extend long ride to 50–60 miles (~180min); long run to 90 minutes.
9.6	SM	
5.6	SM	
7.2	SM	
10.4	SM	Continue long rides and runs, with longest brick adding 15–20 minute run. Add Zone 3 intervals of 2–3x10 minute on bike and 4–6x800m on run. Extend long swim workout to 6x300 @ 20 second rest.
11.2	SM	
12.0	SM	
6.4	SM	
9.0	SM	
11.2	None	
12.0	SM	
8.0	SM	
7.2	SM	Mostly Zone 1 with crisp accelerations to Zone 3 on the bike and run. Practice transition 5–6 times over two weeks.
6.4	None	
4.0	AA	Unstructured, light training
5.6	AA	Structured, moderate training
9.6	SM	Back to long rides (180min) and runs (90min), mostly Zone 2.
10.4	SM	
11.2	SM	
5.6	SM	

CONTINUED

TABLE **12.1** CONTINUED

WEEK	DATE	RACES	PRIORITY	PERIOD	
33	13-Aug.			Base 3	
34	20-Aug.			Base 3	
35	27-Aug.			Base 3	
36	3-Sep.			Base 3	
37	10-Sep.			Peak	
38	17-Sep.	Local Half-Iron	A	Race	
39	24-Sep			Transition	
40	1-Oct			Transition	
41	8-Oct			Transition	
42	15-Oct			Base 3	
43	22-Oct			Base 3	
44	29-Oct	5K run	C	Race	
45	5-Nov			Transition	
46	12-Nov			Transition	
47	19-Nov			Transition	
48	26-Nov			Transition	

climbs. To rectify this limiter, he plans to increase "bridge-ramp" hill repeats to 16 repetitions on the only grade near home over 6 percent, and to make two or three journeys inland to hillier terrain for two- to five-day "climbing camps" alone and with other riders. The strong coastal winds near home have trained him to maintain a good aero position and he can push a big gear into a headwind for hours if necessary—no need for special effort here.

His muscular strength is good for his body type, which only needs regular maintenance with two short sessions per week—anything more simply slows his running and increases the risk of injury. Losing five to ten pounds would provide the necessary power-to-weight ratio

HOURS	STRENGTH	GOALS/METHODS
10.4	SM	Continue long rides and runs, with longest brick at 30–60-minute run. Perform course-environment simulations (nutrition, grade, temperature, wind).
11.2	SM	
12.0	SM	
8.0	SM	
6.4	SM	Mostly Zone 1 with crisp accelerations to Zone 3 on the bike and run. Practice transition 5–6 times over two weeks.
4.8	None	
4.0	None	Week off, light activity
4.0	SM	Moderate, unstructured activity
5.6	SM	Moderate, structured activity
8.0	SM	Bike volume low, increase run intensity to prepare for 5K race (8x400m @ LT).
8.8	SM	
4.0	None	
4.0	None	Week off, light activity
4.8	AA	Moderate, unstructured activity
5.6	AA	
5.6	AA	

411.4 Total annual hours
7.9 Average hours per week

to move him toward top cyclists in his age group, making nutrition a critical limiter.

Vince's plan calls for an early-season half-marathon to gauge LT running speed and heart rate, and some shorter races near home. He has a secondary goal of reaching the top ten of his "regional rankings" in a very competitive four-state USAT region, and these are based primarily on performance in local sprint- and Olympic-distance races. He chose the regional (Olympic) and state (sprint) championships as B races to earn the greatest possible rankings points.

His first half-Ironman is a very difficult course in Lubbock, Texas, with steep grades on the bike and run, strong winds, and finishing temperatures

TABLE 12.2 VETERAN VINCE'S ANNUAL TRAINING PLAN AND GOALS

WEEK	DATE	RACES	PRIORITY	PERIOD
50	4-Dec.			Preparation
51	11-Dec.			Preparation
52	18-Dec.			Preparation
53	25-Dec.			Preparation
1	1-Jan.			Preparation
2	8-Jan.			Base 1
3	15-Jan.	Half-Marathon Run	C	Base 1
4	22-Jan.			Base 1
5	29-Jan.			Base 1
6	5-Feb.			Base 2
7	12-Feb.			Base 2
8	19-Feb.			Base 2
9	26-Feb.			Base 2
10	5-Mar.			Base 3
11	12-Mar.			Base 3
12	19-Mar.			Base 3
13	26-Mar.			Base 3
14	2-Apr.			Build 1
15	9-Apr.	Sprint Duathlon	C	Build 1
16	16-Apr.			Build 1
17	23-Apr.	Sprint Triathlon	C	Build 1
18	30-Apr.			Build 2
19	7-May			Build 2
20	14-May			Build 2
21	21-May			Build 2
22	28-May	International Triathlon (Regionals)	B	Race
23	4-Jun.			Base 3
24	11-Jun.			Base 3
25	18-Jun.			Peak

HOURS	STRENGTH	GOALS/METHODS
8.0	AA	Acclimate to training. Improve swim technique with underwater video and prescribed stroke drills. Use fixed-gear or PowerCranks for bike pedal stroke.
9.0	AA	
10.0	AA	
10.0	AA	
7.0	AA	
8.0	MT	Gradually increase bike volume in solo workouts. Test running threshold via half-marathon race. Begin more structured swim intervals. Transition to more mass lifted with weights.
9.0	MT	
10.0	MT	
7.0	MT	
12.0	MT	Long ride of 3–4 hours; long run of 90 minutes. Increase length of bike and run intervals at moderate intensity. Six heavy weight-lifting sessions.
13.0	MS	
14.0	MS	
8.0	MS	
13.0	SM	Ease off on mass lifted. Extend to maximum volume on long bike and long run. Increase bike intervals to 3x10 minutes threshold and run intervals to 3x1-mile tempo.
14.0	SM	
15.0	SM	
9.0	SM	
12.0	SM	Gauge threshold speed via duathlon and triathlon races. Reduce volume and increase intensity of longer sessions, including tempo period in second half of workout. Run intervals at 6x800.
12.0	SM	
12.0	SM	
7.0	SM	
12.0	SM	Use speed and intensity tests from races to determine Build 2 interval sessions. Cut to three weeks if tired, increase intensity if fresh. Actual international distance race simulations.
12.0	SM	
12.0	SM	
7.0	SM	
7.0	None	Race hard, measure HR and note perceived exertion.
14.0	SM	Back to Zone 3 base workouts in all three sports, plus including 6x400m swim intervals, 6x800m run intervals, 3x10-minute bike sessions at threshold.
15.0	SM	
12.0	SM	Race simulation: 30-minute swim, 120-minute bike, 90-minute run.

CONTINUED

TABLE **12.2** CONTINUED

WEEK	DATE	RACES	PRIORITY	PERIOD	
26	25-Jun.	Buffalo Springs Lake Half-Ironman (70.3)	A	Race	
27	2-Jul.			Transition	
28	9-Jul.			Transition	
29	16-Jul.			Base 3	
30	23-Jul.			Base 3	
31	30-Jul.	State Championship Triathlon (sprint)	B	Race	
32	6-Aug.			Base 3	
33	13-Aug.			Base 3	
34	20-Aug.			Build 1	
35	27-Aug.			Build 1	
36	3-Sep.			Build 1	
37	10-Sep.			Peak	
38	17-Sep.	Half-Iron Nationals	A	Race	
39	24-Sep.			Transition	
40	1-Oct.			Transition	
41	8-Oct.			Transition	
42	15-Oct.			Base 3-run	
43	22-Oct.			Base 3-run	
44	29-Oct.	Local 10K run	B	Race	
45	5-Nov.			Transition	
46	12-Nov.			Transition	
47	19-Nov.			Transition	
48	26-Nov.			Transition	

HOURS	STRENGTH	GOALS/METHODS
8.0	None	Practice first 5 miles of hilly bike course in pre-race brick. Otherwise, stay out of heat.
5.0	AA	Rest, unstructured activity, mostly swim and bike. Later, add some moderate running.
7.0	AA	
12.0	MT	Brief return to moderate weight lifting to ensure strength for hilly race in September.
14.0	MT	
7.0	None	Recovery week with spirited Zone 5a–b accelerations and transition practice. Arrive early and ride racecourse.
12.0	SM	Continue Base 3 cycle, emphasizing muscular endurance and longer tempo and interval workouts.
13.0	SM	
12.0	SM	Specific preparation for hilly half-Iron nationals. Increase climbing intensity and frequency.
13.0	SM	
14.0	SM	
12.0	SM	Course simulation: 30min swim, 120min hilly bike, 90min hilly run.
8.0	None	Arrive in time to drive bike course, practice transition area.
5.0	None	Rest, unstructured activity; mostly swim and bike.
6.0	SM	Light activity, maintain running endurance.
7.0	SM	
8.0	SM	Increase running intensity to prepare for 10K local rivalry.
8.0	SM	
7.0	None	Light activity
5.0	None	
6.0	AA	Moderate, unstructured activity
6.0	AA	
7.0	AA	
545.0	**Total annual hours**	
10.5	**Average hours per week**	

up to 104° F. The heat tolerance is not a difficult problem for Vince, since he already trains in these conditions at home, but the hills will require improvement in cycling strength. The field is also very strong, with several former age-group champions from Kona and speedy elites from Texas, so finishing top ten in his large age group would be a worthy achievement.

His best time in previous years was only 5:31, and this year he would like to break 5:15, perhaps by a significant margin depending on conditions. He will not make a precise goal until training tests about four weeks before the race. He plans to pace mostly on heart rate for the bike and early run, and then begin "racing" in the second half of the run.

His second half-Iron event this season is the national championship in the fall, on a faster course but with an equally difficult field. Provided he makes his time goal in Lubbock (guaranteeing his qualification to the national age-group championship), it's a realistic goal for him to break 5:05 on this flatter, calmer, and cooler course. Since he has never raced in nationals before, Vince has no idea how he might place in the field, so he will wait until the run is well in progress before "dueling" with his age-group rivals.

If he meets his goals in these two half-Iron races—and can adequately recover from the annual volume—he is considering moving up to the full-Iron distance the following season.

DIVISION CHAMP DAVE

Dave believes, however immodestly, that this is his year to "win the big one" at the Buffalo Springs Lake Half-Ironman 70.3 and get his slot to Kona. He has come close before, only to be thwarted by superior runners from afar who won their age-group division at Ironman® Hawaii last year, passing him in the final miles of the run. He is bound and determined to avoid repeating this heartbreak for a second year in a row.

Such is the intensity of age-group competition in his state that Dave will have to follow a program not far removed from a professional triathlete preparing for this event: His annual volume is suitable for a full Ironman, but he trims the early year to emphasize the speed required to win his division at the half-Ironman. Fortunately, there is enough time between the two long-course events to peak sharply for both of them.

Dave's strengths are fast swimming, based on his university team experience, and bike training with the top triathletes in the Texas hill country, including a couple of pros in his weekend riding group. In most local and even some national age-group events, he is one of the first two to three off the bike in the overall race. Although he runs well, he has been known to fade in half- or full-Ironman runs, slowing considerably and losing a place or two on the way. Relative to his stellar swimming and biking, it is indeed a limiter.

His training goals this year are to maintain swimming and cycling speed by continuing the same workouts as in previous years, but with more attention to subtle pedaling technique and position issues on the bike, and extension of muscular endurance so that he can maintain lactate threshold power for most of a 2:20 bike split without hurting his run split.

To work on his running limiter, he plans to deconstruct his stride in the late fall and redesign it using video analysis and prescribed technique drills, building to a full marathon race in late January. In this period, he will begin to incorporate some intervals of anaerobic endurance well above lactate threshold, a practice he avoided in previous years. What he does *not* need is more running volume (a common mistake to improve running), which would likely have him running more miles but not as fast—and risking soreness and injury. Better to increase muscular endurance on the bike, promoting fast recovery for better running form in the race.

In his three short early-season races, he will no longer be satisfied with merely winning his age group, but rather staying with the overall leaders through the race and placing in the top two or three overall. This will require considerable suffering on the run to stay with younger athletes and pros, but it will accustom him to VO_2max efforts.

Dave knows the half-Ironman course very well, this being his seventh race there in the last ten years. There is no need for a special course survey, and the hilly terrain near his home is at least as steep as that of the bike and run course. The only thing that has bothered him in the past is the running heat, and he plans to increase heat tolerance on the run by doing a few (but not all) of his long runs in the afternoon instead of the morning. He will arrive two days before the race to give himself some extra time to recover from the six-hour drive and relax, getting the pre-race brick and registration chores done early in the morning before the sun gets hot.

He will experiment with different electrolyte concentrations on the bike and run in longer bricks to see if that helps maintain his running form

TABLE 12.3 DIVISION WINNER DAVE'S ANNUAL TRAINING PLAN AND GOALS

WEEK	DATE	RACES	PRIORITY	PERIOD	
50	4-Dec.			Preparation	
51	11-Dec.			Preparation	
52	18-Dec.			Preparation	
53	25-Dec.			Preparation	
1	1-Jan.			Preparation	
2	8-Jan.			Base 1	
3	15-Jan.			Base 1	
4	22-Jan.			Base 1	
5	29-Jan.	Marathon Run	C	Base 1	
6	5-Feb.			Base 2	
7	12-Feb.			Base 2	
8	19-Feb.			Base 2	
9	26-Feb.			Base 2	
10	5-Mar.			Base 3	
11	12-Mar.			Base 3	
12	19-Mar.			Base 3	
13	26-Mar.			Base 3	
14	2-Apr.			Build 1	
15	9-Apr.	Sprint Duathlon	C	Build 1	
16	16-Apr.			Build 1	
17	23-Apr.			Build 1	
18	30-Apr.	Sprint Triathlon	C	Build 2	
19	7-May			Build 2	
20	14-May			Build 2	
21	21-May			Build 2	
22	28-May	International Triathlon (Regionals)	B	Race	
23	4-Jun.			Base 3	
24	11-Jun.			Base 3	
25	18-Jun.			Peak	
26	25-Jun.	Buffalo Springs Lake Half-Ironman (70.3)	A	Race	

HOURS	STRENGTH	GOALS/METHODS
14.0	AA	Acclimate to training. Improve swim technique with underwater video and prescribed stroke drills. Use fixed-gear or PowerCranks for bike pedaling.
15.8	AA	
17.5	AA	
17.5	AA	
12.3	AA	
14.0	MT	Increase run volume for marathon; 8x800m intervals and tempo training. Test late-run speed in marathon.
15.8	MT	
17.5	MT	
12.3	MT	
21.0	MT	Increase bike volume. Increase structured swim intervals. Brief, heavy weight lifting.
22.8	MS	
24.5	MS	
14.0	MS	
22.8	SM	Longer bricks and runs with tempo intervals in second half. Increase swim intervals to 6x400m.
24.5	SM	
26.3	SM	
15.8	SM	
21.0	SM	Reduce volume and increase intensity of longer session. Add one long, hard peloton ride on weekend. Gauge speed with sprint duathlon.
21.0	SM	
21.0	SM	
12.3	SM	
21.0	SM	Continue hard riding; increase LT intervals to 6x800m. Include one ME swim and one anaerobic swim.
21.0	SM	
21.0	SM	
12.3	SM	
12.3	None	Win age-group regional championship, place top three overall.
21.0	SM	Maintain bike intensity and extend run intervals to 8x800m.
22.8	SM	
14.0	SM	Course simulations, including immediate climbs after open-water swim.
14.0	None	Practice first 5 miles of hilly bike course in pre-race brick. Otherwise, stay out of heat. Win age-group to qualify for Kona.

CONTINUED

TABLE 12.3 CONTINUED

WEEK	DATE	RACES	PRIORITY	PERIOD	
27	2-Jul.			Transition	
28	9-Jul.			Transition	
29	16-Jul.			Base 3	
30	23-Jul.			Base 3	
31	30-Jul.			Base 3	
32	6-Aug.			Base 3	
33	13-Aug.			Build 1	
34	20-Aug.			Build 1	
35	27-Aug.			Build 1	
36	3-Sep.			Build 1	
37	10-Sep.			Base 3	
38	17-Sep.			Base 3	
39	24-Sep.			Base 3	
40	1-Oct.			Peak	
41	8-Oct.			Peak	
42	15-Oct.	Ironman® Hawaii	A	Race	
43	22-Oct.			Transition	
44	29-Oct.			Transition	
45	5-Nov.			Transition	
46	12-Nov.			Transition	
47	19-Nov.			Transition	
48	26-Nov.			Transition	

HOURS	STRENGTH	GOALS/METHODS
8.8	AA	Rest, unstructured activity, mostly swim and bike. Later, add some moderate running.
12.3	AA	
21.0	MT	Brief return to moderate weight lifting to maintain strength. Longer bike and swim intervals to prepare for Kona.
24.5	MT	
26.3	MT	
17.5	MT	
19.3	SM	Reduce weights and increase intensity in all three sports. Reduce volume and focus on technique and speed.
19.3	SM	
19.3	SM	
12.3	SM	
22.8	SM	Specific "push period" to prepare for Kona: very long rides with tempo finish, longer runs with Zone 4 finish, 6–8x400m swim intervals.
24.5	SM	
26.3	SM	
15.8	SM	After 3 days recovery, begin course simulations for Kona; hot afternoon runs.
12.3	SM	
8.8	SM	Practice swim-bike transition. Run Energy Lab hill. Otherwise stay out of heat.
3.0	None	Unstructured activity, tour islands.
5.0	AA	Return home. Light activity, moderate eating.
5.0	AA	Watch nutrition over holidays.
5.3	AA	
7.0	AA	
7.0	AA	

865.3 **Total annual hours**

16.6 **Average hours per week**

for longer periods in the heat. The long runs will also involve accelerations to lactate threshold in the second half. There is a major risk of heat fatigue and overtraining with these "blast-furnace runs," so an extra day of recovery is required, and meticulous attention should be paid to hydration both during workouts and throughout the day and night. If recovery is not possible for a certain level of heat training, Dave will go back to early-morning runs. Do not confuse desirable "heat tolerance" for potentially catastrophic "heat fatigue."

After successfully achieving his half-Ironman goal, Dave will split his season with a Transition period (avoiding some of the peak summer heat) and a gradual rebuilding of Base 3 volume in preparation for Ironman® Hawaii. Dave has been there before, but several years ago as a considerably slower athlete.

Those winning Dave's age group at Buffalo Springs have a good record of finishing in the top five in their Kona age group, and this would fulfill a decade-long dream, stepping onto the podium in Hawaii. He realizes that he will only be able to invest this much time to training for one or two more years, with job and family forcing less training volume after that.

His motivation could be termed *urgent.* This creative tension is a double-edged sword, providing the impetus for very difficult breakthrough workouts, but increasing the risks. Being an elite age-grouper for long-course events places Dave on a "razor's edge" between champion performance and overtraining. We recommend he seeks the assistance of an outside coach with strong long-course experience, if not on a weekly basis, at least for occasional consultation.

And he will have to become just as serious about rest, sleep, and nutrition as he is about workouts, cutting out all unnecessary activity from his life other than family and his profession. It's a choice that perhaps only one out of a thousand triathletes pull off, but Dave has confidence that he can be that one.

CHAPTER 13

Strength and Flexibility

There is strength in numbers and those numbers come in pounds.
—Mike Berry

THE REUNIFICATION OF STRENGTH AND ENDURANCE

Once upon a time athletes came in two distinctly separate groups: Those who did regular strength training with weights and those who did not. Bodybuilders, American football players, shot or discus throwers, wrestlers, and power-lifters spent a lot of time in the gym sweating over iron bars and machines. Golfers, baseball players, distance runners, martial artists, and even some cyclists stayed away from weight lifting, viewing it as unnatural, unnecessary, and downright dangerous to the fine motor skill and flexibility required in their sport.

We can safely say that those days are gone for good. It's rare to find a current world leader in a major sport—based in skill, speed, or endurance—who does not do at least some strength training with weights. Golfer Tiger Woods has put on twenty pounds of muscle since winning his first major championship and hits the ball farther with less backswing and hence reliably straight. When I played competitive golf in the seventies, most touring and teaching pros said to avoid weight lifting altogether—don't even chop wood or do heavy lifting around the yard. Distance runners were once discouraged from lower-body lifting, possibly allowing some light upper-body weights to prevent arm fatigue in marathons. Mark Allen had won three Ironman® Hawaii world championships before lifting a bar. But he said that adding strength training made a big difference in his later career when he broke all the records.

How did things change so dramatically for endurance athletes and strength training in only a few decades? The evolution of strength training has paralleled scientific study, and the same wave of periodization that flowed from Eastern Europe to the West brought with it a different attitude toward strength training. Not only were Eastern-bloc athletes making inroads in aerobic events, they were dominating the medals in weight lifting and wrestling, using a periodized model of strength training combined with flexibility.

The other factor is less scientific but still important: the legitimatization of bodybuilding and weight lifting in the United States, marketed by people like Arnold Schwarzenegger. Before that milestone, weight lifters were sometimes seen as freaks, incapable of maintaining flexibility or agility.

Speedier participants in team sports began to disprove these prejudices as millions watched. World records in sports not previously associated with muscular strength were regularly broken, and athletes began to tout their strength and flexibility programs as primary causes. Add to that the retail fitness-center expansion into malls, shopping centers, and the mass market, with the awareness of aging baby boomers that strength training is especially beneficial after age 40. As triathlon continues to grow, more beginners are coming from a fitness-center background of indoor weight lifting, bike ergometer, and treadmill training rather than the previous paths of outdoor competition. Pumping iron is here to stay.

The key question for triathletes: How do we tailor knowledge from strength events and periodization to develop specific strength for swimming, biking, and running? The answer is relatively simple: Keep weight training at a low volume and moderate to high intensity, limiting exercises to specific muscle groups required for the three sports. The bulging biceps and huge chests found on bodybuilders and football players are unnecessary for endurance sports, as are many of the classic weight-room exercises. In fact, many endurance athletes have achieved career milestones by reducing upper-body bulk, controlling nutrition, and focusing on sport-specific muscle groups—Lance Armstrong is a prime example of this effect.

Most triathletes can achieve optimal results by spending two hours or less per week actually lifting weights. The remainder of the time should focus on stretching, developing core strength through calisthenics, and other drills easily done at home or in a gym. Those making a transition from strength-based sports will find it takes considerably less time. Male athletes under 35 can usually put weight lifting aside during the racing season without losing significant strength. The KISS principle, "Keep it simple, stupid!" is good strength-training advice for endurance athletes.

Coordinating Strength with Endurance

In previous chapters we emphasized the importance of muscular endurance to long-course triathlon, the blending of endurance and strength energies. In constructing our strength training, we must interweave periodized endurance training, so that key races can utilize peak levels of strength *and* endurance.

Strength training must meet the demands of a busy life outside of triathlon. The reason most triathletes falter in strength training is not the difficulty of the exercises, but the lack of time and discipline to do them at all. Few multisport athletes willfully miss a bike or run workout, but it's easier to ditch a weight lifting session when you are tired or pressed for time. This priority is understandable, since sport-specific training is most important. But once a strength-training program is realistically designed, it should become a consistent habit—and a very valuable habit indeed. The relatively small amount of time spent in strength training can be leveraged into large chunks of time saved, especially on the bike and later run segments of a half-Iron race.

To gain maximum benefit from a strength program, it is preferable (but not required) to perform the strength workouts first or at least early in the day. They can be done before sunrise and during cold or wet weather indoors. Since many swim facilities also have nearby weight rooms, they can be slotted immediately after a moderate swim workout, still leaving time to get to work or school. Core exercises using only body mass can be done at home before heading out for the day. If you find strength training a chore compared to the outdoor fun of cycling and running, best to get it out of the way early.

There are two magnetic poles that affect strength training, seemingly in conflict but resolving in harmony:

1. Keep strength exercises as simple and straightforward as possible. Avoid excessive variation in weight, rest, or numerous exercises, because it can produce injury or inconsistent results in sport-specific performance.
2. The body needs variation and change to grow. The best way to develop muscles is to surprise them with different workouts.

Both of these points of view are good and correct when taken in balance and only become limiting or dangerous when taken to extremes. Since this book focuses on fundamental training for the half-Iron distance, we'll prefer the first principle of simplicity, but realize that elites and endurance athletes from specialized racing may benefit from wider variation. As with endurance training, consistency pays more dividends in the long run than excessive intensity when developing strength. The strength workout you can do consistently with gradual progress over time—and without injury—is the right one for you.

TABLE 13.1 PERIODIC STRENGTH TRAINING

PERIOD	STRENGTH PHASE	WEEKS	WEEKLY FREQUENCY	INTENSITY
Prep, Base 1	Anatomical Adaptation (AA)	2–4	2–3	Low
Base 2	Transitional Strength (TS)	4–8	1–2	Moderate
Base 3	Maximum Strength (MS)	2–4	1–2	High
Build 1, Build 2, Peak	Strength Maintenance (SM)	7–26	1–2	Moderate
Race	Off	1	0	—

Strength Training and Periodization

Although the exact choice of exercises and weights may vary, successful triathletes follow a synchronized progression of strength and endurance development (Table 13.1).

Once you have determined the exercises that work best for you, the most important thing about weight training is flexibility, and by that we mean the mental kind along with the physical. Fortunately, the half-Iron distance does not usually cause the bone-deep fatigue that full Ironman training brings on, so you are likely to be able to maintain a twice-a-week schedule. But if you find yourself overstressed or under-rested during weeks of high volume or intensity, put your ego aside and lift less weight or skip the weight room entirely.

It's amazing how much good you can accomplish with only three exercises done moderately and regular core work during the strength maintenance period. If you're trying to cut your losses in an overbooked workweek, a workout including leg press, lat pull-down, lower-body limiter, and core exercises can be finished in thirty minutes or less. If you're building sport-specific strength by climbing on the bike and run, and doing some paddle sets or other power drills in the water, you won't

SETS/ REST (SEC)	REPS	DESCRIPTION
1–2 / 40	25	Do not strain. Focus on form, slowness, and neuromuscular coordination. Full-body exercises.
2 / 40	13–18	Moderate strain, but not to failure. Maintain form. More focus on lower-body and core muscles.
4 / 150	6–10	Heavy strain. Last two sets to failure. Lower-body free weights may require spotter on last set.
1–2 / 30	8–10	Moderate intensity, constrained by fatigue from hard endurance workouts. May skip a week if overtrained.
—	—	No weight training on race week. Stretching only.

TABLE 13.2 BASIC TRIATHLON STRENGTH EXERCISES

EXERCISE	PRIORITY	WEIGHT GOAL (BW=BODY WEIGHT)	COMMENTS
Squat	High	1.3–1.7 x BW	Difficult and dangerous, but uses most unsupported muscle groups. Important for cycling. Do not bend knees over 90°. Back straight, head and eyes forward.
Leg press (inverted sled or seated)	High	2.5–2.9 x BW	Preferable for most triathletes. Important for cycling. Back flat against seat, no arm-assistance allowed. For safety, most athletes doing the leg press should not combine with the squat in the same workout.
Standing bent-arm lat pull-down	High	0.3–0.5 x BW	Requires cable machine. Useful for swimming. May substitute swim stretch cords.
Knee extension	Medium	Variable	Slow and steady. Range of motion from 110–180°, reaching fullest extension.
Hamstring curl	Medium	0.5–0.7 x Knee extension weight	Careful, slow, and steady—jerky movements can lead to injury. Do not rock hips. Ideal balance with hamstring at 60% of quadriceps strength.
Core	High	Body weight, mechanical	Critical to all three sports. Can be done 3–6 times per week, 10–20 minutes per session. Avoid adding heavy weight, use higher reps year-round. Balance lower abs and obliques with stronger upper abs.

CONTINUED

TABLE 13.2 CONTINUED

EXERCISE	PRIORITY	WEIGHT GOAL (BW=BODY WEIGHT)	COMMENTS
Calf raise	Low	Variable based on method	Helps climbing on bike and run, but should be avoided if sore or prone to lower-leg tendinitis, Achilles problems, etc.
Seated row	Moderate	0.5–0.8 x BW	Do not rock upper body. Hold hands with thumbs facing up to mimic cycling grip.
Triceps extension	Low	Variable based on method	Useful for swimming and bike climbing. Keep elbows as stationary pivot. Can be done with machine, barbell, or dumbbells.

lose significant muscular strength by cutting weight lifting in half. Athletes under 35 won't lose much by eliminating it entirely during the maintenance phase.

The important thing is to focus on increasing strength during the off-season and maintaining a flexible discipline during the build, peak, and race periods.

Choose Exercises Wisely

For those new to weight lifting or endurance-specific strength training, it's useful to experiment in the anatomical adaptation (AA) phase. If there's a weight machine or exercise that you think might help a muscle group used in triathlon, you can give it a try. But once you find what works—and what does not work—stick to a relatively set routine. Unless you're a pro or lucky soul with unlimited training time, messing around with too many fancy exercises feeds the ego more than racing speed. A good starting point includes some, but not necessarily all, of the exercises in Table 13.2, preferably done in order.

During the prep and early base period, with less volume and more time to spend on weights, you can attempt all of these exercises. As three-sport workout intensity increases and more mass is lifted, focus on the high-priority exercises. It's better to do only three exercises correctly with the optimal weight than to rush eight or more exercises with sloppy form.

Tips and Myths about Weight Training

- **Start out with less weight than you think you need and increase weight gradually.** Take six to eight weeks in the AA phase before worrying about mass lifted.
- **Good form trumps mass lifted in strength training.** When using proper technique, you are developing balanced muscularity, avoiding injury, and *training your nervous system* to control stressful body movements. This neuromuscular control is essential to maintaining form and efficiency during late-race fatigue.
- **Limit the maximum strength (MS) phase to four weeks maximum,** even if you are very strong and experienced in weight training. In fact, it's these already muscular athletes who should spend less time in the weight room.
- **When you have reached maximum body weight (BW) multipliers for an exercise, do not increase weight further.** For example, coming from a strength-sports background prior to triathlon, I reached the squat and leg press maximums in only my first year of triathlon training and have had little purpose to increase the squat weight for many years. Yet I still turn in top age-group bike splits and continue to improve my force in climbing and longer time trials, focusing on the power-to-weight ratio. My goal is simply to maintain this squat mass into my early 50s while keeping body mass down.
- **Do not schedule high-intensity workouts after lifting.** Avoid running entirely just after lifting weights, as well as 24–48 hours before a very fast or very long run. Other breakthrough workouts deserve caution and preferably similar recovery. Swimming technique usually degrades after hard lifting, so swimming is best done before weight training.
- **Myth: "Weight training will bulk you up and slow you down."** While this may be true for the casual exerciser, those engaged in regular and vigorous aerobic training will not be likely to gain muscle bulk. If you are gaining weight in the winter, it's probably a result of

nutritional lapses and lower endurance volume rather than time in the weight room. You can, however, increase leg strength (and muscle mass) for cycling to the point where it begins to slow your running. Should this occur, reduce the mass lifted or number of sets in lower-body exercises.

- **Myth: "Weight training will hurt flexibility and agility."** If you try to mimic the weight-lifting practices of bodybuilders, power-lifters, and football linemen, you might have a problem. But the low-volume, moderate intensity of endurance strength training, combined with regular stretching during and after weight-room workouts, has little chance of hurting flexibility. In fact, modern techniques with free weights and nonlinear-resistance machines (Nautilus, for example) have actually been shown to improve range of motion when done with good form. Athletes in the "maximum stretch" sports like golf and gymnastics are moving in the widest ranges ever while still doing weight training. Most athletes experience some loss of speed during the MS phase, which is why it is best limited to the middle Base period, well before the fastest workouts of the Build and Peak periods.
- **Myth: "Weight training will increase the risk of injury."** There is some truth to this rumor, since overly aggressive muscle building, especially the kind associated with banned substances, can leave connective tissue open to injury. In my years of racing and coaching endurance events, I've found most weight-related injuries come from incorrect form in the lift itself, insufficient recovery after a race or very long run before lifting, or insufficient recovery after weight lifting before a high-intensity or very long run. Just as you are likely to stumble on the run or fall off your bike a few times during years of training, even if cautious, you can have a "bum lift" every few years of weight training that strains a muscle or joint. But I find this is about as likely as pulling a muscle while doing house- or yard-work, with similar recovery time—a reasonable risk for the significant gains. Some athletes have biomechanical limitations and chronic injuries that require limitations on strength training, and you should seek the treating physician's approval for the strength exercises.

Core Exercises

These important muscles include the lower back, abdominals, obliques, and glutes. They are perhaps the most important in all of triathlon, and they work differently than muscle groups in the extremities. They respond to higher weekly frequency, less resistance, and more repetitions than other strength exercises. You can perform body-weight core exercises three to five times a week with relatively high repetitions. Since most do not require fancy equipment, they can be done at home, poolside, or toward the end of a weight workout.

There has been a tremendous explosion in the abdominal exercise industry. Many exotic devices are available at the gym and in the home. Some fitness experts claim that traditional core exercises are obsolete, but our own experience indicates that some of the traditional ones remain effective for triathletes if done with good form:

- **Sit-ups:** Best done on a flat to *moderately* inclined bench, with arms folded across chest, with only partial descent back to bench. These are still useful for the upper abs, and you can add a twist to work the obliques.
- **Crunches:** For those with lower back problems or dislike of the traditional sit-up, the crunch is the modern alternative. Crunches better isolate the abdominals from the hip flexors. Lie down flat on your back with your knees bent and your feet on the floor. Hold your hands wherever you feel comfortable (on your chest or beside your head—just be sure you don't pull on your head). For the basic crunch roll your upper torso forward. To increase the effectiveness of the crunch movement, push your chest and head up toward the ceiling, pushing your lower back flat onto the floor. Your anatomy will automatically cause you to follow a crunching pattern. Trying to crunch up toward the ceiling will increase the tension on the abs. Hold at the top of the movement for a second and squeeze hard. Do not lift up into a sit-up, as this works the hip flexors and can strain your back.
- **Leg raises:** For the simplest form, lie on the ground or on an elevated bench and raise legs from parallel to the ground to about 35-degree angle with knees slightly bent. Return to parallel or slight angle with the ground and repeat. Once you are able to do 25–35 of these without undue fatigue, you can add more complex motion by lifting your legs about 6 inches off the ground, and then pulling your heels in toward the buttocks. Return to extended position and then rise to straight-up 90-degree angle with the ground. Return to 6

inches from parallel and repeat. Once you reach 50–75 reps on the leg raises, you can do them on a *moderately* inclined bench (with upper body above the legs) to increase resistance.

- **Standing twists:** With a wooden broomstick, flagpole, or light weight bar positioned across the neck and shoulders and held with the arms, spread legs to shoulder width and bend forward about 30 degrees. Then smoothly rotate the shoulders 90 degrees in each direction. Do not overtwist, and rotate slowly. Keep back straight and spine centered as the axis of rotation.
- **Back extensions:** This important exercise is not easily done without a machine, a Swiss (or exercise) ball, or at least a bench where you can bend forward. Do not use too much resistance (body weight is enough without a machine) and move from a 90-degree spine-thigh angle up to full extension. Move smoothly and slowly, since this exercise can aggravate lower-back problems. This is an excellent exercise for promoting good aerodynamic position on the bike over long distances and run posture at the end of long races.

Most exercises beyond these are just variations on the fundamental theme, creating more leverage and subtle angles using body weight. Beginners should best achieve some mastery of the basic core exercises before moving on to something more challenging, such as:

- **Swiss ball:** Very popular and relatively safe, with hundreds of possible exercises. You should receive detailed exercise charts or even a video if you purchase one of these, or simply check the Internet under a "Swiss ball" search.
- **Medicine ball:** Heavier and smaller than the Swiss ball, available in various weights. Good for twists and unusual angles, integrating obliques and abs with other muscle groups. As with the Swiss ball, many exercises are possible.
- **Stretch cords:** In addition to sport-specific exercises for swim stroke development, these can be used with the lower body for core development.

FLEXIBILITY

Prepare yourself for the world, as the athletes used to do for their exercise; oil your mind and your manners, to give them the necessary suppleness and flexibility; strength alone will not do.

—Earl of Chesterfield

We have stated that long-course triathlon is primarily a test of strength and endurance. So you may ask the question, "Why is flexibility important?" Triathlon exhibits seesaws and polar opposites, and flexibility is a complement to both strength and endurance.

As strength increases and muscle mass grows, there is a tightening tendency, which reduces muscle-fiber length and range of motion. Strength is only useful if we can apply it without injury and in the full range of motion required for economy in the three sports. We need flexibility to safely apply force over the greatest displacement, which defines the real work (directed force over a certain distance) we can do when training and racing.

To build endurance for half-Ironman races, we train over longer distances. As volume grows, especially the longest ride, swim or run, soreness and natural muscular fatigue decrease range of motion and degrade economy. The best long-course athletes are the ones who can postpone this degradation for as long as possible. Starting the race with high flexibility means that even when tired, we can still maintain good range of motion and hence economy. The same theory holds for progression through a training period and finishing the muscle-tightening breakthrough workouts.

Combine these two notions—muscle tightening and fatigue-induced restriction—and you find that it's very difficult to develop muscular endurance for the half-Iron distance without good flexibility. This flexibility requirement is not entirely obvious, since the actual motions required to swim, bike, and run are not extreme. While it's true that triathletes do not need the extreme flexibility of ballet dancers or gymnasts, they must maintain flexibility for more repetitions over a much longer time.

Flexible Methods

Methods of increasing and maintaining flexibility fall roughly into two groups:

- The traditional stretching exercises familiar to most athletes from track-and-field events, swimming, and team sports. These are still useful to modern triathletes, provided they are done with the right form and emphasis. If you learned to do these properly as a school-age athlete, they can continue to form the foundation of your flexibility program. I still do many of the same stretching exercises I did as an adolescent thirty years ago, but with more conscientious technique, variation, and a renewed faith in the results.
- The so-called "modern" techniques are mostly variations on ancient yoga practices. These include hatha (physical) yoga itself, and Western techniques, branching into things like Pilates, stretch cords, and periodic force variations of static and active methods. These techniques are more complex and require more practice for full effectiveness. What they provide for all triathletes is a different *attitude* toward stretching: slowing down, rhythmic breathing, nonlinear range of motion, and much-needed patience. Remember that to the original practitioners of yoga, it was considered a meaningless exercise without the proper mental attitude. Yoga's emphasis on conscious-awareness is useful to the entire training process.

As with our strength-training philosophy, we will remain "flexible" and choose exercises from both schools of thought.

Traditional Stretching

Ballistic stretching

Western athletic stretching was influenced by the calisthenics movement in the 1950s and 1960s, and the flexibility exercises resembled the strength-building exercises, leading to what was known as *ballistic* stretching. This involved quick movements and bouncing, where flexibility became confused with warming up. In fact, ballistic stretching can tighten muscles and result in injury—hence its modern demise. Stretching is best done slowly and *after* warming up for 10–15 minutes.

Static stretching

The static method came along later from various sources, with a common theme of moving slowly to a stationary position and holding for several seconds. This method is simple, safe, and draws on the theme of ancient yoga methods where *asanas* (postures) were held for at least fifteen seconds up to several minutes to stretch muscles, promote blood flow, and harmonize nerve electrical flow. Because of its simplicity, it is the most popular with athletes from various sports. It's the method many of us learned in school with traditional sports.

Modern Stretching and PNF

PNF (Proprioceptive Neuromuscular Facilitation) stretching is perhaps the fastest and most effective way known to increase static-passive flexibility. Although it requires more practice initially than static stretching, we recommend experienced triathletes give it a try. It is not really a type of stretching, but rather a technique of combining static and isometric stretching to achieve maximum static flexibility. Although classified as a modern technique and using more analytical experiments, there is nothing within it that has not been tried by yogis for thousands of years. PNF force variation closely resembles the practices yoga. Actually, the term of PNF stretching is itself a misnomer, since it was originally developed as a method of rehabilitating stroke victims. PNF now refers to any of several post-isometric relaxation stretching techniques where a muscle group:

- is passively stretched,
- contracts isometrically against resistance while in the stretched position, and
- is passively stretched again through the resulting increased range of motion.

PNF stretching usually employs a partner to provide resistance against the isometric contraction and then passively take the joint through its increased range of motion. You can try it without a partner, though it is usually more effective with assistance.

Most PNF stretching techniques employ isometric agonist (the stretch target) contraction/relaxation, where the stretched muscles are contracted isometrically and then relaxed. Some PNF techniques also employ isometric antagonist (opposing muscle group) contraction where the antagonists of the stretched muscles are contracted. In all cases, the stretched muscle should be rested and relaxed for at least twenty seconds before performing another PNF technique. The most common PNF stretching techniques are:

- **Hold-relax:** This technique is also called the contract-relax. After assuming an initial static stretch, the muscle being stretched is isometrically contracted for 7–15 seconds, then is briefly relaxed for 2–3 seconds, and then immediately stretched passively, stretching the muscle even farther than the initial passive stretch. This final passive stretch is held for 10–15 seconds. The muscle is then relaxed for 20 seconds before performing another PNF technique.
- **Hold-relax-contract:** This technique is also called the contract-relax-contract, and the contract-relax-antagonist-contract (or CRAC). It involves performing two isometric contractions: first of the agonists, then of the antagonists. The first part is similar to the hold-relax where, after assuming an initial passive stretch, the stretched muscle is isometrically contracted for 7–15 seconds. Then relax the muscle is relaxed while its antagonist performs an isometric contraction that is held for 7–15 seconds. Then relax for 20 seconds before performing another PNF technique.
- **Hold-relax-swing:** This method involves some dangerous motions similar to ballistic stretching and is not recommended for triathletes.

Notice that in the hold-relax-contract technique, there is no final passive stretch. Because there is no final passive stretch, this PNF technique is considered one of the safest PNF techniques to perform, less likely to result in torn muscle tissue. Some make the technique even more intense by adding the final passive stretch after the second isometric contraction. Although this can result in greater flexibility gains, it also increases the likelihood of injury.

PNF stretching is not recommended for children and adolescents whose bones are still growing. It is very strenuous and should be performed for a given muscle group no more than once per day (ideally, no more than once every thirty-six hours). If you are tired or insufficiently recovered to stretch with PNF, fall back on simple static stretching as an easier alternative.

Stretching Exercises

There are hundreds of potentially useful stretching exercises available to triathletes, ranging from ancient yoga to traditional Western exercises to techniques requiring exotic equipment. In keeping with this book's philosophy of the simplest, most fundamental approach to long-course training, we are going to outline a few that are suited to all triathletes. Once you have mastered these, we encourage you to explore some of the variations found in yoga and other stretching sources listed in the bibliography. As with strength training, the most useful stretch for you is the one that addresses your specific limiters and can be performed consciously and consistently without risk of injury.

INTRODUCTION TO STRETCHING

Stretch slowly without bouncing. Stretch to where you feel a moderate, easy stretch. Hold this feeling for 15–30 seconds. As you hold, the feeling of tension should diminish; if not, ease off some. The easy stretch reduces tension and readies the tissues for the developmental stretch.

After holding the easy stretch, move a fraction of an inch farther into the stretch until you feel mild tension again. This developmental stage is held for 5–30 seconds. Tension should slightly diminish or remain the same. If tension increases, ease off.

Stretching is best done after workouts or after a 10–15 minute warm-up. Stretching "stone cold" first thing in the morning is not recommended, although stretching in the evening before bed is useful and relaxing. Some light stretching may be done immediately before a race if you are prevented from warming up, but at only half the regular duration.

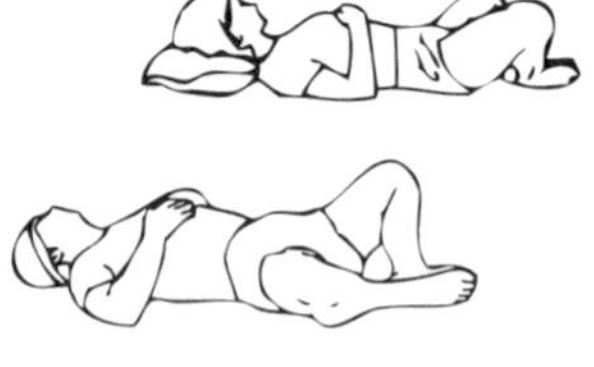

A. **Hip flexor stretch:** Gently lie back with your knees bent and the soles of your feet together, relaxing completely, to stretch the groin. Hold 30 seconds.

B. **IT band stretch 1:** Recline and bend your knees, then lock your fingers behind your head and lift the left leg over the right. Use the left leg to pull the right one toward the floor, stretching along the side of your hip and lower back. Stretch and relax. Upper back, shoulders and elbows remain flat on the floor. Avoid touching the floor with the right knee. Hold 20–30 seconds. Repeat stretch for other side.

C. **Hamstring stretch 1:** Relax and straighten legs. Pull the left leg toward chest. Head preferably remains on the mat, but do not strain. Hold for 30 seconds. Repeat using other leg.

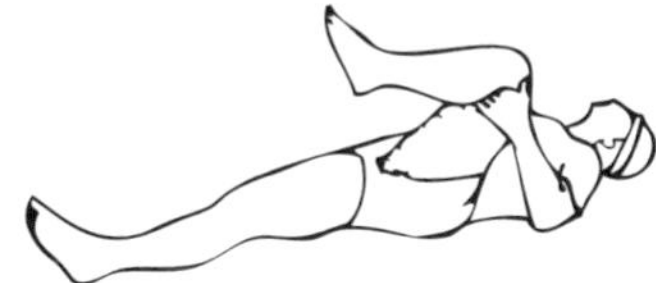

D. **IT band stretch 2:** Bend the left leg and pull it up with the right hand over the right leg. Turn the head and see the hand of the arm that is straight. Rest the head on the mat. Keep back of shoulders flat on the mat. Using the hand on the thigh, just above the knee, pull the bent leg down, stretching the lower back and side of hip. Relax feet and ankles. Hold for 20–30 seconds. Repeat other side.

E. **Groin stretch:** Place your feet together with your heels a comfortable distance from your groin. Place hands around feet and slowly contract abdominals, moving forward until groin stretches. Move from the hips, not the shoulders. Keep elbows outside the lower legs for greater stability during the stretch. Hold for 20–30 seconds.

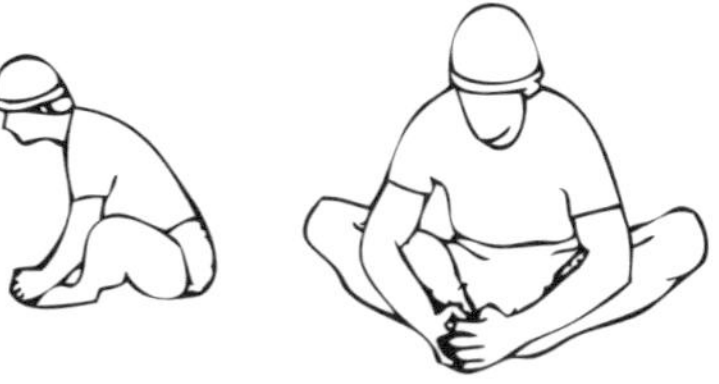

F. Hip stretch 1: With right leg straight, put left foot down flat on the other side of right knee. Reach over the left leg with the right arm with the elbow outside the left leg. Leaving the left hand on the ground behind back, slowly turn head and look over the left shoulder. Simultaneously turn the upper body (not the hips) toward left hand and arm. Bend the right elbow and gently push against the bent leg. Hold for 5–15 seconds for each side, stretching the outside of the upper leg and lower back. Repeat on other side.

G. Hip stretch 2: Keep shoulders and face relaxed, breathing normally. Hold the outside of ankle with left hand, with right hand and forearm around the bent knee. Gently pull the leg toward chest, easily stretching the rear upper leg. If needed, use a pillow or some other form of support. Hold for 15–30 seconds. Provide adequate support while holding the leg to prevent stress on the knee. Repeat with other leg to stretch upper hamstrings and hip.

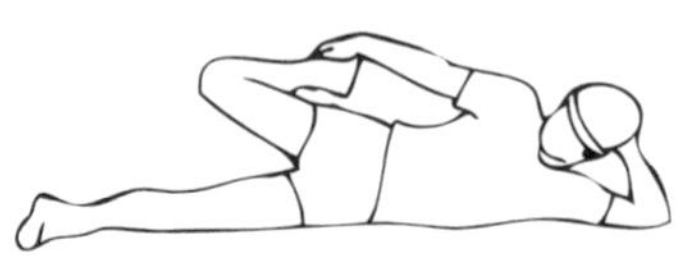

H. Quadriceps stretch: Lie on side, resting the head in the palm of the left hand. Hold the top of the right foot with the right hand between the toes and ankle joint. Move the front of the right hip forward by contracting the right buttock muscles, pushing the right foot into the right hand, stretching the front of the thigh. Hold for 10–15 seconds, keeping body aligned. Repeat on other side.

I. **Hamstring stretch 2:** Sit with right leg straight and the sole of the left foot resting near the inside of right leg. Slowly lean forward from the hips to stretch the right hamstring. Use a towel if you cannot reach your feet with your hands. Avoid locking the knee. Relax breathing along with the right quadriceps, ankles, and toes, keeping the right foot upright. Hold for 30 seconds. Repeat with other leg.

J. **Lower back stretch 1:** Place feet shoulder-width, with toes pointed out at 15-degree angles. Bend at the knees and squat down with back straight. If unstable, hold rigid object for support. Stretch Achilles tendon, groin, lower back, and hips for 20–30 seconds. Those who experience pain or have existing knee problems should omit this stretch.

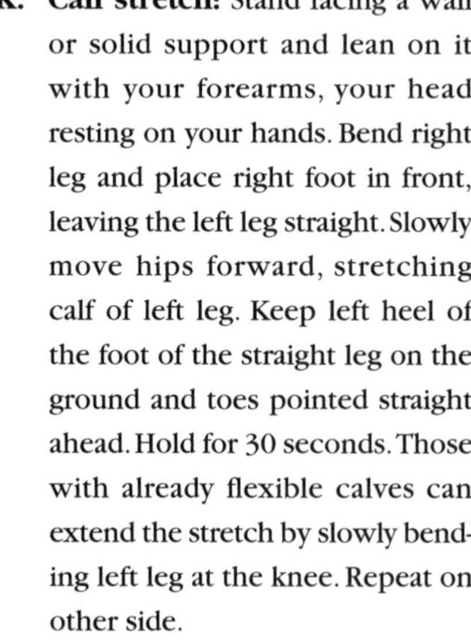

K. Calf stretch: Stand facing a wall or solid support and lean on it with your forearms, your head resting on your hands. Bend right leg and place right foot in front, leaving the left leg straight. Slowly move hips forward, stretching calf of left leg. Keep left heel of the foot of the straight leg on the ground and toes pointed straight ahead. Hold for 30 seconds. Those with already flexible calves can extend the stretch by slowly bending left leg at the knee. Repeat on other side.

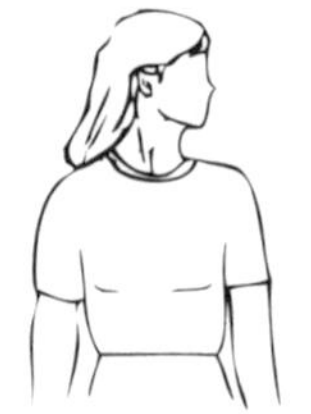

L. Neck stretch: Turn chin toward left shoulder, stretching the right side of the neck. Hold moderate tension for 10–15 seconds. Repeat twice each side.

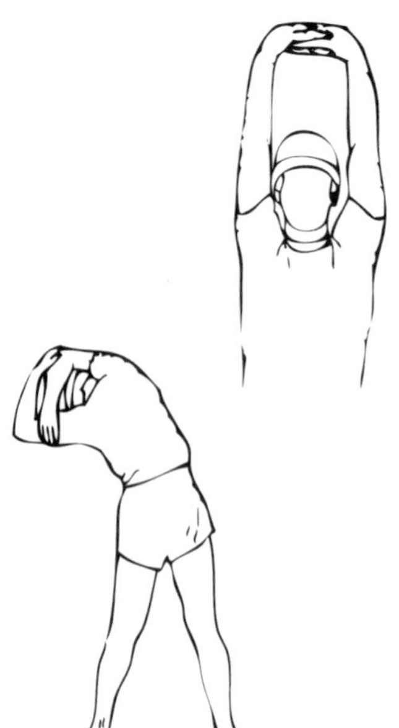

M. Shoulder stretch: Lock fingers above head. Push arms slightly back and up with palms facing skyward, stretching the arms, shoulders, and upper back. Hold for 15–20 seconds, breathing normally.

N. Oblique stretch: Lift arms overhead and hold the elbow of the right arm with left hand. With knees slightly bent for balance, pull elbow behind the head, bending from the hips to the side. Hold for 10–15 seconds. Repeat on other side.

O. **Lower back stretch 2:** Place both hands at shoulder-width on a fence or ledge, dropping upper body with knees slightly bent, keeping the hips directly above the feet. To vary the stretch, bend the knees slightly more or place hands higher. Hold for 30 seconds, and keep knees bent when standing up again.

A Final Word on Flexibility

The large majority of age-group triathletes do not pay enough attention to flexibility; it's a bigger limiter than strength training for many nowadays. It is also proven that increased flexibility produces faster times for most athletes, and this with little time investment. But as with strength training, it is possible to become *too* obsessed with flexibility. Some joints and muscle groups can actually become weaker and more prone to injury if they are too flexible. If you stretch at the wrong time, before warming up, or in the wrong way, you can cause more trouble than it's worth. Some stretching techniques that come from sprinting, gymnastics, or dancing are not well suited to triathlon. Genetic variations produce athletes who naturally hyperextend certain joints, sometimes significantly with elite athletes: Legendary swimmer Mark Spitz could hyperextend his knee beyond straight when kicking, for example. These people should modify, limit, or avoid stretching these areas—perhaps consult an orthopedic. The very qualities that make some athletes very fast can contribute to injury.

Given a choice between a good warm-up and a good stretch before an intensive workout or race, go with the warm-up as the first priority.

APPENDIX A

Swim Workouts

PRACTICE MAKES PERFECT

Remember that swimming sessions are really more skill practice than fitness workout. For the overwhelming majority of triathlete swimmers, this is doubly true. Once you have established a sound technique (and this can take years for the beginner), you do eventually have to learn to "swim hard," but not at the expense of technique.

However good you are, if continually wear yourself out in the pool but you don't get any faster, it's probably time to go back to more technique workouts and stroke drills. As with a good golfer or baseball hitter, it's a good idea to have a coach inspect and preferably videotape your stroke every year, sometimes more often if you are still learning technique. An hour or two spent here can be worth a hundred times the duration of other sessions.

No other triathlon sport has as much session variety as swimming. There are literally thousands of possible workouts published on paper and the Internet. If you need more, seek them out!

TECHNIQUE WORKOUTS

Technique 1 (easiest)

Swim several long, easy sets. Focus on form. Count strokes per length, trying to reduce them with efficient technique. Cadence should be in the range of 45–55 strokes per minute.

Technique 2

Warm-up: 200 easy

Main Set:

10×50 alternate side kick (25 each side) with freestyle

100 back

10×50 alternate opening fist drill with freestyle

100 back

10×50 alternate band only (most swimmers will need to use band or buoy) with freestyle

100 back

10×50 alternate catch-up with freestyle

Cool-down: 200 easy

Total = 2,700

Comments:

- Opening fist: 25 freestyle with closed fist, focus on using forearm to catch the water. Slowly open one finger at a time for the second 25.
- On catch-up, focus on front end of stroke, bend in elbow, keep elbow above wrist during catch.
- Band only will elevate your heart rate, requiring more rest.

Technique 3

Warm-up: 200 easy

Main Set:

10×50 alternate side kick (25 each side) with freestyle

100 back

10×50 alternate single change with freestyle

100 back

10×50 alternate triple change with freestyle

100 back

10×50 alternate breathe every stroke catch-up with freestyle

Cool-down: 200 easy

Total = 2,700

Comments:

- For freestyle let the leading hand *float* while breathing; a common mistake is pushing down.
- Side kick can vary between chin-up (breathing) and chin-down (kicking). Most can roll slightly onto the back when breathing. Resist the urge to lift the head. Nose and mouth only above waterline when breathing. When kicking on side, extend the low arm with high arm clear of the water from shoulder to wrist. Spine is straight; "press the buoy" on your side to lift your hips.

- All freestyle swims should either be catch-up, or 3/5/7 stroke swimming. Focus on leaving the leading arm floating when breathing.
- Single change and triple change use underwater arm recovery.

Technique 4

Warm-up: 200 easy

Main Set:

10×50 alternate side-kick change with freestyle
100 back
10×50 alternate two-stroke drill with freestyle
100 back
10×50 alternate triple catch-up with freestyle
100 back
10×50 alternate bilateral breathing with freestyle

Cool-down: 200 easy

Total = 2,700

Comments:

- Side-kick change: Three breaths on each side, then slowly rotate to the other side while exchanging leading arms (underwater). Maintain buoy pressure throughout rotation to ensure hips stay up. Remain calm.
- Two-stroke drill: Two left strokes, breathe, two right strokes, breathe, repeat. Rotate strongly during transition. Breathe on the second stroke for each side.
- Triple catch-up: Bilateral breathing with catch-up swimming. Body rotation is paramount.

Technique 5

Warm-up: 200 easy

Main Set:

10×50 alternate side-kick change with freestyle
100 back
10×50 alternate triple change with freestyle
100 back
10×50 alternate triple catch-up with freestyle
100 back
10×50 alternate offside with freestyle

Cool-down: 200 easy
Total = 2,700

Comments:

- Triple catch-up: Head down and hips up. Start breathing at hips, rotating to air.
- Offside: 50 breathing on your least favorite side. Remember to let leading arm float while breathing.

Technique 6

Warm-up: 200 easy
Main Set:

10×50 alternate side kick (25 each side) with freestyle
100 back
10×50 alternate buoy bilateral with freestyle
100 back
10×50 alternate rear emphasis with freestyle
100 back
10×50 alternate triple catch-up with freestyle

Cool-down: 200 easy
Total = 2,700

Comments:

- Buoy bilateral: Slow stroke down and focus on stroke length; ensure that you push through. Less-balanced swimmers might find a buoy helpful.
- Rear emphasis: Focus on back end of stroke; speed arm in second half of stroke and ensure that you push through.

Technique 7

Warm up: 200 easy
Main Set:

10×50 alternate side kick (25m each side) with freestyle
100 back
10×50 alternate buoy bilateral with freestyle
100 back

10×50 alternate three-stroke breathing with five-stroke breathing

100 back

10×50 alternate catch-up with freestyle

Cool-down: 200 easy

Total = 2,700

Comments:

- Ensure hands enter wide of the body. If you cross over, it will feel like you are reaching *way* outside.
- Have a friend watch or video to ensure your entry is correct. Check for bending spine after entry—this is not good. Some swimmers twist toward the air creating the illusion of a crossover when they are actually twisting at the spine.

ENDURANCE WORKOUTS

Endurance 1

Warm-up: Start slow and gradually build pace and effort.

4×200 done as 100 swim, 100 kick

10×50 done as 25 drill (your limiter), 25 swim

Main Set:

8×200 (10-sec. rest) at T-Pace + 5 sec.

Cool-down: 200 easy. Stretch out your stroke.

Total = 3,100

Endurance 2

Warm-up: 500 swim easy

8×50 done as 25 drill and 25 swim

Main Set:

7×100 (20-sec. rest); first is easy. Descending time for each interval.

Rest 1–2 minutes.

3×100 (20-sec. rest) each same pace as seventh of first set

300 kick steady effort

Cool-down: 200 easy swim

Total = 2,400

Endurance 3

Warm-up:

100 swim easy

50 kick easy

100 swim moderate

50 kick moderate

100 swim building speed throughout

50 kick building speed throughout

Main Set:

400 constant pace, moderate effort. Rest one minute.

4×100 (20-sec. rest) Start easy. Make each 100 faster. Rest one minute after last one.

300 constant, moderate pace. Rest one minute.

3×100 (20-sec. rest) Start easy. Make each 100 faster.

200 constant, moderate pace. Rest one minute.

2×100 (20-sec. rest) Start easy. Make each 100 faster.

Cool-down: 200–300 easy swim.

Total = 2,450–2,550

Endurance 4

Warm-up: Build effort on each rep.

100 swim, 50 kick, 100 swim, 50 kick, 100 swim

Main Set: Each numbered set is done nonstop as a 200.

1: 100 easy, 50 mod, 50 fast (10-sec. rest)

2: 50 easy, 100 mod, 50 fast (20-sec. rest)

3: 50 easy, 50 mod, 100 fast (30-sec. rest)

4: 100 fast, 50 easy, 50 mod (20-sec. rest)

5: 50 fast, 100 easy, 50 mod (10-sec. rest)

6: 50 fast, 50 easy, 100 mod (60-sec. rest)

Repeat 1, 2, 3.

Cool-down: 150 easy with drills

Total = 2,350

Endurance 5

Warm-up:

200 swim, 100 kick

6×100 done as 25 kick, 25 R arm, 25 L arm, 25 swim

Main Set:

8×100 (20-sec. rest) moderate, alternating 100 paddles and 100 fins

300 kick moderate

Cool-down: 200 easy swim

Total = 2,200

Endurance 6

Warm-up:

4×150 easy each done as 50 pull, 50 kick, 50 swim

200 kick easy

4×50 (10-sec. rest) moderate

Main Set:

6×100 at T-Pace (10-sec. rest)

500 time trial

Cool-down:

100 easy, 300 kick easy, 100 form

200 pull easy

Total = 2,800

MUSCULAR ENDURANCE WORKOUTS

Muscular Endurance 1

Warm-up: 100 drill, 50 kick, 100 drill, 50 kick

Main Set:

300 at T-Pace, 50 kick easy

250 at T-Pace, 50 kick easy

200 at T-Pace, 50 kick easy

150 at T-Pace, 50 kick easy

100 at T-Pace, 50 kick easy

Cool-down:

100 drill, 50 kick easy

300 swim good form

Total = 2,000

Muscular Endurance 2

Warm-up: 6×50 increasing pace slightly each 25

Main Set: All are at T-Pace:

100 (10-sec. rest), 200 (15-sec. rest), 300 (15-sec. rest), 400 (30-sec. rest), 500 (40-sec. rest), 400 (30-sec. rest), 300 (15-sec. rest), 200 (15-sec. rest), 100

Cool-down: 300 easy with emphasis on form

Total = 3,100

Muscular Endurance 3

Warm-up: 6x50 done as 25 drill of choice, 25 building speed

Main Set:

500 at T-Pace (50-sec. rest)
5×25 fast (20-sec. rest)
400 at T-Pace (40-sec. rest)
4×25 fast (20-sec. rest)
300 at T-Pace (30-sec. rest)
3×25 fast (20-sec. rest)
200 at T-Pace (20-sec. rest)
2×25 fast (20-sec. rest)
100 at T-Pace

Cool-down: 200 easy kicks and swims of your choice

Total = 2,350

Muscular Endurance 4

Warm-up: 5–10 minutes of swimming and kicking

Main Set:

4×100 at T-Pace (10-sec. rest)
30-sec. rest recovery
4×100 at T-Pace (10-sec. rest)
30-sec. rest recovery
4×100 at T-Pace (10-sec. rest)
30-sec. rest recovery

Cool-down:

500 steady swim
6×50 kick easy

Total = 2,100+

Muscular Endurance 5

Warm-up: 5–10 minutes of swimming and kicking

Main Set:

6×100 at T-Pace (10-sec. rest)
30-sec. rest recovery
6×100 at T-Pace (10-sec. rest)
30-sec. rest recovery
6×100 at T-Pace (10-sec. rest)
30-sec. rest recovery

Cool-down:

600 steady swim
6×50 kick easy

Total = 2,700+

Muscular Endurance 6

Warm-up: 100 drill, 100 kick, 100 drill, 100 kick

Main Set:

4×500 at T-Pace (45-sec. rest)

Cool-down:

100 drill, 50 kick easy
500 swim good form

Total = 3,050

ANAEROBIC ENDURANCE WORKOUTS

Anaerobic Endurance 1

Warm-up: 400 easy swim

Main Set:

4×50 very fast (30-sec. rest)
50 kick easy
4×50 very fast (30-sec. rest)
50 kick easy
4×50 very fast (30-sec. rest)
50 kick easy
4×50 very fast (30-sec. rest)
50 kick easy
4×50 very fast (30-sec. rest)
50 kick easy

Cool-down: 400 easy swim

Total = 2,050

Anaerobic Endurance 2

Warm-up:

3×100 descending times (30-sec. rest)

4×50 kick descending times (30-sec. rest)

Main Set:

6×200 fast with 50 kick easy between 200s

200 kick steady

Cool-down: 200 easy swim

Total = 2,350

Anaerobic Endurance 3

Warm-up: 200 pull for form, 200 swim easy, 100 kick

Main Set:

6×100 descending times (20-sec. rest)

50 kick easy

6×100 descending times (30-sec. rest)

Cool-down: 100 kick easy, 200 pull easy

Total = 2,050

TEST WORKOUTS

Test 1

Warm-up: Start slow and gradually build pace and effort.

100 swim, 100 kick, 100 swim, 100 kick

Main Set: This set will establish your T-Pace. After the warm-up, swim 1,000 yards/meters at a constant pace and good effort—as if racing. Record the time in your log. Record your average pace per 100, which becomes your T-Pace.

Cool-down: 500 swim easy

Total = 1,900

Test 2

Warm-up: 200 building speed each 50 (slow-mod-faster-fastest). Rest 30 sec.

Main Set:

Then 5×400 (10-sec. recoveries) building speed on each 100 (slow-mod-faster-fastest). Recover 10 seconds after last one. Then swim a 500 time trial, all out. Your average 100 pace for this is your T-time for future workouts.

Cool-down: 100 swim easy

Total = 2,850

FORCE WORKOUTS

Force 1

Open water swimming with partners. Do several short race efforts. Work on sighting and swimming straight. (If open water is not possible do the same type of sighting swim in a pool looking at a landmark above the deck every fourth to sixth stroke.)

APPENDIX B

Bike Workouts

VOLUME OR INTENSITY—TO BE OR NOT TO BE?

Such is the fundamental riddle of cycling: Should I ride more miles or ride the miles harder? This question is pondered by all, from the beginner trying to make it through their first 50-mile ride up to the pro riding more than 500 miles per week for the Ironman or Tour de France. Most modern coaches will quickly retort: "Intensity!"

Definitely, advances in heart rate monitoring and power metering have greatly enhanced our understanding of intensity. Before these tools, all we knew was that hammerheads who trained harder more of the time won more races, and the new technology has not proved this notion wrong. Even in long-course triathlons, where seasoned athletes are supposedly saving something for the run, the best of them in the pro division and even the masters age groups seem to be going all out in the half-Iron bike segment.

The problem with the "intensity is paramount" philosophy is that it is often espoused by those who already have considerable volume, more than their counterparts. They have been riding long distances for a long time. It's not unlike rich people saying that "money isn't the most important thing"—easy to say when you already have it.

As with other physiological factors, volume and intensity flow in a wave across the spectrum of athlete types. Most beginners moving up to the half-Iron distance need to increase volume without necessarily any increase in intensity beyond Zone 2 or 3. Simply riding more miles will improve their economy and VO_2max, making them faster. For long-course veterans riding 150 or more miles per week, they are more likely to improve performance by increasing intensity. For pros and division winners who win half-Iron races and usually compete at the full Iron distance, they must judiciously mix big mileage *and* high intensity to keep up with their peers.

Indeed, the reason for most long-course triathletes riding overdistance is to optimize fat burning and extend endurance for a faster *run,* not to improve the bike split. At the head of the bike pack, it's still strength and intensity that pushes the pedals harder and makes the bike go faster.

Managing intensity is highly variable, depending on genetics, age, life stress, season, and many other factors. It is much more variable than optimal volume, which is fairly simple to calculate based on your race distance, experience, and lifestyle. Yet in this dilemma there is one universal truth: If you are going to increase intensity, you must become more serious about recovery. Some masters athletes have maintained the speed of their younger days by focusing mostly on intensity while decreasing volume and increasing rest days.

ENDURANCE WORKOUTS

Endurance 1

Recovery ride: Very easy recovery spin on a mostly flat course in small chainring. Heart rate Zone 1. Pedal lightly with a comfortably high rpm, focusing on "drawing two circles" with the feet.

- People sometimes laugh at this workout, but it can be as important as your hardest ride. We hereby make it "official" so you can do it without remorse.
- Pro cyclists have called the intensity of this workout "guilt-provokingly slow." You should almost feel embarrassed about doing it—touring and mountain bikes may pass you.
- Great ride to do with spouse and kids or noncompetitive friends.

Endurance 2

Longer Aerobic Threshold (AeT): Warm up 20–30 minutes. Then ride 2–2.5 hours steady at 20 beats per minute below your lactate threshold heart rate (Zone 5a). Observe power if you have a meter and record average power after warm-up.

- This ride can serve as the basic long ride of half-Iron training.
- Once you've started an AeT ride, resist the temptation to go into Zone 3. The only exception to this rule is an occasional steep climb, but even these should be done in the easiest gear.

Endurance 3

Basic rolling ride: Ride primarily at Zone 1–2 on a rolling course, staying mostly in saddle on hills to build and maintain hip strength. Small and big chainrings.

Endurance 4

Group ride (conservative): Sit in middle or back of pack with no hard, sustained pulls. Mostly Zone 1–3. Avoid Zone 5.

Endurance 5

100-plus-mile rally: Join large charitable group for catered ride. Advanced triathletes can attempt to stay with lead peloton, but most age groupers should just ride with friends and have fun. Fall in love with the fraternity of cycling.

FORCE WORKOUTS

Force 1

Long climbs: Steady climbs of six or more minutes on moderate 4-6 percent grade. Climb mostly in saddle at 60–70 rpm. Stay in Zone 1–5a, but not above.

Force 2

Variable stepper climbs: Ride several 1–2-minute climbs of varying grades. Shift to a higher gear than you would normally use for any given climb. Cadence is 50–60 rpm to build strength, remaining seated with heart rate no higher than Zone 5a.

Force 3

Short hill attacks: On a course with long and short hills, long climbs in the saddle. Attack short hills. Spend 10 percent or more of time; should be in the Zone 4–5b. Work hard on climbs.

SPEED WORKOUTS

Speed 1

Isolated-Leg Training (on trainer): After warm-up, alternate 20–60 seconds with one leg, leaving the other on a chair. Get a total of 7–10 minutes on each leg in workout. Alternate legs as you feel like it with a comfortably high cadence. Focus on eliminating dead spot at top of stroke by pushing toes forward in shoes at top.

Speed 2

Spin-ups: Slowly spin up to your maximum rpm (100–120) over 30 seconds. When you begin to bounce, back off and then hold it for several seconds. Recover completely and repeat several times. *Stay relaxed.*

Speed 3

Pedal-stroke drills: Ride in the Zone 1–2 on a mostly flat course. Perform pedaling drills:

- Drive pedal straight forward from nine to three o'clock
- Foot against the top inside of your shoe trying to avoid touching the insole
- Touch toes to end of your shoes at top of downstroke.

Stay as relaxed with no tension in feet, legs, hands, and so on.

Speed 4

Ride fixed gear bike on a rolling course. Ride mostly in Zone 2–3 with some 4–5a on small uphills.

MUSCULAR ENDURANCE WORKOUTS

Muscular Endurance 1

Tempo intervals: Do 4–5×6 minutes in Zone 3 with 2-minute recoveries. Relaxed, smooth pedaling at 80–90 rpm in aero position. On road or trainer.

- As long-course racing approaches, extend to 3×15 minutes in Zone 3 with 3-minute recoveries.

Muscular Endurance 2

Cruise intervals: Do 4–5×6 minutes in Zone 4–5a with 2-minute recoveries. Smooth pedaling at 80–90 rpm in aero position. On road or trainer.

- As long-course racing approaches, extend to 3×10 minutes in Zone 4–5a with 3-minute recoveries.

Muscular Endurance 3

Tempo ride: Warm up well for 15–30 minutes, then ride 40–60 minutes nonstop in Zone 3 on a mostly flat course at 85–95 rpm. Pedal smoothly in aero position.

Muscular Endurance 4

Half-Iron intervals: Warm up 20–30 minutes, then complete 4×20 minutes in Zone 3–4 with 5 minutes recovery. Maintain aero position and refuel as in race.

Muscular Endurance 5

Do 3–4 climbs on a 6–8 minute hill (4–6 percent grade) in Zone 4–5a. Shift up for 30 seconds, down for 60 seconds.

- Lower cadence to build strength at 50–70 rpm (optional).
- Recover on the descents at low heart rate and higher cadence.

Muscular Endurance 6

Crisscross threshold: Warm up and then ride 20 minutes on a flatter course in Zone 4–5a. Crisscross from lower Zone 4 to higher Zone 5a every 1–2 minutes. Pedal at 85–100 rpm in aero position.

Muscular Endurance 7

Time-trial cruise intervals: Do 3–4×6–8 minutes on a 2 percent hill (or into a headwind) in Zone 3 with 2-minute recoveries. Choose a big gear at 60–75 rpm to build strength in aero position.

ANAEROBIC ENDURANCE WORKOUTS

Anaerobic Endurance 1

Variable-paced intervals: Warm up and then ride 5 minutes in Zone 4 with 3-minute recovery followed by 2 minutes in Zone 5b with 1-minute recovery. Follow this pattern three times nonstop. Pedal smoothly at 95–110rpm in aero position.

Anaerobic Endurance 2

30-30 intervals: Warm up well and then do 15–20×30 seconds at 90 percent effort with 30-second spin recoveries. Stop if speed drops by one mph. Rolling starts, standing in big gear. Get to top end quickly. Cool down easily and stretch.

- Heart rate is not an accurate indicator of shorter anaerobic intervals.
- Power meter should register at 125 percent of LT power.
- Good for early season to provide variety in longer, slower rides.
- Good for division contenders who already have good muscular endurance and speed.

Anaerobic Endurance 3

Time-trial intervals: Warm-up and then do 5×3 miles building to Zone 5a–5b with 5-minute recoveries on a flat course. Increase gear size for first three intervals. Pedal at 85–100 rpm in aero position.

Anaerobic Endurance 4

Group ride: Treat parts of group ride with triathletes or roadies as a race. Ride aggressively. Experiment with race strategies and test yourself.

- Not recommended for beginners.
- Intermediate and advanced triathletes should avoid the hammerhead peloton within two weeks of a long-course race: It can make you go out too hard in your upcoming triathlon.

Anaerobic Endurance 5

Course review: Ride course with race-ready bike setup. Attack 2–3 short hills on this ride. Otherwise, keep it very easy. Stay off of legs afterward and make sure everything on bike is tight and race-ready.

APPENDIX C

Run Workouts and Interval Tables

WHAT IS FAST?

Once you become a veteran race finisher, you often want to see posted race results of those whom you passed or those who ran past you. If you're racing locally or perhaps even internationally, you recognize the names of certain people and say to yourself, "Oh well, he or she is just a really fast runner." Perhaps you are lucky enough to have that top run split yourself, thinking, "I am the fleet-footed gal or dude today!"

Unless you are at the finish line of the Summer Olympics or a pro ITU race, a reality check will tell you that indeed these times are not that fast. Twenty-seven minutes is a fast 10K run, 29–30 minutes off the bike in an ITU triathlon. Under 2:10 is a fast marathon time for the world's best. Fortunately, these world-class runners are too busy dominating their sport to race in triathlons. The coach of a famous triathlete considered an elite runner with one of the top run splits in Ironman® Hawaii once said, "If he could run a 28-minute 10K, he would not be doing triathlons."

So for long-course athletes, running fast enough to win does not require blazing foot speed, anymore than a top triathlon swimmer has to be as fast as Ian Thorpe or Michael Phelps in the pool.

The important skill in long-course triathlons is to be able to run relatively fast after a longer bike and to maintain running form and pace to the finish line. The half-Iron distance is probably the longest triathlon that strong runners can hope to "negative split" on the run. Even the best Ironman times usually show some degradation in pace (and visibly deteriorating form) for the second half of the marathon—the champions just degrade less.

The other factor in running is recovery and injury: It takes longer to recover from long or hard running workouts than from swimming or cycling intervals—and the risk of injury is greater. Many good half-Iron triathletes can hammer on most bike workouts as hard as their roadie friends and get away with it, but few if any could avoid chronic injury attempting two hard track workouts per week as top runners do.

So when choosing the right run workouts for triathlon performance, remember that you must do *some* fast running to become a better runner, but not too much. Also know that running fast in a long-course triathlon may well be merely a high-aerobic endeavor, even though stand-alone runners are sometimes racing at VO_2max for distances shorter than the marathon.

It does not pay to risk injury or overtraining to get in a few more hard intervals or beat your training buddy. You could consider very fast training runs the riskiest investment in all of triathlon, the equivalent of mining for gold or drilling for oil in the financial realm. Only those with considerable experience and the ability to endure suffering and potential loss should attempt it.

INTERVAL TABLES

The world of running, especially in cyberspace, is overflowing with tables recommending work versus recovery time and predicting performance. Many of them are useful, but there is wide variation in how individuals respond to the workout and how they perform in a race. Throw in the additional factor of running after a hard bike, and it makes generalization difficult.

That being said, we include two tables for stand-alone 10K running in metric (Table C.1) and mile (Table C.2) units, since it's a classic distance for gauging performance for longer races in running and triathlon. It's very likely that you can find one or more local 10K events on which to baseline your running speed during the year.

Many coaches have ingenious physiological formulas to calculate actual run performance, including off the bike. We resisted the temptation to include a derivative table for predicting run splits in triathlons because:

- Top triathletes are high on the scale of mental toughness.
- Triathletes exceed formula predictions because of their additional aerobic fitness from swimming and cycling, proving that "less is more" when optimizing intervals. Beginners may fixate on their limiters with run speed, which for them has more to do with overall

endurance than interval or time-trial testing splits. They may attempt too many intervals too fast.

- Triathlon course conditions are more variable than stand-alone run courses: higher heat, variable winds, pavement mixed with trails, and a higher incidence of mismeasurement for classic distances like 10K and the half-marathon (21.1km). Recently a professional world championship triathlon turned out to be only eight kilometers instead of ten!
- Unrealistic expectations can cause confusion. The running track is usually the only way to be sure about objective testing and interval evaluation, though GPS and accelerometer systems are becoming more accurate every year.

Our hesitation should not stop you, the industrious athlete, from guesstimating your own table of likely triathlon splits based on a 10K race or time trial. You can then backtrack to the correct interval workout for your triathlon race goal. Veteran triathletes and strong cyclists can often do *fewer repetitions* than recommended in the table to meet the goal.

TABLE C.1 SUGGESTED METRIC INTERVAL TRAINING BASED ON 10K RACE PACE

10K TIME	RACE SPLITS		2,000 METERS		
	km	400m	Interval	Recovery	Reps
50:00	5:00	2:00	9:40–10:05	5:00	3
48:00	4:48	1:55	9:20–9:40	5:00	3
46:00	4:36	1:50	9:00–9:20	5:00	3
44:00	4:24	1:46	8:30–8:50	5:00	3–4
42:00	4:12	1:41	8:10–8:30	4:00	3–4
40:00	4:00	1:36	7:40–8:05	4:00	3–4
38:00	3:48	1:31	7:20–7:40	4:00	3–4
36:00	3:36	1:27	6:50–7:15	4:00	3–4
34:00	3:24	1:22	6:30–6:50	3:00	4–5
32:00	3:12	1:17	6:00–6:25	3:00	4–5
30:00	3:00	1:12	5:40–6:05	3:00	4–5
28:00	2:48	1:07	5:20–5:40	3:00	4–5

1,000 METERS			400 METERS		
Interval	Recovery	Reps	Interval	Recovery	Reps
4:50–5:00	4:00	6	1:48–1:53	3:00	8
4:40–4:50	4:00	6	1:45–1:50	3:00	8
4:25–4:35	4:00	6	1:40–1:45	3:00	8
4:15–4:25	4:00	6	1:36–1:40	2:00	9
4:00–4:10	3:00	6	1:32–1:36	2:00	9
3:50–4:00	3:00	6–8	1:28–1:32	2:00	9
3:40–3:50	3:00	6–8	1:25–1:30	2:00	10
3:25–3:35	3:00	6–8	1:18–1:22	1:30	12
3:15–3:25	2:00	6–8	1:12–1:14	1:30	12
3:05–3:15	2:00	6–8	1:08–1:10	1:30	14
2:50–3:00	2:00	8–10	1:04–1:07	1:00	16
2:40–2:50	2:00	8–10	0:58–1:02	1:00	16

TABLE C.2 SUGGESTED MILE TRAINING BASED ON 10K RACE PACE

10K TIME	RACE SPLITS		ONE MILE (1,609 meters)		
	mile	1/4 mile	Interval	Recovery	Reps
50:00	8:03	2:01	7:45–8:05	5:00	3
48:00	7:43	1:56	7:30–7:45	5:00	3
46:00	7:24	1:51	7:15–7:30	5:00	3
44:00	7:05	1:46	6:50–7:05	5:00	3–4
42:00	6:45	1:41	6:30–6:40	4:00	3–4
40:00	6:26	1:37	6:15–6:25	4:00	3–4
38:00	6:07	1:32	5:55–6:05	4:00	3–4
36:00	5:48	1:27	5:35–5:50	4:00	3–4
34:00	5:28	1:22	5:15–5:30	3:00	4–5
32:00	5:09	1:17	4:55–5:10	3:00	4–5
30:00	4:50	1:12	4:35–4:50	3:00	4–5
28:00	4:30	1:08	4:20–4:30	3:00	4–5

HALF MILE			QUARTER MILE		
Interval	**Recovery**	**Reps**	**Interval**	**Recovery**	**Reps**
3:50–4:00	4:00	6	1:48–1:53	3:00	8
3:40–3:50	4:00	6	1:45–1:50	3:00	8
3:30–3:40	4:00	6	1:40–1:45	3:00	8
3:20–1:30	4:00	6	1:36–1:40	2:00	9
3:10–3:20	3:00	6	1:32–1:36	2:00	9
2:55–3:05	3:00	6–8	1:28–1:32	2:00	9
2:50–2:55	3:00	6–8	1:25–1:30	2:00	10
2:40–2:50	2:00	6–8	1:18–1:22	1:30	12
2:30–2:35	2:00	6–8	1:12–1:14	1:30	12
2:20–2:25	2:00	6–8	1:08–1:10	1:30	14
2:10–2:15	2:00	8–10	1:04–1:07	1:00	16
2:00–2:05	2:00	8–10	0:58–1:02	1:00	16

ENDURANCE WORKOUTS

Endurance 1

Walk 30-60 minutes. Or go for a long trail hike or a round of golf carrying your own clubs. We include this workout so you'll remember that walking is indeed an aerobic exercise, a great way to relax before or recover after a race. I walked up all the stairs to the top level of the Eiffel Tower in Paris two days after Ironman® Europe—almost as much fun as the race!

Endurance 2

Run in Zone 1 on a flat, soft surface, *very* easy—guilt-provokingly slow. Take recovery workouts seriously.

Endurance 3

Run in Zone 1-2 on a gently rolling course. Check cadence by counting left foot strikes every 15 seconds, aiming for 22 or higher.

Endurance 4

After warming up, run on a mostly flat course for 60 minutes at 20bpm below Zone 5a (lactate threshold heart rate).

- Focus on good form with a high cadence (88-92rpm) and mid- to ball-of-foot strike, not on toes.
- Just before foot strike the foot should paw back slightly.
- Primary tool of long-course run training and should be standard for most of your longest runs.

Endurance 5

Keep heart rate in Zones 1-3 on a rolling course. Focus on relaxed, upright form. Heart rate gradually rises to Zone 3 as pace builds, but don't force it. Do this workout on trails when possible.

Endurance 6

Aerobic training marathon: Enter a local half or full marathon in the Preparation or early Base period, but start 20bpm below race pace (over one minute per mile slower). Stay in Zone 1-2 for the first three-quarters of the race, pacing on heart rate instead of speed. If you feel good, move into Zone 3 for the final miles. Avoid Zone 4 or higher and do not duel with other runners. Nevertheless, you will probably pass a lot of people toward the end of a full marathon.

- This serves as an effective race strategy for a first-time marathon runner.
- If you are going to race long-course triathlons, do not attempt more than one "fast" stand-alone marathon per year, but you can do an aerobic training marathon more often. Let's face it—the atmosphere of a big marathon is fun.

FORCE WORKOUTS

Force 1

Run in Zone 1–4 on hilly course. Only move into Zone 5 on steepest hills. Don't force heart rate up: Allow it to rise with hills.

Force 2

If you have no hills in your area, run stadium steps at a local facility. Go slowly at first until you develop this skill.

- Avoid when tired, on rainy days, or in darkness.
- Avoid trying to take two steps at a time, focusing more on gradual increase in cadence up the stairs. Skill development is as important as strength.
- Avoid when injured or if you have chronic orthopedic limiters: knees, tendinitis, Achilles heel, plantar fasciitus, and so on.
- Prefer stadium steps to indoor stair-master machine, which is as stressful as actually running on pavement.
- Prefer natural road hills to stadium steps when available.

MUSCULAR ENDURANCE WORKOUTS

Muscular Endurance 1

Tempo intervals: Warm up well, and then run 3–4×6 minutes in Zone 3 heart rate with 2-minute jogging recovery interval. Relax and listen to your breathing and try to keep it relaxed.

Muscular Endurance 2

Cruise intervals: Warm up well, and then run 3–4×6 minutes in Zone 4–5a heart rate with 2-minute jogging recovery intervals. Controlled and moderate breathing.

Muscular Endurance 3

Cruise intervals: Warm up well, including four strides. Then on a track, run 4–6×800 meters at 10K mile pace plus 10–20 seconds (90-second jogging recoveries, about 200 meters). Record times and heart rates.

- Those also preparing for a full Ironman or full marathon can increase to 8–10×800 meters.
- These are not the same as the well-known "Yasso 800s," which are usually run in Zone 5b with longer (sometimes walking) recoveries of 400 meters. Your actual pace could be about 10 seconds or more slower than Yasso's 800 splits. Note that Yasso himself was rather flexible with the number of repetitions or recovery. We believe a slightly slower pace with less recovery is more applicable to long-course triathlon training.
- Many triathletes with allied cycling volume can expect even better performance in stand-alone running events than the Yasso scale would predict (e.g., 3:10 average 800m split could produce a sub-three-hour marathon using our modified method, which I experienced personally at 2:59:51). Remember the rule that "cycling usually helps your running, but running rarely if ever helps your cycling."

Muscular Endurance 4

Long cruise intervals: Warm up well, including four strides. Then run 3×1 mile at LTHR (10K mile pace plus 10–20 seconds) with 200–400m recovery. Record times and heart rate averages for each.

- Those preparing for full Ironman or full marathon can extend to 4-6×1 mile.
- Even for a fast stand-alone marathon, there is usually no need for triathletes to extend intervals to the 10–13×1-mile intervals recommended by some running coaches to achieve a marathon PR, provided bike mileage is maintained in the off-season. Many triathletes report their best winter marathon time involved the least intervals, but included a good mix of swimming and cycling continued through the off-season.

- Recovery is paramount for longer running intervals. If you don't have the time or capacity to recover from them, it's best not to do them at all.

Muscular Endurance 5

Hill intervals: On a moderate hill of around 4–6 percent grade, run 3–4×5 minutes building to Zone 4–5a. Recover during the descent, maintain good form.

Muscular Endurance 6

Tempo run: Complete a long warm-up building heart rate to Zone 3. Then run 20 minutes continuous at heart rate Zone 4–5a on flat course, with relaxed breathing and form.

Muscular Endurance 7

Step-ups: Run 10 miles with first 3 miles warm-up; miles 4–6 in Zone 3, miles 7–9 in Zone 4–5a; then cool down for 1 mile. Record pace for Zone 4–5a.

Muscular Endurance 8

Tempo finish: First part of run Zone 1–2 for 20–90 minutes, with the last 30 minutes in Zones 3–5a steady, recording pace. This is an excellent long run strategy as half-Iron race nears.

SPEED WORKOUTS

Speed 1

Strides: Warm up 10–15 minutes, then run 6–8×20-second strides on soft, slight downhill (90-second walk back recoveries).

- Focus on technique (cadence, pawback, foot lift, or your limiter).
- If possible, do this barefoot on grass to build foot strength.
- Be sure to check for sharp objects or dog poop in grass. Don't run barefoot if there are any breaks in the skin on your feet.

Speed 2

Strides and Hops: Warm up 10–15 minutes, and then stride 4–5×20 seconds fast on soft, gentle downhill. Run approximately 400m race pace, not all out, with relaxed form. Walk and hop back to start point during each recovery. Hop 30 times on right leg and then 30 times on left leg to build foot and leg strength; then cool down easy.

Speed 3

Hill skips: Warm up and then go to a moderate 4–6 percent hill over 25 meters long. Skip up the hill for 20 seconds focusing on the height of each skip. Then turn and run down the hill, with gravity setting your pace (not all out). Land flat on your foot toward the forefoot with quick turnover and leaning slightly forward. The downhill run should take 10 seconds, which means you may go beyond your starting point, finishing on flatter terrain. Turn and walk back to start. Repeat eight times and cool down.

ANAEROBIC ENDURANCE WORKOUTS

Anaerobic Endurance 1

Track intervals: Warm up and do four strides; then run 6–8×600m at 3–5 seconds/faster per 400 than 5km pace with 400m recovery. Control pace.

Anaerobic Endurance 2

Track intervals: Warm up and do four strides, then run 2×600m (recover for 300m), 2×800m (recover for 400m), 2×1,000m (recover for 500m). Five seconds faster per 400 than 5K race pace. Maintain good form and high cadence.

Anaerobic Endurance 3

Thirty-thirty intervals: Warm up well and then run 15–20×30 seconds at a pace about 20 seconds faster per mile than your 5K race pace per mile. Recover by jogging easily for 30 seconds after each.

- You should cover half of the fast rep distance during your jog (for example, run 150 in 30 seconds, jog 75 in 30 seconds).
- Stop when you can no longer maintain the targeted pace.
- It's best to run on a track or other measured course so that pace may be monitored.

Anaerobic Endurance 4

Taper repeats: Warm up including four pickups; then run 4×90 seconds (recover 3 minutes) at next race pace. Relaxed speed! Do not run all out. This workout can be done on racecourse if possible.

Anaerobic Endurance 5

Jog easily for 2 miles, then:

1. 800 meters at 10K pace with the last 100 at top speed; then jog for 400 meters.
2. 800 meters at 10K pace with the last 200 at top speed; then jog for 400 meters.
3. 800 meters at 10K race pace with the last 300 at mile speed; then jog for 400 meters.
4. 800 meters at 10K race pace with the last 400 at mile speed; then jog for 400 meters.

Cool down with 2 miles of easy running. When your opponent comes up on your shoulder with 800 meters to go in a race, this workout will help you put the hammer down.

TEST WORKOUTS

Test 1

Maximum Aerobic Function (MAF) test: Warm up about 15 minutes, raising heart rate to 10bpm below Zone 5a (lactate threshold heart rate). Then run 3, 4, or 5 miles on track maintaining a heart rate that is exactly 9–11bpm below lowest Zone 5a number. Press lap-counter for each mile during the test. Cool down in Zone 1.

- Only long-course veterans with a good running base should test over 4 or 5 miles: Others should limit this test to 3 miles (5K).
- If you warm up properly, the mile splits should go up gradually for each mile at a constant heart rate.
- The average of these mile splits is your Maximum Aerobic Function or Aerobic Pace. This is often very close to the pace many athletes will be capable of in a half-Iron triathlon run.
- Do this test early in the morning with moderate temperatures and low wind. Fatigue or environmental extremes will invalidate the test results.
- Athletes have gauged their progress from beginner to world champion with this test.

APPENDIX D

Combined Workouts

IS THE BRICK WORKOUT FADING?

When triathlon first started, it was all about combining different events, whether they included swimming in the ocean and running along the beach to your bike, or just about any variation to see what happened. Training reflected this, with athletes spending a lot of time experimenting with combinations. And everyone has initial trouble transitioning the frontal leg muscles used in cycling over to more use of the hamstrings, calves, and glutes for running.

In recent years, popular coaches and athletes have moved away from so much brick training, or at least from the long brick workouts that dominated full and half-Iron training for past masters like Dave Scott and Mark Allen. Some of this has to do with the higher speeds that short- and long-course professionals can now generate. In order to run very fast, you need to do more of your training very fast, and this is difficult to maintain consistently after cycling.

The other factor is recovery, where long bricks are blamed for overtraining or "garbage Zone" cycling and running. Beginning athletes mistakenly try to start with the long, advanced bricks and quickly find themselves worn-out or hurt.

I believe, however, there can be something lost in this bargain for the average age-group veteran who can still benefit from moderate pacing and frequent practice of transitions and fatigue management via brick workouts. Since these athletes probably should not train as intensively as elites, one of the only other ways to challenge muscle tissue for greater endurance at race pace is to rapidly switch sports in the middle of a workout. I'm amazed at how many slower triathlon runners have done little or perhaps no brick training, yet they read in books and magazines that the reason to avoid them was so they could run faster while avoiding injury.

Most triathletes need to master the fundamental skill of running off the bike efficiently before running faster still in stand-alone workouts.

There are creative methods to vary workouts to suit different physiological types, and avoiding a certain class of workouts simply because it requires conscientious recovery seems unwise for the large majority of long-course athletes. The key is to find the right balance, right recovery, and optimal volume and intensity—this balance is highly variable for individual athletes. And few would have anything bad to say about mixing swim workouts with bike or run training, something many triathletes never attempt except in a race.

ENDURANCE WORKOUTS

Endurance 1

Medium endurance brick: Bike moderate to long, mostly in Zone 2. Transition to medium run in Zone 3. Refuel as in race.

- This workout is the "fundamental brick" of triathlon, doable by beginner and advanced alike. Most will benefit by *at least* a 2:1 margin of bike to run. For example: 60-minute bike plus 20–30 minute run. For half- and full Iron-distance athletes, improve endurance by gradually extending bike length more than the run to something like 90- to 90–120-minute bike and 30-minute run.
- Practice transitions most of the year, especially shoe changes, starting and ending workout with bike cleats clipped in.

Endurance 2

Long brick: Ride long on a course that simulates the racecourse as best you can. Do not exceed heart rate Zone 4 with most of the ride in Zone 2 and 3. Then transition to a medium- to long-duration run on a course that approximates your next A-priority racecourse. Run mostly in heart rate Zones 2 and 3. Eat and drink just as you will in the race. Focus on recovery for two hours after this workout.

- More advanced version of fundamental brick. Veteran half-Iron athletes can extend as far as three-hour ride plus 60-minute run—anything more has diminishing returns unless you are also preparing for a full Iron race.

Endurance 3

Swim-to-run workout: For an infrequent swimmer or someone with low running base, this could be termed a muscular-endurance workout. But since it is likely done in the summer, most athletes will be swimming farther and running steadily. Instead of doing a morning swim workout and an afternoon or evening run, do the run immediately after the swim before the sun rises high. The swim can be as hard as usual, even a longer ME workout, but the run should start in Zone 1–2 and gradually build no higher than Zone 3. Heart rate will probably be low on the early run from the cooling effect of the water and lower morning temperature.

If you live in an area where late afternoon runs can be 95–105°F, this may be your only way to maintain running volume for your long-course training without dehydration and heat fatigue. Swimming in an early-morning masters group can make it impractical to find pool time later in the day. Or you might want to try it just for variety.

A good rule of thumb is to shorten your usual late-day run by 30–50 percent. For example, a one-hour swim followed by a 30–45-minute run instead of your usual 60-minute evening run. Once you are fit, you can use this as a "harder" aerobic function test, jogging to a running track and doing 2–3 test miles at a steady Zone 3 heart rate. As swimming endurance and running economy improves, the average mile-pace of the test will come down.

MUSCULAR ENDURANCE WORKOUTS

Muscular Endurance 1

Half-Iron pacing brick: Start bike easy first hour in Zone 1. Then ride 40 minutes steady in Zone 2. For the next 20 minutes increase to Zone 3 (moderately hard). Repeat 40-20 pattern 1–2 more times for a total of 2–3 hours.

- This is controlled pacing—beginners to intermediates avoid Zone 4 or higher except in very steep climbs. Division contenders can push final 10–15 minutes of each hour in Zone 4–5a.
- After warm-up of 15–30 minutes, this ride should be on the aerobars except for steep climbing. Easy run off the bike for 15–30 minutes.
- Good baseline for half-Iron pacing.
- Note heart rate, power, and perceived exertion during workout.
- Eat and drink as planned for the race.

Muscular Endurance 2

Pre-race brick: Bike 30 minutes plus run 15 minutes. Include three short (45–75-second), race efforts for bike and run, but without undue fatigue.

- On the racecourse, if possible; note landmarks.
- Tighten all bolts on your bike and inspect tires for cuts, cracks, or debris.
- Good preparation for most triathlon and duathlon race distances. Resist temptation to bike longer before half- and full Ironman races.
- Best done the morning of the day before the race.

Muscular Endurance 3

Tempo brick: Bike 1 hour building effort with a 10K time trial near the end. After a fast transition, run 20 minutes at 10K race effort. Walk 5 minutes for cool-down.

- Good for veteran and advanced triathletes preparing for a shorter race or faster half-Iron performance.
- Better done later in base period or during actual race season.

Muscular Endurance 4

Half-Iron race simulation: Ride 2 hours on a flat to rolling course. Warm up 30 minutes and ride 5×12 minutes at Zone 3 in aero position (3-minute recovery spins). Transition to a 30-minute run in Zone 3.

- Beginners can shorten intervals to 5×6 minutes in Zone 3.
- Advanced athletes can extend run to 60 minutes for true race-distance simulation.
- Add steeper climbs to intervals if A-race venue is hilly.

Muscular Endurance 5

Long swim-bike transition with spin class: Swim 60 minutes at a health club pool, using long-interval ME swim workout (or 10-minute warm-up plus 40 minutes continuous moderately hard pace). Transition smoothly to a 60–90-minute bike on flat to rolling terrain, then return in time for the spin class of 50 minutes.

- This work resulted from training for my first Ultraman Hawaii triathlon held in late November, where you have to swim 10K, mount your bike, and climb at 8–10 percent grade for 1,500 feet in 90°F heat, then climb another 3,500 feet for a total of 90 miles—and that's just the first of three stages.

- This workout is not for the beginner, nor does it have year-round utility, but you learn to bike strongly after a long, hard swim.
- Developed while swimming at a health club with regular spin classes, which were too short and anaerobic for a long-course athlete. By prefacing them with a longer swim and bike, they became good training for triathlons.
- Can be done completely indoors with a stationary bike near the pool.

Muscular Endurance 6

Multiple swim-bike intervals: 3× (500 swim plus 5-mile bike).

- Useful for beginners having trouble with transitions or longer swim or bike sessions; should stay in Zone 2–3. Also useful for veteran athletes who want to improve transitions and speed, pushing into Zone 4–5a.
- The bike is usually done harder than the swim, but into the later reps, the swim can become quite challenging.
- You get six sessions with five transitions, which also makes this a speed workout.

Muscular Endurance 7

Multiple run-bike intervals: 3–4× (10-mile bike plus 1.5–2-mile run)

- As with the swim/bike workout above, good for beginners maintaining steady pace in Zone 2–3.
- Experts can do the run harder, perhaps on a track to promote speed and experience progressive stages of fatigue, which challenge good running form.
- All triathletes can benefit from the transition practice.
- Can be done in cold weather on an indoor trainer going outside for the run, or completely indoors in a gym with stationary bike and treadmill.

ANAEROBIC ENDURANCE WORKOUTS

Anaerobic Endurance 1

Running-track interval brick: Set up your bike on a trainer at a track or other site with a measured, out-and-back, or circular course. Warm up on bike for 15 minutes to Zone 3. Transition to 400m run at 10K pace. Get back on the bike for a 5-minute ride, as follows: Spin easily for 2 minutes to recover and then build heart rate to Zone 4–5a and hold this for 3 minutes. Transition to an 800m run at 5K race pace. Repeat this pattern of 5 minutes on the bike followed by an 800m run three more times. After the last one, cool down on the bike by spinning easily for 10 minutes. This workout will take approximately 1 hour.

- Good for veteran and advanced triathletes, but not for beginners.
- Use only as preparation for shorter B races or well before half-Iron A race.
- Useful for elites trying to win division and stay with faster runners.

SPEED WORKOUTS

Speed 1

Transitions: Practice swim to bike and bike to run. Review stall setup, wet suit off, helmet on, shoe changes, and so on. Focus on rehearsing the transition you have the most trouble with. Can be used as an active recovery day workout, maximizing rest while improving skill.

Speed 2

Transitions: Practice bike to run. Review stall setup, dismount, helmet off, shoe change, start run. More challenging with running practice.

Speed 3

Out-in bike transition repeats in driveway or parking lot: Mount bike with shoes already clipped in, pedal, and step off (right leg steps between left leg and frame). Repeat 3–5 times.

- Can be combined before/after regular brick workout.
- Flying mount and dismount has several possibilities, but is hindered by bottles in behind-the-seat cages, which may need to be removed before race day. Watch ITU/Olympic pros for fastest technique possible.
- Beginner, older, or less flexible athletes may do better focusing more on safety, smoothness, and consistency than speed.

BIBLIOGRAPHY

Allen, H. and A. R. Coggan. *Racing and Training with a Power Meter.* Boulder, CO: VeloPress, 2006.

Armstrong, L. and S. Jenkins. *It's Not About the Bike: My Journey Back to Life.* New York, NY: G. P. Putnam's Sons, 2000.

———. *Every Minute Counts.* New York, NY: Broadway Books, 2003.

Bailey, A. A. *The Light of the Soul: The Yoga Sutras of Patanjali.* New York, NY: Lucis Publishing Company, 1927.

Borysewicz, E. *Bicycle Road Racing: The Complete Program for Training and Competition.* Brattleboro, VT: VeloNews, 1985.

Burke, E. R. *Serious Cycling.* Champaign, IL: Human Kinetics, 1995.

Burke, E. R., ed. *Precision Heart Rate Training.* Champaign, IL: Human Kinetics, 1998.

Byrn, G. and J. Friel. *Going Long.* Boulder, CO: VeloPress, 2003.

Cobb, J. *Wind Tunnel Magic.* VHS Video. Rollout Productions, Inc., 1996.

Cordain, L. and J. Friel. *The Paleo Diet for Athletes: A Nutritional Formula for Peak Athletic Performance.* Emmaus, PA: Rodale, 2005.

Friel, J. *The Cyclist's Training Bible.* Boulder, CO: VeloPress, 1996.

———. *The Triathlete's Training Bible.* Boulder, CO: VeloPress, 1998.

Galloway, J. *Marathon.* Atlanta, GA: Phidippides Publication, 2000.

Herrigel, E. and D. T. Suzuki. *Zen in the Art of Archery.* New York, NY: Pantheon Books, Inc., 1953.

Jackson, S. A. and M. Csikszentmihalyi. *Flow in Sports.* Champaign, IL: Human Kinetics, 1999.

Jonas, S. *Triathloning for Ordinary Mortals.* New York, NY: W. W. Norton & Company, Inc., 1999.

Maffetone, P. *Training for Endurance.* Stamford, NY: David Barmore Productions, 1996.

———. *Eating for Endurance.* Stamford, NY: David Barmore Productions, 1999.

Mierke, K. *The Triathlete's Guide to Run Training.* Boulder, CO: VeloPress, 2005.

———. *Evolution Running: Run Faster with Fewer Injuries.* DVD Video. VeloPress, 2004.

Murphy, M. *Golf in the Kingdom.* New York, NY: Viking Press, 1972.

Noakes, T. D. *The Lore of Running.* Champaign, IL: Human Kinetics, 2002.

Svensson, T. "The Total Triathlon Almanac—4." Palo Alto, CA: The Trimarket Company, 1999.

Tarpinian, S. *Swim Power.* VHS Video. SwimPower.com, 2000.

Tinley, S. *Triathlon: A Personal History.* Boulder, CO: VeloPress, 1998.

Zinn, L. *Zinn and the Art of Road Bike Maintenance.* Boulder, CO: VeloPress, 2000.

INTERNET SOURCES

All internet sources and URL addresses were stable for over a year and still valid as of August 2006 but are subject to change. Some are collections of contributions without listing an editor or full name of the contributor.

Byrn, G. "Aerobic Threshold Summary." http://www.coachgordo.com/gtips/endurance_essentials/aerobic_threshold_summary.html

Empfield, D., ed. "Tech Center." http://www.slowtwitch.com/mainheadings/techctr/techctr.html.

"Quotations about Running." http://www.quotegarden.com/running.html.

http://www.runnersworld.com/channel/0,5032,s6-51-0-0-0,00.html.

"Widgets: Calculators, Charts, etc." http://www.runnersweb.com/running/rw_widg.html.

INDEX

ABOUT THE AUTHOR

Tom Rodgers started endurance sports later in life, doing his first marathon and triathlon at age 37. A former electrical and biomedical engineer, his work at NASA's Johnson Space Center in Houston, Texas, included developing experiments for the International Space Station to measure endurance during long-term spaceflight. However, Rodgers quickly became hooked on training and racing, retiring from engineering to become a full-time multisport coach and accomplished age-group racer.

He has coached triathletes, road cyclists, ultracyclists, and runners ranging from Hawaii to Slovakia. Some of his clients have competed in world championships. Some have moved on to the professional level, yet he still enjoys training beginners and the average athlete who participates for the pure joy of achievement. He was invited to join Joe Friel's prestigious Ultrafit Coaching Association after only three years in the sport.

Rodgers continues to compete as a top masters competitor in triathlon and ultracycling events. He has been a Texas State Triathlon Age-Group Champion and the top-ranked masters triathlete in the USA Triathlon South-Midwest Region, as well as a USA Triathlon Age-Group All-American. He has been an age-group champion at Ironman events and finished the Ironman® Hawaii World Championship many times, including a time of 9:56 in Kona at age 46. He has also finished three Ultraman Hawaii World Championships, winning his age-group and third-place overall. In ultracycling events, he has placed second at national championships and participated in solo Race Across America (RAAM).

Rodgers has written for popular magazines, scientific journals, and for the multisport publications *Inside Triathlon* and *Runner Triathlete News*. He also delivers commentaries on public radio, writes screenplays, and enjoys sports photojournalism with his wife, Tuula.

In his beloved state of Texas, he still swims, bikes and runs every week. When he's not training, he's coaching, writing, studying philosophy, reading science-fiction, serving with United Nations educational groups, or helping his wife edit thousands of her multisport photographs, some of which are included in this book.

For more information on camps, training plans, and personal coaching, see his website at http://www.half-iron.com or e-mail tom@half-iron.com.